THE SUBJECTS OF
OTTOMAN INTERNATIONAL LAW

THE SUBJECTS OF OTTOMAN INTERNATIONAL LAW

Edited by Lâle Can, Michael Christopher Low, Kent F. Schull, and Robert Zens

Indiana University Press

This book is a publication of

Indiana University Press
Office of Scholarly Publishing
Herman B Wells Library 350
1320 East 10th Street
Bloomington, Indiana 47405 USA

iupress.org

Manufactured in the United States of America

DOI: 10.2979/subjectsottomaninternationallaw.0.0.00

Library of Congress Cataloging-in-Publication Data

Names: Lâle Can, editor. | Michael Christopher Low, editor. |
Kent F. Schull, editor. | Robert Zens, editor.
Title: The subjects of Ottoman international law /
edited by Lâle Can, Michael Christopher Low,
Kent F. Schull, and Robert Zens.
Description: Bloomington, Indiana : Indiana University Press,
2020. | Includes bibliographic references and index.
Identifiers: LCCN2020025893 (print) | LCCN 2020025894
(ebook) | ISBN 9780253056610 (paperback) | ISBN
9780253056634 (ebook)
Subjects: LCSH: law—Turkey—History. | Turkey—
History—Ottoman Empire, 1288–1918.
Classification: LCC KZ4242 .S83 2020 (print) | LCC
KZ4242 (ebook) | DDC 341.0956/0903—dc23
LC record available at https://lccn.loc.gov/2020025893
LC ebook record available at https://lccn.loc.gov/2020025894

First Printing 2020

Contents

Foreword

THE CORE OF this edited volume originates from a special issue of the *Journal of the Ottoman and Turkish Studies Association* (*JOTSA*). This volume, however, goes well beyond the special issue to incorporate the stimulating discussions and insights of two Middle East Studies Association roundtables and the important work of additional scholars in order to create a state-of-the-field volume on Ottoman socio-legal studies, particularly regarding Ottoman international law from the eighteenth century to the end of the empire. It makes several important contributions to Ottoman and Turkish studies, namely, by introducing these disciplines to the broader fields of trans-imperial studies, comparative international law, and legal history. It also combines the best practices of diplomatic history and history from below to integrate the Ottoman Empire and its subjects into the broader debates of the nineteenth-century trans-imperial history. These broad debates include the creation of and contestation over citizenship, contestations over sovereignty, geopolitical rivalries, legal literacy on individual and imperial levels, the intersectionality of law and society within and between various states, and how the status or plight of an individual can mobilize geopolitical forces for imperialist agendas. These contributions upend Orientalist notions that the Ottomans did not engage in international law until the nineteenth century and simply copied what European powers had created. They also bring together the best of statist and history-from-below methodologies and approaches to this field by looking at non-elites affected by and effecting the contours, engagement, power struggles, manipulation, development, and transformation of Ottoman international law. This volume represents the exciting work and cutting-edge scholarship on these topics that will continue to shape the field moving forward.

It has been our pleasure to work on this edited volume with our co-editors, Lâle Can and Michael Christopher Low, and all its contributors. Volumes, such as this one, are always a labor of love and dedication that rely on the various talents and good humor of many individuals in order to assemble, review, advise, coordinate, consult, revise, to obtain publication permissions, copy edit, index, and shepherd to publication such an important work as this one. We are all very grateful to Indiana University Press and the Ottoman and Turkish Studies Association (OTSA) for their support of this scholarly contribution.

Kent F. Schull
Robert Zens

The Subjects of Ottoman International Law (2020): vii
DOI: 10.2979/subjectsottomaninternationallaw.0.0.1

THE SUBJECTS OF
OTTOMAN INTERNATIONAL LAW

1   Introduction

Lâle Can and Michael Christopher Low

THE IMPETUS FOR this volume grew out of a series of workshops and panels, all of which pointed toward a critical mass of new research on Ottoman engagement with questions of sovereignty, citizenship, and extraterritoriality. In heated discussions about what it meant to be an Ottoman "national" versus a "citizen" or "subject," and conversations about the provenance of the legal advisors in the Ottoman Foreign Ministry who did the day-to-day work of defending the empire's sovereignty, there was a clear consensus that these topics merited greater attention and precision in terms. As editors of this volume, our own paths toward these subjects grew out of a recognition of what was missing in our work on different facets of Ottoman management of the steamship-era hajj. While neither of us set out to make international law a central concern of our research, questions of jurisdiction and protection, nationality and subjecthood, mobility regulation and passports, and the documentary practices underpinning them seemed to continually redirect our efforts. At every turn in the Ottoman archive, catalog searches for "foreign pilgrims" directed us to a trove of documents produced by the jurists at the Ottoman Office of Legal Counsel (Hukuk Müşavirliği İstişare Odası), the Hamidian-era bureau formed to navigate the landscape of Eurocentric international law. These archival sources provided unparalleled insight into the mechanics of empire, and disrupted long-held assumptions about imperial logic and governance. However, as we began to grasp the significance of this bureau for studying the Hamidian era, we became acutely aware of the deep disconnect between its omnipresence in the Ottoman archive and its curious absence in the extant historiography. In trying to understand the role that the Hukuk Müşavirliği İstişare Odası played in diplomacy and statecraft, we quickly found that many of the most basic institutions and practices related to the Ottoman state's formulation and dissemination of international legal expertise had barely garnered more than stray remarks.[1]

---

1. For noteworthy titles on Ottoman international legal institutions, see Aimee M. Genell's dissertation and forthcoming book project, "Empire by Law: Ottoman Sovereignty and the British Occupation of Egypt, 1882–1923" (PhD diss., Columbia University, 2013); Turan Kayaoğlu, *Legal Imperialism: Sovereignty and Extraterritoriality in Japan, the Ottoman Empire, and China* (Cambridge, UK: Cambridge University Press, 2010); Umut Özsu, "Ottoman Empire," in *The Oxford Handbook of the History of International Law*, ed. Bardo Fassbender and Anne Peters (Oxford: Oxford University Press, 2012), 429–48; idem, "The Ottoman Empire, the Origins of Extraterritoriality, and International Legal Theory," in *The Oxford Handbook of the*

The Subjects of Ottoman International Law (2020): 001–016
DOI: 10.2979/subjectsottomaninternationallaw.0.0.02

The work of addressing these lacunae resulted in collaborations with colleagues that revealed a wider constellation of shared frustrations. Foremost among them was the pervasive assumption that Ottoman legal reforms, both international and domestic, were merely reactions to the pressures of the Eastern Question. An interrelated problem has been the conflation of the diplomatic history of the Eastern Question with the history of international law, both of which have been marred by an over-reliance on European sources. While there is a recognition that the Ottoman state struggled to prove its acceptance of the emerging civilizational norms of "international society" in a bid for full and equal membership in the European family of nations, the story of this effort remains skewed.[2] Previous studies of Ottoman engagement with international law have tended to overemphasize certain aspects of public international law that grew out of the Eastern Question: peace treaties, annexation, border demarcation, and territorial losses.

Likewise, existing scholarship has generally put forward a rather narrow vision of private international law associated with consular jurisdiction over European merchants and their non-Muslim protégés.[3] This myopic emphasis on non-Muslim minorities has reinforced a reading of late Ottoman history that foregrounds the salience of religious and identity politics. Another consequence of this approach has been the tendency to ignore the empire's Muslim populations, or to analyze Ottoman relations with Muslim colonial subjects outside an international legal framework.[4] But when we consider, for example, how the

Theory of International Law, ed. Florian Hoffman and Anne Orford (Oxford: Oxford University Press, 2016), 123–37; Mustafa Serdar Palabıyık, "International Law for Survival: Teaching International Law in the Late Ottoman Empire (1859–1922)," *Bulletin of the School of Oriental and African Studies* 78, no. 2 (2015): 271–92; Nobuyoshi Fujinami, "The First Ottoman History of International Law," *Turcica* 48 (2017): 245–70. Also see Umut Özsu and Thomas Skouteris's recent collection of symposium articles, "International Legal Histories of the Ottoman Empire," *Journal of the History of International Law/Revue d'histoire du droit international* 18 (2016).

2. On the standard of civilization and the Ottoman Empire's awkward place in the European family of nations, see Cemil Aydın, *The Politics of Anti-Westernism in Asia: Visions of World Order in Pan-Islamic and Pan-Asian Thought* (New York: Columbia University Press, 2007); Anthony Anghie, *Imperialism, Sovereignty, and the Making of International Law* (Cambridge, UK: Cambridge University Press, 2002); Gerrit Gong, *The Standard of Civilization in the International Society* (Oxford: Clarendon Press, 1984).

3. On the undervaluation of private law in international legal history, see Will Hanley, "International Lawyers without Public International Law: The Case of Late Ottoman Egypt," *Journal of the History of International Law* 18 (2016): 98–119.

4. For recent work on legal pluralism, consular protection, and protégés, see Karen Barkey, "Aspects of Legal Pluralism in the Ottoman Empire," in *Legal Pluralism and Empires, 1500–1850*, ed. Lauren Benton and Richard Ross (New York: NYU Press, 2013); Lauren Benton, Adam Clulow, and Bain Attwood, eds., *Protection and Empire: A Global History* (Cambridge, UK: Cambridge University Press, 2017); Ziad Fahmy, "Jurisdictional Borderlands: Extraterritoriality and 'Legal Chameleons' in Precolonial Alexandria, 1840–1870," *Comparative Studies in So-*

Porte responded to Ottoman Muslims assuming "borrowed" European nationalities, or to European protégés—Christian, Muslim, and Jewish alike—seeking to benefit from capitulatory privileges, it becomes apparent that its vision of the relationship between defending the empire's territorial sovereignty and the reconfiguration of imperial subjecthood/citizenship and definition of nationality was not filtered exclusively through the prism of religion.

After decades of scholarship focused on Ottoman diplomacy and European legal imperialism, we have substantial insight into the kinds of questions that preoccupied European statesmen and jurists, as well as how their exercise of legal imperialism and extraterritoriality vis-à-vis the Ottoman Empire shaped the overall development of international legal thought. It is clear that the Ottoman Empire was a critical laboratory in which Europe experimented with a broad range of international legal instruments. On the other hand, how international law gained prominence and was translated and internalized within the Ottoman state remains an open question that this collection of essays seeks to address. How did Ottoman jurists, statesmen, and ordinary people apply and/or experience international legal thought? What novel solutions came out of these Ottoman experiments? Did they reproduce European expertise or did they contribute something uniquely Ottoman that shifted the parameters of what Europeans accepted as a valid perspective on international law? And, if so, what subjects and problems were most prominent in this Ottoman vision of international law? In answering these questions, this collection endeavors to reconstruct an Istanbul-centered history of "the law of nations" (*hukuk-ı düvel*) as it evolved over the course of the long nineteenth century. It also seeks to capture the messy, improvised process of incorporating international legal norms into existing patterns of domestic Ottoman governance.

As Umut Özsu points out in his concluding essay, "international law has never been merely an instrument for the coordinated regulation of inter-state relations; it has also been a means of reconfiguring the link between the state and the individual, with far-reaching implications for the latter's self-understanding." To this we could add that international law has never been exclusively driven by a single state, or even the collective will of European international society. In the "age of steam and print," the meanings of subjecthood, nationality, mobility controls, treaties, and even international law itself were all being challenged,

ciety and History 55, no. 2 (2013): 305–29; Mary Dewhurst Lewis, *Divided Rule: Sovereignty and Empire in French Tunisia, 1881–1938* (Berkeley: University of California Press, 2013); Willem Maas, ed., *Multilevel Citizenship* (Philadelphia: University of Pennsylvania Press, 2013); James Meyer, *Turks Across Empires: Marketing Muslim Identity in the Russian-Ottoman Borderlands, 1856–1914* (Oxford: Oxford University Press, 2014); Paolo Sartori and Ido Shahar, "Legal Pluralism in Muslim-Majority Colonies: Mapping the Terrain," *Journal of the Economic and Social History of the Orient* 55, no. 4/5 (2012): 637–63.

reshaped, and subverted by non-state actors, whether they be Ottoman or foreign nationals, Muslims or Christians, prisoners of war, migrants, smugglers, or pilgrims.[5] During this era of accelerating mobility, the proliferation of border-crossers was simultaneously forcing government officials across Europe, Africa, and Asia to define the parameters of subjecthood, nationality, and citizenship, and to clarify where their respective jurisdictional claims of territorial sovereignty or extraterritorial protection began and ended. In turn, as states tried to "cast shadows of sovereignty" beyond their realms, individuals seeking their protection were eager to know just how far these shadows extended and under what conditions they might recede.[6]

Our attention to these questions is not meant to detract from the importance of Ottoman treaty-making or the impact of European diplomacy on both the empire's external and internal affairs. However, the nature of our sources and the complex stories of statesmen and ordinary people engaging with international legal norms in novel ways all highlight the need for a fuller picture of what international law meant in the everyday practice and mechanics of empire. From Ottoman prisoners of war who learned to use treaty law to secure their release from Tsarist Russia to Ottoman provincial officials in Beirut and Anatolia who realized the interconnectedness of domestic policing and international mobility controls, we argue that international law was not something confined to European diplomats negotiating territorial losses or the fine print of treaties. We see international legal considerations engrained in the central state's day-to-day affairs, and also becoming integral dimensions of questions, periods, and geographies that scholars have either overlooked or failed to emphasize. With this in mind, this collection seeks to give greater visibility to a wider range of issues playing out across the Mediterranean, Balkans, and Russo-Ottoman frontier, as well as Anatolia, the Levant, Egypt, Libya, and the Anglo-Ottoman frontiers of the Indian Ocean basin in the Hijaz, Yemen, and Iraq.

One of the most glaring historiographical blind spots that this collection makes more visible is the overwhelming tendency to associate European international society, diplomacy, and international law exclusively with the Tanzimat period. In part, this is a legacy of the stubborn, artificial divide between a West-

---

5. On mobility and the "age of steam and print," especially see James L. Gelvin and Nile Green, eds., *Global Muslims in the Age of Steam and Print* (Berkeley: University of California Press, 2014); Nile Green, "Spacetime and the Muslim Journey West: Industrial Communications in the Making of the 'Muslim World'," *American Historical Review* 118, no. 2 (2013): 401–29; On Barak, *On Time: Technology and Temporality in Modern Egypt* (Berkeley: University of California Press, 2013); Valeska Huber, *Channelling Mobilities: Migration and Globalisation in the Suez Canal Region and Beyond, 1869–1914* (Cambridge, UK: Cambridge University Press, 2013).

6. Lauren Benton, "Shadows of Sovereignty: Legal Encounters and the Politics of Protection in the Atlantic World," in *Encounters Old and New: Essays in Honor of Jerry Bentley*, ed. Alan Karras and Laura Mitchell (Honolulu: University of Hawai'i Press, 2017), 136–50.

ern-facing era of Tanzimat modernization and an Eastern- (read backward-) facing Hamidian period characterized by Pan-Islamic legitimacy and outreach to the Muslim world. A closer look at the evolution of the state's international legal apparatus, however, suggests considerably more continuity than the oft-posited divisions between the Tanzimat and Hamidian eras would suggest. Conventional wisdom links the rise of Ottoman international legal thought to the Crimean War and the Treaty of Paris (1856), which begrudgingly invited the empire into the European family of nations and afforded it all of the advantages of public law and the Concert of Europe. By the 1860s and 1870s Ottoman officials regularly employed international legal arguments in order to defend the empire's territorial integrity and navigate the hostile world wrought by European colonialism. Yet, the formalization of Ottoman international institutions, expertise and the full articulation of what we might call an Ottoman vision of international law were Hamidian-era creations. Although this might be surprising to some, it should not be.

As it turns out, the Hamidian Pan-Islamic turn and the Ottoman experience of international law and diplomacy after 1876 were mutually constituted phenomena. In the wake of the disastrous Russo-Ottoman War of 1877–78 and the Treaty of Berlin, the French occupation of Tunisia in 1881, the British occupation of Egypt in 1882, and the acceleration of the Scramble for Africa, the Hamidian regime understood that a more systematic engagement with international law was necessary to the state's survival.[7] The exact timing of the creation of the Foreign Ministry's Office of Legal Counsel in 1883 makes this point explicit and shows that it was a quintessentially Hamidian institution. The unequal treatment to which the only Muslim member of the Concert of Europe was subjected, however, compromised the sultan's faith in European international society. In this context, the promotion of the caliphate and state-sponsored Pan-Islam was a complementary strategy designed to bolster the empire's position on the international stage.

The caliphate's inclusion in the Office of Legal Counsel's arsenal of legal tools and concepts shows how Ottoman international legal institutions and Hamidian Pan-Islam were parallel, sometimes contradictory, projects rather than diametrically-opposed or unrelated subjects. After all, Pan-Islam was a Janus-faced discourse aimed at shoring up legitimacy vis-à-vis both a domestic Muslim constituency and Islamic lands that were conquered by non-Muslim powers. International legal considerations led to radical redefinitions of Ottoman nationality and subjecthood that affected the empire's Muslim populations just as much as they changed the position of certain non-Muslim groups. Likewise, international

7. On the rapidly changing Ottoman position in European diplomacy from 1878 through the Scramble for Africa, especially see Mostafa Minawi, *The Ottoman Scramble for Africa: Empire and Diplomacy in the Sahara and the Hijaz* (Stanford: Stanford University Press, 2016).

legal expertise was also needed to reconsider the empire's foreign relations with the rest of the *umma*. As various forms of indirect and direct colonial rule extended across Central Asia, India, and Southeast Asia, by the closing decades of the nineteenth century virtually all non-Ottoman Muslims interacting with the Ottoman state had become subjects of European colonial empires. The result was a major reconfiguration of relations between the sultan and vast segments of the Muslim world.[8] In an era often defined by vague terms like Pan-Islamic unity, brotherhood, loyalty, and allegiance, even the state's highest foreign-policy objectives were being evaluated against—and frequently contradicted by—the empire's international legal establishment. Although counterintuitive to the dominant historiographic image of the Hamidian state, these calculations and counter-measures were necessary in order to guard against conflicts over questions of extraterritoriality, jurisdiction, nationality, protection, and subjecthood.[9]

* * *

At the outset of this collaboration we posed several overarching questions to our colleagues: What did international law mean to the late Ottoman Empire? How was this Ottoman vision of international law translated into the administrative mechanics of the state? How was international law translated into material documentary practices? For Ottomanists, how might a more precise understanding of international law contribute to a rethinking of the empire's engagement with Europe and colonialism? Likewise, how can Ottomanists contribute to conversations about nationality, protection, subjecthood, and citizenship beyond the field of Ottoman and Middle Eastern studies?[10] And, finally, what do we gain by

---

8. For a critical genealogy of the idea of the Muslim World and its emergence during this period, see Cemil Aydın, *The Idea of the Muslim World: A Global Intellectual History* (Cambridge, MA: Harvard University Press, 2017).

9. For studies of how the Hamidian state promoted Pan-Islam to counter European encroachments on its sovereignty and legitimize its Islamic authority among both Muslims within the empire and under colonial rule, see Selim Deringil, *The Well-Protected Domains: Ideology and Legitimation of Power in the Ottoman Empire 1876–1909* (London: I.B. Tauris, 1998); Kemal Karpat, *The Politicization of Islam: Reconstructing Identity, State, Faith, and Community in the Late Ottoman State* (Oxford: Oxford University Press, 2001); Azmi Özcan, *Pan-Islamism: Indian Muslims, the Ottomans and Britain, 1877–1924* (Leiden: Brill, 1997). On the different forms of Pan-Islam in this period, also see Adeeb Khalid, "Pan-Islamism in Practice: The Rhetoric of Muslim Unity and its Uses," in *Late Ottoman Society: The Intellectual Legacy*, ed. Elisabeth Özdalga (London: RoutledgeCurzon, 2005), 201–24.

10. For recent efforts to locate these Ottoman questions of citizenship and subjecthood in wider comparative and inter-imperial frameworks, see Dina Rizk Khoury and Sergey Glebov, "Citizenship, Subjecthood, and Difference in the Late Ottoman and Russian Empires," *Ab Imperio* 1 (2017): 45–58; Michelle U. Campos, "Imperial Citizenship at the End of Empire:

placing the Ottoman Empire in broader international, global, and comparative frameworks?

The scholars invited to contribute to this volume were given free rein to explore any aspect of the late Ottoman Empire's engagement with international law. The result is a provocative set of essays covering topics as disparate as the empire's highest international legal authorities, prisoners of war, Indian Ocean consulates, and Armenian migrants. They range from overviews of how the central state's approach to international law and diplomacy evolved over time to more discrete studies of how specific international legal concepts were brought to bear in domestic legislation, interstate contexts, and their blurry points of contact. Where the essays cohere is in their commitment to translating abstract concepts in the fine print of the Capitulations, the 1869 Ottoman Nationality Law, consular jurisdiction, and passport legislation, and integrating them into narratives that extend well beyond the narrow confines of legal history. The contributions reveal the multi-layered processes involved in translating international legal norms and instruments between international and Ottoman institutions. Equally important, they are careful not to flatten the "Ottoman state" by collapsing the differences between Istanbul and the empire's peripheries. They demonstrate both the complex interplay between the goals envisioned in Istanbul and the difficulties in implementing these new legal concepts across the empire's varied landscapes, especially in the empire's so-called exceptional provinces (*eyalat-ı mümtaze*) and semi-autonomous frontiers.[11]

Another critical contribution is the dizzying array of geographies featured in this collection. Within the empire, these essays draw upon examples from Balkan, Anatolian, Armenian, and Arabian frontier contexts. In the arena of interstate relations, they connect different parts of the empire not only to Western Europe, but also to Russia, Afghanistan, the Indian Ocean, the Muslim colonial world, and even the United States. We believe that this geographical breadth is more than a perfunctory nod to all things comparative, transnational, and global. It is indicative of how the field has evolved. Rather than seeking to decenter Europe or write the Ottomans into European history, this volume examines the global scope and tensions inherent in the state's simultaneous engagement with European international society, the colonial world, and its unique position as the world's last great Muslim empire. At the same time, we also hope that these previously overlooked Ottoman cases will bring something new to the study of

The Ottomans in Comparative Perspective," *Comparative Studies of South Asia, Africa and the Middle East* 37, no. 3 (2017): 588–607.

11. On the exceptional legal status of the empire's autonomous provinces, see Ayhan Ceylan, *Osmanlı Taşra İdarî Tarzı Olarak Eyâlet-i Mümtâze ve Mısır Uygulaması* (Istanbul: Kitabevi, 2014); Aimee M. Genell, "Autonomous Provinces and the Problem of Semi-Sovereignty in European International Law," *Journal of Balkan and Near Eastern Studies* 18, no. 6 (2016): 533–49.

international legal history as it relates to the Ottoman Empire and the Islamic world more broadly. To that end, Umut Özsu concludes this volume with an Afterword. Writing from his perspective as an expert on international law, rather than as a historian or Ottomanist, Özsu's panoramic evaluation of the volume as a whole allows us to think more broadly about what this collection might contribute not just to Ottoman studies but how it might also fit into a wider interdisciplinary conversation on "comparative international law" in non-European settings and through non-European archival materials.

In this volume's opening chapter, Will Smiley challenges our most basic assumptions about the timing and sources of the Ottoman gravitation toward international legal thought. As Smiley argues, even as the empire lost a series of wars against Russia, it became increasingly forceful in asserting the legal right to demand the release of its prisoners of war. By examining the evolution of Ottoman-Russian treaty-making, Smiley reveals how the liberation of Ottoman prisoners of war, especially Muslim captives, became enshrined in Ottoman conceptions of treaty and customary law.[12] As he points out, the story of captivity and the development of legal rights surrounding their return challenges assumptions that concepts of diplomacy, law, and sovereignty were static, modular categories that could simply be imported and assimilated during the Tanzimat period. By contrast, Smiley demonstrates how Ottoman ideas and practices surrounding sovereignty, inter-imperial treaty law, and subjecthood had already begun to develop along the Ottoman-Russian frontier during the eighteenth century. These developments were initiated by captives who learned how to use the language of treaty and customary law to assert their rights as Ottoman subjects. In addition to challenging the conventional periodization of Ottoman engagement with international law, Smiley raises the question of whether this pre-Tanzimat right to liberation from Russian captivity might suggest the development of a sort of "proto-citizenship" produced not only through domestic reforms but also through the legal logics of interstate relations.[13]

In Chapter 2, Aimee M. Genell underscores that while historians have long agreed that the Ottoman Foreign Ministry embraced international law as a necessary adjunct to European diplomacy, there remains no clear consensus on the exact timing of this legal turn. As she points out, we know very little about how international legal concepts were handled at the procedural level or the Ottoman

---

12. For parallel developments in early-modern practices surrounding inter-imperial treaty law related to questions of piracy, captivity, and diplomacy in the Mediterranean, see Joshua M. White, *Piracy and Law in the Ottoman Mediterranean* (Stanford: Stanford University Press, 2018).

13. On the concept of Ottoman "proto-citizenship," also see Ariel Salzmann, "Citizens in Search of a State: The Limits of Political Participation in the Late Ottoman Empire," in *Extending Citizenship, Reconfiguring States*, ed. Michael Hanagan and Charles Tilly (Lanham, MD: Rowman and Littlefield, 1999), 37–66.

officials tasked with executing such complex policy objectives. In a much-needed intervention, Genell provides an overview of the rise and fall of international law through an analysis of the Foreign Ministry's Office of Legal Counsel and a prosopography of the jurists employed there in the Hamidian and Committee of Union and Progress (CUP) eras. While Ottoman lawyers and statesmen viewed international law as a critical defensive strategy throughout the Hamidian era, Genell shows how and why their faith in its efficacy dramatically declined in the wake of the Italian invasion of Libya (1911) and the Balkan Wars (1912–13). By the First World War, she argues that "many one-time evangelists of international law" came to view it as little more than "an instrument of European imperialism used to justify the unequal treatment of the Ottoman state in the international arena."

Genell also catalogues the most common—and thorniest—issues brought to the attention of the empire's legal advisors. On the one hand, we find Ottoman lawyers occupied with questions of public international law, such as protecting autonomous provinces from being annexed, claimed as European protectorates, or even gaining their independence. On the other, we also find them involved in disputes between individuals, requiring a mastery of private international law. Such cases often grew out of the Capitulations, questions over consular protections, jurisdiction, or disputes over an individual's nationality, passport, or travel documents. In this sense, Genell's essay provides an overview that frames and contextualizes the case-studies that follow.

In Chapter 3, Will Hanley's analysis of the 1909 revision of the 1869 Ottoman Nationality Law takes up one of the central themes that occupied the Office of Legal Counsel: the slippery relationship between the legal definitions of nationality, subjecthood, and citizenship.[14] As Hanley argues, recent scholarship on the 1869 Ottoman Nationality Law has consistently sought its origins in the Tanzimat edicts of 1839 and 1856. He contends that interest in the question of Ottoman citizenship has led to a misreading of the word *tebaa*, and that the Tanzimat edicts referred to subjects, *not* citizens.[15] This "citizenship misreading" has

14. For a more complete "glossary" of terms surrounding Ottoman nationality, subjecthood, and citizenship, see Will Hanley, *Identifying with Nationality: Europeans, Ottomans, and Egyptians in Alexandria* (New York: Columbia University Press, 2017), 53–66, 236–55.
15. Hanley's essay engages and critiques recent debates on citizenship in the late Ottoman Empire and the colonial Middle East more broadly. For example, see Michelle U. Campos, *Ottoman Brothers: Muslims, Christians, and Jews in Early Twentieth-Century Palestine* (Stanford: Stanford University Press, 2010); Julia Phillips Cohen, *Becoming Ottomans: Sephardi Jews and Imperial Citizenship in the Modern Era* (New York: Oxford University Press, 2014); Engin Fahri Isin, "Citizenship after Orientalism: Ottoman Citizenship," in *Citizenship in a Global World: European Questions and Turkish Experiences*, ed. Fuat Keyman and Ahmet İçduygu (London: Routledge, 2005), 31–51; Karen M. Kern, *Imperial Citizen: Marriage and Citizenship in the Ottoman Frontier Provinces of Iraq* (Syracuse: Syracuse University Press, 2011); James H.

obscured the 1869 law's original connection to the Capitulations and an 1863 decree designed to restrict the proliferation of foreign protégés. This law presented foreign protégés with a choice: they could either naturalize as foreign subjects or submit to Ottoman territorial jurisdiction to maintain their status as subjects of the sultan. The unintended consequence was that many of them chose to naturalize with a foreign state, while remaining in residence and continuing to benefit from the rights of Ottomans. Thus, while the number of protégés dropped, the number of naturalized foreigners increased precipitously. This development prompted firmer legislation, which took the shape of the 1869 law. Set against this backdrop, Hanley puts forward the provocative conclusion that neither the 1863 protégé legislation nor the 1869 Ottoman Nationality Law were intended to form a citizenry. Rather, he argues that both were primarily aimed at safeguarding the empire's sovereignty over its residents against the threat of European extraterritoriality. Hanley then analyzes a 1909 proposal for the revision of the 1869 law in order to chart the evolution of Ottoman readings of nationality and naturalization from the Tanzimat through the CUP period. While the 1909 proposal was never enacted, Hanley considers what it reveals about ongoing struggles to implement the 1869 law, as well as two specific issues that it failed to fully address: denaturalization and marriage to Iranians.[16]

If Hanley's analysis of nationality legislation reexamines the changing definitions of what it meant to be Ottoman, in Chapter 4 Michael Christopher Low takes up a related question: what did it mean to be a foreigner after 1869? Low focuses specifically on an understudied group in relation to the Capitulations—non-Ottoman Muslims who had become foreigners both by virtue of the 1869 law and the expansion of colonial rule—and moves this issue's focus into the realm of inter-imperial competition for allegiance and influence in the Hijaz. Low brings to the fore the messy nature of implementing international law, while also considering its impact on Muslims caught in the middle of Anglo-Ottoman legal battles and proxy wars. After tracing how traditional distinctions between Muslims and *dhimmi* (People of the Book) were theoretically leveled by the 1856 Islahat Fermanı and more fully realized with the promulgation of the 1869 Ottoman Nationality Law, Low considers the impact on non-Ottoman Muslims who were designated as foreigners. By the early 1880s, when virtually all of the Islamic world was ruled by European powers, Low argues that foreign Muslims (*ecanib-i müslimin*) fell under a cloud of suspicion. This was especially true in the

Meyer, "Immigration, Return, and the Politics of Citizenship: Russian Muslims in the Ottoman Empire, 1860–1914," *International Journal of Middle East Studies* 39, no. 1 (2007): 15–32; Sarah Abrevaya Stein, *Extraterritorial Dreams: European Citizenship, Sephardi Jews, and the Ottoman Twentieth Century* (Chicago: University of Chicago Press, 2016).

16. On denaturalization and marriage along the Ottoman-Iranian frontier, especially see Kern, *Imperial Citizens*.

Hijaz, where foreign Muslims and their consular representatives began to assert their rights to European protections. Low argues that this previously unthinkable scenario opened up a paradox in the basic logic of the Capitulations: Ottoman authorities were forced to grapple with the stranger-than-fiction claim that foreign Muslims in Islam's holiest cities were entitled to capitulatory privileges and consular protections in order to avoid the supposedly arbitrary nature of Ottoman rule and Islamic law. By highlighting the unintended consequences of the 1869 Ottoman Nationality Law, Low demonstrates how the pervasive logics of international jurisprudence and extraterritoriality threatened to alter and undermine the Hijaz's previously exceptional autonomous, sacred, and ideological positions within the empire. In turn, his contribution offers an antidote to conventional wisdom about the Hamidian era, and urges us to consider Pan-Islam not as a religious discourse, but "a set of policies and discourses defined as much by sovereignty and international legal considerations as by Islamic legitimacy."

In an empire historically ruled by difference, Lâle Can's contribution in Chapter 5 shows that the status of non-Ottoman Muslims hinged on a variety of factors that included their subject status vis-à-vis European empires in the context of international law. Whereas Low's story revolves around non-Ottoman Muslims originating from formally colonized territories like British India, French Algeria, or the Dutch East Indies, Can tackles the even more vexing question of whether or not Central Asian pilgrims and migrants from the "informally colonized" protectorates and inter-imperial borderlands of Afghanistan, Bukhara, and Chinese Turkestan had legitimate claims to Russian and British nationality and their attendant capitulatory privileges. By tracing how the Office of Legal Counsel distinguished "protected persons" (*mahmi*) from so-called "real" (*asıl, sahih*) European subjects, she demonstrates that these mobile Central Asians were the exceptions that helped to define the rules and boundaries of an emerging "protection question." As opposed to colonial subjects like Indians and Jawis, whom the Ottomans begrudgingly accepted as foreign nationals, the Ottoman state repeatedly denied and resisted Central Asian claims to European nationality and protection. As Can cautions, this was a complex and deeply ambivalent strategy. On the one hand, it was designed to thwart the expansion of European consular protections to those taking on "borrowed nationalities." At the same time, while the Ottoman state had no hope of dismantling the expansion of extraterritoriality to the vast majority of the *umma*, Central Asians who had fallen between the cracks of empires represented a unique opportunity for the Ottoman state to assert its jurisdiction. As she demonstrates, Ottoman legal advisors in the Office of Legal Counsel engaged in a multi-pronged strategy to deny these foreign Muslims the rights of European nationals and protégés, while simultaneously promoting the sultan-caliph's right to protect them via the very novel claim that they fell under the exclusive protection of the caliphate.

Here, she challenges the conventional wisdom that late Ottoman approaches to Turkic-speaking Central Asians were primarily a function of ethno-linguistic kinship ties. Instead, Can shows how the Porte recast the religious authority of the caliphate and Pan-Islamic rhetoric, melding them together with emerging international legal norms to assert a kind of spiritual protection over the Central Asian pilgrims and migrants residing in Ottoman lands. Through attention to the complex stories of Bukharans, Afghans, and Kashgaris who sought, often unsuccessfully, to exploit competing regimes of imperial protection, the chapter also presents a different picture of legal pluralism than in the more plentiful examples documented in the Mediterranean and Indian Ocean worlds. As Can argues, practices such as affiliation switching and forum shopping often led to dead ends and legal limbo for subjects and states alike.

In Chapter 6, Julia Stephens shifts our focus from the Hijaz to Iraq and deepens our understanding of the inherent uncertainties in imperial legal regimes. While her chapter examines the same kinds of dilemmas explored by Low and Can, Stephens provides a non-Ottoman view of how inter-imperial law and extraterritoriality functioned along the Ottoman Empire's Indian Ocean frontiers. Thus, while most of the essays in this collection primarily focus on the Ottoman state's own internal understandings of the varied threats to the empire's sovereignty, Stephens explores how Ottoman frontier provinces like Iraq served as a kind of "transnational legal laboratory," in which the principal actors were just as likely to be the mobile subjects and consular representatives of other empires as Ottoman authorities dispatched from Istanbul. Given the constant flow of Shi'i Indian pilgrims, funds for pious endowments, and merchant capital moving between India, Persia, and Ottoman Iraq, British consular authorities cast a long jurisdictional shadow over the region. As a result, this Ottoman territory "could at times feel distinctly British" to its Indian residents. By viewing Iraq's conflicted imperial legal regimes through the eyes of these mobile subjects, Stephens reveals strikingly divergent lived realities than those "presented in the legal treatises written from the centers of empire."

To tell this story, Stephens examines the lives and what she terms "legal afterlives" of Iqbal al-Daulah and Taj Mahal Begam, members of the princely family of the Nawab of Awadh who had settled among the Shi'i Indian migrant communities of Ottoman Iraq. By tracing the fate of the estates and inheritances of these border-crossing subjects, Stephens details how Ottoman officials and British consular authorities squabbled over who was responsible for administering the properties of deceased Indians. In theory, the administration of their estates, whether in Iraq or India, should have been a matter of Islamic law. However, as Stephens points out, the intractable disputes over where these cases should be adjudicated revealed a vast gulf between the interpretation of Islamic law in Istanbul, Iraq, and India. As was the case in the Ottoman Hijaz, British officials in

Iraq and India repeatedly claimed special legal privileges and asserted the British Empire's right to protect its subjects from laws and legal regimes, whether Ottoman or Islamic, that it "deemed uncivilized." In the process, Britain defined its own judicial authority as territorial, secular, and universal, and subordinated non-European laws under the rubric of personal law. This limited their scope to familial and religious domains and denigrated them as irrational and arbitrary. By doing so, British consular authorities in Iraq sought to "discipline plural legal regimes" along India's frontiers "into clear and consistent hierarchies." Yet, as the reams of legal correspondence that Stephens draws on make clear, colonial legal regimes were constitutive of the very uncertainties and inconsistencies they purported to rectify.

In Chapter 7, Faiz Ahmed's examination of Anglo-Ottoman rivalry extends the discussion of intersections between extraterritoriality, Pan-Islam, and private international law across Afghanistan, British India, and the Indian Ocean. Similar to Can, Low, and Stephens, Ahmed shows how itinerant Afghan and Indian Muslims became caught up in larger geopolitical struggles over jurisdiction between the British Foreign Office and the Sublime Porte. In this way, his contribution traces how the battle lines over extraterritoriality shifted to include Muslim subjects of protected states such as Afghanistan, as well as how Indians and Afghans were able to "pull in" multiple state actors in order to maximize their rights and protections. As Ahmed argues, one of the main points of contention for the British was whether the Ottoman sovereign could claim "anything more than a symbolic authority over Afghans." The case-studies he presents—which include Ottoman attempts to expand the empire's consular presence in the Indian Ocean world, to Afghans who were able to activate the sultan-caliph's protection and become Ottomans—show how Pan-Islam was indeed more than a matter of faith and had become deeply imbricated in international legal considerations. Here, Ahmed also makes clear how Abdülhamid II's Pan-Islamic outreach bore fruit among Afghans. As Ahmed argues, these "transborder subjects *par excellence*" were not only claiming to be Afghans and Indians, but also subjects of the Ottoman sultan-caliph. In the contested terrain of nationality, we again see Pan-Islam as much more than a religious discourse.[17]

As Ahmed, Can, Low, and Stephens all point out, the symbiotic relationship between colonialism and cheap steamship and rail travel led to a multiplication of new dilemmas surrounding extraterritoriality, consular protection, and jurisdictional quarrels. It also led to an increased interest in documenting, monitoring, and sorting the nationalities, identities, and commercial affairs of both Ottoman subjects and foreigners residing and traveling within and beyond the empire's

17. For a fuller treatment of Anglo-Ottoman relations surrounding Afghanistan, see Faiz Ahmed, *Afghanistan Rising: Islamic Law and Statecraft between the Ottoman and British Empires* (Cambridge, MA: Harvard University Press, 2017).

borders. Especially after the opening of the Suez Canal in 1869, the Porte began to recognize the increasing commercial and legal entanglements linking Ottoman ports like Jidda and Basra to major maritime transportation hubs across the colonial Indian Ocean from Bombay and Karachi to Singapore and Batavia.

In Chapter 8, Jeffery Dyer shows how this increased connectivity prompted the Ottoman state to establish a network of consulates across the region. Conventionally the rise of more formalized diplomatic contacts with South and Southeast Asia has primarily been understood as an outgrowth of the Hamidian state's strategy of Pan-Islamic outreach to Muslim subjects living under European colonial rule. However, as Dyer points out, the civil servants dispatched to "politically sensitive Indian Ocean territories were not one-dimensional Pan-Islamic firebrands." Rather, the expansion and standardization of full-time, salaried Ottoman consular postings was a global phenomenon. In the 1870s and 1880s, they joined a maturing cadre of Tanzimat-style professional civil servants and consular officers with experience in diplomatic postings from Europe and North America. In addition to experience in previous consular postings, the men tasked with representing Istanbul in the Indian Ocean were often drawn from the Foreign Ministry's Translation Bureau (Tercüme Odası) or the Office of Legal Counsel. As Dyer demonstrates, their professional backgrounds gave them the diplomatic and international legal expertise needed to navigate the Porte's increasingly complicated relations with a Muslim world populated by subjects of European colonial rule. Whether defending the rights of Ottoman subjects living abroad or regulating the flow of Indian Ocean pilgrims through newly erected passport and visa regulations, this emerging consular network met the evolving challenges of European colonialism across the Muslim Indian Ocean armed with the latest instruments of international law and diplomacy.

Just as Dyer tracks the rise of hajj-related passport and mobility controls managed by Ottoman consular officials in the Indian Ocean, in Chapter 9, David Gutman shows how the post-Tanzimat state embraced new documentary practices to manage the explosion of migration and mobility across the Mediterranean and Atlantic. Gutman specifically explores intersections and cleavages between the emergence of international systems of passport and mobility regulation and the idiosyncrasies and contradictions inherent in the parallel development of Ottoman domestic identity and mobility controls.[18] At the heart of his

---

18. On the international passport system, see Jane Caplan and John Torpey, eds., *Documenting Individual Identity: The Development of State Practices in the Modern World* (Princeton: Princeton University Press, 2001); John Torpey, *The Invention of the Passport: Surveillance, Citizenship, and the State* (Cambridge, UK: Cambridge University Press, 2000); Adam McKeown, *Melancholy Order: Asian Migration and the Globalization of Borders* (New York: Columbia University Press, 2011).

analysis is the creation of the *mürûr tezkeresi*, or internal passport.[19] Its development was meant to render domestic mobility legible to the state. In theory, the ability to permit or deny applications for this document allowed the state to distinguish between legitimate forms of mobility such as trade, labor, or pilgrimage, and those considered illegitimate or dangerous, such as smuggling, banditry, and illegal overseas migration. Gutman also interrogates the contradictions between post-Tanzimat visions of standardized nationality and subjecthood against the deep anxieties provoked by mass migration and human smuggling. He deftly exposes these contradictions by presenting the Hamidian state's divergent approaches to the management of documentary practices and mobility networks surrounding mass overseas migration among two Christian communities: Maronite Christians from Mount Lebanon and Armenians from Eastern Anatolia.

In the final contribution to the volume, Stacy Fahrenthold extends the previous chapter's discussion of Ottoman migration to the Americas into World War I, and traces the afterlife of empire in distant lands and legal regimes. Through a focus on the exceptional immigration and nationality statuses of the Syrian diaspora (*mahjar*), Fahrenthold examines the origins of American wartime legal ideas about Syrians and Syria as a people and a "territory simultaneously *a part of* and *apart from* the Ottoman Empire." According to Ottoman nationality laws requiring Ottomans to seek permission from the state before renouncing their subjecthood and naturalizing as foreign nationals, prior to 1915, Syrian migrants found it difficult to renounce their ties to the Ottoman Empire and become American citizens. On the other hand, Arab Christian migrants struggled to distinguish themselves from "Turkish" Muslims or so-called subjects of "Turkey in Asia." In both cases, their conflation with Islam and Asians placed them in distinctly undesirable groups according to the United States' increasingly restrictive immigration laws. In order to overcome these obstacles, Arab Christian activists worked to be classified as "Syrians" and racially white. By redefining themselves in this way, they sought to avoid Ottoman laws designed to prohibit their naturalization. And by claiming to be white, they sought to skirt legislation designed to limit Asian labor migration.

Beginning in the summer of 1917, Fahrenthold shows, the United States Congress began to distinguish "Syrians and Mount Lebanese claimed by Turkey as subjects" as a separate category from other Ottoman nationals. This legal adjustment, in addition to making Syrians and Lebanese eligible for military service and the draft, would have far-reaching consequences extending well-beyond the status of the migrants themselves. In effect, this change recast Syria and Mount Lebanon "not as sovereign Ottoman territories but as contested spaces held by Istanbul also claimed by America's allies." This case provides a perfect example of

---

19. On the *mürûr tezkeresi*, see Nalan Turna, 19. *Yüzyıldan* 20. *Yüzyıla Osmanlı Topraklarında Seyahat, Göç ve Asayış Belgeleri: Mürûr Tezkereleri* (Istanbul: Kaknüs Yayınevi, 2013).

how Ottoman practices of autonomy were used as evidence in the court of international legal opinion to undermine and even discount Ottoman sovereignty. As Fahrenthold points out, this move was based, in part, on an American reading of the pre-1914 status of Mount Lebanon as an autonomous province under French extraterritorial supervision. This reading also implicitly rejected the Ottoman state's abolition of Mount Lebanon's autonomous status in 1914. This discourse of exception allowed the United States and its army to enlist and deploy Syrian migrants as military labor. More importantly, the same American wartime laws that ignored the Ottoman Empire's identity documents and claims of sovereignty over its migrants abroad simultaneously helped France to construct and bolster its Mandate-era claims to Lebanon and Syria in the 1920s. This American precedent provided the French Foreign Ministry with a novel way of selectively claiming certain Ottoman migrants under their protection. Similarly, it provided a model for the French issue of safe conduct passports in order to claim and repatriate Syrian migrants and establish sovereignty over their lands.

Fahrenthold's essay underscores how Ottoman nationality regulations and the larger goal of turning Ottoman subjects into citizens remained incomplete projects. In the empire's final decades, international law had provided important tools in the defense of Ottoman sovereignty. However, the protections theoretically provided by international law were always a porous defense system. Ultimately, the Ottoman adoption of international legal norms and practices was only successful to the extent that other states and empires respected Ottoman law and territorial sovereignty. As was frequently the case in the empire's final decades, interpreting and applying international law to the Ottoman Empire was primarily in the hands of other states. Just as Ottoman nationality could be redefined, built up, and protected by international legal thought, as Fahrenthold's American case study reveals, those very same concepts could just as easily be turned against Istanbul. Indeed, on the eve of World War I, even Ottoman statesmen began to realize that it simply did not matter "however many books we write on international law or however many human rights laws we implement." The only way to command respect from other states was through military might. In the end, the Ottoman Empire and the Turkish Republic that succeeded it would survive or die "by war," not "by those old books of international law."[20]

---

20. Mustafa Aksakal, "Not 'by those old books of international law, but only by war': Ottoman Intellectuals on the Eve of the Great War," *Diplomacy and Statecraft* 15, no. 3 (2004): 507–44.

2 Freeing "The Enslaved People of Islam": The Changing Meaning of Ottoman Subjecthood for Captives in the Russian Empire*

Will Smiley

Between 1677 and 1918, the Ottoman Empire fought (and mostly lost) eleven wars to the Russian Empire in a nearly ceaseless competition for imperial supremacy in the Black Sea, Balkans, and Caucasus. As lives were lost, borders moved, local notables altered allegiances, and Eurasian geopolitics shifted, thousands of Ottoman subjects also fell into Russian hands as captives. This is a story that has only begun to be told, primarily through the social history of captivity in the late Ottoman period.[1] This chapter, drawing on Ottoman archival documents and embassy accounts as well as Russian and British archival sources, will instead take a different approach—asking what captivity meant for Ottoman diplomacy, law, sovereignty, and subjecthood in the eighteenth and early nineteenth centuries.[2]

* I am grateful to Lâle Can, Y. Hakan Erdem, Tolga Esmer, Ben Fortna, Leslie Peirce, Kent Schull, Robert Zens, *JOTSA*'s reviewers, and the participants in the Central European University workshop "Honor in Ottoman and Contemporary Mediterranean Societies" for their comments on earlier versions of this essay. I also thank the Gates Cambridge Trust, the Skilliter Centre for Ottoman Studies, and the Harvard-Cambridge Center for History and Economics for supporting the underlying research.

1. See Yücel Yanıkdağ, *Healing the Nation: Prisoners of War, Medicine and Nationalism in Turkey, 1914–1939* (Edinburgh: Edinburgh University Press, 2013); İbrahim Köremezli, "Kırım Harbi Sırasında Rusya'daki Esir Osmanlı ve Müttefik Askerleri (1853–1856)," *Belleten* 77, no. 280 (2013): 983–1030; Yücel Yanıkdağ, "Ottoman Prisoners of War in Russia, 1914-22," *Journal of Contemporary History* 34, no. 1 (1999): 69–85; Mahmut Akkor, "I. Dünya Savaşında Çeşitli Ülkelerdeki Türk Esir Kampları" (master's thesis, Sakarya University, 2006). I have written about foreign captives in Ottoman hands during the same period elsewhere: Will Smiley, *From Slaves to Prisoners of War: The Ottoman Empire, Russia, and International Law* (Oxford: Oxford University Press, 2018).

2. An alternative approach, which has proven fruitful in Western European contexts, focuses on captivity narratives, but there are few Ottoman narratives of captivity, particularly captivity in Russia, from this period. See Linda Colley, *Captives: Britain, Empire and the World, 1600–1850* (London: Jonathan Cape, 2002); Robert C. Davis, *Christian Slaves, Muslim Masters: White Slavery in the Mediterranean, the Barbary Coast, and Italy, 1500–1800* (Basingstoke: Palgrave Macmillan, 2003); Claire Norton, "Lust, Greed, Torture, and Identity: Narrations of Conversion and the Creation of the Early Modern Renegade," *Comparative Studies of South*

The Subjects of Ottoman International Law (2020): 017–035
DOI: 10.2979/subjectsottomaninternationallaw.0.0.03

I argue that the legal and diplomatic importance of Ottoman subjecthood changed over this period, pushed both by the contingent development of inter-imperial treaty law and by the initiative of captured Ottomans themselves.[3] As the Ottoman state gained legal rights to demand its subjects' release, it became increasingly assertive in vindicating these rights—even as it lost one war after another. I argue that the liberation of Ottoman subjects, and especially Muslim Ottoman subjects, transformed from an abstract issue of little direct importance to state elites, into a legal right, and then into an imperative in which the honor of the sultan and his state were at stake. At the same time, Ottoman subjects seem to have learned that their subjecthood entitled them to release, and they channeled their requests through the language of subjecthood and treaty law. The story of captivity therefore offers us a chance to move beyond Western European comparisons, and beyond the assumption that "European diplomacy" or "international law" were set categories that the Ottomans could either reject or accept, in total.[4] It allows us, instead, to explore how sovereignty, inter-imperial treaty law, and Ottoman subjecthood were defined and used, and what was at stake, in one particular context. In doing so, I aim to open a new perspective on questions of subjecthood and citizenship before the Tanzimat—questions which have received increasing attention recently, with some scholars perceiving aspects of Ottoman "citizenship" in the early modern era.[5] I suggest that some of

Asia, Africa and the Middle East 29, no. 2 (2009): 259–68; Gillian Weiss, *Captives and Corsairs: France and Slavery in the Early Modern Mediterranean* (Stanford: Stanford University Press, 2011). As discussed below, Weiss's story is particularly comparable to the argument here. Two prominent Ottoman exceptions are the narratives of Temeşvarlı Osman Ağa and Necati Efendi: Harun Tolasa, *Temeşvarlı Osman Ağa: Bir Osmanlı Türk Sipahisi ve Esirlik Hayatı* (Istanbul: Akçağ Yayınları, 2004); Frédéric Hitzel, "Osmân Ağa, captif ottoman dans l'Empire des Habsbourg à la fin du XVIIe siècle," *Turcica* 33 (2001): 191–213; Erhan Afyoncu, "Necati Efendi: Târih-i Kırım (Rusya Sefâretnâmesi)" (master's thesis, Marmara University, 1990).

3. I use "subjecthood" here in the sense of legal affiliation with, and assumed loyalty to, the Ottoman dynasty. How the states determined the *fact* of someone's subjecthood—before considering what that legally implied—was a vexed question beyond the scope of this essay. For other perspectives on subjecthood, citizenship, and rights in the Ottoman and Russian contexts, see E. Natalie Rothman, *Brokering Empire: Trans-Imperial Subjects between Venice and Istanbul* (Ithaca: Cornell University Press, 2012); Jane Burbank, "An Imperial Rights Regime: Law and Citizenship in the Russian Empire," *Kritika* 7, no. 3 (2006): 397–431; Will Hanley, "Foreignness and Localness in Alexandria, 1880–1914" (PhD diss., Princeton University, 2007).

4. For example, see Thomas Naff, "The Ottoman Empire and the European States System," in *The Expansion of International Society*, ed. Hedley Bull and Adam Watson (Oxford: Oxford University Press, 1985); Rifa'at A. Abou-el-Haj, "The Formal Closure of the Ottoman Frontier in Europe: 1699–1703," *Journal of the American Oriental Society* 89, no. 3 (1969): 469. For a more recent and nuanced perspective, see A. Nuri Yurdusev, ed., *Ottoman Diplomacy: Conventional or Unconventional?* (Basingstoke: Palgrave Macmillan, 2004).

5. See Baki Tezcan, *The Second Ottoman Empire: Political and Social Transformation in the Early Modern World* (Cambridge, UK: Cambridge University Press, 2010); Virginia H. Ak-

these aspects emerged out of the inter-imperial legal context, through contests over captivity and liberation.

This story begins in the early eighteenth century, in the aftermath of the 1735–39 Russo-Ottoman War—the first conflict in which Russia clearly gained the upper hand. It continues through subsequent wars, and especially the aftermath of those wars, in 1768–74, 1787–92, and 1806–12.[6]

From the Treaty of Belgrade (1739) to the Treaty of Küçük Kaynarca (1774)

Captivity was a common phenomenon all along the early modern Ottoman frontiers, from the Mediterranean to Hungary to the Black Sea steppes to the Caucasus. From the fifteenth through the eighteenth centuries, hundreds of thousands of captives flowed back and forth, most notably Slavic-language speakers captured by the Crimean Tatars and sold into slavery in the Ottoman Empire. Scholars have studied, and attempted to reconstruct, how systems of captivity functioned in different places along the frontiers.[7] The Hanafi Islamic legal tradition held that Muslim rulers had a duty, when making peace with non-Muslims, to secure the release of Muslim captives.[8] Yet in practice, when Ottoman subjects fell into enemy hands, they generally had to rely upon ransom for

san, *Ottoman Wars 1700–1870* (London: Longman, 2007); Y. Hakan Erdem, "'Do Not Think of Them As Agricultural Labourers': Ottoman Responses to the Greek War of Independence," in *Citizenship and the Nation-State in Greece and Turkey*, ed. Thalia G. Dragonas and Faruk Birtek (London: Routledge, 2005), 67–84.

6. For an overview of these conflicts, see Aksan, *Wars*.

7. For the Black Sea frontier, see Liubov Kurtynova-D'Herlugnan, *The Tsar's Abolitionists: the Slave Trade in the Caucasus and Its Suppression* (Leiden: Brill, 2010); Brian J. Boeck, *Imperial Boundaries: Cossack Communities and Empire-Building in the Age of Peter the Great* (Cambridge, UK: Cambridge University Press, 2009); Michael Khodarkovsky, *Russia's Steppe Frontier: The Making of a Colonial Empire, 1500–1800* (Bloomington: Indiana University Press, 2002); Brian J. Boeck, "Identity as Commodity: Tournaments of Value in the Tatar Ransom Business," *Russian History* 35, no. 3/4 (2008): 259–66; Alan W. Fisher, "Muscovy and the Black Sea Slave Trade," in *A Precarious Balance: Conflict, Trade, and Diplomacy on the Russian-Ottoman Frontier*, ed. Alan W. Fisher (Istanbul: Isis Press, 1999), 27–46. For other frontiers, for example, see Géza Pálffy, "Ransom Slavery along the Ottoman-Hungarian Frontier in the Sixteenth and Seventeenth Centuries," in *Ransom Slavery Along the Ottoman Borders: (Early Fifteenth-Early Eighteenth Centuries)*, ed. Géza Dávid and Pál Fodor (Leiden: Brill, 2007), 41–84; Weiss, *Captives and Corsairs*; Pál Fodor, "Piracy, Ransom Slavery and Trade: French Participation in the Liberation of Ottoman Slaves from Malta during the 1620s," *Turcica* 33 (2001): 119–34; Eyal Ginio, "Piracy and Redemption in the Aegean Sea during the First Half of the Eighteenth Century," *Turcica* 33 (2001): 135–47; Peter F. Sugar, "The Ottoman 'Professional Prisoner' on the Western Borders of the Empire in the Sixteenth and Seventeenth Centuries," *Études Balkaniques* 7, no. 2 (1971): 82–91; Karl Jahn, "Zum Loskauf Christlicher Und Türkischer Gefangener Und Sklaven Im 18. Jahrhundert," *Zeitschrift Der Deutschen Morgenländäsche Gesellschaft* 111 (1961): 63–85.

8. Mohammad Fadel, "International Law, Regional Developments: Islam," *Max Planck Encyclopedia of Public International Law* (Oxford: Oxford University Press, 2010), ¶ 21.

liberation, and this ransom was typically raised from among their families and associates. Pál Fodor has found that in the Mediterranean, the Ottoman central state took little role in liberating ordinary subjects, whether through financing or through logistics. Instead, the sultan devoted attention only to the "so-called 'principal captives' or to those with influential relatives or acquaintances."[9] This was true on the Hungarian frontiers as well.[10] Ransom was largely an individual, or communal, responsibility: the British observer Thomas Thornton claimed that each janissary unit kept a communal account, to be used in part for "the ransom of captives."[11] Ottoman subjecthood itself did not confer any particular right to state aid in securing release.

Elite captives were still the Ottoman state's main priority when the Sublime Porte signed the 1739 Treaty of Belgrade with Russia, ending a four-year war. The agreement banned the payment of ransom, and required both states to ensure that they, and their subjects, released all captives. Importantly, the agreement provided that those slaves who had converted to Christianity in Russia, or to Islam in the Ottoman Empire, would not be returned.[12] The terms applied equally to both states, but the initiative likely came from Russia.[13] The tsarist state and Orthodox Church had tired of paying large sums to recover Orthodox Christians enslaved in the Ottoman Empire,[14] and after a series of military victories in the recent war, Empress Anna (r. 1730–40) had a strong bargaining position. Her forces had captured thousands of Ottoman subjects, including (they claimed) 3,200 military men and 1,400 noncombatants when the Ottoman coastal fortress of Ochakov/Özü (in modern-day southern Ukraine) fell in 1737.[15] Two years

9. Fodor, "Piracy," 126.

10. Pálffy, "Ransom," 46.

11. Thomas Thornton, *The Present State of Turkey* (London: Joseph Mawman, 1809), 2:34. Elsewhere Thornton claimed that, "[t]he prisoners of their own nation are abandoned to the mercy of their enemies: the Turkish government expresses no anxiety as to their fate: they are neither ransomed, nor exchanged" (ibid., 1:291). All other evidence indicates that this was an exaggeration, and in the case of captives held in Russia, entirely false by the time Thornton's book was published.

12. Treaty of Belgrade (Cemazeyilahir 1152), Başbakanlık Osmanlı Arşivi (BOA), Divan-ı Hümayun Düvel-i Ecnebiye dosyaları (DVEd) 83/1, p. 85. Over the next few years, at least 2,600 Russian subjects were released from captivity and sent to Russia. On the Ottoman release process for captives in the eighteenth century more broadly, see Smiley, *Slaves to Prisoners of War*, ch. 3–4. The Ottomans and Habsburgs signed a separate peace treaty, also at Belgrade, on the same day.

13. It is revealing that Peter the Great had demanded a release without ransom during peace negotiations in 1699. See Boeck, *Boundaries*, 137.

14. Michael Khodarkovsky estimates that Muscovy paid five million rubles in ransoms during the first half of the seventeenth century, funded by a special tax. Khodarkovsky, *Steppe*, 22, 223.

15. "Manifest'" (1737), Rossiiskii Gosudarstvennii Voenno-Istoricheskii Arkhiv (RGVIA), Russko-Turetskaya Voina 1735-1739 collection (RTV-1735), *fond* 460, *opis'* 1, *del'* 1.

later, at Khotyn on the Dniester River, they claimed another 2,121 captives, 700 of them military.[16] This was critical to the treaty: the British ambassador, Everard Fawkener, believed the Ottomans accepted the terms because "there are a great Number of Turks Prisoners in Muscovy, the Price of whose Liberty is to be that of the Muscovites here."[17] The Ottoman state itself presented this reasoning in justifying its orders for Ottoman slaveowners to release Russian captives, declaring that in exchange for "the insignificant number of Muscovites" they would set free, "all of the enslaved people of Islam" (*üserâ-yı ehl-i İslâm*) in Russia would be released.[18]

This statement was intended only to persuade reluctant Ottoman slaveowners—it did nothing, in itself, to liberate those "enslaved people of Islam." The most pressing captivity issue for state officials remained, as it had been before, the liberation of well-connected elites—in other words, those who held important positions and had connections to the Imperial Council (Divan-ı Hümayun). Such captives included Kolçak İlyas Pasha, commandant of Khotyn, and even more importantly, Yahya Pasha, commandant of Ochakov.[19] Yahya was not merely a military commander, a vizier, and a pasha of three horsetails (*trekhbunchuzhnoy*, as the Russians referred to him)—he was also son-in-law to the former (and future) grand vizier and noted war hero Hekimoğlu Ali Pasha.[20] The Russians were well aware of Yahya's importance, and that of other elite captives—as they demonstrated by preparing an official list of captured pashas and beys.[21] The Russians threatened that if their own captives were not released, they would not return Yahya, İlyas, and other prominent captives. Perhaps convinced by this

16. Fawkener to the Secretary of State (11 Sept. 1739, 22 Sept. 1739, and following), The National Archives [of the United Kingdom] (TNA), State Papers (SP) 91/23; Cevat Erbakan, *1736-1739 Osmanlı-Rus ve Avusturya Savaşları* (Istanbul: Askeri Matbaa, 1938), 61–62.
17. Fawkener to the Secretary of State, (15 Feb. 1740), TNA, SP 97/31.
18. Imperial orders (Rabiulahir 1155), BOA, DVEd *defter* 84/9, hüküm #59, pp. 20–21. Also see Ahmet Refik, *Hicrî on Ikinci Asırda Istanbul Hayatı (1100-1200)* (Istanbul: Devlet Matbaası, 1930), #177. Amusingly, the order nearly contradicted itself in its attempts at propaganda—while this line presents the Russian prisoners as a small number, compared to the greater number of Ottomans who would be released, the preface to the order declares triumphantly that in the past war, "so many" Muscovites has been captured, and only "some" Ottomans.
19. Fawkener to the Secretary of State (11 Sept. 1739, 22 Sept. 1739, and following), TNA, SP 91/23; M. Münir Aktepe, ed., *Mehmed Emnî Beyefendi (Paşa)'nin Rusya Sefâreti ve Sefâret-Nâmesi* (Ankara: Türk Tarih Kurumu, 1974), 49.
20. "Manifest'" (1737), RGVIA, RTV-1735 460/1-1. Yahya's relationship to Ali is confirmed in Mehmed Süreyyâ, *Sicill-i Osmanî Yahud Tezkire-i Meşâhir-i Osmâniyye*, ed. Ali Aktan, Abdülkadir Yuvalı, and Metin Hülâgû (Istanbul: Sebil, 1996), IV/2:243–44. Also see Michael Robert Hickok, *Ottoman Military Administration in Eighteenth-Century Bosnia* (Leiden: Brill, 1997).
21. "Manifest'" (1737), RGVIA, RTV-1735 460-1-1.

threat, and hoping to aid his son-in-law, Hekimoğlu Ali himself visited the galleys to secure the release of enslaved Russians.[22]

The Ottoman envoy sent to Russia 1740–42, Mehmed Emnî Efendi, made no such systematic efforts to find and release his own sovereign's subjects. The Russian government issued general orders for releasing captives,[23] but there is no indication Mehmed Emnî influenced those orders. His embassy report (*sefaretname*) echoes Mahmud's official line in abstractly invoking Muslims' freedom—he described freeing "the people of Islam who fell captive to the snare of enslavement by the infidels" as "the obligation of the imperial embassy and the responsibility of the zeal of our religion."[24] But this is presented only as a preface to an account of how Mehmed Emnî met the captured commandants of Ochakov and Khotyn (Yahya and İlyas) on the road as they returned to the Ottoman Empire. The Ottoman state's generalized claim to be concerned about its captured subjects did not translate into action, and with the exception of certain prominent officials, the recovery of captives was not a diplomatic priority.

Captives' liberation was, of course, a priority for the captives themselves—and at least some of them learned that they now could press the Ottoman state to demand their release through treaty law. This became clear to the next Ottoman ambassador, Şehdî Osman Pasha, when he visited the Russian Empire in 1757–58. Soon after crossing the frontier, Osman was approached by a woman named Fatma, who presented herself as the daughter of a certain Şahin Ağa, the apprentice (çırak) of an Ochakov janissary named Yusuf Pasha.[25] One by one, others took refuge with Osman, claiming ties to specific individuals or residences in Ochakov.[26] Clearly understanding the provisions of the Treaty of Belgrade, these prisoners claimed that they had not converted to Christianity. They proved this by describing previous escape attempts or by reciting the shahada, which "in any circumstances must be accepted according to the requirement of the imperial treaty and the requirement of religion."[27] They seemed to see the Ottoman state's treaty rights as coterminous with its religious duties, and they argued that both of these entitled them, as Ottoman Muslims, to demand state aid in gaining release.

Osman's mission officially included seeking out such captives, marking a greater state commitment to the task than had been the case during Mehmed Emnî's mission fifteen years earlier. He continued to take in captives over ob-

22. Russian memorandum to the Porte (est. 1153), BOA, İrade Hariciye (İHR) *gömlek* 1830.
23. Köremezli, "Rusya'daki Esir," 985.
24. Aktepe, *Emnî*, 49–50.
25. Faik Reşit Unat, ed., "Şehdi Osman Paşa Sefaretnamesi," *Tarih Vesikaları* 1 (1941–42): 77. He transcribes the name as "Fatıme."
26. Ibid., 156.
27. Ibid., 78, 156–57.

jections from Russian slaveowners and officials. As he passed through Kiev on his return journey, angry Russians even attacked his retinue while he attended a feast with the city's military commander. The attack was repulsed, however, and Osman returned to Ottoman territory, via Poland, with the freed Muslims.[28] Their assertiveness, and Osman's willingness to protect them, foreshadowed the increasing Ottoman commitment to captive release that was to come later in the century.

From the Treaty of Küçük Kaynarca (1774) to the Treaty of Jassy (1792)

War erupted between the Ottoman and Russian Empires again in 1768, and after a series of devastating defeats, the Ottomans signed the humiliating Treaty of Küçük Kaynarca in July 1774. The treaty is famous for its requirement that the Ottomans grant autonomy to the Crimean Tatar Khanate, and for the later Russian claim that the treaty entitled them to "protect" Ottoman Christians.[29] However, in its application to Ottoman captives in Russia, it was less novel, and did little to change the rules established at Belgrade thirty-five years earlier.[30] As in the 1735 war, the Russians had taken many captives, and they again began returning them in large groups after peace was concluded.[31] Once again, the Russians and Ottomans ordered their respective subjects to release captives (the Ottomans, as after the Treaty of Belgrade, justified their orders as necessary to ensure freedom for Muslims in Russia).[32] Thus the Russian Chargé d'Affaires in Istanbul, Christopher Peterson, successfully used a threat to halt the return of captives to exert pressure on the Porte in a dispute over the return of Russians in the Ottoman Empire.[33]

For the most part, however, it still fell to captives themselves, or their families, to take the lead in pursuing their release. As Şehdî Osman had found during his mission in the 1750s, many captives knew the law—and they pressed the Ottoman state to enforce it. Families communicated the names of their captured relatives to the Porte (something which elites were probably far better positioned

---

28. Ibid., 397.
29. See Roderic H. Davison, "'Russian Skill and Turkish Imbecility': The Treaty of Kuchuk Kainardji Reconsidered," *Slavic Review* 35, no. 3 (1976): 463–83.
30. See Will Smiley, "Let *Whose* People Go? Subjecthood, Sovereignty, Liberation, and Legalism in Eighteenth-Century Russo-Ottoman Relations," *Turkish Historical Review* 3, no. 2 (2012): 196–228.
31. Certificates of prisoner return (Receb 1188), BOA, Cevdet Hariciye collection (CHR) 7198; Panin to Abdülkerim (1775), Arkhiv Vneshnei Politiki Rossiiskoi Imperii (AVPRI), Snosheniya Rossii s Turtsei (SRT), 89/8-934.
32. Imperial orders (Şaban 1188), BOA, CHR 8060; Osman Köse, *1774 Küçük Kaynarca Andlaşması* (Ankara: Türk Tarih Kurumu, 2006), 199; Köremezli, "Rusya'daki Esir," 985.
33. Peterson to Field Marshal Pyotr Rumyantsev (30 June 1775), AVPRI, Konstantinopol'skaya Missiya (KM), 90/1-616, ff. 50–51.

to do). When the Ottoman ambassador, Abdülkerim Pasha, travelled to Russia in 1775–76, he took these lists of names with him, and presented them to Russian Prime Minister Nikita Panin.[34] The information they presented was detailed, but idiosyncratic: Molla Mehmed, the son of a janissary from Bender, sought his captured mother Ayşe and two sisters; Hacı Mustafa, also of Bender, had been released with his family when peace was made, but a Russian major had taken his twelve-year old son, Halil; Beşir Mehmed of Gümülçine/Yumurtina requested the release of his three eunuchs, allegedly held by a Russian count; and Fatma, an elderly woman from Bender, had been released with her husband, but her son, Şerif Mehmed, had been retained by a "colonel's sergeant" in the town of Tirepol.

Panin replied dismissively, going through the Ottoman lists individual-by-individual and in many cases denying any knowledge of the named captives and captors. The count had no eunuchs in his custody (a *different* count, Orlov, had captured three eunuchs but already released them); Panin claimed he had never heard of Ayşe or her sisters-in-law, or of the sergeant holding Fatma's son, or even of the town of Tirepol.[35] Moreover, the Russians argued, many Ottoman captives had converted to Christianity, and, therefore, were required to stay in Russia.[36] Abdülkerim eventually abandoned his claims, although he did accept eighty captives who escaped custody and took refuge with his retinue. According to the embassy report, Russian officials deliberately looked the other way.[37]

Abdülkerim, then, went beyond Şehdî Osman and Mehmed Emnî in his commitment to free captives. Presenting the Russian state with lists was an important step, but the initiative still came more from Ottoman subjects themselves than from the state. Captives' families had submitted the names for these lists, while most of the actual captives who followed Abdülkerim home had joined his retinue themselves. It was captives and their families, more than the Ottoman state, who sought to enforce the sultan's treaty rights.

Far more vexing to the Porte than its subjects' captivity in Russia, was its loss of territory to that empire, especially Crimea, which Empress Catherine (r. 1762–96) formally annexed in 1783. Regaining the peninsula became a major goal of Ottoman foreign policy, and this helped prompt Sultan Abdülhamid I (r. 1774–89) to declare war in 1787. He and his successor, Selim III (r. 1789–1807), launched unsuccessful campaigns to recover the Crimea, and repeated losses to Russian and Austrian forces eventually led to a peace treaty, signed at Jassy in 1792. This treaty's eighth article, pertaining to prisoners, virtually duplicated the provisions of Küçük Kaynarca. Thus, once again all Ottoman and Russian captives, whether

---

34. Written in French and Russian, these lists are contained in AVPRI, SRT, 89/8-933, ff. 4–7.
35. Panin to Abdülkerim (1775), AVPRI, SRT 89/8-934.
36. Ibid.; Norman Itzkowitz and Max Ethan Mote, eds., *Mubadele: An Ottoman-Russian Exchange of Ambassadors* (Chicago: University of Chicago Press, 1970), 100–01.
37. Mote and Itzkowitz, *Mubadele*, 98, 101–02.

in state or private hands, were to be released, without ransom, unless they had converted to the captor state's religion.[38]

It is not surprising, then, that the account of Mustafa Rasih Efendi's embassy to Russia in 1793–94 partly echoes those of Şehdî Osman and Abdülkerim. Thousands of Ottoman subjects were held in Russian state custody, and many more by private Russian owners. These private captives were, in essence, serfs or slaves, even though Catherine had decreed an end to enserfing war captives in 1781.[39] Many such captives sought out Rasih and took shelter with him, but the Russians raised a variety of objections: captors denied having received orders to release their captives, while state officials argued that captives had converted to Christianity.[40] The Russians even placed guards around Rasih's delegation to prevent fugitives from reaching them, and used force to pry a few escapees away from him.[41] As before, Ottoman subjects asked the Porte for help in liberating their relatives held in Russia. Some, despite the treaty, even paid ransoms to Russian captors.[42] Rasih found that many Russian officials claimed they had no authority to deal with captives, and the Russian minister A. A. Bezbordoko would not meet with him to discuss the matter—indeed, this was a major factor in Rasih's eventual return to Istanbul.[43]

---

38. Treaty of Jassy, Art. 8, BOA, DVEd 83/1, 192–93; *Polnoe Sobranie Zakonov Rossiiskoi Imperii, 1649 Goda* (St. Petersburg, 1830), I/23:291 (#17008); Gabriel Noradounghian, ed., *Recueil d'Actes Internationaux de l'Empire Ottoman* (Paris: Pichon, 1897), 2:20; Mahmud Mesud, ed., *Muahedat Mecmuası* (Istanbul, 1876), 4:11.

39. This is an intriguing question deserving of more attention than can be given to it here. For an overview of Russian slavery (generally seen as ending under Peter the Great in the early eighteenth century), see Richard Hellie, *Slavery in Russia 1450–1725* (Chicago: University of Chicago Press, 1982). For Catherine's decree (which may or may not have applied to non-Christian captives), see Isabel de Madariaga, *Russia in the Age of Catherine the Great* (London: Weidenfeld and Nicolson, 1981), 552–53; Aleksandr S. Lappo-Danileskii, "The Serf Question in an Age of Enlightenment," in *Catherine the Great: A Profile*, ed. Marc Raeff (London: Macmillan, 1972), 276–77.

40. Rasih to the Russian Court (1794), AVPRI, SRT 89/8-784; Halil İnalcık, "Yaş Muahedesinden Sonra Osmanlı-Rus Münasebetleri: Rasih Efendi ve Ceneral Kutuzof Elçilikleri," *Ankara Üniversitesi Dil ve Tarih-Coğrafya Fakültesi Dergisi* 4, no. 2 (1946): 201.

41. Ibid., 200–01.

42. Rasih to the Russian Court (1794), AVPRI, SRT 89/8-784; Summary of petitions (20 Zilhicce 1209/8 July 1795), BOA, Hatt-ı Hümayun (HAT) 221/12359.

43. İnalcık, "Yaş," 201. Thomas Naff and Stanford Shaw have incorrectly asserted that it was Ottoman, rather than Russian, intransigence about returning captives that soured relations between the two empires. See Thomas Naff, "Reform and the Conduct of Ottoman Diplomacy in the Reign of Selim III, 1789–1807," *Journal of the American Oriental Society* 83, no. 3 (1963): 304; Stanford J. Shaw, *Between Old and New: The Ottoman Empire under Sultan Selim III, 1789–1807* (Cambridge, MA: Harvard University Press, 1971), 189. Also see Valeriy Morkva, "Russia's Policy of Rapprochement with the Ottoman Empire in the Era of the French Revolutionary and Napoleonic Wars, 1792–1806" (PhD diss., Bilkent University, 2010).

Rasih's mission, however, demonstrated a stronger state commitment to retrieving captives than in the 1770s. The Ottoman state used ever-more-specific diplomatic measures to enforce its legal rights to the benefit of its own subjects. After peace was agreed at Jassy in 1792, the Ottoman state kept records of captives returning from Russia,[44] and braced itself for a diplomatic showdown with the Russians. The Imperial Council consulted Sultan Selim III about how to proceed "if in the matter of the release of captives there arise futile types of perfidies" from Russia.[45] Selim, however, warned that "bargaining [done] at home does not suffice in the market."[46] Following Selim's instructions, Rasih raised the issue of captives repeatedly, and brought with him lists of those believed to be held in Russia (over 7,000, according to the British ambassador to Istanbul, Robert Ainslie).[47] Rasih himself prepared lists of over 1,500 captives whom he found, or heard rumors of, during his mission. He presented this list to the Russians, accusing them also of moving other captives out of his route so he would not hear of their presence.[48] The Ottomans were quite concerned about two particular notables, Battal Hüseyin and Tayyar Pasha of the prominent Caniklizâde family, who were both captured during the war.[49] However, a large portion of Rasih's dealings with the Russians involved other, non-elite captives.

Russian geopolitical power still allowed them to dismiss Ottoman concerns at times, but this level of Ottoman diplomatic pressure on Russia, on behalf of less prominent captives, was nevertheless unprecedented. Legally, Rasih based his demands on the wording of the Treaty of Jassy, and thus on the captives' status as "the subjects of my [the sultan's] Sublime state."[50] This meant Rasih could reclaim *both* Ottoman Muslims and Ottoman Christians—as he tried to do when he objected that "thousands" of Armenians had been forced into Russian territory from the Ottoman fortress city of Akkerman.[51] But he also complained about the deportation of fifty-four *ulema* from the Crimea—people who probably

---

44. For example, see the lists (17 Receb 1206/11 March 1792) in BOA, Cevdet Askeriye collection [hereinafter CAS] 29740.
45. Council to Selim and reply (Zilhicce 1207), BOA, HAT 239/13343.
46. Ibid.; this wording is based on Itzkowitz's translation in Mote and Itzkowitz, *Mubadele*, 101 n. 55.
47. Robert Ainslie to the Secretary of State (10 Feb. 1794), TNA, Foreign Office (FO) 78/15, letter #3; İnalcık, "Yaş," 200.
48. Rasih to the Russian Court (1794), AVPRI, 89/8-784.
49. See BOA, HAT 226/12583; BOA, HAT 226/12600; BOA, HAT 240/13444; BOA, HAT 258/14869; Canay Şahin, "The Rise and Fall of an *Ayân* Family in Eighteenth Century Anatolia: The Caniklizâdes (1737–1808)" (PhD diss., Bilkent University, 2003), 64.
50. Treaty of Jassy, Art. 8, BOA, DVEd 83/1, 192–93. The Hanafi tradition, in fact, expected that Muslim rulers would seek to liberate both Muslim and *dhimmi* captives: Fadel, "International Law," ¶ 21.
51. Rasih to the Russian Court (1794), AVPRI, 89/8-784.

were not legally Ottoman subjects, at least not since 1774, so were not included in the treaty.[52]

When officials in St. Petersburg were intransigent about releasing captives, Sultan Selim personally expressed his frustration, noting that "in this matter we have a problem with the Russians."[53] The Porte raised the issue with the Russian ambassador to Istanbul, General Mikhail Kutuzov. After Rasih reported that Ottoman Muslims were being held against their will based on their alleged conversion to Christianity, the Ottomans threatened to retaliate in kind by making it more difficult to recognize Russian captives' conversion to Islam within the Ottoman Empire.[54]

As Selim's comments indicated, he and his Council were determined to support Rasih. Why was the sultan so dedicated to redeeming non-elite captives? Halil İnalcık has suggested that Selim, frustrated by his failure to reclaim Crimea during the war, sought consolation by becoming "extremely fastidious" in returning captives.[55] The sultan himself articulated this concern in terms of imperial honor, ordering Rasih to guide his actions on the prisoner question in order to advance "the glory of my state" (*şan-ı devletim*).[56] But this concern for individual captives' return was not simply a matter of Selim's individual priorities[57]—as we have seen, such concerns had been increasing since the 1739 Treaty of Belgrade.

After the Treaty of Bucharest (1812)

These state concerns became even more prominent in Ottoman-Russian diplomacy in the early nineteenth century. Sultan Mahmud II (r. 1808–39), like Selim, frequently saw the matter as vital to the honor of his state. This is apparent when we consider the 1806–12 Russo-Ottoman War—the next in the two empires' long series of conflicts. The Russians overran a number of Ottoman fortress cities, and captured perhaps 40,000 Ottoman subjects, both military and civilian, holding them in the southern governorates of the Russian Empire.[58] Mahmud dispatched hundreds of thousands of silver piasters to aid the captives after peace was made, and also presented substantial gifts to Ottoman military units freed

52. Ibid.
53. İnalcık, "Yaş," 201.
54. AVPRI, SRT 89/8-784-5; for the diplomatic background, see Morkva, "Rapprochement," 57–64.
55. İnalcık, "Yaş," 200.
56. Council to Selim and reply (Zilhicce 1207), BOA, HAT 239/13343.
57. That said, such "fastidiousness" fits well with Betül Başaran's portrait of Selim as a categorizing, "statistical" ruler. See Betül Başaran, *Selim III, Social Control and Policing in Istanbul at the End of the Eighteenth Century* (Leiden: Brill, 2014).
58. Council to Mahmud and reply (22 Cemaziyülahir 1227/3 July 1812), BOA, HAT 986/41741; Alexander Bitis, *Russia and the Eastern Question: Army, Government, and Society, 1815–1833* (Oxford: Oxford University Press, 2006), 352–53.

from captivity.[59] He dispatched a commissioner, Ahmed Pasha, to Russia to oversee the return of captives, though the matter was greatly complicated by the fact that Napoleon invaded Russia almost immediately after the Russo-Ottoman War ended.[60]

Two particular incidents from this conflict, one concerning military captives and the other civilians, are particularly valuable in revealing the changing meanings of captivity and subjecthood. The first resulted from a military success-turned-catastrophe: in September 1811, Grand Vizier Ahmed Pasha took 36,000 men—the main body of the Ottoman army—across the Danube to the north (left) bank to face the Russian forces under Field Marshal Mikhail Kutuzov (the same Kutuzov who had been ambassador to the Ottoman Empire in the 1790s). Kutuzov, however, did not retreat in the face of Ahmed's offensive; he responded by himself crossing to the south (right) bank of the Danube, severing Ahmed's supply lines and dispersing the Ottoman reserves. Now, Ahmed's army was trapped on the wrong side of the river (though he himself escaped).[61] Soon, according to Russian observers, "[t]he elite of the Turkish army" was starving; "[h]orses were either dead or eaten. Poor Turks had to eat rotten meat and had no salt. They cropped and ate the grass and roots on the territory of the camp, often paying with their lives for such terrible food and dying under the Russian artillery and musket fire."[62] As winter set in, the Ottoman army had dwindled to about 12,000 men, so "Kutuzov intervened on behalf of the surviving soldiers, and as a means of propelling the [ongoing peace] negotiations, took them under his protection."[63]

This sounded like surrender, but it was not. Kutuzov "instructed Count Langeron to escort the Turks to designated settlements, some 50 *versts* [33 miles] behind the Russian army, and demonstrate to them that 'they are not our prisoners of war, but our guests, willingly staying here.'"[64] This was a semantic distinction, but it mattered to Mahmud. Repeatedly, in conversation with his advisers, the sultan refused to consider the army to have the status of "prisoners of war" (*üsera-yı harb*), and he insisted that the Russians not treat them in that manner.[65] The Ottoman-Russian armistice signed on 8 December 1811 formalized this

59. Ibid.; Council to Mahmud and reply (est. 1227), BOA, HAT 1296/50382.
60. Council to Mahmud and reply (9 Muharrem 1228/12 Jan. 1813), BOA, HAT 1000/41997.
61. Aksan, *Wars*, 276–77.
62. Quoted in ibid.
63. Ibid., 277.
64. Quoted in ibid.
65. See, e.g., Council to Mahmud and reply (6 Receb 1227/16 July 1812), BOA, HAT 963/41253; Council to Mahmud and reply (15 Cemaziyülahir 1227/26 June 1812), BOA, HAT 986/41776; Council to Mahmud and reply (26 Cemaziyülahir 1227/7 July 1812), BOA, HAT 1001/42027; Ziya Yılmazer, ed., *Sânî-Zâde Târîhî: 1223–1237/1808–1821* (Istanbul: Çamlıca, 2008), 1:527.

demand,[66] but Mahmud continued to complain that "despite saying previously to our soldiers remaining on the far side [of the Danube] '[they are] my guest[s],' now they are considered prisoner[s] of war."[67]

The Russians recognized Mahmud's sensitivity on this issue, and as a negotiating tactic in early 1812, they renounced the armistice, "treat[ing] the beleaguered Ottoman troops as prisoners of war."[68] This, coupled with other "humiliating terms," prompted Mahmud to consider renewing the war, before he realized that this was a military impossibility.[69] Treating the army on the left bank as "guests" rather than "prisoners of war" was largely a matter of language; they were militarily useless, and might as well have surrendered. Indeed, to the extent that the designation did make a difference, it actually hurt Ottoman financial interests. This was because the Porte bore the burden of paying the Russians to feed and maintain the army.[70] By contrast, the Russians paid to support Ottoman subjects held as prisoners, and the terms of the final Treaty of Bucharest decreed that neither side would reimburse the other for such expenses.[71] And regardless of their categorization, it seems everyone knew that they would be returned at the end of the war. This was a new concern, not apparently shared by previous sultans. State honor, Mahmud seemed to believe, was implicated by his subjects' captivity, and particularly by their categorization under international law as "prisoners of war."

Soon after the war ended, the status of Ottoman captives again became a major subject of diplomatic debate, but now, the subjects in question were civilians, and they clearly *were* prisoners. The matter arose in mid-1812, after the war had ended, as the thousands of Ottoman civilians captured during the conflict, and mostly held in state custody, began to return home.[72] In late 1812, 500 or 600 Ottoman captives traveled through rural southern Russia on their way to the

---

66. Fehmi Ismail, "The Making of the Treaty of Bucharest, 1811–1812," *Middle Eastern Studies* 15, no. 2 (1979): 170.
67. Yılmazer, *Sânî-Zâde*, 1:527.
68. Ismail, "Bucharest," 171.
69. Ibid., 172.
70. Ibid., 170.
71. Mahmud Mesud, *Muahedat*, 4:54–55.
72. This account is based on Grand Vizier to the Kaymakam (est. 1227), BOA, CHR 2382; Russian memorandum to the Porte (1 Şevval 1227/8 Oct. 1812), BOA, HAT 989/41821H; Council to Mahmud and Reply (est. Zilhicce 1227), BOA, HAT 1164/46049; Liston to the Secretary of State (12 Nov. 1812), TNA, FO 78/78 #16; B.P. Milovidov, "Turetskie Voennoplennye v Rossii v 1812 Goda," *Voprosy Istorii* 10 (2008): 91–96. The Ottoman chronicler Câbî tells a generally similar version of the story: Câbî Ömer Efendi, *Câbî Târihi (Târîh-i Sultân Selîm-i Sâlis ve Mahmûd-ı Sânî) Tahlîl ve Tenkidli Metin*, ed. Mehmet Ali Beyhan (Ankara: Türk Tarih Kurumu, 2003), 920–21.

frontier, to be returned to Ottoman lands.[73] While passing through the small city of Valki, near Kharkov in modern-day Ukraine,[74] the captives encountered two young Ottoman Muslim girls or young women from Sistova, enslaved by a Russian named Bulychev. According to the Russians, these captives had converted to Christianity, but the Ottoman prisoners, led by an officer named Yusuf Bey, rejected that claim and demanded that the women be set free and turned over to them. A fight broke out, and the villagers soon armed themselves. Along with a few soldiers, these residents overwhelmed the largely unarmed Ottoman captives, killing between 380 and 538 and recapturing 138. Only fourteen Russians were killed or mortally wounded, while more than a hundred suffered minor wounds.

The responses of Mahmud II, his Council, and his subjects to this incident illuminate the changing meaning of Ottoman subjecthood for captives. The sultan and his advisers were outraged when they learned of the incident, and the Council demanded the Russians punish the perpetrators. The fault, Russian Ambassador Andrei Italinskii assured the Porte, lay with the locals and with the governor of Kharkov, who would be disciplined appropriately. Many on the Council, however, were unsatisfied with this answer, and demanded that the Russians execute a number of guilty subjects equal to the number of dead Ottomans—along with the governor.[75] The British ambassador, Robert Liston, even claimed that some Ottoman officials wished to execute an equal number of Russian military captives in Ottoman state custody.[76]

Mahmud did not follow this advice. However, many soldiers, and residents of Istanbul, continued to demand justice—and some went so far as to attack Italinskii while he walked near the Süleymaniye Mosque in central Istanbul. The Porte executed some of these attackers, and exiled others—providing further ammunition to those Ottomans who asked why the Russians did not similarly punish their own criminal subjects.[77] Others on the Council, however, were more cautious, preferring to demand monetary reparations from the Russians. In these discussions, the Ottomans cast their concerns in both Islamic and international

---

73. This is the number given in Ottoman sources, while Milovidov gives the numbers as 622 or 642. The British ambassador, Robert Liston, seems to be incorrect in quoting a figure of "three to four hundred."

74. Most Ottoman documents refer to this as the "Kharkov matter," but more detailed accounts agree with the Russian sources that the event did occur in Valki; Council to Mahmud and replies (1227), BOA, HAT 980/41607A, 980/41607C, 1093/44372A. The confusion may be explained by the fact that Valki was near Kharkov (in fact, the Ottomans referred to the region as the "Kharkov governorate") or by the similarity in names. Liston refers to the town as "Halkova," which phonetically is halfway between "Valki" and "Kharkov."

75. Council to Mahmud and replies (est. Zilhicce 1227), BOA, HAT 1295/50336, 1164/46049.

76. Liston to the Secretary of State (12 Nov. 1812), TNA, FO 78/79 #16.

77. Council to Mahmud and reply (est. Zilhicce 1227), BOA, HAT 1295/50336.

legal terms. They referred to reciprocal executions as *kısas*, and payments as *diyet* (blood money), while also seeing their demands as required by the "laws" or "rights" of states (*hukuk-ı devlet/hukuk-ı düvel*).[78]

The Ottomans dispatched a special envoy, Abdülhamid Efendi, to look after this matter, which dragged on for months as each side blamed the other's subjects for starting the fight.[79] The Russian state—initially distracted by its life-and-death struggle against Napoleon's invading army—eventually conducted a series of inquiries. The District Court of Valki finally found, in April 1816, that the Ottoman captives had been the aggressors, so the Russian soldiers and villagers had acted in self-defense. The Criminal Court of the Kharkov governorate agreed in 1817, as did the Senate in 1819.[80]

Leaving aside the Russian state response, what is most relevant here is how Ottoman officials and subjects reacted, and how they couched their concerns. As we have seen, Ottoman officials up until the 1740s largely had looked out for each other, and devoted less attention to non-elite captives. The furor after the Valki incident demonstrates how this had changed in the later eighteenth century, since there is no indication that any of the Ottoman victims were well-connected. Indeed, Mahmud and his Council did not even refer to them by name or as individuals. Instead, they were important to the state simply through their status as Ottoman subjects, and especially as Muslims. They were "the captive people of Islam."[81] This gave new emphasis to the term Mehmed Emnî had used seventy years earlier, but the Porte now put its diplomatic and legal power behind the liberation of those people, as it lodged complaints and even sent out a special envoy. Here, as with the army stranded north of the Danube, the Porte was concerned about the Ottoman state's honor. The Council, in discussing how to respond, noted that "completely looking the other way at this [incident] would also necessarily cause shame among the other states."[82]

Ottoman subjects' viewpoints and actions on this matter are also intriguing. Like the captives who approached Şehdî Osman and Rasih, they understood that they were entitled to protection due to their status as Ottoman subjects. Soon after the incident, several janissary officers among the surviving captives presented a note to the Russian authorities, in which they laid out their side of the story. Most interestingly, they protested that as "prisoners, taken in battle[,] by the laws

---

78. Ibid.; Council to Mahmud and replies (est. Zilhicce 1227), BOA, HAT 1164/46049. See also E. Tyan, "Diya," *Encyclopaedia of Islam*, 2nd ed. (*EI²*), ed. P. Bearman, Th. Bianquis, C.E. Bosworth, E. van Donzel, W.P. Heinrichs. (2012), http://dx.doi.org/10.1163/1573-3912_islam_COM_0172; J. Schacht, "Ḳiṣāṣ," *EI²*, http://dx.doi.org/10.1163/1573-3912_islam_SIM_4400.
79. Grand Vizier to the Kaymakam (Zilkade 1227), BOA, HAT 999/41944.
80. Milovidov, "Voennoplennye," 95–96. Many villagers had also appropriated the captives' property, but only one Russian subject was found guilty of theft, and he was soon pardoned.
81. For example, see Council to Mahmud and reply (est. Zilhicce 1227), BOA, HAT 1295/50336.
82. Ibid.

of all nations [they] must be protected from everyone."[83] Furthermore, these captives recognized that Ottoman-Russian treaties guaranteed their return, and that this could be a point of leverage against the Russian state. The Ottoman janissary commander announced that he and his men would not accept repatriation until eight other janissaries, held in custody after the Valki incident, were also allowed to return. This exasperated the governor of Slobodsko-Ukraine, who wanted these troublesome captives gone, and recognized that delaying their return would violate the Treaty of Bucharest. Thus, he complied and sent all of them home, including the eight arrestees.[84] And as noted above, in Istanbul at least some Ottoman subjects felt that if the state would not secure justice for the captives, they would take it into their own hands by attacking the ambassador.[85]

Conclusion

This overview, then, illustrates the central Ottoman state's growing concern over the fate of non-elite captives in Russian hands over the course of the eighteenth century, and how it grew alongside the Ottoman state's legal rights to liberate such captives. This might be seen as a story of Russian initiative and Europeanization. Indeed, Russia won every war during this period and drove the new captivity rules introduced at Belgrade in 1739, but it would beg the question to assume that there was a set category of "European" diplomacy and treaty law, including these captivity rules, which the Ottomans could be forced to adopt. In fact, recent scholarship has suggested that Europeanization is an inadequate model, which does not capture the changing and pragmatic nature of Ottoman diplomacy.[86] At the same time, historians of international law have focused our attention on *how* particular norms have been used at particular moments, rather than assuming that they have meant the same thing across different contexts.[87]

We might, instead, consider the role of honor and subjecthood at this historical moment. Scholars of European history have shown that international law

83. Milovidov, "Voennoplennye," 94.
84. Ibid., 95. Twenty years earlier, after the Treaty of Jassy, Russian sailors held in Ottoman custody used the same tactic, though with less success, to press their demands against the Porte. See Will Smiley, "'After Being so Long Prisoners, They Will Not Return to Slavery in Russia': An Aegean Network of Violence between Empires and Identities," *Journal of Ottoman Studies* 44 (2014): 221–34.
85. Council to Mahmud and reply (Zilhicce 1227), BOA, HAT 1295/50336. The Council decided to exile some of the offenders and to execute others.
86. Compare Yurdusev, *Ottoman Diplomacy*, with Naff, "Ottoman Empire and the European States System."
87. For example, see John Fabian Witt, "A Social History of International Law: Historical Commentary, 1861–1900," in *International Law in the U.S. Supreme Court: Continuity and Change*, ed. David L. Sloss, Michael D. Ramsey, and William S. Dodge (New York: Cambridge University Press, 2011), 164–87.

and diplomacy served to demonstrate, and protect, monarchical honor, while the social place of prisoners of war was also a critical site for negotiating aristocratic honor.[88] In the early nineteenth century (though perhaps not the eighteenth) war itself could be seen as an expression of European states' honor.[89] Ottoman officials also had a sense of their own empire's honor, and since at least the sixteenth century they had seen it as bound up with protecting its subjects' lives and freedom within the empire.[90] As Ottoman sultans began making lasting peace treaties with their rivals after 1699, they came to see "the honor and dignity of my Sultanate" as also being at stake in upholding their end of each agreement.[91] Now, as the Ottomans became enmeshed in ever more treaties with Russia over the course of the eighteenth century, state honor reached further. It obligated the state not only to fulfill its own commitments but also to ensure that other states fulfilled theirs, even in ways that had not previously seemed vitally important (such as the release of captives).

This occurred because the treaties connected Ottoman state honor to Ottoman subjecthood. Russo-Ottoman treaties made Ottoman subjecthood legally meaningful in a new way, but they did not immediately compel the Ottoman state to put its resources into enforcing their articles. Indeed, the state initially did not pay much attention to non-elite captives, even when it could—as the missions of Mehmed Emnî in the 1740s and, to a lesser extent, Şehdî Osman in the 1750s, demonstrate. The Ottoman state turned a legal right into a perceived political obligation, to be pursued even in the face of mounting costs, and repeated failures. This paralleled the process that Gillian Weiss has noted in France, as slavery became "an extraordinary and unacceptable state of being rather than simply a horrible but sometimes inescapable condition"—especially as Bourbon subjects became French citizens following the Revolution.[92] It may be that in the Ottoman case, as in France, possibility preceded obligation. As Weiss argues, "the notion that all Frenchmen should be free followed from the possibility that

88. See Jan Hennings, *Russia and Courtly Europe: Ritual and the Culture of Diplomacy, 1648–1725* (Edinburgh: Edinburgh University Press, 2016); Renaud Morieux, "French Prisoners of War, Conflicts of Honour, and Social Inversions in England, 1744–1783," *The Historical Journal* 56, no. 1 (2013): 55–88.

89. See James Q. Whitman, *The Verdict of Battle: The Law of Victory and the Making of Modern War* (Cambridge, MA: Harvard University Press, 2012), 223.

90. See Leslie Peirce, "Abduction with (Dis)honor: Sovereigns, Brigands, and Heroes in the Ottoman World," *Journal of Early Modern History* 15 (2011): 311–29. I thank Tolga Esmer for stimulating my thinking about issues of honor in this period.

91. Abou-el-Haj, "Closure," 475.

92. Gillian Weiss, "Barbary Captivity and the French Idea of Freedom," *French Historical Studies* 28, no. 2 (2005): 232–64. In Britain, too, changes in imperial politics went hand-in-hand with changing attitudes toward British subjects in captivity. See Colley, *Captives*.

all Frenchmen could be."[93] For the French, this possibility came from imperial power and from national ideology; for the Ottomans, it came from the provisions of inter-imperial treaty law. As Janice Thompson has said in a different context, "an is became an ought."[94] Once the state gained a legal right through treaties, its honor came to depend on vindicating that right.

Captured Ottoman subjects were quick to realize what this meant. From the moment captives approached Şehdî Osman to vindicate "the requirement of the imperial treaty and the requirement of religion," up through the Valki incident in 1812, Ottoman subjects seem to have come to recognize that they were able to mobilize the Ottoman state's abstract religious commitments, and its theoretical treaty rights, to their own advantage. In a strictly legal sense, Russo-Ottoman treaties granted rights only to the states themselves, not to individual captives. The right to demand release was held by the Ottoman state, against the Russian state, but it did work to the benefit of Ottoman subjects.[95] In practice, individual Ottomans, especially Ottoman Muslims, could use the treaties to make claims on the Russian and Ottoman states, almost as if they had a treaty right themselves. They did so not as well-connected elites, or as members of corporate groups such as the janissaries, but simply as Ottoman subjects.

Even so, while treaty law applied to all Ottoman subjects equally, it helped some more than others in practice. Rasih's demands on behalf of captured Armenians aside, Ottoman official concern for slaves had a religious tinge—they assumed that captured Ottoman subjects, by default, could be thought of and referred to as Muslims.[96] Thus, Mehmed Emnî could speak of "the obligation of the imperial embassy and the responsibility of the zeal of our religion," and by the early nineteenth century, Mahmud and his Council referred to all captive Ottomans simply as the "people of Islam." The international legal rights of the empire, the sultan's duty as a Muslim ruler, and the honor of the empire were all joined together in recovering captives.

---

93. Ibid., 263.

94. Janice Thomson, *Mercenaries, Pirates, and Sovereigns* (Princeton: Princeton University Press, 1994), 152.

95. This was common in European international law at the time, which, classically, is said to have applied only to states and never to individuals. On this topic, see Kate Parlett, *The Individual in the International Legal System: Continuity and Change in International Law* (Cambridge, UK: Cambridge University Press, 2011).

96. Molly Greene has noted that in the Mediterranean, religious and political identifications were intertwined for longer than often believed. In the Ottoman-Russian context, only subjecthood, or a certain politically defined type of conversion, had *legal* weight under treaty rules. Yet in this story of captivity and liberation, we see that even in the legal world of subjecthood, religion still had great weight. See Molly Greene, *Catholic Pirates and Greek Merchants* (Princeton: Princeton University Press, 2010); Will Smiley, "The Burdens of Subjecthood: The Ottoman State, Russian Fugitives, and Interimperial Law, 1774–1869," *International Journal of Middle East Studies* 46, no. 1 (2014): 87.

Other scholars have offered models of Ottoman "citizenship" in the pre-Tanzimat era that may help understand these developments. Y. Hakan Erdem and Virginia Aksan see Sultan Mahmud II using the language of religious duty to persuade his male subjects to fight the empire's enemies, even as he abolished the janissary corps. Indeed, Erdem argues, Mahmud sought to create a sense of unity among Ottoman Muslims—of all social ranks—as a "nation" (*millet*).[97] Baki Tezcan reaches further back, arguing that during the "second Ottoman Empire," from the late sixteenth to early nineteenth centuries, a "proto-democratization" of society meant that male, Muslim Ottoman subjects, possessing legal rights, "moved up to become citizens of sorts much before the autocratic political modernization of the Tanzimat era."[98]

These narratives may provide a model for the changing status of Ottoman subjects held in Russia. An abstract, theoretical state concern to free "the enslaved people of Islam" became a legal obligation, and then a perceived state duty in which the sultan's honor was at stake. Ransom-free release from captivity became, in a sense, a right attaching to Ottoman subjecthood. While all Ottoman subjects could claim liberation, in practice such claims were somewhat limited by religion, as Ottoman Muslims—even non-elites—became the state's main priority. Through the lens of captivity, we see changes in subjecthood occurring in the eighteenth century, not in the seventeenth or nineteenth centuries. By 1800, unlike in 1700, Ottoman subjects in captivity looked like Tezcan's "citizens of sorts," and like members of Erdem's unified Muslim community. This was not the result of a monolithic Europeanization, but also was not solely an internal Ottoman matter. These changes in captives' status were reflected in, and arose partly from, the contingent negotiation and enforcement of treaty law and honor between two early modern Eurasian empires.

97. See Aksan, *Wars*, 343–44; Erdem, "Responses."
98. Tezcan, *Second Ottoman Empire*, 236–37.

3 The Well-Defended Domains: Eurocentric International Law and the Making of the Ottoman Office of Legal Counsel*

Aimee M. Genell

In the spring of 1883, the Ottoman Foreign Ministry established a new office to manage questions related to international law. From the creation of the Office of Legal Counsel (Hukuk Müşavirliği İstişare Odası) to its reconfiguration within the Turkish Foreign Ministry in the 1920s, Foreign Ministry legal advisors (*hukuk müşavirleri*) generated thousands of legal opinions in response to a wide range of problems from issues of personal status to matters of high diplomacy. Staffed initially by European and later Ottoman lawyers, legal advisors provided much of the raw legal material and arguments for the Ottoman diplomatic engagement with Europe. The Office of Legal Counsel systematized the longstanding Ottoman practice of hiring European lawyers for assistance in public and private legal matters, but it was pressure from territorial losses in the Balkans and the British military occupation of Egypt that added urgency to the creation of a special department dedicated to international law. In the absence of military strength, territory recently lost or endangered on the battlefield could be preserved through law.

Foreign ministries across Europe absorbed international legal experts into their diplomatic arsenals in the 1880s and 1890s, and similarly created new offices to deal with international law, but the Ottoman Empire was the first to formalize a legalistic approach to foreign policy. For much of the period between the reign of Abdülhamid II and the Balkan Wars, Ottoman international lawyers appealed to positive international law, particularly treaty law, as a viable means to protect the imperial domains.[1] While European foreign ministries harnessed

* I wish to thank International Security Studies at Yale University and the Middle East Institute at Columbia University for their generous research support for this project. I thank Nahed Samour and Martii Koskenniemi for inviting me to present an earlier iteration of this project at the Erik Castrén Institute of International Law and Human Rights in Helsinki. I would also like to thank the anonymous reviewers for their helpful comments, as well as Beth Baron, Lâle Can, Patrick O. Cohrs, Will Hanley, Sinan Kuneralp, Michael Christopher Low, Marcus Payk, Christine Philliou, Steffen Rimner, Will Smiley, and Adam Tooze for their counsel, comments, and suggestions.
1. The Ottoman use of international law in foreign policy is one of the main subjects of my current manuscript project and my dissertation. See Aimee M. Genell, "Empire by Law: Ottoman

The Subjects of Ottoman International Law (2020): 036–054
DOI: 10.2979/subjectsottomaninternationallaw.0.0.04

international law to justify imperial expansion, the Ottoman state relied on international law as a defensive strategy against Europe and as a tool to consolidate power within the empire.[2] Simply put, international law mattered more for a weak empire at the margins of an expansive Europe.

Historians of the late Ottoman Empire have long argued that the Foreign Ministry embraced international law as an instrument of European diplomacy, particularly after the conclusion the Crimean War and the Treaty of Paris (1856), which ostensibly invited the Ottoman Empire into the ranks of the Great Powers of Europe.[3] However, we know very little about the precise mechanisms that the Ottoman state relied upon in order to make international law a centerpiece of its foreign policy.[4] Though historians have drawn upon records contained within the Office of Legal Counsel, no one has attempted to examine the department on its own as a particular Ottoman institution, nor considered the lawyers who

Sovereignty and the British Occupation of Egypt, 1882–1923" (PhD diss., Columbia University, 2013).

2. The relationship between international law and empire has been taken up by a number of legal scholars recently, including Antony Anghie, *Imperialism, Sovereignty, and the Making of International Law* (Cambridge, UK: Cambridge University Press, 2005); Jennifer Pitts, "Empire and Legal Universalisms in the Eighteenth Century," *American Historical Review* 117, no. 1 (2012): 92–121. Also see Mark Mazower, *Governing the World: The History of an Idea* (New York: Penguin, 2012), ch. 3.

3. Research concerning the Ottoman engagement with European international law has grown significantly over the last few years. For recent works, see Umut Özsu and Thomas Skouteris, "International Legal Histories of the Ottoman Empire: An Introduction to a Symposium" and accompanying articles especially, Berdal Aral, "The Ottoman 'School' of International Law as Featured in its Textbooks," Will Hanley, "International Lawyers without Public International Law: The Case of Late Ottoman Egypt," and Will Smiley, "War without War: The Battle of Navarino, the Ottoman Empire and the Pacific Blockade," in *Journal of the History of International Law / Revue d'histoire du droit international* 18 (2016); Umut Özsu, "Ottoman Empire," in *The Oxford Handbook of the History of International Law*, ed. Bardo Fassbender and Anne Peters (Oxford: Oxford University Press, 2012); Cemil Aydın, *The Politics of Anti-Westernism in Asia: Visions of World Order in Pan-Islamic and Pan-Asian Thought* (New York: Columbia University Press, 2007); Mustafa Serdar Palabıyık "International Law for Survival: Teaching International Law in the Late Ottoman Empire (1859–1922)," *Bulletin of the School of Oriental and African Languages* 78, no. 2 (2015): 271–91; For older approaches, see Richard S. Horowitz, "International Law and State Transformation in China, Siam, and the Ottoman Empire during the Nineteenth Century," *Journal of World History* 15, no. 4 (2004): 445–86; Carter Findley, *Bureaucratic Reform in the Ottoman Empire: The Sublime Porte, 1789–1922* (Princeton: Princeton University Press, 1983); Roderic Davison, *Essays in Ottoman History, 1774–1923: The Impact of the West* (Austin: University of Texas Press, 1990).

4. Apart from Sinan Kuneralp's collection of Foreign Office legal opinions there is no secondary literature on the Office of Legal Counsel. Sinan Kuneralp and Emre Öktem, eds., *Chambre des conseillers légistes de la Sublime Porte: Rapports, avis et consultations sur la condition juridique des ressortissants étrangers, le statut des communaités non musulmanes et les relations internationals de l'empire ottoman* (İstanbul: Isis Press, 2012).

occupied the post of legal advisor over the course of its existence. Yet, doing so reveals a strikingly more inventive and dynamic empire than we are accustomed to seeing in the older diplomatic histories of the Eastern Question.

This chapter examines the rise and fall of international law within the late Ottoman state through an analysis of the Foreign Ministry's Office of Legal Counsel and the small group of international lawyers employed there. Foreign Ministry lawyers generated legal fodder for the exercise of Ottoman diplomacy abroad, but rather critically, they also served an important interpretive function for the state and translated the meaning and practices of European international law for the empire. Between the early 1880s and the mid-1920s, the role of international law in Ottoman state practice transformed dramatically. In the late nineteenth century, Ottoman lawyers viewed international law positively as a tool of the weak and an instrument to establish sovereign equality in inter-imperial relations. In the years leading up to the First World War, however, Ottoman enthusiasm for international law dropped precipitously against the unprovoked Italian invasion of Ottoman Libya (1911) and the Balkan Wars (1912–13). Ottoman officials and lawyers increasingly doubted that international law was the best way to preserve the state. By 1914, many one-time evangelists of international law saw the field as an instrument of European imperialism used to justify the unequal treatment of the Ottoman state in the international arena.[5]

Finally, the lawyers of the Office of Legal Counsel, while few in number, exemplified the diversity of the Ottoman Empire and imperial possibilities that would be permanently foreclosed by 1923. In the aftermath of the First World War, the erstwhile guardians of the empire found themselves in a variety of positions vis-à-vis the new Turkish state. Former colleagues dedicated to the preservation of empire through law found themselves on opposite sides of the bargaining table at Lausanne. Some remained within Turkey as architects of the national order, others lived in permanent exile. But across the board, it was clear that war had achieved what law ultimately failed to do, namely preserve the state.

Inside the Ottoman Foreign Ministry's Office of Legal Counsel

Before examining the circumstances that brought the Foreign Ministry's Office of Legal Counsel into existence, it will be useful to consider briefly how international law came to play a central role in Ottoman diplomatic practice. While historians agree that international law was critical to the Ottoman engagement with Europe, the precise moment that the Foreign Ministry self-consciously embraced European international law as a defensive strategy is a matter of some de-

---

5. Mustafa Aksakal, "Not 'by those old books of international law, but only by war': Ottoman Intellectuals on the Eve of the Great War," *Diplomacy and Statecraft* 15, no. 3(2004): 507–44.

bate.[6] Whether that moment was in the 1880s, the 1850s, the 1830s, or even earlier, the Treaty of Paris (1856) fundamentally reshaped the content of Ottoman legal claims in the international arena. The treaty concluding the Crimean War explicitly invited the Ottoman Empire as the first non-Christian state to "participate in the advantages of the public law and system (concert) of Europe."[7] While many European international lawyers would later argue that the Treaty of Paris had extended international legal personality to the Ottoman Empire too soon, Ottoman lawyers seized upon the treaty as an instrument of positive international law to defend the territorial integrity of the empire.[8] By the 1870s Ottoman officials regularly relied upon international legal arguments in their dealings with Europe, Persia, and the wider world—and never more so than in attempts to outmaneuver European powers over colonial questions.[9]

At the same time, European-imposed legal, economic, and administrative restrictions on Ottoman sovereignty compelled the state to deal with international law on a procedural level. The unevenness of Ottoman sovereignty during this period engendered numerous legal dilemmas that could only be solved ad-

6. The question of when international law came into being shaped the debate on the history of international law in Europe as well. Martti Koskenniemi has argued that modern international law was a product of a late nineteenth century discourse and that the field emerged only after a small group of liberal publicists began thinking of themselves as international lawyers and their ideas as distinct from contemporary diplomatic practices. Martti Koskenniemi, *The Gentle Civilizer of Nations: The Rise and Fall of International Law 1870–1960* (Cambridge, UK: Cambridge University Press, 2002). Will Smiley has made the most convincing case that the Ottoman Empire did indeed rely upon treaties and international legal precedent when dealing with European powers before 1856. Will Smiley, "When Peace Comes, You Will Again Be Free: Islamic and Treaty Law, Black Sea Conflict, and the Emergence of 'Prisoners of War' in the Ottoman Empire, 1739–1830" (PhD diss., Cambridge University, 2012) and his article "The Burdens of Subjecthood: The Ottoman State, Russian Fugitives, and Interimperial Law, 1774–1869," *International Journal of Middle East Studies* 46, no. 1 (2014): 73–93. Also see Mustafa Serdar Palabıyık, "The Emergence of the Idea of 'International Law' in the Ottoman Empire before the Treaty of Paris (1856)," *Middle Eastern Studies* 50, no. 2 (2014): 233–51; Turan Kayaoğlu, *Legal Imperialism: Sovereignty and Extraterritoriality in Japan, the Ottoman Empire, and China* (Cambridge, UK: Cambridge University Press, 2014).
7. T.E. Hall, ed., *The European Concert in the Eastern Question: a Collection of Treaties and Other Public Acts* (Oxford: Clarendon Press, 1885), 241–59.
8. See Aimee M. Genell, "Ottoman Autonomous Provinces and the Problem of 'Semi-Sovereignty' in European International Law," *Journal of Balkan and Near Eastern Studies* 18, no. 6 (2016): 533–49.
9. For example, see Michael Christopher Low, "Ottoman Infrastructures of the Saudi Hydro-State: The Technopolitics of Pilgrimage and Potable Water in the Hijaz," *Comparative Studies in Society and History* 57, no. 4 (2015): 942–74; Mostafa Minawi, "Telegraphs and Territoriality in Ottoman Africa and Arabia during the Age of High Imperialism," *Journal of Balkan and Near Eastern Studies* 18, no. 6 (2016): 567–87. My dissertation examines the Ottoman international legal arguments used to maintain Egypt and Sudan as part of the internationally recognized boundaries of the empire, see Genell, "Empire by Law."

vantageously through recourse to international law. For instance, disputes arising from the Capitulations—those foreign privileges that exempted European
subjects from taxation, local courts, and search of domicile—forced the Ottoman Foreign Ministry to master private international law in order to establish
jurisdiction and to settle differences between private persons.[10] Similarly, Ottoman autonomous provinces—such as Egypt and Lebanon that where legally
part of the empire, but where authority was exercised locally rather than at an
imperial level—created legal and administrative puzzles that prompted Ottoman
officials to search for public international law solutions to protect such provinces
from further European intervention or independence.[11] European restrictions
on the full exercise of Ottoman imperial control were themselves framed and justified in international legal terms. In other words, international law was not just
a weapon of last resort against a rapacious Europe; it was how European empires
had framed the entire problem of Ottoman sovereignty.

Beyond the problem of when the Foreign Ministry began relying upon international law as a tool of diplomacy, we might consider instead when and why
international lawyers were incorporated in the state's Foreign Ministry apparatus. After the Crimean War, the Foreign Ministry intermittently called upon European legal experts who resided in the empire for support on a broad range of
foreign policy questions.[12] In the period leading up to the establishment of the
Office of Legal Counsel, the Foreign Ministry employed a handful of European
subjects as occasional legal advisors—the need for international legal expertise
was pressing, and in the 1860s there was no pool of Ottoman lawyers upon whom

10. Consular protection originally applied to European residents in the Ottoman Empire.
However, over the course of the nineteenth century, European powers extended consular protection to local Ottoman subjects, who then became protected subjects (*protegé*) of the various
empires. A protected subject might claim to be a French protected subject in one legal arena
and an Ottoman subject in another. Protection was a legal feature of the Eastern Mediterranean during this period and one of which the Ottomans were very wary. Will Hanley has done
extensive research on this problem in the Ottoman Egypt. Will Hanley "When Did Egyptians
Stop Being Ottomans? An Imperial Citizenship Case Study," in *Multilevel Citizenship*, ed.
Willem Maas (Philadelphia: University of Pennsylvania Press, 2013); Mary Dewhurst Lewis,
Divided Rule: Sovereignty and Empire in French Tunisia, 1881–1938 (Berkeley: University of
California Press, 2013).
11. Ottoman autonomous provinces, as well as those provinces under permanent military occupation such as Egypt and Bosnia-Hercegovina, generated many of the same legal problems
caused by the Capitulations and consular jurisdiction. International lawyers—both Ottoman
and European—were deeply troubled by the fact that sovereignty and administration were
cleaved in such provinces.
12. Kuneralp and Öktem, *Chambre des conseillers légistes*, 10.

the state might depend.[13] Provisional legal consultations were increasing regularly and eventually laid the groundwork for the Office of Legal Counsel.

During this period, most of the European lawyers hired by the Foreign Ministry obtained their expertise working within the European consular court system in the Ottoman Empire. They were part of the great network of European lawyers circulating through consular courts in North Africa and the eastern Mediterranean.[14] For instance, William Parnis, a British-Maltese subject, worked at the Supreme British Consular Court in Istanbul before acting as a legal advisor starting in the 1860s, he also served as a legal consultant for the Ottoman Empire during the Congress of Berlin in 1878 and worked as a legal advisor for the Foreign Ministry until his death in 1883. Similarly, Carl Gescher, a German subject, worked as a legal advisor within the Office of Legal Counsel until he was appointed by the German government to the Mixed Courts in Egypt in 1894.

It was the disasters of the Russo-Ottoman war in 1877–78 that prompted the Foreign Ministry and Sultan Abdülhamid II to institutionalize this ad-hoc approach. Berlin ended in the first major Ottoman territorial loss since Greek independence. In addition to independence for Serbia, Montenegro, and Romania, Bulgaria was divided into the autonomous province of Eastern Rumelia and the principality of Bulgaria under the suzerainty of the sultan. The Great Powers awarded the three provinces (*vilayat-ı selase*) of Ardahan, Batum, and Kars to Russia; the Habsburg Empire occupied Bosnia-Hercegovina; and Britain permanently occupied Cyprus—an agreement that was only made possible by Britain agreeing to recognize a future French military occupation of Tunisia.[15] On the heels of the Berlin calamity, France occupied Tunisia in 1881, quickly followed by the British occupation of Egypt in 1882. All of these events unfolded against the Scramble for Africa, which European powers increasingly justified through appealing to international law and legalized through formalizing the rules of im-

13. Kuneralp lists the ad-hoc advisors as Émile Tarin, Louis Amiable, and Benjamin Édouard Cor, who were French. William Parnis was a British-Maltese subject and the brothers Alfred and Carl Gescher were German. Ibid., 10–12.
14. European lawyers, who worked within the consular court system in the Ottoman Empire, as well as the Mixed Courts in Egypt, knew one another and often circulated between legal venues, as well as within the imperial court system of their respective empires. For instance, when the British arrested Colonel Ahmed 'Urabi in 1882, Wilfred Blunt tracked down and hired A. M. Broadley to defend him. Broadly had first worked as an assistant magistrate in India, but later moved through the British Consular Court system and was defending the Bey of Tunis at the time of 'Urabi Rebellion. He later acted as a legal advisor to the ex-Khedive Ismail. There are numerous cases like this, especially of lawyers moving between consular courts in the Ottoman Empire and the Mixed Courts of autonomous Egypt. See A. M. Broadley and Frederick Villiers, *How We Defended Arabi and His Friends: A Story of Egypt and Egyptians* (London: Chapman and Hall, 1884).
15. *British Documents on Foreign Affairs*, Part I, Series B, Vol. 8 "The Ottoman Empire in North Africa: the Suez Canal, Red Sea, and Tunisian Problems, 1859–1882," doc. 231, p. 363.

perial expansion.[16] The international context is critical for understanding why the Ottoman state not only formally adopted international law as a tool of diplomacy, but why the state officials thought they needed an office dedicated to international law.

In 1883, the Foreign Ministry established the Office of Legal Counsel (Hukuk Müşavirliği İstişare Odası) and created the position of legal advisor (*hukuk muşaviri*).[17] The special department was intended to deal more systematically with questions related to international law, but should also be seen as a Hamidian institution and part of the project to extend Ottoman control more firmly throughout the empire, to reduce the influence of European powers in the empire, and to assert equality with the powers of Europe.[18] Much like the improvisational approach of the 1860s and 1870s, the Ottoman Foreign Ministry appointed European legal experts who had already provided legal counsel. While it is not entirely clear from the archival record, it appears that Carl Gescher (Şarl Geşir) and Gabriel Noradounghian [Kapriel Noradunkyan] were among the first legal advisors appointed to the formalized Office of Legal Counsel. Carl Gescher's Ottoman employment record notes that he was appointed to service within the "Foreign Ministry's Office of Legal Counsel (Hukuk Muşavirliği)" on 19 April 1883 (11 Cümadelahire 1300)—the same day as the Ottoman subject Gabriel Noradounghian.[19] Though European lawyers originally occupied the position of legal advisor, Ottoman subjects eventually took over these posts entirely.

From its inception in the 1880s through its demise in the early 1920s, the Office of Legal Counsel was more often than not staffed by a first and second legal advisor, posts which were generally held by one Armenian and one Muslim Ottoman subject, as well as a handful of directors (*müdir*) and legal assistants (*muavin*).[20] This structure was not permanently fixed and there was some flex-

16. For an excellent analysis of the Ottoman engagement with the Scramble for Africa, see Mostafa Minawi, *The Ottoman Scramble for Africa: Empire and Diplomacy in the Sahara and the Hijaz* (Stanford: Stanford University Press, 2016).
17. Findley, *Bureaucratic Reform*, 260.
18. Selim Deringil, *The Well-Protected Domains: Ideology and the Legitimation of Power in the Ottoman Empire, 1876–1909* (New York: I.B. Tauris, 1998); Thomas Kuehn, *Empire, Islam, and Politics of Difference: Ottoman Rule in Yemen, 1849–1919* (Leiden: Brill, 2011); Benjamin Fortna, *Imperial Classroom: Islam, State and Education in the Late Ottoman Empire* (Oxford: Oxford University Press, 2002); Engin Akarlı "The Problems of External Pressures, Power Struggles, and Budgetary Deficits in Ottoman Politics under Abdülhamid II, 1876–1909" (PhD diss., Princeton University, 1976).
19. Bab-ı Ali Hariciye Nezareti, *Salname-i Nezaret-i Hariciye*, 1:252–53. Findley also dates the establishment of the Office to 1882 or 1883. BOA/BEO/DH./SAİD./2/510. "Kişer"; BOA/BEO/ HR.SAİD./4/12 (29 C. 1313/17 Dec. 1895).
20. This practice was not abandoned during World War I. Throughout the entirety of the war into the early 1920s, the chief legal advisor at the İstişare Odası, Hrant Abro Bey, was Armenian.

ibility within the organization of the office. For example, for several years leading up to the Young Turk Revolution there were three rather than two legal advisors. The number of directors and legal assistants also swelled and contracted over time.[21] Most of the directors and legal assistants, and later the legal advisors themselves, were graduates from the Imperial Law School (Mekteb-i Hukuk) and the Law Faculty at the Darülfünun—the main European-style university of the empire.[22] After the Hamidian era (1876–1909), the first and second legal advisors were promoted from within the Office of Legal Counsel. Though legal advisors might have studied law in Europe as well, the fact that the Foreign Ministry had a trained body of international lawyers upon which it could rely, indicates the expansion of legal education, in general, and the development of international law in the Ottoman Empire, in particular.[23]

In many ways, the Hamidian era was the highpoint of the Office of Legal Counsel. During that period, the Office shifted from being a domain of European international law experts, who had cut their teeth in the Capitulation Courts, to an office staffed entirely by Ottoman subjects who were trained and professionalized as international lawyers. When the Foreign Ministry first recognized the diplomatic need for international legal expertise in the 1860s and 1870s, the Ottoman state did not have a qualified group of international lawyers upon whom it could rely for legal advice. But by the mid-1890s, the Foreign Ministry no longer required European lawyers for the functioning of the office. The Hamidian period is also noteworthy for the fact that the empire's most authoritative international law experts occupied the post of legal advisor for much of the period: Gabriel Noradounghian and İbrahim Hakkı Bey (later pasha).

Almost immediately after the Foreign Ministry formalized the Office of Legal Counsel, Grand Vizier Said Pasha (Küçük), appointed Noradounghian, an Ottoman-Armenian, to the post of legal advisor. According to Noradounghian's secretary, the Foreign Ministry wanted to limit European influence within the office, and when Parnis Efendi died in 1883, Said Pasha proposed Noradounghian

---

21. For instance, during the same period when there were three legal advisors, the Office of Legal Counsel had nearly fifty *muavin* listed on the books. Kuneralp notes that these figures were inflated and instead that the number of staff hovered around eight assistants. In any case, by the period leading up to World War I, the numbers dropped to about eight *muavin*, which is still a significant number of staff for the office and tells us something of its importance. See Kuneralp and Öktem, *Chambre des conseillers*, 10–12; Bab-ı Ali Hariciye Nezareti, *Salname-i Nezaret-i Hariciye* (1320/1902), 220–22.

22. This observation is born out through an examination of employment registers (*sicil-i ahval*) as well as documents detailing the inner-workings of the Office of Legal Counsel.

23. Ekmeleddin İhsanoğlu, *Darülfünun: Osmanlı'da Kültürel Modernleşmenin Odağı* (Istanbul: IRCICA, 2010); Murteza Bedir, "Fikh to Law: Secularization through Curriculum," *Islamic Law and Society* 11, no. 3 (2004): 378–401.

for the job.[24] Knowledge of European languages, especially French and English were critically important for the post. Noradounghian had studied law in Paris and in addition to French, Ottoman Turkish, and Armenian knew English and Italian—a linguistic profile that was in no way unusual for the staff at the Office of Legal Counsel. Like İbrahim Hakkı Pasha, Noradounghian taught law at the Mekteb-i Hukuk before entering the Foreign Ministry.[25] For nearly ten years Noradounghian worked alongside Carl Gescher producing legal opinions on questions of public and private international law.[26] The advisors authored a wide assortment of legal opinions for the Foreign Ministry, covering everything from issues related to the laws of war to Ottoman territorial claims to Egypt and Sudan. Alfred Gescher returned to Germany in 1889 and his brother, Carl, left Istanbul for the Mixed Courts of Egypt in the early 1890s.[27] Abdülhamid II personally appointed İbrahim Hakkı Pasha to take his place in 1894.[28]

Hakkı Pasha had a long and varied career in the Ottoman civil service during the Hamidian and Young Turk period. In the early 1880s, he worked in the palace (*mabeyn*) for Abdu'lhamid as a translator. He also taught international law at the Law Faculty in Istanbul.[29] During the CUP period İbrahim Hakkı obtained a number of ministerial posts. Noradounghian and İbrahim Hakkı had much in common and were later appointed to the highest bureaucratic positions within

24. Raymond H. Kévorkian, "Gabriel Noradounghian (1852–1936): extraits des memoires recueillies par Aram Andonian," *Revue d'histoire arménienne contemporaine* 1(1995). The manuscript of Noradounghian's memoirs has never been located. His private secretary, Aram Andonian, recorded fragments of the text, which are now housed in the Nubar Library and Archive in Paris.

25. BOA/DH.SAİD/81/238 "Noradunkyan, Gabriel." Also see Y.G. Çark, *Türk Devlet Hizmetinde Ermeniler, 1453–1953* (Istanbul: Yeni Matbaa, 1953). Noradounghian was elected the *Institut de Droit International* in 1922. Peter Macalister-Smith, "Bio-Bibliographical Key to the Membership of the Institut de Droit International, 1873–2001," *Journal of the History of International Law* 5 (2003): 77–159.

26. Kuneralp notes that the brothers Alfred and Carl Gescher both worked as legal advisors, but that it is not clear which legal opinions were authored by whom as they never used their first names. Moreover, Alfred appears to have been appointed as the German representative on the Ottoman Public Debt Administration. I have found far more evidence linking Carl Gescher to the Office of Legal Counsel than Alfred. See Kuneralp and Öktem, *Chambre des conseillers*, 11.

27. Carl Gescher, "Egypten," *Jahrbuch der Internationalen Vereinigung für vergleichende Rechtswissenschaft und Volkswirtschaftslehre zu Berlin Jahrbuch der Internationalen* 8 (1904): 1489–1505.

28. Kévorkian, "Gabriel Noradounghian (1852–1936)," 16.

29. BOA/İ.HR./354/23 (8 S 1312/11 Aug. 1894). "*Bab-ı Ali hukuk müşavirliği'ne mabeyn mütercimlerinden Hakkı Bey'in tayini.*" M.K. İnal, *Osmanlı Devrinde son Sadriazamlar* (Istanbul: Milli Eğitim Basımevi, 1965), 3:1763–1804; Ali Çankaya, *Mülkiye Tarihi ve Mülkiyeliler* (Ankara: Örnek Matbaası, 1954), 54–58; F. Ahmad, "İbrāhīm Ḥaḳḳī Pasha." *Encyclopaedia of Islam*, 2nd ed. Brill Online, 2013.

the empire—a point that underlines the significance of this posting within the Ottoman administration. İbrahim Hakkı Pasha was briefly grand vizier, while Noradounghian served as the minister of foreign affairs from the summer of 1912 through the Bab-ı Ali Coup in January of 1913. Before that, they were dedicated to the cause of preserving the empire. Both lawyers evangelized the benefits of international law for the Ottoman state through publishing and teaching.

In addition to generating legal opinions for diplomatic use, each wrote extensively on positive international law, both public and private. While Noradounghian wrote in French and consequently his work was widely available and cited by European readers, Hakkı Pasha wrote in Ottoman Turkish, with only one of his textbooks being reviewed in a European international law journal.[30] Hakkı Pasha wrote for pedagogical use, but Ottoman Turkish-reading intellectuals and non-experts avidly read his textbooks and treatises as well.[31] Like their counterparts in Europe and the United States, Noradounghian and Hakkı Pasha argued for the ameliorative effects of international law on international relations and viewed international law as an alternative to Great Power politics. They relied heavily upon existing treaty law to shore up Ottoman territorial claims and to attempt to assert Ottoman equality with Europe. It was no mistake that Noradounghian's massive "compendium of international treaties," *Recueil d'Actes Internationaux,* was a collection of treaties and international legislation to which the Ottoman Empire was a signatory.[32]

The Ottoman effort to incorporate international lawyers into the Foreign Ministry was not far off the mark from developments elsewhere in the world. The Office of Legal Counsel was established at roughly the same time as similar offices in Europe and the United States. The German Foreign Ministry created a Legal Department (Rechtsabteilung) within the Auswärtiges Amt in 1885. British Foreign Office officials had long relied upon ad-hoc legal advice, as well as opinions generated by the law officers of the Crown, but it was not until 1886, and after a contentious public debate, that the legal assistant to the Foreign Office emerged as a formal office. Similarly, France created the office of the Jurisconsulte within their Foreign Ministry in 1890. The US State Department followed suit and ad-

---

30. İbrahim Hakkı Pasha's chief international law works include: *Tarih-i Hukuk-ı Beyn'ed-düvel* (Istanbul: Karabet ve Kasbar, 1303 [1885–86]); *Medhal-ı Hukuk-ı Beyn'ed-düvel* (Istanbul: Karabet ve Kasbar, 1303 [1885–86]); *Hukuk-ı düvel* (Dârülhilâfe: Matbaa ve Kütüphane-yi Cihan, 1327 [1911]).

31. According to Findley, non-specialists broadly read his textbooks as well. For information on Hakkı Pasha, see Carter Findley, *Ottoman Civil Officialdom: A Social History* (Princeton: Princeton University Press, 1989), ch. 5.

32. Gabriel Noradounghian, *Recueil d'actes internationaux de l'empire ottoman,* 4 vol. (Paris: F. Pichon, 1897–1903).

opted a similar position, the legal advisor, in 1891.[33] The fact that the Great Powers incorporated international lawyers into the workings of their foreign ministries does not mean of course that law conquered politics. On the contrary, the Foreign Ministry officials brought international law under control to justify their respective foreign policies. The fact that the Ottoman state was the first to do so shows the degree to which a weak state recognized the importance of knowing international law in order to engage with European states.

From the Young Turk Revolution to the Italian Invasion of Libya

The Young Turk Revolution pulled Noradounghian and İbrahim Hakkı Pasha out of the Office of Legal Counsel and into other important administrative offices. Hrant Abro Bey and Ahmed Reşid replaced them in the early days of the revolution. Hrant Abro had been the first law clerk for most of the early twentieth century, while Ahmed Reşid worked as a legal assistant (*muavin*) in the Office of Legal Counsel starting in 1322 (1904/1905). Hrant Abro was educated in Europe, where he graduated from the University of Lausanne and continued his legal studies in literature and law at the Faculty of Law in Nantes.[34] His father, Sahak Abro Efendi, had been a reformer during the Tanzimat and was reportedly favored by Ali and headed the Office of Foreign Correspondences after the Crimean War.[35] In contrast, Ahmed Reşid graduated from the Law Faculty (Mekteb-i Hukuk) in Istanbul and held a series of posts within the Ottoman Foreign Ministry between the second constitutional period and the end of World War I.[36] In 1913, Mehmed Münir Bey (Ertegün) succeeded Ahmed Reşid as legal advisor.[37] He was from a religious family in Üsküdar, and he too received his

33. Marcus Payk, "Institutionalisierung und Verrechtlichung: Die Geschichte des Völkerrechts im späten 19. und frühen 20. Jahrhundert," *Archiv für Sozialgeschichte* 52 (2012): 861–83. Herbert C. L. Merillat *Legal Advisers and Foreign Affairs* (Dobbs Ferry: American Society of International Law, 1964); Raymond Jones, *The Nineteenth-Century Foreign Office: An Administrative History* (London: London School of Economics and Political Science, 1971); Robert B. Mowat, *The Life of Lord Pauncefote, First Ambassador to the United States* (London: Constable and Co., 1929); M.B. Hayne, *The French Foreign Office and the Origins of the First World War 1898–1914* (Oxford: Oxford University Press, 1993); Lester H. Woolsey, "The Legal Adviser of the Department of State," *American Journal of International Law* 26, no. 1 (1932): 124–26.
34. BOA/DH.SAİD./88/143. Sezai Balcı "Bir Osmanlı Ermeni Aydın ve Bürokrati: Sahak Abro (1825–1900)," in *Osmanlı Siyasal ve Soysal Hayatında Ermeniler*, ed. İbrahim Erdal and Amhet Karaçavuş (Istanbul: IQ Kültür Sanat Yayıncılık, 2009); Doğan Gürpinar, *Ottoman Imperial Diplomacy: A Political, Social and Cultural History* (London: I.B. Tauris, 2013); Findley, *Bureaucratic Reform*, 208.
35. Gürpinar, *Ottoman Imperial Diplomacy*, 114.
36. BOA/HR.SAİD./19/21. Late in the war he was appointed as the Ottoman ambassador to Persia, but never occupied the post.
37. BOA/İHR./431/9 (27 M. 1331/6 Jan. 1913). "Bab-ı Ali istişare odası müdüriyeti'ne hukuk müşaviri Münir Bey'in tayini."

doctorate in law from the Law Faculty in Istanbul.[38] Mehmed Münir started in the Office of Legal Counsel as a legal assistant in 1909 or 1910 (1326) and followed the path charted by Hrant Abro and Ahmed Reşid. These three lawyers were the last of the important legal advisors and in many ways the last officials to cling to international law as the redeemer of the empire. They continued to furnish legal opinions to stave off Europe, but by 1914 their confidence in the law had already been profoundly shaken.

Hrant Abro and Ahmed Reşid acted as legal advisors for much of the Young Turk period. Hrant Abro continued to author legal opinions into the 1920s and was one of the last, if not the last, Ottoman legal advisor. These were difficult days for the Foreign Ministry in which the old strategy of appealing to international law in dealing with the powers of Europe came under increased strain. Abdülhamid and his ministers managed to arrest the territorial losses and occupations of the 1878–82 period, but almost as soon as the Young Turk Revolution began in 1908, the territorial hemorrhaging began anew—Bulgaria declared its independence and the Habsburg Empire annexed Bosnia-Hercegovina. During this period, the Office of Legal Counsel scrambled to stave off further territorial losses through independence and annexations. The search for more persuasive legal arguments led to an overhaul of the office's library.

In the years leading up to the Italian invasion of Libya, the lawyers undertook a massive project to rebind, update, and expand the holdings of the library of the Office of Legal Counsel.[39] While it appears that Hrant Abro and Ahmed Reşid spearheaded the initiative, the assistants carried out much of the work.[40] The records of this improvement project are significant for a number of reasons. They enable us to see very generally what the lawyers were reading, what they wanted to read, and ultimately what counted as sources of international law. At the same time, the project stretched out during the periods of the war in Libya, the Balkan Wars and the beginning of World War I. Foreign Ministry lawyers

---

38. Mehmet Münir's grandfather on his mother side was the Sheykh Ethem Efendi from the Uzbek sufi lodge (Özbekler Tekkesi) in Üsküdar, while his father was the under-secretary of the Religious Endowments Ministry. See George S. Harris, "Cementing Turkish-American Relations: The Ambassadorship of (Mehmet) Münir Ertegün," in *Studies in Atatürk's Turkey*, ed. George S. Harris and Nur Bilge Criss (Leiden: Brill, 2009); George S. Harris, *Atatürk's Diplomats & Their Biographies* (Istanbul: Isis Press, 2010).
39. Sezai Balcı's work on the Translation Office (Tercüme Odası) has shown the intellectual alignments within the office by focusing upon the content of the office's library. Arguably we might do the same for the Office of Legal Counsel. See Sezai Balcı, *Babıali Tercüme Odası* (Istanbul: Libra Kitapçılık, 2013).
40. Many of the documents related to improving the library, show that the legal advisors needed specific titles in order to negotiate a particular issue. For example, see BOA/HR.HMŞ. İŞO./101/14 (9 Şubat 1332) where Reşid Bey requested a book on international law in order to negotiate in Berlin.

pressed Ottoman ambassadors and consuls throughout Europe to buy books on their behalf even in the midst of war. While Libya and the Balkan Wars may have eroded the lawyers' confidence in the law, they did not forgo it entirely and continued to shape their diplomatic claims in international legal terms.

The library of the Office of Legal Counsel was packed with European as well as Ottoman international textbooks. The Ottoman preoccupation with positive international law was quite clear from the holdings of the library. In addition to Noradounghian's *Recueil d'Actes Internationaux* and the *Düstur*, the library held around ten collections of treaties and international agreements written in Ottoman Turkish under the heading "Turkish books."[41] On the European side, the lawyers amassed a huge number of treaty collections from the British, Italian, and French foreign ministries, the vast majority of which dealt with the Scramble for Africa and Eastern Question. One entire section of the library was dedicated to the vexing foreign policy and colonial "questions" of the era, many of which concerned places to which the Ottomans had territorial claims. Several volumes dealt with the question of Ottoman autonomous provinces in Egypt, Eastern Rumelia, Bulgaria, and Crete. Before the new volumes were added to the library, the collection contained treaties, reports from international diplomatic conferences related to the codification of international law, the International Sanitary Conferences as well as individual volumes on subjects that the lawyers deemed most pressing in terms of Ottoman foreign policy—such as Bulgaria, Egypt, and the Ottoman-Italian legal contest in the Red Sea and North Africa.[42] There were also several volumes in Ottoman and European languages on private international law, as well as colonial law.

The inter-imperial colonial contest over North Africa and the Red Sea was especially well represented in the library, particularly questions related to Massawa. The titles included a number of volumes by French international lawyers who had written about the colonial occupation following the Congress of Berlin in 1884–85, including Franz Despagnet's *Essai sur les protectorats*, Gaston Jézé's *Étude théorique et pratique sur l'occupation comme mode d'acquérir les territoires en droit international*, as well as Charles Salomon's *L'occupation des territoires sans maitre: etude de droit international*. In each of these texts, the lawyers wrote critically about the Italian occupation and annexation of Massawa. The Red Sea port city had been part of the imperial domains since the conquest of Egypt in 1517 and was occupied by Italy as part of their burgeoning Red Sea empire in 1885. Despagnet had earlier condemned the British reconquest of Sudan as a usurpation of the sultan's sovereign rights.[43]

---

41. BOA/HR.HMŞ.İŞO./109/13 (28 Mayıs 1327), s. 2 "Türkçe Kitapları."
42. BOA/HR.HMŞ.İŞO/109/13.
43. Franz Clément Despagnet, "Égypte et Grande-Bretagne," *Revue générale de droit international public* 6 (1899).

The renewed weakness of the Ottoman Empire's international position appears to have prompted the lawyers to revamp their existing international law collection. The legal advisors and assistants compiled a list of desiderata for the library, which were then sent out to all Ottoman ambassadors and consuls in Britain, France, Germany, Switzerland, Austria-Hungry, Spain, Sweden, the Netherlands, and the United States.[44] The project was not an inexpensive undertaking and it should tell us something about the role of international law in the Ottoman Foreign Ministry: a state strapped for cash was devoting economic resources to obtaining several hundred books for a handful of lawyers.

The Office of Legal Counsel requested books on a variety of international legal questions, but also other administrative questions related to the organization of state. For instance, Mehmet Münir, then legal assistant, requested books "containing a critical study of French laws on separation of church and state and associations and congregations."[45] The lawyers requested new treaty and European foreign ministry diplomatic collections. Added to this, however, was an emphasis on some of the classic works of European international law including works by Henry Bonfils, John Westlake, Lord Bryce, Sir Robert Phillimore, Travers Twiss, James Lorimer, and T.J. Lawrence.[46] The lawyers at the Foreign Ministry had access to at least some of these texts before 1912. Bonfils was translated into Ottoman Turkish on more than one occasion and Ottoman international law textbooks written as pedagogical material for Mekteb-i Hukuk also referred to some of the classic European treatises, notably James Lorimer.[47] The lawyers also requested a number of books on the British occupation of Egypt. More than a few of these volumes concerned the problem of Egypt's status in international law, but also popular titles including Cromer's *Modern Egypt* and Wilfred Blunt's *Secret History of the English Occupation*.[48] In addition to books on Egypt, the greatest hits of European international law and volumes on private international law, the legal advisors asked for several books on the laws of war, the treatment

44. BOA/HR.HMŞ.İŞO./105/38. Assim Pasha approved book requests and sent letters to Ottoman ambassadors and consuls in Europe and the United States. BOA/HR.HMŞ.İŞO/109/16 (28 Mayıs 1327). This document included both specific book requests as well as responses from various ambassadors on which books they were able to obtain.
45. BOA/HR.HMŞ.İŞO./108/23 (19 Temmuz 1332). Telegram to the Berne Legation.
46. BOA/HR.HMŞ.İŞO.109/16 (28 Mayıs 1327). The titles included among many others: Sir Travers Twiss, *The Law of Nations Considered as Independent Political Communities*; Henry Sumner Maine, *International Law*; T.J. Lawrence, *The Principles of International Law*; S. Kitabian, *Conséquences Juridiques Des Transformations Territoriales Des États Sur Les Traités*; John Westlake, *A Treatise on Private International Law* and *Chapters on International Law*; T.E. Holland, *The Wars of Law on Land*; James Lorimer, *Institutes of the Laws of Nations*; Viscount James Bryce, *The American Commonwealth*.
47. Palabıyık has shown that Henry Bonfils was of particular interest to Ottoman international lawyers. Palabıyık "International Law for Survival," 290.
48. BOA/HR.HMŞ.İŞO.109/16.

of prisoners of war, as well as other titles on the creation of new states in international law including a book by Arthur Berriedale Keith entitled *Theory of State Succession with special reference to the English and Colonial Law*.[49]

Strikingly, the prized item missing from the library was Georg Friedrich von Martens's *Nouveau recueil général de traités et autres actes relatifs aux rapports de droit international*, prepared by Felix Storerk and published between 1876 and 1908.[50] The pressure to obtain this book coincided with the Italian invasion of Libya. The Ottoman state protested the unprovoked war in Libya on the grounds that it violated international law. Hrant Abro and Ahmed Reşid wrote the legal opinions that provided fodder for Ottoman diplomats in Europe to make this protest.[51] While they underlined that the war was unprovoked, and contrary to international law, their legal opinions focused on *jus in bello* questions and attacked the Italians for abrogating the Hague Conventions through their use of poisonous and asphyxiating gases. The lawyers also argued that the Italian occupation contravened the Treaty of Paris (1856).[52] Hrant Abro and Ahmed Reşid argued that the Italians had broken long-standing rules related to the use of blockade in warfare. Their primary source of international law on the matter was Georg Friedrich von Martens on the Russo-Japanese war.[53] If the lawyers' perseverance to obtain the Martens treatise was linked to an urgent matter of foreign policy, we might interpret their other book requests along similar lines.

The awareness that old legal order was coming undone was acutely felt in the Office of Legal Counsel in the aftermath of the Italian invasion and annexation of Libya. Hrant Abro Bey and Mehmet Münir, the wartime legal advisors, continued to write legal opinions, but their confidence in law was shaken and increasingly it appeared that force was the only way to maintain the state. In 1915, they

---

49. Ibid.

50. BOA/HR.HMŞ.İŞO./108/45 (7 Mayıs 1328); BOA/HR.HMŞ.IŞO./105/43 (12 Mayıs 1328). This file includes the receipt for the Martens text, *Nouveau recueil général de traités et autres actes relatifs aux rapports de droit international*; continuation du Grand Recueil de G. Fr. Martens par Felix Storerk.

51. They also defended Ottoman interests at the Hague Court of Arbitration in 1911 and 1912. Russian Arbitration Case—The Hague Court Reports.

52. BOA/HR.HMŞ.İŞO./203/25 (12 Za. 1329/4 Nov. 1911). Asim Bey to Nizami Bey in Berlin. He noted that the legal advisors believed that the Italians launched projectiles and deleterious gases in their attack on Trablusgarb, which contravene the Hague rules of 1899. The problem of Italy's illegal occupation of Libya, as well as the use banned weapons, bothered lawyers beyond the Ottoman Foreign Ministry. A member of the Law Faculty as the Darülfünun wrote a short but critical analysis of the perspective of international law. See Örikağasızade Hasan Sırrı, Hukuk-i düvel nokta-yı nazarından Osmanlı-İtalya muharebesi (Kostantiniye: Matbaa-yı Ebüzziya, 1330 [1914]).

53. BOA/HR.HMŞ.İŞO./203/15 (9 L 1329/24 Sept. 1911). "İtalya tarafından Osmanlı İmparatorluğu'nun işgal edilen bazı bölgeleri ve abluka altına mermi attığı ve uluslararası savaş kurallarına aykırı davrandığı."

prepared a legal opinion for İbrahim Hakkı Pasha, who was then the Ottoman ambassador to Berlin. Their task was to consider the empire's international legal status vis-à-vis main treaties guaranteeing the territorial integrity of the empire. The lawyers argued that the Ottoman-German alliance put the Ottoman Empire on equal footing with the states of Europe—it was a military alliance rather than a territorial guarantee. The lawyers recommended that the empire announce that it no longer recognized restrictions imposed by the Treaty of Paris (1856) and the Treaty of Berlin (1878). [54]

Abandoning the territorial guarantees provided by the Treaties of Paris and Berlin amounted to a diplomatic revolution in Ottoman foreign affairs. Drawing upon this legal opinion, İbrahim Hakkı Pasha argued that the Allied Powers had so often violated the positive articles of the 1856 and 1878 treaties, which recognized "the independence and the territorial integrity of the Ottoman Empire," that the imperial government now considered them "null and void and completely without any contractual value." [55] In order to justify the new Ottoman view of the treaties, Hakkı Pasha enumerated European violations of Ottoman territorial integrity and outlined explicit infringements upon Ottoman territorial rights by the European powers. He provided the German foreign minister with a history of European treaty violations and listed every European demand for autonomous administration from Mt. Lebanon to Serbia to Crete, as well as provinces lost to annexation and permanent military occupation.

İbrahim Hakkı argued that the imperial government has "scrupulously executed the onerous clauses" of the various treaties but the clauses that were favorable to the Ottoman Empire "remained a dead letter" as European governments actively obstructed administrative and economic reforms in the empire. [56] Despite the fact that the Ottoman government denounced the treaties of 1856 and 1878, Hakkı Pasha noted that the empire would "not fail to take advantage of the principles of international law in order to enforce its rights to its advantage by the aforementioned treaties and which have hitherto been ignored." [57]

The Office of Legal Counsel continued to function well after the end of the First World War, but the legal advisors seemed less sure about international legal instruments as the best means to safeguard the Ottoman Empire's precarious position in Europe. Rather than appeal to the Treaty of Paris, or the territorial integrity of the Ottoman Empire as lawyers had done since the 1860s, legal advisors now pushed for complete sovereignty without conditions. In late 1918, Mehmed Münir (Ertegün) wrote an important opinion on the Ottoman interpretation of

54. BOA/HR.HMŞ.İŞO./65/20 (17 Temmuz 1332). İbrahim Hakkı Pasha was then posted to Berlin as the Ottoman ambassador between 1915 and his death in 1918.
55. BOA/HR.HMŞ.İŞO./65/9-14.
56. BOA/HR.HMŞ.İŞO./65/11.
57. BOA/HR.HMŞ.İŞO./65/20 (17 Temmuz 1332).

Wilson's Fourteen Points. It presented a vision of the empire reconstructed as a Muslim federation with little said about Christians and Jews. While the Arab provinces under European occupation would be given administrative autonomy, no agreements would be carried out to give Europe any power to interfere in Ottoman internal affairs. The opinion was widely circulated through the wartime and armistice governments and became the basis of Ottoman diplomacy emanating out of Istanbul as well as Ankara.[58]

Conclusion: International Law and the State

World War I destroyed the Ottoman Empire, but it also completely crushed the foundations upon which the empire had engaged in international diplomacy. The old Ottoman conviction that international law would preserve the state through Great Power territorial guarantees, embedded in the positive international law of treaties, was simply no longer tenable. Even before the Allied Powers legalized the partition of the Ottoman Empire in 1920 with the Treaty of Sèvres, it was clear to Ottoman officials and lawyers that what mattered was force not treaties. The destruction of the Ottoman state and the birth of the Republic of Turkey by force sidelined international law as a viable foreign policy strategy. In some respect the Ottoman Foreign Ministry's Office of Legal Counsel survived the war, but only in the way that other Ottoman institutions were reconfigured in the Republic of Turkey.

The international lawyers who operated the Office of Legal Counsel from the Hamidian period through the Treaty of Lausanne found themselves in wildly different positions vis-à-vis the new republic. As a further testament to the importance of the office, each of the former advisors directly engaged in matters of high diplomacy either during the war or in its many aftermaths following the armistice in 1918. İbrahim Hakkı Pasha spent the bulk of the war in Berlin. He negotiated the Treaty of Brest-Litovsk for the Ottoman government and with Leon Trotsky arranged for the return of territories lost to Russia in 1878, the "three provinces" (*vilayat-ı selase*)—Ardahan, Batum, and Kars.[59] He died in Berlin in 1918. Noradounghian left the Ottoman Empire for Paris in 1913. The state that he had faithfully protected confiscated his family properties in Istanbul and promptly forgot his contribution to Ottoman statecraft.[60] Noradounghian

58. BOA/HR.HMŞ.İŞO/214/14 (15 M 1337/21 Oct. 1918).
59. On negotiating the return of the "three provinces" to the Ottoman Empire, see Michael Reynolds, *Shattering Empires: The Clash and Collapse of the Ottoman and Russian Empires 1908–1918* (Cambridge, UK: Cambridge University Press, 2011).
60. Lerna Ekmekçioğlu, "Republic of Paradox: The League of Nations Minority Protection Regime," *International Journal of Middle East Studies* 46, no. 4 (2014): 657–79; eadem, *Recovering Armenia: The Limits of Belonging in Post-Genocide Armenia* (Stanford: Stanford University Press, 2016). Also see Fatma Müge Goçek, *Denial of Violence: Ottoman Past, Turkish Present,*

represented Armenian interests at Lausanne and pleaded for a "national home" to remain within the new Turkey.[61]

Hrant Abro's story is somewhat less certain. A bewildering number of sources claim that he worked at the Foreign Ministry until 1917.[62] This is entirely wrong, as he continued to issue legal opinions into the early 1920s, including a very important one criticizing the Permanent Court of International Justice, which disavowed the Middle East Mandates of the League of Nations.[63] According to Sezai Balcı, he retired from service in 1924, a date which accords with his presence in the archive. It is unclear if he remained in Turkey; it is only certain that he no longer worked for the state.

Ahmed Reşid had an uneasy relationship with the new order. Following the war, he stayed out of politics and was appointed as a law professor at the Darül-fünun, which later became Istanbul University. In many ways he remained tied to an older conception of international law, where the law might improve international relations. More than any of the other former legal advisors, Ahmed Reşid was most engaged with international lawyers in Europe—he even did a stint at The Hague Academy of International Law in the 1930s. But the fact that Turkey emerged as an independent state after the war and was freed from the Capitulations and other European restrictions on sovereignty meant that the state had to jealously guard this newfound freedom. There was no room for the kind of concessions that might invite Europe to meddle once again in the affairs of the state—an idea that saturated his post-war writing. During the interwar years, Ahmed Reşid published books and articles on international law, including work on the Capitulations and the minority rights regime under the League of Nations.[64] In 1935 he wrote an article on minorities in which he claimed that Turkey's great success, compared to the other new states of Europe, was that its minorities were not legally recognized as such.[65]

and the Collective Violence against Armenians, 1789–2009 (Oxford: Oxford University Press, 2015).

61. Bilal N. Şimşir, *Lozan Telgrafları* (Ankara: TTK Yayınları, 1990), 1:192.
62. The only plausible explanation appears to be that this is the last year the *salname* lists him as the chief legal advisor, but it was the last year for any mention of the İstişare Odası.
63. BOA/HR.HMŞ.İŞO./148/19.
64. Ahmed Reşid's arguments about minorities conform to Ekmekçioğlu's argument about minority citizenship in Turkey after Lausanne in "Republic of Paradox." See the various works of Ahmed Reşid, "Kapitülasyonlar," *Dârülfünûn Hukuk Fakültesi Mecmuası* 6/37 (1928): 1–38; "Kuvve-i Müessese Nazariyyesi," *Dârülfünûn Hukuk Fakültesi Mecmuası* 6/38 (1928): 1299–328; *Hukuk-u umumiye-i düvel* (Istanbul: Arkadaş Matbaası, 1928); "Les droits minoritaires en Turquie dans le passé et le présent," *Revue générale de droit international public* (1935): 293–341; "La condition des étrangers dans la République de Turquie," *Recueil des cours* 4 (1933).
65. Réchid, "Les droits minoritaires en Turquie dans le passé et le présent," 293–341.

Given the painful situation of minorities in other countries, those in Turkey have proved profoundly happy upon seeing the entry of their communities into the National Assembly. And the new members have proven to be wise enough to not see themselves as representatives of their "nations" in Parliament in Ankara: all have publically stated they were entering not as representatives of minorities of which they are a part. The Armenian deputy, Keretédjian, was most explicit: "In Turkey," he said, "there is no longer a question of minorities or non-Muslims. The Armenians do not constitute a distinct element of the population called 'minorities'."[66]

Ahmed Reşid argued further that the privileges bestowed upon non-Muslims during the Ottoman era, were "incompatible with the concept of state sovereignty." Unlike the minorities of Central Europe, Turkey's minorities submitted themselves to the state as citizens.

Mehmed Münir Bey was the only legal advisor to remain within the state apparatus. He was deeply engaged in wartime diplomacy as well as settling the peace. He joined İbrahim Hakkı Pasha at Brest-Litovsk. In 1918, he acted as a legal advisor for the Ottoman delegation to the Paris Peace Conference. In 1920 he abandoned the sultan's government in Istanbul for the rival government in Ankara. Like his former boss, Gabriel Noradounghian, Mehmed Münir acted as a legal advisor at Lausanne, but for the Turkish government. Due in part to his success as Lausanne, Mehmed Münir Bey was awarded the position of chief legal counsel to the republican government on 1 April 1924. He unsuccessfully negotiated for the return of Mosul at the League of Nations and was a key figure in establishing the new Foreign Ministry in the Turkish Republic. He ended his career as the Turkish ambassador to the United States.[67]

Arguably, the breakup of the empire affected offices throughout the Ottoman bureaucracy in the much same way, with former colleagues finding themselves on different sides of state boundaries and ranging from support to disavowal of the new regime. What is distinct about the Office of Legal Counsel is that this group of intellectuals and legal experts were firmly committed to international law and legalism in diplomacy before the war—a idea that none of them fully retained afterwards.

---

66. Ibid., 295.
67. See George S. Harris, "Cementing Turkish-American Relations."

4 What Ottoman Nationality Was and Was Not

Will Hanley

NATIONALITY LEGISLATION WAS a nineteenth-century invention, and the Ottomans were early adopters. The Ottoman Nationality Law (Tabiiyet-i Osmaniye Kanunnamesi) of 1869 appeared at a time before any commonly-agreed international understanding of the basic elements of such legislation—this consensus emerged only after the First World War. In the third quarter of the nineteenth century, only a minority of states had enacted specific legislation to govern nationality. Many more defined state membership as part of a fundamental law, such as a constitution (United States), a civil code (France, Greece) or even a compendium (Egypt).[1] In these cases, membership boundaries developed directly out of legal definitions of the civil and political rights of members. In independent nationality regulations such as the 1869 Ottoman law, on the other hand, acquisition and loss of nationality (rather than the rights and obligations that nationality conveyed) was the primary concern. As membership became more narrowly and thoroughly defined, ambiguities unresolved in comprehensive codes and constitutions required the sort of focused directives that nationality laws contain. Thus independent nationality laws, as in the Ottoman case, represent an evolution in procedure based on practical experience.

In many of its aspects, the Ottoman Nationality Law resembled nationality laws of other states issued before 1869 and after. All such laws seek to regulate the core scenarios for the acquisition of nationality—birth, descent, naturalization through residence or marriage—with minor variance in the particulars of implementation. Yet the Ottoman Nationality Law has been identified as the origin point of a very different set of practices: those of modern political identity and citizenship. Semantically, the term *tabiiyet* supports various shades of meaning: nationality, subjecthood, affiliation, allegiance, "under the sovereignty of."[2] It does not support translation as "citizenship," however; those inscribing the 1869 law into a genealogy of citizenship must therefore be referring to the func-

---

1. Major collections of nationality laws include George Cogordan, *Droit des gens: la nationalité au point de vue des rapports internationaux*, 2nd ed. (Paris: L. Larose et Forcel, 1890); Richard W. Flournoy and Manley O. Hudson, eds., *A Collection of Nationality Laws of Various Countries, as Contained in Constitutions, Statutes and Treaties* (New York: Oxford University Press, 1929); United Nations, *Laws Concerning Nationality*, United Nations Legislative Series 4 (New York: United Nations, 1954).
2. Thanks to one of my anonymous reviewers for this last suggested translation.

tion of the law. But when one examines the content of the legislation, it is clear that the law is not concerned with functions typically associated with citizenship. Citizenship is practiced by those whose full membership is most secure, while nationality is the concern of those whose membership is least certain. The Ottoman Nationality Law concerns these latter individuals: children and wives of foreigners, orphans, emigrants, and immigrants.

I am not arguing that there was no Ottoman citizenship during the closing decades of the empire. Certainly there was. But the 1869 law describes forms of affiliation that do not constitute citizenship according to any useful understanding. The law was one step in the gradual imagination and constitution of a secular, state-centered membership regime. Was it the end of an 1839–69 trajectory of civil emancipation, or the beginning of a trajectory of political participation recurring in 1876 and 1908? Or is Ottoman nationality situated along another timeline, or a cul-de-sac of its own?

This chapter approaches these questions in five sections. The first maps out the major patterns of scholarly reference to the 1869 law. The second examines the content of the law itself and the circumstances of its promulgation. The third section traces the evolution and interpretation of law from 1869 to the second constitutional period, with particular emphasis on a detailed 1909 draft revision of the law that has not previously been analyzed. The fourth section takes up the broad question of acquisition of Ottoman nationality. The fifth section treats two issues particular to Ottoman nationality: marriage to Persian subjects and naturalization of Ottomans abroad. In sum, the essay argues that Ottoman nationality functioned not as a headwater of late imperial or national identity, but as a dike or bank shored up by the 1869 law that sought to hold a fluid population within the Ottoman watershed.

Citizenship, Ethnicity, Sect, or Nationality?

Scholars exploring the last half-century of Ottoman history frequently invoke the 1869 Ottoman Nationality Law. They define its character using a variety of labels of belonging, notably ethnicity, sect, and citizenship. These categories are ascribed to the law, but their pertinence is rarely explained. As a result, the particulars of the law itself remain indistinct and its functions uncertain. A remedy for murkiness in scholarly treatment of the Ottoman Nationality Law is to consider with greater precision what the law meant, and for whom: it is no surprise that different people made different things of it. The late Ottoman state was a functionally differentiated entity, and so there are several answers to this question, each valid but also discreet from others. Moreover, nationality was a novel legal concept in the last decades of the nineteenth century, not only in the Ottoman Empire but also worldwide. Nevertheless, the 1869 Nationality Law had positive content and well-defined limits which must be observed if its meaning is to be understood.

One line of scholarship situates the 1869 law in the course of the long rise of sectarianism and ethnic nationalism in the Ottoman Empire. In his study of nationalist divisions in the late Ottoman Empire, Feroz Ahmad treats nationality as a form of sectarian or ethnic identity (akin to the use of nationality in the Russian imperial context), while translating the term *tabiiyet* in the 1869 law as "citizenship." Ahmad suggests that the 1869 law was meant to encode a "patriotic identity" in the Ottoman population, which the reformers hoped would "transform subjects into citizens."[3] Kemal Karpat's widely-cited 1982 essay on millets and nationality suggests that nationality "in the sense of ethnic-national identity, drew its essence from the religious-communal experience in the millet, while citizenship—a secular concept—was determined by territory."[4] This distinction between nationality and citizenship proves difficult to unpack: the 1869 law made no reference to religion or ethnicity. Citizenship and territory, meanwhile, are not congruous concepts in the Ottoman Empire: unlike the United States of America, Ottoman law attributed nationality by territory of birth only rarely—in fact, a good part of the Nationality Law was devoted to specifying the conditions of *jus soli* acquisition. In Karpat's view, nationality was rooted in religion and language, while *tabiiyet* was a term that reconciled millet status and European citizenship.[5] He argues that by 1850, non-Muslim Ottoman subjects (millet members) were already treated as Ottoman citizens, and that the 1869 law was a "mere technicality that legalized and clarified further an already established concept."[6]

This is a moment to consider what it meant to be "treated as an Ottoman citizen." Ottoman membership was a meaningful and difficult question for many branches of the empire's administration. The Interior Ministry, the Office of the Şeyhülislam, the Chamber of Deputies (Meclis Vükela), the Population Bureau (Sicill-i Nüfus), and the Council of State itself all engaged with questions of nationality. As the other chapters in this volume show, the law bore various shades of meaning for all of these authorities. They exercised control over citizens through conscription, taxation, censorship, mobility controls, education, registration, and prosecution. Nationality was never essential to any of these administrative practices; however, its core functions belonged to the Foreign Ministry. The 1869 text, legal in nature and focused on external questions, was written us-

3. Feroz Ahmad, *The Young Turks and the Ottoman Nationalities: Armenians, Greeks, Albanians, Jews, and Arabs, 1908–1918* (Salt Lake City: University of Utah Press, 2014), 3–4.
4. Kemal H. Karpat, "Millets and Nationality: The Roots of the Incongruity of Nation and State in the Post-Ottoman Era," in *Christians and Jews in the Ottoman Empire*, ed. Benjamin Braude and Bernard Lewis (New York: Holmes & Meier Publishers, 1982), 141.
5. Ibid., 165.
6. Ibid., 162.

ing the language of international law in order to address other states. It was only secondarily a piece of domestic legislation. Acknowledging this fact can help to explain the various and contradictory roles that law has been assigned in the scholarly literature.

Like Karpat, Bruce Masters locates nationality in the field of sectarianism, but he does so without confusing it with citizenship (which he assigns to the 1876 constitution).[7] He describes the "reconfiguring of religious identity as nationality," as against the development of a unifying Ottoman nationalism, during the closing decades of the nineteenth century.[8] For Ussama Makdisi and Selim Deringil, the 1869 law represented a decoupling of religion and citizenship.[9] Because Ottoman subjecthood remained tightly associated with Muslims, however, the law created myriad problems, not least in cases of Muslims (including new converts) who were nationals of other states, as Michael Christopher Low shows in this volume.[10]

A second approach to the Nationality Law is pursued by scholars interested in political citizenship.[11] This approach seizes on the 1869 law as the referent for the Ottoman subjects of Article 6 of the 1876 constitution: "All subjects of the Empire are called Ottoman [*Devlet-i Osmaniye tabiiyetinde bulunan fertlerin*]... the status of an Ottoman is acquired and lost according to conditions specified by law [*Osmanlı sıfatı kanunen muayyen olan ahvale göre istihsal ve izaa olunur*]."[12] These scholars emphasize the ways in which residents of the empire came to articulate their aspiration to political participation, whether through representation (for example, in the 1876 parliament, secret societies, or the governments of the second constitutional period) or through discourse, notably in the press. For these scholars, the importance of the Nationality Law is its formal designation of membership in the class of Ottomans. Scholars who have examined the "imperial citizenship" of Ottomans have been alert to the question of legal mem-

---

7. Bruce Alan Masters, *Christians and Jews in the Ottoman Arab World: The Roots of Sectarianism* (Cambridge, UK: Cambridge University Press, 2001), 140.

8. Ibid., 196. Note, however, that he does not cite the 1869 law in this study.

9. Ussama Makdisi, "Ottoman Orientalism," *American Historical Review* 107, no. 3 (2002): 778; Selim Deringil, *Conversion and Apostasy in the Late Ottoman Empire* (Cambridge, UK: Cambridge University Press, 2012), 157.

10. Deringil, *Conversion and Apostasy*, 181–86.

11. Ariel Salzmann, "Citizens in Search of a State: The Limits of Political Participation in the Late Ottoman Empire," in *Extending Citizenship, Reconfiguring States*, ed. Michael P. Hanagan and Charles Tilly (Lanham, MD: Rowman & Littlefield Publishers, 1999), 37–66; Engin Fahri Isin, "Citizenship after Orientalism: Ottoman Citizenship," in *Citizenship in a Global World: European Questions and Turkish Experiences*, ed. Fuat Keyman and Ahmet İçduygu (London: Routledge, 2005), 31–51.

12. This attribution comes in İsmail Aydıngün and Esra Dardağan, "Rethinking the Jewish Communal Apartment in the Ottoman Communal Building," *Middle Eastern Studies* 42, no. 2 (2006): 325.

bership in the empire.[13] Too often, though, this citizenship seeks a referent that simply does not exist. Karpat's rich study of late Ottoman membership attributes a political character to the "Citizenship Laws of 1864 [*sic*]" that it simply did not possess: "Ottomanism implied that the country belonged, or should belong, to its citizens and that their ownership of the state was based on their citizenship status as 'Osmanli' or Ottomans, regardless of religious affiliation."[14] The few Ottomans who might have conceived of themselves as citizens owning the country did not do so because of the Nationality Law of 1869, which only admitted the state's ownership of its subjects.

Lawyers have engaged with the 1869 law using a third approach. Some see it as the fundament of Ottoman private law—it is, for example, the first law printed in Aristachi Bey's massive six-volume collection of Ottoman legislation. More recently, Cihan Osmanağaoğlu's book offers a detailed legal reading of the law.[15] Lawyers interested in nationality in Ottoman successor states have looked back on the 1869 law in order to understand subsequent statutes in Turkey and elsewhere. Gianluca Parolin's study of citizenship in the Arab world gives a brief but serious treatment of the 1869 law itself, in the context of his broader argument about kin, religious, and national belonging.[16] Constantin Iordachi's work on Balkan nationality and Mutaz Qafisheh's work on Palestinian nationality also elaborate continuities with the 1869 law.[17] Accounts of citizenship in the Republic frequently take 1869 as their point of departure.[18] These legal accounts are concerned with continuities with the present day, rather than understanding Ottoman nationality on its own terms. Nevertheless, their specialized domain clarifies the law's own vocabulary.

13. For example, Michelle Campos, *Ottoman Brothers: Muslims, Christians, and Jews in Early 20th Century Palestine* (Stanford: Stanford University Press, 2010); Julia Phillips Cohen, *Becoming Ottomans: Sephardi Jews and Imperial Citizenship in the Modern Era* (New York: Oxford University Press, 2014).

14. Kemal H. Karpat, *The Politicization of Islam: Reconstructing Identity, State, Faith, and Community in the Late Ottoman State* (Oxford: Oxford University Press, 2001), 315.

15. Cihan Osmanağaoğlu, *Tanzimat Dönemi İtibarıyla Osmanlı Tâbiiyyetinin (Vatandaşlığının) Gelişimi* (Istanbul: Legal, 2004).

16. Gianluca Paolo Parolin, *Citizenship in the Arab World: Kin, Religion and Nation-State* (Amsterdam: Amsterdam University Press, 2009), 73–74 and passim.

17. Constantin Iordachi, "The Ottoman Empire: Syncretic Nationalism and Citizenship in the Balkans," in *What Is a Nation?: Europe 1789–1914*, ed. Timothy Baycroft and Mark Hewitson (Oxford: Oxford University Press, 2006), 130–31; Mutaz M. Qafisheh, *The International Law Foundations of Palestinian Nationality : a Legal Examination of Nationality in Palestine Under Britain's Rule* (Leiden: Martinus Nijhoff, 2009).

18. For instance, Zeynep Kadirbeyoğlu, "Changing Conceptions of Citizenship in Turkey," in *Citizenship Policies in the New Europe*, ed. Rainer Bauböck, Bernhard Perchinig, and Wiebke Sievers (Amsterdam: Amsterdam University Press, 2007), 419–38.

Historians who are interested in the law as a means of accessing social history pursue a fourth path. Karen Kern (on marriage), James Meyer (on migration), Abdul-Karim Rafeq and Sibel Zandi-Sayek (on property), and Julia Phillips Cohen and Sarah Abrevaya Stein (on Jews) each find uses for the 1869 law.[19] Again, however, the mechanisms by which political citizenship relates to acquisition and loss of legal membership (the main subjects of the 1869 law) are not important concerns in the literature on citizenship.[20] So, for instance, we do not discover the administrative location of citizenship, or understand why nationality was the purview of the Ottoman Foreign Ministry, rather than of mayors (as was the case in Greece and Hungary) or the Interior Ministry.[21] The literature has not managed to disaggregate political questions from questions of unitary subjecthood. Hence Iordachi's assertion:

> Until the advent of the First World War, the Ottoman state organization was thus dominated by the contradiction between the emergence of a generic Ottoman citizenship based on the legal equality of all its inhabitants, irrespective of their religion or ethnicity, and calls for an Islamic based Ottoman nationality, supported by a legal order that would favour the political and socioeconomic interests of the Muslims.[22]

He seems to confuse domestic and foreign ministry questions, and political and property rights. Tanzimat legal equality was a different question altogether, figuring not at all in the nationality laws, though the questions are certainly mingled in the secondary literature, which often (and imprecisely) substitutes "citizenship" for *tabiiyet*. Scholars seeking to use nationality as an avenue to ad-

19. Karen M. Kern, *Imperial Citizen: Marriage and Citizenship in the Ottoman Frontier Provinces of Iraq* (Syracuse: Syracuse University Press, 2011); James H. Meyer, "Immigration, Return, and the Politics of Citizenship: Russian Muslims in the Ottoman Empire, 1860–1914," *International Journal of Middle East Studies* 39, no. 1 (2007): 15–32; Abdul-Karim Rafeq, "Ownership of Real Property by Foreigners in Syria, 1869 to 1873," in *New Perspectives on Property and Land in the Middle East*, ed. Roger Owen (Cambridge, MA: Harvard University Press, 2001), 175–240; Sibel Zandi-Sayek, *Ottoman Izmir: The Rise of a Cosmopolitan Port, 1840–1880* (Minneapolis: University of Minnesota Press, 2012); Cohen, *Becoming Ottomans*; Sarah Abrevaya Stein, "Protected Persons? The Baghdadi Jewish Diaspora, the British State, and the Persistence of Empire," *American Historical Review* 116, no. 1 (2011): 80–108; eadem, "Citizens of a Fictional Nation: Ottoman-Born Jews in France during the First World War," *Past & Present* 226, no. 1 (2015): 227–54.
20. Consider the careful explanation of 1869's acquisition rules in Campos, *Ottoman Brothers*, 61.
21. Intriguingly, in his archivally vivid 2012 study of Ottoman belonging, Selim Deringil frequently thanks Sinan Kuneralp for reference to sources, but he does not cite any document from the Foreign Ministry Legal Bureau, about which Kuneralp published an extensive document collection in the same year. Is this an indication of the isolation of the bureau from the administrative mainstream?
22. Iordachi, "Syncretic Nationalism," 133.

dress other historical topics have been poorly served by a literature that does not specify what Ottoman nationality was and was not.

The Ottoman Nationality Law of 1869

The four lines of interpretation described above put a lot of weight on narrow shoulders: the 1869 Nationality Law contains just nine articles.[23] The first three articles deal briskly with the three main means of nationality acquisition: descent (children of Ottoman fathers are Ottomans), birth (foreigners born in the Ottoman domains may acquire Ottoman nationality at the age of majority), and residence (foreigners may acquire Ottoman nationality after five years of residence). The middle articles concern the empire's sovereignty over its nationality, offering the executive a full range of possible powers over the nationality status of individual subjects: the Imperial Council may make exceptions to the requirements just listed, it may refuse permission for Ottomans to quit Ottoman nationality, and (conversely) it can strip those who acquire foreign nationality of their Ottoman nationality and bar them from Ottoman territory. The seventh and eight articles concern the nationality of wives and children who do not share the nationality of their husbands or fathers. The ninth article states that anyone inhabiting the empire is considered an Ottoman by default, unless they can demonstrate otherwise.

Although it resembles European nationality legislation, the 1869 law was also marked by influences particular to the empire. Foremost among these was the Capitulations, a set of long-standing extraterritorial privileges and exemptions for foreign subjects in the Ottoman domains.[24] By the middle of the nineteenth century, the professionalizing Tanzimat bureaucracy was combatting all and any limitations on Ottoman sovereignty. A modern state required a well-defined territory and a well-defined population. Clarifying and standardizing membership was no simple undertaking for a complex empire characterized by decentralized authority and differentiated status and jurisdiction.

After the Islahat Fermanı of 1856, which leveled civil distinctions between Muslim and non-Muslim Ottoman subjects, the reformers could tackle the next great membership problem: protégés (*beratlılar*) of foreign states. Protégés, Ottoman subjects who enjoyed the exemptions and privileges of foreigners, possessed

---

23. The law was published in *Düstür* 1 (1289/1872): 16–18. A French translation appears in Gregorius Aristarchi Bey, *Législation ottomane, ou Recueil des lois, réglements, ordonnances, traités, capitulations et autres documents officiels de l'Empire ottoman*, 6 vols. (Constantinople: Freres Nicolaïdes, 1873), 1:7-8.

24. For background on the capitulations, see Maurits H. van den Boogert, *The Capitulations and the Ottoman Legal System: Qadis, Consuls, and Beratlis in the 18th Century* (Leiden: Brill, 2005); Umut Özsu, "Ottoman Empire," in *The Oxford Handbook of the History of International Law*, ed. Bardo Fassbender and Anne Peters (Oxford: Oxford University Press, 2013), 429–48.

a hybrid status that became intolerable for the reformers. In 1863, the Ottoman administration issued a regulation that dramatically restricted the possibility of protection.[25] Because Ottoman subjects now possessed equal rights, the legislation asserted, there was no more need for foreign protection. Foreign embassies and consulates and Christian and Jewish religious institutions could continue to protect a limited number of employees, but all other protégés now faced a choice: they had to naturalize as foreign subjects, or submit to the territorial jurisdiction that went along with their Ottoman subjecthood and residence.

The 1863 protégé regulation did not clarify everyone's status overnight. Individuals discovered the practical implications of the legal change only gradually, as occasions to investigate and clarify their status arose. But the Ottoman bureaucracy now had the legal basis to clarify and simplify the state's relationship with the greatest part of its population. Having made this stride, it discovered the next stumbling block in defining a well-bounded population subject to its sovereignty. Quite naturally, many protégés (especially those possessing wealth or power) reacted to the 1863 regulation by naturalizing with a foreign state, but these newly-minted foreign nationals also remained Ottoman residents and (in most cases) Ottoman subjects. Thus the 1863 regulation, intended to clarify whether an individual was an Ottoman or a foreigner, led many to establish status as Ottomans *and* foreigners. It was this problem that the 1869 Ottoman Nationality Law aimed to solve.

As we have seen, scholarship citing the Ottoman Nationality Law of 1869 has quite consistently traced its lineage to the Tanzimat edicts of 1839 and 1856.[26] An interest in Ottoman citizenship—unquestionably a key concern of the Tanzimat edicts—can quite innocently lead to this reading of the 1869 law (which entails the need to explain away a problem of terminology, because the text refers to *tebaa*, which means subjects, not citizens). This "citizenship" misreading misses the immediate context of the law: its most direct connection was to the protégé regulation of 1863. Ali Pasha, the grand vizier who promulgated the law, made this connection plain in an April 1869 memorandum circulated to foreign powers through the Ottoman ambassadors abroad.[27] He stated that the Ottoman government supports the individual freedom to choose nationality, but that the capitulations had perverted that freedom in the Ottoman domains. The privileges of foreigners naturally led Ottomans to seek foreign protection, and protégés came to outnumber foreigners themselves. "The imperial government believed that it

---

25. *Règlement relatif aux consulats étrangers d'août 1863*, and an 1865 addendum, reproduced in Pierre Arminjon, *Étrangers et protégés dans l'Empire ottoman* (Paris: A. Chevalier-Maresq & cie, 1903), 325–30.
26. Karpat, "Millets and Nationality," 163; Salzmann, "Citizens in Search of a State," 39–45; Campos, *Ottoman Brothers*, 61; Kern, *Imperial Citizen*, 14–16.
27. This memorandum is reproduced in Cogordan, *Droit des gens*, 547–51.

had partially remedied this situation with the 1863 regulation...but our hope was not realized": the number of protégés dropped, but the number of naturalized foreigners rose apace. The administration tried to be patient, Ali's memorandum continues, believing that no foreign state would encourage Ottomans to naturalize in order to further its own interests in the empire. Furthermore, he points to Ottoman expectations invested in a different 1856 document: the Treaty of Paris, which promised a revision of the capitulations. When these hopes were "cruelly denied," the Ottoman government had no choice but to pass its nationality law of 19 January 1869.

Specification of nationality law was a trend. French Civil Code provisions were refined many times, notably with a comprehensive law in 1883.[28] Russia's mid-nineteenth-century collection of laws (*svod zakonov*) governed personal status generally, but the question of naturalization required far more detailed specification, which came in a separate edict in 1864.[29] States without fundamental compilations of laws, like the Ottoman Empire, introduced independent nationality legislation. German nationality, for instance, depended on the stand-alone law of 1 June 1870.[30] Britain produced a Naturalization Act in the same year, developing its Nationality Acts of 1730 and 1844. The Ottoman law of 1869 was less detailed than these acts, but roughly contemporary to them. Kuneralp has shown that a French and a British lawyer advised the Ottoman Foreign Ministry during the 1860s; these men would have considered these European laws when consulted on the Ottoman Nationality Law.[31]

In addition to these general influences, Ottoman nationality law was shaped by the policies of the empire's neighbors, who "competed" for its subjects. Kern's work details the Ottoman-Iranian contest over nationality at the frontier.[32] Iordachi suggests that "the Ottoman citizenship law can be characterized...as reactive to nationality laws passed by neighbouring Christian states, a feature highlighted by the delegation of citizenship matters to the Ministry of Foreign Affairs."[33] He argues that the "inclusive" nationality rules of Greece and other Balkans states antedated the 1869 law and, as its direct competitors, shaped its

---

28. For a comprehensive study, see Patrick Weil, *How to Be French: Nationality in the Making since 1789* (Durham: Duke University Press, 2008).
29. Cogordan, *Droit des gens*, 519–24.
30. *British and Foreign State Papers* 79 (1887–88), 147–51. A stimulating comparison of German and French nationality is Rogers Brubaker, *Citizenship and Nationhood in France and Germany* (Cambridge, MA: Harvard University Press, 1992).
31. Sinan Kuneralp and Emre Öktem, eds., *Chambre des conseillers légistes de la Sublime Porte: rapports, avis et consultations sur la condition juridique des ressortissants étrangers, le statut des communautés non musulmanes et les relations internationales de l'Empire ottoman (1864–1912)* (Istanbul: Isis Press, 2012), 10.
32. Kern, *Imperial Citizen*.
33. Iordachi, "Syncretic Nationalism," 131.

provisions. Greek nationality was governed by its Civil Code of 1856.[34] Bulgaria introduced comprehensive nationality laws in 1883 (revising the constitution of 1879) and in 1903.[35] Before its final division from the Ottoman Empire in 1878, Romania's Civil Code of 1864 and Constitution of 1866 based membership on religion; in 1878 these restrictions were lifted, and an 1880 rule allowed the naturalization of any Ottoman residents, except those visiting temporarily to work lands they owned.[36]

The most important and controversial provisions of the 1869 law were the controls over expatriation contained in Articles 6 and 7. By refusing to acknowledge any nationality change by an Ottoman subject without permission, the empire aimed to reassert its sovereignty over its own subjects on its own territory, badly eroded as a result of the capitulations. While early twentieth-century commentators hinted that this measure constrained individual freedom, they also had to acknowledge that many other states had provisions similar to the Ottomans.[37] In any event, the Ottomans were not claiming anything so pervasive as Russia's perpetual allegiance.[38] Thus the great powers (if grudgingly at times) agreed that, in the words of a French Foreign Ministry committee that studied the 1869 law, it contained "nothing contrary to international law in general, and it does not infringe on the rights and privileges granted under the capitulations and established by custom."[39]

Evolution and Interpretation of the Nationality Law

It is not surprising that the 1869 law, meant to curb widespread jurisdiction dodging through expatriation, met considerable opposition. This controversy was mentioned in an *izahname* (explication) sent to provincial governors in March 1869 and in Ali Pasha's April memorandum to foreign consuls. These two documents were among a number of clarifications and supplemental laws that the Ottoman government issued in the years after 1869 in order to elaborate the law's provisions. The *izahname*, dated 4 Zilhicce 1285 (26 March 1869) and addressed to provincial governors and distributed as well to foreign consulates in the empire, shows that questions requiring clarification arose just weeks after

---

34. Cogordan, *Droit des gens*, 486.
35. Flournoy and Hudson, *Collection of Nationality Laws*, 161–69.
36. Estanislao Severo Zeballos and André Bosq, *La nationalité au point de vue de la législation comparée et du droit privé humain* (Paris: L. Tenin, 1914), 1:297–98.
37. Emmanuel R. Salem, "De la nationalité en Turquie," *Journal du droit international privé (Clunet)* 32 (1905): 585–91, 872–83; 33 (1906): 1032–41; 34 (1907): 51–56.
38. On Russian nationality, see Eric Lohr, *Russian Citizenship: From Empire to Soviet Union* (Cambridge, MA: Harvard University Press, 2012).
39. "Avis du comité de contentieux auprès du ministère des affaires étrangères," reprinted in Cogordan, *Droit des gens*, 554.

the law was promulgated.[40] The text emphasized that the law's force was not ret-roactive, which supports my contention that its function was to complement and extend existing instruments defining and refining the Tanzimat membership re-gime. The document also states that nationality change under the new law cannot be used to dodge any existing criminal or civil case; cases antedating the law will be pursued in their original venue. Certain lacunas of the law are addressed: the age of majority is to be defined by the norms of each community. The *izahname* cautions provincial authorities that only the central authorities can dispense the permission to expatriate (under Article 5) and order the banishment or expulsion of those who expatriate without permission (Article 6). Again, this suggests that the purpose of the Nationality Law was to settle otherwise intractable puzzles, rather than to manage everyday administration on the ground.

Ali Pasha's April 1869 memorandum responds at some length to the claim that the Sublime Porte lacked the legal authority to legislate Ottoman nationality independent of foreign assent. "The question of nationality in Turkey, we are told, is a European question, involving all Powers which have treaties with the Sublime Porte. Any law or regulation of this question must be a joint product [*oeuvre com-mun*] of the Sublime Porte and representatives of the Powers."[41] The memoran-dum argues that the law carefully avoided any retroactive effect or infringement on existing treaties, and denounces this attempt of foreign powers "to interfere in the relations of the Sultan with his subjects." It seems that this assertion was largely respected in the years that followed. In the case of nationality legislation, at least, it appears that the Ottomans achieved some ground in their mid-century efforts to have their sovereignty recognized by the community of nations.

As in many aspects of international law, most of Europe considered the Ot-toman laws a curiosity rather than a mainstay. Von Bar and other general treatise writers in international law gave no attention to the 1869 Ottoman Nationality Law; the interest of these authors in the Ottoman example was limited to the question of extraterritoriality. Valéry states simply that the Ottomans follow the French practice of *sanguinis* nationality with a strong *soli* aspect, alongside Bel-gium, Spain, Greece, Italy, the Netherlands, Sweden, Denmark, Russia, Bulgaria, Persia, and China.[42] Lehr's survey includes Turkey in the community of nation-alities.[43] The serious examinations of Ottoman nationality came in the context of specialized study of Ottoman law. Pierre Arminjon's 1903 *Étrangers et proté-*

---

40. A French translation appears in Aristarchi Bey, *Législation ottomane*, 1:9–11.
41. Cogordan, *Droit des gens*, 549–50. One of the grounds for this claim was an Ottoman-Rus-sian convention of April 1863 that regulated the implementation of the protégé law of that year.
42. Jules Valéry, *Manuel de droit international privé* (Paris: Fontemoing, 1914), 144–45.
43. Ernest Lehr, *La nationalité dans les principaux États du globe (acquisition, perte, recouvre-ment)* (Paris: A. Pedone, 1909), 215–18.

gés dans l'Empire ottoman was the closest study of the topic.[44] Emmanuel Salem published a four-part study of Turkish nationality in the leading international law journal in 1905–07.[45] George Young's seven-volume collection of Ottoman law treats nationality under the field of personal status (at odds with its classification as a matter for the Foreign Ministry).[46]

We have seen that the 1869 Nationality Law was the product of a series of steps toward more positivist determination of membership, beginning with the Tanzimat and the 1856 reform edict, but depending especially on the 1856 Treaty of Paris and the 1863 protégé regulation. After each step, new and exceptional cases arose revealing the need for further regulation and clarification. After 1869 and through the long Hamidian period, officials in the Foreign Ministry made a good number of piecemeal adjustments to Ottoman nationality policy.[47] The second constitutional period was a political watershed that offered the occasion for an update, and in 1909 the Foreign Ministry produced a major revision of the forty-year-old Ottoman Nationality Law.[48] This revision entailed a line-by-line evaluation of the successes and failures of the 1869 law, and it integrated many nationality policies adopted in the intervening years. The proposed revision, though never implemented, offers the clearest indication of what nationality law meant for those charged with implementing it. The revision was both a response to particular pressures as the empire sought to realign loyalty to the state and staunch internal and external opposition movements and part of the general global movement to standardize statuses in the first decades of the twentieth century.

The typeset revision shares its archival folder with a dozen auxiliary documents, carefully copied on the letterhead of the Nationality Directorate (Tabiiyet Müdiriyeti) of the Foreign Ministry, which the drafters of the law considered necessary appendices to support their work.[49] As Aimee Genell's pioneering essay in

---

44. For a brief biographical sketch of Arminjon, see Will Hanley, "International Lawyers without Public International Law: The Case of Late Ottoman Egypt," *Journal of the History of International Law* 18 (2016): 108.

45. Salem, "De la nationalité en Turquie."

46. George Young, *Corps de droit ottoman; recueil des codes, lois, règlements, ordonnances et actes les plus importants du droit intérieur, et d'études sur le droit coutumier de l'Empire ottoman*, 7 vols. (Oxford: The Clarendon Press, 1905), 2:223–41.

47. In addition to the evidence given elsewhere in this volume, see the rich collection of examples from the 1870s and 1880s published in Kuneralp and Öktem, *Chambre des conseillers légistes*.

48. BOA, HR.HMŞ.İŞO, 221/11.

49. In addition to the comments discussed below, the appendices include two further items: item 3 is a *firman* of 11 Rebiülevvel 1297 (11 Feb. 1880), and item 10 is a copy of the minute (*mazbata*) of opinion (*ray*) of the Devlet-i Tanzimat Dairesi number 2607, dated 13 Receb 1310 (31 Jan. 1893), which is a response to request from the Tabiiyyet Kalemi, about a specific person seeking French nationality in Salonika.

this volume shows, the history of the legal work of the Ottoman Foreign Ministry is only beginning to emerge, and so it is difficult to gauge how well integrated this Directorate, the Legal Bureau, and the Foreign Ministry itself were with the other administrative conduits that governed the Ottoman membership regime.[50] The draft law was never implemented. Although unimplemented ideas can exert influence on legal practice and on subsequent legislation, such influence has proven difficult to track in this case.[51] At the very least, the draft law offers the Foreign Ministry's verdict on its own 1869 Nationality Law.

No end of internal reasons influenced the 1909 revision. Its relatively conservative modernization of existing nationality practices is entirely in step with the conservative aims of the new government, which sought to preserve the empire rather than transform it. And new nationality problems would continue to arise in the months to come: Deringil reports that in 1912–13, the Council of State returned to the question of nationality, declaring that converts to Islam would no longer automatically acquire Ottoman nationality.[52] But external influences are also clear. The Legal Bureau was a competitor with its counterparts in other states and empires. The Ottomans needed to show their currency and competence on all fronts. The update was not merely a question of keeping up, however. Other states had developed means of dealing with particular kinds of nationality problems, and the Legal Bureau—which followed such developments closely— would have chosen to adopt and import these means where feasible. The Foreign Ministry was under tremendous pressure to account for Ottoman treatment of its subjects. Major conflicts with the Armenian community and the influx of refugees from Balkan wars each posed nationality problems. "Minority protection" was the euphemism that emerged to describe international interest in these questions, and the Ottomans knew that there was an intense need for response in 1909, in order to forestall further intervention.

The Purview of Nationality

The meaning of the 1869 Nationality Law is confirmed by the content of the 1909 revision, which shows what the Ottoman administrators responsible for nationality thought it was. Nationality, in the Ottoman Empire as elsewhere, begins with acquisition—the most basic grounds on which a person can be considered

---

50. The classic account is Carter Vaughn Findley, *Bureaucratic Reform in the Ottoman Empire: The Sublime Porte, 1789–1922* (Princeton: Princeton University Press, 1980), 319.
51. On this question, see Tatiana Borisova, "The Digest of Laws of the Russian Empire: The Phenomenon of Autocratic Legality," *Law and History Review* 30, no. 3 (2012): 903. For a history of Republican Turkish nationality tracing continuity to Ottoman law, see Osman Fazû Berki, "Türk Vatandaşlığı Kanununun Aslî Tabiiyete Müteallik Hükümleri," *Ankara Üniversitesi Hukuk Fakültesi Dergisi* 7, no. 1–2 (1950): 146–59.
52. Deringil, *Conversion and Apostasy*, 187; this issue is also treated in Salem, "De la nationalité en Turquie," 1038–41.

a subject. The opening articles of the 1909 regulation and the 1869 law treats the same three topics—descent, place of birth, and naturalization—but the 1909 draft is much more extensive and specific, accounting for a broad range of exceptions. First comes *jus sanguinis*: a male or female, regardless of birthplace, who is the legitimate child of an Ottoman father or the illegitimate child of an Ottoman mother, is an Ottoman national. (The legitimate child of an Ottoman mother and a non-Ottoman father would take the nationality of her or his father). Second comes a quite pervasive definition of subjecthood by residence: any individual, irrespective of birthplace, who is resident in the Ottoman dominions is considered an Ottoman subject—except those who can convince Ottoman officials that they are foreigners. This blanket provision serves to establish a default assumption in cases which otherwise would be open to debate. After these two basic categories, Article 1 details five less frequently occurring forms of basic membership. None of these categories figured in the 1869 law, though some were the subject of directives in the intervening years. The following also counted as Ottoman:

- the foundling children of persons of unknown identity in the Ottoman domains;

- any man or woman who is legally stateless (*kaideten vatansız*) and not subject to any foreign government, irrespective of birthplace, who is present on Ottoman territory (*Osmanlı ülkesinde*);

- Muslim Ottoman women who had married Iranian men despite the ban on such marriages, and the sons and daughters of these marriages;

- unregistered persons (*nüfus*) in localities where the Ottoman census was not carried out; and

- "concealed" (*mektûme*) persons from localities where the census had been carried out.

Most of these exceptional categories are addressed in greater detail in the articles that follow. The great increase in the kinds of unknowns and exceptions in this article embodies a response to experience. Already, it is clear that this law is the product of the very men in the Legal Bureau of the Foreign Ministry who had been charged with decades of complex problems resulting from the ambiguities of the 1869 law.

Jus soli is the concern of Article 2, which specifies that children born in the Ottoman domains to foreign parents may be considered Ottoman subjects, and may hold dual nationality if they apply to the government according to procedures which the draft spells out in considerable detail. Naturalization is the subject of Article 4, which stated that the foreign born persons could apply for Ottoman naturalization after three years of residence. These applicants must be of the age of majority and free of bankruptcy or criminal conviction, or have been rehabilitated (*iade-i itibar eden*). Like the previous article, this article describes the application procedure, and goes so far as to state that following investigation of the application, officials have the right either to accept or refuse the request. The injection of procedural details into the statute, as well as the insistence on administrative discretion, shows that the framers of the draft were especially concerned with its application. This concern with spelling out all possibilities is sustained throughout the 1909 draft, which also introduces regulation of acquisition through adoption (Article 3), and the case of children born on ships in Ottoman waters (Article 5). Executive discretion featured in Article 4 of the 1869 law (borrowed from Article 9 of the French Civil Code), which gave the government the power to admit exceptional individuals to Ottoman nationality in extraordinary circumstances.[53] The 1909 law much surpassed this general power, carefully encoding in Articles 6, 7, and 8 the government's power to make exceptions to the standard avenues of acquisition. A sign of the times, Article 9 gave the government special powers to enforce nationality during wartime. In addition to allowing for obscure possibilities and procedures, the regulation greatly expanded administrative prerogative.

As Kern has established, Persia had a major influence on Ottoman nationality; it is not surprising that the 1909 draft looks east as much or more than west or north. In many of its articles, the draft shows a marked resemblance to the first comprehensive Persian nationality law, dated 5 Safer 1312 (8 August 1894).[54] The Persian law took its first four articles almost verbatim from the Ottoman Nationality Law of 1869, adding only, in Article 3, a provision that naturalizing foreigners must (in addition to being of majority and having resided in Persia for five years) have a clean penal record and be free of military service obligations. Other articles were original, however. Articles 5–7 of the Persian law concern the resumption of Persian nationality by expatriates and children of expatriates (they are excused from the five-year residence requirement), foreign wives of Persian subjects (they become Persian nationals, but may revert to their original nationality in widowhood or divorce), and foreign wives of foreign subjects (who may only naturalize if their husbands also do so). None of these provisions appear in the 1869 law, but Articles 6 and 7 anticipate Articles 20 and 21 of the 1909 draft law. Similarly, Article 10 of 1894 (on children's independence from their father's nationality) anticipates Article 23 of 1909, and Article 11 of 1894 (on Persian women following their husband's nationality) resembles Article 19 of 1909.

53. Arminjon, *Étrangers et protégés*, 84.
54. Translations of this law appear in *British and Foreign State Papers* 86 (1893–94), 180–82 and in James Brown Scott, David Jayne Hill, and Gaillard Hunt, "Citizenship of the United States, Expatriation, and Protection Abroad," [59th Cong., 2nd sess., HR Doc. 326] (Washington DC: State Department, 1906), 484–86.

Most intriguing are Articles 13 and 14 of the Persian law. Article 13 mimics Article 9 of 1869, stating that "those who appear to be Persian subjects, and yet claim to be subjects of a foreign state, must prove their nationality...." But Article 14 turns this idea on its head: "Aliens who have come to Persia, and have concealed their nationality while residing in the Shah's dominions, and have been treated as Persian subjects, or have purchased property, which is the exclusive right of Persian subjects, shall be recognized as Persian subjects, and their claim to foreign protection shall not be admitted." Presumably both articles of the Persian law were intended to address the twin problem of false Ottomans and Ottomans pretending to be Persians. These articles seem to anticipate Article 1 Section 8 of 1909, which makes "concealed" persons found on the territory Ottoman nationals.

"Concealed" persons were typical of the marginal subjects that were the focus of nationality legislation. The only discussion of the kinds of rights that a citizen might possess concerned the political and property rights of immigrants and refugees. Article 15 of the 1909 regulation stipulates that the acquisition of Ottoman political rights (*hukuk-i siyasiye*) by a person entering into Ottoman nationality through naturalization or special government dispensation (Articles 4–8) is contingent on ten years' residence in the Ottoman domains from the date of nationality change.[55] For refugees (*muhacirin*), however, the period of residence is five years. Extended residence was an important loyalty test. In Ali Pasha's 1869 narrative of the reasons for the promulgation of the law, he complains bitterly that in the years before 1869, "several states changed their naturalization laws; the condition making residence for a number of years mandatory [before naturalization] was reduced, and even abolished in certain countries."[56] Forty years later, the Ottomans were careful to test loyalty with time before according political rights. This two-step naturalization shows again that nationality and citizenship rights followed separate tracks. Presumably the loyalty of refugees, who had few other places to go, was more easily (and quickly) assured.

Marriage and Expatriation

Ottoman administrators demonstrated creative agency during the Hamidian period, but they did so by adapting international norms to local conditions. While most Ottoman nationality legislation duplicates laws found elsewhere, in the case of marriage and expatriation Ottoman lawyers sought to extend control over its subjects beyond the generally-accepted limits of international law. The

55. In 1894, a regulation of the Council of State made it possible for foreign converts to Islam who did not fulfill all of the requirements for naturalization to acquire a sort of provisional Ottoman nationality (including the requisite identification documents). Deringil, *Conversion and Apostasy*, 187.
56. Cogordan, *Droit des gens*, 549.

1909 draft deals with both of these questions in detail, summarizing four decades of experience and describing a trajectory for the post-Hamidian membership regime.

The 1869 law gave slight attention to marriage, stating only that a woman who acquired Ottoman nationality through marriage could return to her original nationality after her husband's death (Article 7). The framers of the law did not foresee that marriage would form such a major part of their work in the decades that followed, as the legal bureau was called on again and again to issue opinions on marriage problems.[57] These problems also required legislation in the intervening years.

Questions of Iranian nationality figure in two appendices attached to the draft law: the well-known marriage regulation dating 5 Şaban 1291 (24 September 1874) and a 5 Receb 1305 (18 March 1888) circular letter to provincial governors specifying treatment for couples who had broken the prohibition on Ottoman/ Iranian marriage.[58] It is clear that the authors of the 1909 law had just these problems in mind as they sought to clarify rules and procedures for the second constitutional period. Generally speaking, the law shows a greater awareness and specificity concerning questions of gender; as the *istişare odası* nationality opinions of the 1880s and 1890s show, problems arose from the gender vagaries of the 1869 law.[59] Although nationality differentiation by gender is clear, the 1909 draft is careful to specify its applicability to both male and female subjects in the more commonplace categories of acquisition (whereas the 1869 law mentioned a [generic] "person" [*şahıs*]).

The 1909 draft contains six articles concerning marriage. Article 10 states that for the purposes of nationality, the age of majority (twenty-one years of age) is set aside for married Ottoman women and for foreign women married to Ottoman men. Articles 19 and 20 treat the cases of Ottoman women married to foreign men and Ottoman men married to foreign women, respectively. In both cases, wives follow the nationality of their husbands under most circumstances (though the Ottoman/Iranian marriage ban is specifically referenced in Article 19). The following three articles further specify possible circumstances: wives changing nationality along with husbands (Article 21), nationality change after death or divorce (Article 22, which again specifically excludes any coverage for Ottoman/Iranian marriages), and the status of children, who do not follow the nationality of their fathers (Article 23).[60] But the draft of 1909 does not encode

57. Kuneralp and Öktem, *Chambre des conseillers légistes.*
58. The former document appears in Kern, *Imperial Citizen*, 159, appendix two. Portions of the latter document appear in Ibid., 103–4.
59. Kuneralp and Öktem, *Chambre des conseillers légistes.*
60. Articles 22 and 23 of the 1909 draft seem to correspond to Articles 7 and 8 of the 1869 law.

the marriage ban; instead, it states several times that its provisions do not apply to such forbidden marriages.[61]

Marriage is a major driver of nationality law, but the Persian marriage ban was not about marriage *per se* but a part of a broader effort to retain population.[62] This was also the ambit of the second distinctive aspect of Ottoman nationality law: its attempt to restrict naturalization under foreign nationality by Ottoman subjects. The core feature of the 1869 law was the stipulation that the Ottoman state was not bound to recognize any other state's naturalization of an Ottoman subject. This feature, which had been the subject of considerable diplomatic controversy over the intervening decades, was reiterated and further specified in Articles 11–16 of the 1909 draft.[63] Article 5 of the 1869 law tersely stated that foreign naturalization was permitted, but required an imperial *irade*, and reserved for the Ottoman state the right to disregard any unauthorized naturalization.

George Young reported in 1905 that it had become almost impossible to procure this *irade*. To do so, the consular authorities of the state to which the petitioner had naturalized had to send a copy of the certificate to the Ottoman Ministry of Foreign Affairs. He also had to submit a declaration that he would leave the empire as soon as the *irade* was granted. The file was then sent to local authorities at the petitioner's place of residence to ensure that there were no legal, tax, or other issues outstanding. The Porte was then able to request an *irade*, but would only do so if the petitioner had influence; in practice, it happened very rarely.[64] In 1906, the Nationality Bureau published a detailed price list for all of its procedures.[65] Presumably, the standardization of forms and procedures in 1909 was an effort to streamline a process developed in the intervening years.[66]

Most of these procedures were restrictive. Ottoman subjects needed permission to leave the dominions at all (Article 11), and of course could only denaturalize with authorization (Article 12). Article 13 specified the formalities required for such an authorization. Article 14 detailed the registration procedures for naturalized Ottomans. Article 16 explained the consequences of leaving Ottoman residence and Ottoman nationality. Among these consequences was banishment;

---

61. The 1894 Persian Nationality Law does not reciprocate the Ottoman prohibition of marriage with Persian subjects.

62. On global efforts to retain population in this period, see Adam McKeown, *Melancholy Order: Asian Migration and the Globalization of Borders* (New York: Columbia University Press, 2008).

63. On the controversy, see Qafisheh, *International Law Foundations*, 33.

64. Young, *Corps de droit ottoman*, 2:227.

65. Ibid., 7:339.

66. Articles 8 and 9 of the 1894 Persian Nationality Law concern expatriation. Article 8 states that expatriates must be free of criminal sentences, judicial proceedings, military service obligations, and liabilities in Persia, while Article 9 reproduces the sanctions for unauthorized expatriation in Article 6 of the 1869 law.

Article 18 stated that denaturalized Ottomans could not return to the empire. This confirmed and extended practice already present in an *irade* of 9 October 1896 concerning Armenians naturalized in the United States especially, which stated that passports delivered to these persons showed that they "will not be allowed to set foot again on Ottoman territory."[67] Article 25 specified punishment for nationality fraud. Five model forms to accomplish naturalization and nationality formalities are included in the handwritten appendices to the draft. These include a shorter and longer identity form model for those returning to Ottoman nationality (items six and seven), as well as a model authorization letter (*ruhsat-name*) (item eight). Item nine is an oath form for those returning to Ottoman nationality, and item eleven is another medium-sized identification form model.[68]

Territorial access and property rights offered teeth to denaturalization controls. After the 1869 law, a series of regulations attacked the property rights of denaturalized Ottomans. The 1909 draft enshrines these rules in Article 17. Since the 1860s, Ottoman subjects who changed nationalities had been subject to considerable disabilities within the empire. After 1867, they were prohibited from owning real property on Ottoman territory.[69] In 1873, foreign husbands and children were prohibited from inheriting from Ottoman wives and mothers.[70] Appendix 12 in the archival file is a four-article law dated 25 Rebiülahir 1300 (5 March 1883) on the property rights of foreigners (*ecanibin hakk-ı istimlak-i kanunu*). This law prohibited Ottomans who took a foreign nationality without permission from inheriting real property.[71] *Miri* and *vakıf* property would be treated as if there were no heir, while *mülk* land would be apportioned amongst heirs who were Ottoman nationals.[72] Property rights had been reformulated in such a way that nationals and non-nationals felt a difference. Ottoman Zionists realized that participation in the political project required Ottoman nationality,

67. John Bassett Moore, *A Digest of International Law*, 8 vols. (Washington DC: Government Printing Office, 1906), 3:706, cited in Qafisheh, *International Law Foundations*, 33.

68. On the late Hamidian nationality document regime, see Osmanağaoğlu, *Osmanlı tâbiiyyeti*, 282–89.

69. This rule referenced in American dispatches of 1897 and 1898 in Moore, *Digest*, 3:696. Also cited as "Law concerning the Disposition of Foreign Subjects of Property, 6 Safar 1284" ('Arif Ramadan and Yusuf Ibrahim Sadir, eds., *Majmu'at al-qawanin: tahtawi 'ala jami' al-qawanin al-ma'mil bi-mawjibiha fi jami' al-bilad al-'Arabiyah al-munsalikhah 'an al-hukūmah al-'uthmaniyah*, 7 vols. (Beirut: al-Matba'ah al-'Ilmiyah, 1925), 3:139) in Qafisheh, *International Law Foundations*, 32.

70. Cited as "Instructions Concerning Inheritance of Foreigner's Wives Who are Nationals of the State" (Ramadan and Sadir, *Majmu'at al-qawanin*, 3:141) in Qafisheh, *International Law Foundations*, 32.

71. This regulation is discussed in Belkıs Konan, "Osmanlı Devletinde Yabancıların Kapitülasyonlar Kapsamında Hukuki Durumu" (PhD diss., Ankara University, 2006), 106–9.

72. Young cites an Interior Ministry circular to the same effect dated several months earlier on 14 Mart 1299 (26 May 1882). Young, *Corps de droit ottoman*, 4:228.

and they urged Jews resident in the Ottoman domains to take out nationality papers.[73]

What was the source of this draconian approach to foreign naturalization? Qafisheh suggests that the Ottoman prohibition of nationality change was a holdover from Islamic notions of membership, which forbade conversion from Islam.[74] Parolin supports this view.[75] Kern's analysis of marriage regulations and Deringil's work on conversion suggests a sort of religious mercantilism, an effort to stockpile subjects in order to protect the prestige of the sultan-caliph.[76] As the domestic and foreign legal context of the 1909 draft presented in this chapter shows, however, the protectionism was in large measure a reaction to lingering fears of Capitulations abuses. The 1863 protégé regulation and the 1869 nationality laws were not intended to form a citizenry. They aimed to shore up the government's sovereignty over its resident population in the face of extraterritorial claims. It was the responsibility of the Foreign Ministry, not the Interior Ministry, to ensure that a bounded population was established. The greatest threat to Ottoman population was not conversion or emigration—it was subversion from within, through foreign privilege. This is the longstanding fear that the 1909 draft, entirely in line with the anti-Capitulations policy priorities of the Committee of Union and Progress, sought to assuage.

Conclusion

Ottoman nationality aimed to draw a fragmenting group of subjects closer to the centralizing Tanzimat and Hamidian states. It did so with legal tools that seem ill-suited to the rough and ready nature of both Hamidian control and the opposition to it. At the same time, legal status offered a front of comparative advantage to the Ottoman state, which was—despite everything—the most competent bureaucracy and authority in the eastern Mediterranean. The 1909 revision was consonant with other Ottoman bureaucratic developments of the period. What is curious is that the regimes that succeeded Abdülhamid, which strengthened many of his rationalizing procedures, did not see fit to revise Ottoman nationality, even as they pressed their subject populations harder and harder to conform to the state's will.

In the global context, the 1909 revision is an example of modular, standardized legal vision. It aimed to enact the Ottoman claim to commensurate status as a member of the community of nations better than the 1869 law, just as the 1869 law was a more modular, standardized approach to the problems that the 1863 protégé regulation sought to address. In both cases, the lawyers adopted inter-

---

73. Cohen, *Becoming Ottomans*, 104.
74. Qafisheh, *International Law Foundations*, 27.
75. Parolin, *Citizenship*.
76. Kern, *Imperial Citizen*; Deringil, *Conversion and Apostasy*.

national language and sidestepped local idiosyncrasies in favor of flatter, more general, and much more specific provisions. The draft revision of 1909 captures their aim to use nationality to transform a disparate Ottoman population into a homogeneous unit. The literature on the late Ottoman Empire reveals that the empire's other administrative and bureaucratic wings shared the same objective but tackled it using different tools. The workers at the Foreign Ministry's Legal Bureau clearly saw themselves as part of a global community of international lawyers.[77] In the prologue to the 1909 revision, they insisted on only one Ottoman particularity: "Every problem of nationality has greater importance and delicacy for the Ottoman Empire than for any other place."

77. This community is described in Martti Koskenniemi, *The Gentle Civilizer of Nations: The Rise and Fall of International Law, 1870–1960* (Cambridge, UK: Cambridge University Press, 2002); Arnulf Becker Lorca, *Mestizo International Law: A Global Intellectual History, 1850–1950* (Cambridge, UK: Cambridge University Press, 2015).

5   Unfurling the Flag of Extraterritoriality: Autonomy, Foreign Muslims, and the Capitulations in the Ottoman Hijaz

Michael Christopher Low

DURING THE SECOND half of the nineteenth century, the Hijaz and the steamship-era hajj came to be defined by European colonial powers, most notably British India, as vectors responsible for spreading various forms of colonial disorder. The pilgrimage to Mecca became entangled in an inter-imperial web of medical and political surveillance, spies and consular agents, quarantines, passport controls, and documentary practices. Although the British government of India initially imagined the Hijaz as a launching pad for anti-colonial radicalism and Ottoman-sponsored Pan-Islam, over time covert colonial surveillance morphed into a more robust regime of consular protection based on the principles outlined in the Capitulations.[1] From an Ottoman perspective, the nature and direction of these threats took a series of unexpected "international legal" turns, calling into question exactly who was more afraid of political subversion emanating from the Hijaz: European colonial administrators or the Ottoman state itself? As a result, Istanbul came to view foreign (non-Ottoman) Muslims as potential stalking horses for European extraterritoriality and "legal imperialism."[2]

Conventional wisdom suggests that the Hijaz was excluded from the extraterritorial privileges granted by the Capitulations. While this may have been true in theory, following the tentacles of Britain's Indian Ocean empire shows that British consular officials were at least partially successful in extending the privileges of protection to Indian and other colonial subjects travelling or residing in the Hijaz. Concurrent changes in Ottoman legal definitions of nationality, naturalization, and subjecthood—themselves grounded in efforts to defend against the proliferation of European protégés—also exacerbated this problem by subjecting non-Ottoman pilgrims and sojourners to unprecedented levels of suspicion and exclusionary practices.

---

1. John Slight, *The British Empire and the Hajj, 1865–1956* (Cambridge, MA: Harvard University Press, 2015), 13–16.
2. Turan Kayaoğlu, *Legal Imperialism: Sovereignty and Extraterritoriality in Japan, the Ottoman Empire, and China* (Cambridge, UK: Cambridge University Press, 2010), 6.

The Subjects of Ottoman International Law (2020): 076–098
DOI: 10.2979/subjectsottomaninternationallaw.0.0.06

By examining this Anglo-Ottoman clash over the extension of the Capitulations to the Hijaz and the Sharifate of Mecca, this chapter questions some of our most basic assumptions regarding the region's exceptional status. It traces how Ottoman officials struggled to delicately subvert the logics of international law and colonialism threatening the Hijaz. On the one hand, Ottoman officials pointed to the Hijaz's obvious religious exceptionalism and traditional exemption from the Capitulations. On the other hand, they also found it necessary to deploy the new language and logic of international law. Taking advantage of the Sharifate of Mecca's semi-autonomous status, blurry jurisdictional boundaries, and divided sovereignty, both provincial administrators and the empire's highest legal authorities sought to buffer the holy cities from the brunt of European legal imperialism. Although Ottoman officials failed to fully shield the Hijaz from the Capitulations, examining the novelty of their approaches provides new perspective on the fragility of the post-Tanzimat Hijaz's exceptional status. By reframing the Hijaz through international legal lenses, we find that both the increasing pressures of European extraterritoriality and the unintended consequences of the very legal and administrative maneuvers meant to blunt them combined to radically alter and undermine the Hijaz's privileged religious and ideological positions within the empire.

The interconnected problems of autonomy and extraterritoriality were further complicated by the Hijaz's promotion as a pillar of Sultan Abdülhamid II's (1876–1909) Pan-Islamic public image.[3] Probing beneath the surface of Hamidian legitimacy structures, we find a constant tension between the soaring rhetoric of Pan-Islamic outreach to the rest of the Islamic world and the increasingly exclusionary policies adopted to insulate the empire from the extraterritorial threat posed by foreign Muslims and their colonial masters.[4] Although counterintuitive to the dominant historiographic image of the Hamidian state, this friction reveals how the sultan-caliph's Pan-Islamic universalism was continually recalibrated and often subordinated to suit the new realities of territorial sovereignty and international law.

The Most Privileged Province?: Autonomy and the Fragility of Hijazi Exceptionalism

As early as 1889, the Sharif of Mecca, 'Awn al-Rafiq (r. 1882–1905), began to openly express his opinion that the Emirate of Mecca should be made a heredi-

---

3. On Hamidian Islamic symbolism, see Selim Deringil, *The Well-Protected Domains: Ideology and Legitimation of Power in the Ottoman Empire, 1876–1909* (London: I.B. Tauris, 1999); Kemal Karpat, *The Politicization of Islam: Reconstructing Identity, State, Faith, and Community in the Late Ottoman State* (Oxford: Oxford University Press, 2001).
4. For a parallel reading of this friction, especially see Lâle Can, "The Protection Question: Central Asians and Extraterritoriality in the Late Ottoman Empire," in this volume.

tary office. 'Awn al-Rafiq reportedly favored abolishing the overlapping jurisdictions of the Ottoman provincial government and the emirate, arguing for a truly "autonomous administration" (*idare-i muhtare*).[5] In the wake of Mehmed Ali Pasha's successful creation of a hereditary dynasty in Egypt, this ambition was the worst possible trajectory that the central government in Istanbul could imagine for this semi-autonomous province.

Even though the Hijaz province (*vilayet*) and the Sharifate of Mecca had always featured a system of semi-autonomous power-sharing and layered sovereignty, the meanings and usages of autonomy changed dramatically over the course of the nineteenth century. With the rise of positivist international law, autonomy transformed from an accepted tool in the management of a large, multi-ethnic empire into a characteristic of compromised sovereignty.[6] Despite the Hijaz's singularity as the linchpin of the caliphate and a pillar of Hamidian Pan-Islamic image-making, it was not as unique as we often imagine. In reality, it shared core similarities with a host of other vulnerable provinces throughout the Ottoman Empire.

As Aimee Genell argues, one of the most overlooked aspects of Mehmed Ali's sub-empire was its deep impact on the rapidly evolving definitions of autonomy and sovereignty in nineteenth-century international law.[7] In 1840, the Ottoman state was forced to formally recognize Egypt's status as an autonomous or "privileged" province, one of the so-called *eyalat-ı mümtaze*.[8] Over the long nineteenth century this list of special territories grew to include: Serbia, Montenegro, Bulgaria, Eastern Rumelia, Moldavia and Wallachia, Samos, Crete, Cyprus, Mount Lebanon, Egypt, Tunisia, Algeria, and the Sharifate of Mecca.[9] As Genell points out, in most cases their special statuses were byproducts of conflicts that had precipitated some form of European military intervention, occupation, partition, or annexation. Indeed, this list reads like a map plotting the hotspots of Europe's gradual dismemberment of the empire via the Eastern Question and the absorp-

---

5. Başbakanlık Osmanlı Arşivi (hereafter BOA), Y. PRK. AZJ, 16/13 (13 Ra 1307/8 Nov. 1889).

6. Aimee M. Genell, "Ottoman Autonomous Provinces and the Problem of 'Semi-Sovereignty' in European International Law," *Balkan and Near Eastern Studies* 18, no. 6 (2016): 533–549.

7. Aimee M. Genell, "Empire by Law: Ottoman Sovereignty and the British Occupation of Egypt, 1882–1923" (PhD diss., Columbia University, 2013), 7–12.

8. Ayhan Ceylan, *Osmanlı Taşra İdarî Tarzı Olarak Eyâlet-i Mümtâze ve Mısır Uygulaması* (Istanbul: Kitabevi, 2014).

9. Sinan Kuneralp, *Son Dönem Osmanlı Erkân ve Ricali, 1839–1922: Prosopografik Rehber* (Istanbul: İsis Press, 1999), 43. On special autonomous zones (*mutasarrıflık*) in Cyrenaica, Jerusalem, and Mount Lebanon, also see Mostafa Minawi, *The Ottoman Scramble for Africa: Empire and Diplomacy in the Sahara and the Hijaz* (Stanford: Stanford University Press, 2016), 87.

tion of its Arab peripheries as protectorates or colonial possessions of one kind or another.[10]

This new reality did not go unnoticed. The most notable critic of the Sharifate of Mecca was Gazi Ahmed Muhtar Pasha, the Ottoman special commissioner in Egypt (*fevkalade komiser*) between 1892 and 1908. Between 1888 and 1905, Ahmed Muhtar repeatedly urged Abdülhamid II to abolish the emirate, transfer the sharif to Istanbul, and place the Hijaz solely under the governor's control. Although the Hijaz fell well beyond his own jurisdiction, Sharif 'Awn al-Rafiq's corruption and abuses of pilgrims were running scandals in the Indian and Egyptian presses and constant sources of aggravation for the British Embassy. As he warned, the sharifate's oppressive and unjust administration of the hajj was providing Britain, France, and the Netherlands with perfect excuses to intervene more directly in the Hijaz.[11]

From Ahmed Muhtar's perspective, there was nothing to be gained from indirect rule via local notables. Drawing on his experiences from the re-conquest of Yemen in the early 1870s, during which a number of sharifs were sent to assist him, he remarked that contrary to the government's opinion, the sharifs' noble ancestry meant little to the Bedouin. Whatever influence they might have over the tribes was merely a pale reflection of the imperial government's sovereignty. If they were stripped of this connection to the empire, they would have no more "power" (*kudret*) or "influence" (*nüfuz*) than an "ordinary Arab shaykh" (*adi bir Arab şeyh*).[12]

Ahmed Muhtar's varied experiences on the overlapping frontiers of the Ottoman and British Empires provided another dimension to his strident calls for the abolition of the sharifate. Having presided over the occupation of Egypt alongside the British had taught him the dangers posed by the autonomous rulers like the khedive and the sharif. It also left him with a keen sense of how the Scramble for Africa had put the Hijaz in a completely indefensible position at the heart of the colonial world, sandwiched between Egypt, the Suez Canal, Sudan, and the road to India. He pleaded that the Hijaz, the very "object of pride" (*medar-ı iftihari*) of the caliphate, was in imminent danger. To compensate for the loss of Egypt and British naval dominance in the Red Sea, Ahmed Muhtar

---

10. Genell, "Empire by Law," 7–12; Elektra Kostopoulou, "Armed Negotiations: The Institutionalization of the Late Ottoman Locality," *Comparative Studies of South Asia, Africa and the Middle East* 33, no. 3 (2013): 295–309.
11. BOA, Y. PRK. TKM, 28/68 (29 Z 1310/14 July 1893); BOA, Y. PRK. AZN, 11/52 (10 L 1312/6 April 1895); Nurtaç Numan, "The Emirs of Mecca and the Ottoman Government of Hijaz, 1840–1908" (master's thesis, Boğaziçi University, 2005), 144–47, 158–60; Rifat Uçarol, *Gazi Ahmet Muhtar Paşa (1839–1919): Askeri ve Siyasi Hayatı* (Istanbul: Derin Yayınları, 2015), 238–42.
12. BOA, Y. PRK. MK, 4/42 (23 Ra 1306/27 Nov. 1888).

urgently advocated the establishment of land-based rail and telegraph links to better connect the Hijaz to Istanbul.[13]

In response to Ahmed Muhtar's appeals, the eminent statesmen, Ahmed Cevdet Pasha, was consulted. Cevdet cautioned that transferring the sharif to Istanbul would not be prudent because he might become a focal point for discontent and anti-Ottoman intrigues. Cevdet also worried that the abolition of the sharifate might cause a backlash among Ottoman subjects or enflame global Islamic public opinion. Ahmed Muhtar's opinion was so poorly received that it was even suggested that his ideas might have been the product of foreign influence.[14] In the end, Abdülhamid II viewed his proposal as wholly unrealistic, noting that if the sharifate were to become dysfunctional, "holding sway over the Arab public only with appointed governors would be impossible" without turning the region over to a full military occupation.[15]

To be sure, Ahmed Muhtar's call for centralization was completely out of step with the prevailing Hamidian frontier experiments with indirect rule.[16] However, his argument was no less prescient. As Cevdet argued, foreign interference in the Hijaz was completely intolerable; thus, "it is clear that the administration of the holy land of the Hijaz, the cradle of Islam, *could never be comparable* to any of the considerations put forward by foreign powers concerning some [other] imperial provinces."[17] But even Cevdet's firm declaration of the Hijaz's "incomparable" status belies the deepening anxieties over this question. In hindsight, the privileged status of the Hijaz was not as unique as either Cevdet or most present-day scholars imagine. It is too difficult to overlook all of the province's similarities to the other autonomous and irregular provinces on the vulnerable frontlines of European intervention and partition. Indeed, when viewed alongside the lengthy list of *eyalat-ı mümtaze* and other non-Tanzimat-compliant frontier regions like

---

13. BOA, Y. EE, 118/10 (3 C 1315/30 Oct. 1897); Minawi, *The Ottoman Scramble for Africa*, 73, 96–97, 99–139.

14. Butrus Abu-Manneh, "Sultan Abdülhamid and the Sharifs of Mecca, 1880–1890," *Asian and African Studies* 9, no. 1 (1973): 5; William Ochsenwald, *Religion, Society, and the State in Arabia: The Hijaz under Ottoman Control, 1840–1908* (Columbus: Ohio State University Press, 1984), 213.

15. Murat Özyüksel, *The Hejaz Railway and the Ottoman Empire: Modernity, Industrialisation, and Ottoman Decline* (London: I.B. Tauris, 2014), 161–62.

16. On autonomy and indirect rule on the empire's Arab frontiers, see M. Talha Çiçek, "Negotiating Power and Authority in the Desert: the Arab Bedouin and the Limits of the Ottoman State in Hijaz, 1840–1908," *Middle Eastern Studies* 52, no. 2 (2016): 250–79; Thomas Kuehn, *Empire, Islam, and Politics of Difference: Ottoman Rule in Yemen, 1849–1919* (Leiden: Brill, 2011); Michael Christopher Low, "Ottoman Infrastructures of the Saudi Hydro-State: The Technopolitics of Pilgrimage and Potable Water in the Hijaz," *Comparative Studies in Society and History* 57, no. 4 (2015): 942–74; Eugene Rogan, *Frontiers of the State in the Late Ottoman Empire: Transjordan, 1850–1921* (Cambridge, UK: Cambridge University Press, 1999).

17. Emphasis mine. BOA, Y. EE, 5/59 (9 R 1323/13 June 1905).

Iraq, Libya, and Yemen, the Hijaz's "incomparable" status begins to look rather more ordinary.

While it is probably unwise to second-guess the wisdom of Cevdet's cautious approach to the sharifate, the threats posed by British support for a rival caliphate or extraterritorial influence over the Hijaz were more than paranoid figments of the Hamidian imagination.[18] These fears were also byproducts of London's long-term shift toward the promotion of autonomy and decentralization for all of the Ottoman Empire's subject peoples. As Ahmed Midhat Efendi framed the problem for Abdülhamid II:

> It is clear that England—God forbid!—is striving to dissolve the Ottoman Empire into statelets (*müluk* or *küçük devletçikler*). It amounts not to autonomy (*otonomi* or *muhtariyet*) but to anatomy (*anatomi*), by creating for example, an Albanian Albania, an Armenia in the Armenian inhabited places, an Arab government in all the places inhabited by Arabs, and a Turkey in the Turkish-inhabited areas.

> Meanwhile, [England] also wishes to transfer the great caliphate from Istanbul to the Arabian Peninsula, to Jidda, or somewhere in Egypt. And by using the caliphate as a tool in her service, to rule all Muslims as it pleases.[19]

Lurking just beneath the question of autonomy was the British-backed threat of a rival caliphate and Arab separatism. While we know that British attempts to undermine the legitimacy of the Ottoman caliphate surged between 1878 and the early 1880s, the intersections between international legal thought, the British Empire's promotion of autonomy, and its long-term adoption of an ethno-nationalist view of the Sharif of Mecca as the rightful "Arab" caliph has been very poorly articulated in the existing literature on Pan-Islam.[20]

This was the web of concerns underpinning Ahmed Muhtar's warning. In his view, traditional Ottoman conceptions of autonomy and Hijazi exceptionalism carried new risks in the colonial age. Autonomy was the cracked door

---

18. On Hamidian paranoia, see F.A.K. Yasamee, *Ottoman Diplomacy: Abdülhamid II and the Great Powers, 1878–1888* (Istanbul: Isis Press, 1996), 90.
19. BOA, Y. EE, 4/59, undated *muhtıra-ı seniye* from Ahmed Midhat Efendi to Abülhamid, reproduced in Sultan İkinci Abdülhamid Han, A. Atilla Çetin ed., *Devlet ve Memleket Görüşlerim* (Istanbul: Çamlıca, 2011), 2:241.
20. On British attitudes toward the Hijaz and the caliphate, see Ş. Tufan Buzpınar, "Abdulhamid II and Amir Hussein's Secret Dealings with the British, 1877–1880," *Middle Eastern Studies* 31 no. 1 (1995): 99–123; idem, "Opposition to the Ottoman Caliphate in the Early Years of Abdülhamid II: 1877–1882," *Die Welt des Islams* 36, no. 1 (1996): 59–89; Azmi Özcan, *Pan-Islamism: Indian Muslims, the Ottomans and Britain, 1877–1924* (Leiden: Brill, 1997). For the best account of the connection between Pan-Islam and international law, see Cemil Aydın, *The Politics of Anti-Westernism in Asia: Visions of World Order in Pan-Islamic and Pan-Asian Thought* (New York: Columbia University Press, 2007).

through which European extraterritorial influence would inevitably slip. In the long run the sharifate's privileged status and autonomy would always provide a tempting rationale and opportunity for Britain's intervention on behalf of its subjects in the Hijaz. This was the wider inter-imperial environment that helped bring the Capitulations to the Hijaz.

Complicated Subjects: The Capitulations, Nationality, and the Problem of Non-Ottoman Muslims in the Hijaz

While scholars of the Ottoman Empire have long been preoccupied with how the Capitulations and Tanzimat reforms placed Christian protégés and protected persons beyond the reach of Ottoman justice, surprisingly little attention has been paid to the analogous projects of European powers claiming to protect their Muslim colonial subjects from the supposed corruption of Ottoman rule and the arbitrary nature of the Sharia courts of Mecca.[21] At the most basic level capitulatory privileges, tax exemptions, and concessions of consular protection were originally meant to provide early-modern Europeans, generally Christians, with partial, if not complete, immunity from Ottoman jurisdiction. In theory, the Capitulations ought to have been abolished as a result of the 1856 Treaty of Paris. The treaty's signing had ostensibly welcomed the empire into the Concert of Europe, guaranteeing the Ottomans the same legitimacy and rights to international existence and territorial integrity as any other member of the European family of nations. However, far from resulting in their abolition, the Treaty of Paris formalized and further entrenched the Capitulations. Over the course of the nineteenth century European diplomats increasingly came to understand these previously unilateral grants and revocable privileges as binding obligations, which through their incorporation into bilateral and multilateral treaties, essentially gave them the full force of international law.[22]

Even so, the Capitulations had never included the Hijaz. The first article of the original Capitulations granted to France in 1535 provided individual freedom

21. For the only other work addressing this topic, see Can, "The Protection Question." On the Capitulations, see Umut Özsu, "Ottoman Empire," in *The Oxford Handbook of the History of International Law*, ed. Bardo Fassbender and Anne Peters (Oxford: Oxford University Press, 2012), 429–48; Feroz Ahmad, "Ottoman Perceptions of the Capitulations, 1800–1914," *Journal of Islamic Studies* 11, no. 1 (2000): 1–20. On the politics of protégés and protected persons, see Mary Dewhurst Lewis, *Divided Rule: Sovereignty and Empire in French Tunisia, 1881–1938* (Berkeley: University of California Press, 2014); Salahi R. Sonyel, "The Protégé System in the Ottoman Empire," *Journal of Islamic Studies* 2, no. 1 (1991): 56–66. Also see Faiz Ahmed, "The British-Ottoman Cold War, c.1880-1914: Imperial Struggles over Muslim Mobility and Citizenship from the Suez Canal to the Durand Line," in this volume.
22. Umut Özsu, "The Ottoman Empire, the Origins of Extraterritoriality, and International Legal Theory," in *The Oxford Handbook of the Theory of International Law*, ed. Florian Hoffman and Anne Orford (Oxford: Oxford University Press, 2016), 129.

of trade, travel, navigation, residence, and worship, but explicitly exempted the Hijaz.[23] There were also later legal exemptions beyond the Capitulations themselves. The Ottoman state's attempt to construct the Hijaz as an exceptional space deemed unfit for many of the secularizing Tanzimat reforms also provides useful clues. For example, the Hijaz was exempted from the 1857 edict calling for an empire-wide prohibition on the African slave trade.[24] Similarly, when the Ottoman government lifted the ban on foreign real estate ownership throughout the empire in 1867, the Hijaz was again exempt.[25]

Since Christians were forbidden from traveling or residing outside of Jidda or owning real estate in the Hijaz, prior to the advent of regular steamship service there was little real danger of this situation arising anyway. Prior to the 1850s one could safely argue that the Hijaz *was* truly beyond the reach of the Capitulations. But historians have also taken for granted that the Hijaz's exceptional status remained intact from the Tanzimat era right up until the empire's demise.

At first glance, there are a variety of sound reasons for assuming that Mecca's incomparability remained unchanged. Historians have rightly emphasized how the Hijaz theoretically stood outside the framework of most (though not all) Tanzimat-style reforms. And yet, from the 1850s and 1860s onward, both European consular protections enshrined in a post-1856 reading of the Capitulations coupled with Tanzimat redefinitions of Ottoman subjecthood and nationality would have profound impacts on this most exceptional province.

By the conclusion of the nineteenth century millions of Muslims across Africa and Asia found themselves living under various forms of European colonial rule, protectorates, or spheres of influence. As a result of this previously unimaginable scenario, a paradoxical rift in the traditional fabric of the Capitulations was opened. Up until this point, the Capitulations had always been predicated on the idea that the foreign subjects being excused from Ottoman jurisdiction would be non-Muslims. But what if the subjects of states enjoying capitulatory privileges were, in fact, Muslims hailing from European colonies or protectorates? As Muslims became colonial subjects of European states, Ottoman authorities were suddenly forced to grapple with the hypocritical claim that non-Ottoman Muslims sojourning or residing in Islam's holiest cities needed the protection of their colonial masters in order to avoid the "uncivilized" dictates of Sharia law.[26] International legal justifications for humanitarian interventions claiming to pro-

23. Nasim Sousa, *The Capitulatory Régime of Turkey: Its History, Origin, and Nature* (Baltimore: Johns Hopkins University Press, 1933), 71.
24. Ehud Toledano, *The Ottoman Slave Trade and Its Suppression: 1840–1890* (Princeton: Princeton University Press, 1983), 129–35.
25. Belkıs Konan, "Osmanlı Devletinde Yabancıların Kapitülasyonlar Kapsamında Hukuki Durumu" (PhD diss., Ankara University, 2006), 98–111.
26. Deringil, *The Well-Protected Domains*, 60.

tect the Ottoman Empire's Christian subjects had long cited Ottoman despotism, corruption, and the arbitrary nature of Islamic jurisprudence. In many respects, it was a natural progression for these concepts to be applied gradually to Muslim colonial subjects as well.[27] As in other parts of the Ottoman Empire, where European manipulation of the Capitulations often placed Christian protégés and protected persons beyond the reach of Ottoman justice, this new extension of extraterritoriality raised the troubling prospect of European powers claiming to protect their Muslim colonial subjects and even Islam itself from Ottoman despotism.

As Selim Deringil has suggested, by the Hamidian period the Ottoman state had begun to fear "that the Muslim subjects of foreign powers could act as potential fifth columns and infiltrate the holy land of the Hicaz."[28] Istanbul came to view the Hijaz as a kind of colonial frontier, both unsuited to Tanzimat centralization and increasingly vulnerable to European expansion.[29] In an attempt to anticipate some of the problems that the colonial element in Mecca might present, significant thought was put into squaring the Hijaz's exceptional status with Tanzimat-style redefinitions of Ottoman subjecthood and nationality.

As a result of the 1856 Islahat Fermanı, the traditional Ottoman civil distinctions between Muslims and *dhimmi*s (People of the Book) were theoretically leveled. However, the reconfiguration of these older categories was not fully realized until the 1869 Ottoman Nationality Law (Tabiiyet-i Osmaniye Kanunnamesi). Recent scholarship on Ottoman citizenship has made great use of the 1869 Ottoman Nationality Law. However, as Will Hanley argues, this literature has consistently drawn a somewhat misleading link between the term *tabiiyet* and citizenship as opposed to subjecthood or nationality. Whatever the longer-term aspirations of the Tanzimat project might have been, the 1869 law's immediate objective was not to define citizenship. Rather, it was mainly designed to clarify the terms of Ottoman nationality and naturalization. As a result of this slippage in terminology, the 1869 law's relationship to the Capitulations has been obscured.[30] The 1869 legislation was actually the sequel to an 1863 decree designed

27. Davide Rodogno, *Against Massacre: Humanitarian Interventions in the Ottoman Empire, 1815–1914* (Princeton: Princeton University Press, 2012), 29–35, 38–41, 43–47.

28. Selim Deringil, *Conversion and Apostasy in the Late Ottoman Empire* (Cambridge, UK: Cambridge University Press, 2012), 181–82.

29. On the repackaging of older Ottoman practices of autonomy and the articulation of a "colonial policy" (*müstemleke siyaseti*) in frontier regions like Iraq, Libya, Hijaz, and Yemen, see Kuehn, *Empire, Islam, and Politics of Difference*; Minawi, *The Ottoman Scramble for Africa*; Tahsin Paşa, *Sultan Abdülhamid: Tahsin Paşa'nın Yıldız Hatıraları* (Istanbul: Boğaziçi Yayınları, 1999), 205, 341–42.

30. For examples, see Julia Phillips Cohen, *Becoming Ottomans: Sephardi Jews and Imperial Citizenship in the Modern Era* (New York: Oxford University Press, 2014); Will Hanley, "When Did Egyptians Stop Being Ottomans? An Imperial Citizenship Case Study," in *Multilevel*

to restrict the proliferation of foreign protégés. The 1863 legislation sought to force protégés to naturalize as foreign subjects or submit to Ottoman territorial jurisdiction. When these protégés responded by trying to naturalize with foreign states while still retaining their Ottoman residency and nationality, Istanbul was once again forced to tighten the terms of Ottoman nationality.[31]

Under the new Ottoman Nationality Law, the most important differentiating criterion was no longer whether one was Muslim or Christian. The 1869 law changed the practice whereby any non-Muslim converting to (Sunni) Islam on Ottoman soil was to be considered an Ottoman citizen. The bond between confessional and civic identities was radically altered. From 1869 onward, the operative question became whether or not one was an Ottoman national. In addition to formalizing the non-denominational legal status of Ottoman nationality, the law also introduced a new category, *ecnebi* (foreigner), which included all foreign nationals regardless of religious affiliation.[32] Because the distinction between Ottoman and foreigner essentially replaced the old divide between Muslim and *dhimmi*, this also necessitated the creation of a more precise descriptor for foreign or non-Ottoman Muslims (*ecanib-i müslimin*). Since the majority of the nineteenth-century Islamic world had fallen under British, Dutch, French, or Russian rule, this effectively placed non-Ottoman Muslims under a similar cloud of suspicion as non-Muslims claiming the capitulatory protection of foreign states.

As a result, traditional expectations of the Hijaz as a non-territorial space of refuge, a cosmopolitan magnet for foreign *mücavirin*, where the only meaningful bar to claiming rights as an Ottoman subject in the past had been defined by confessional status (i.e., being a Sunni Muslim), were suddenly overturned. To further compound this paradox, in the absence of standardized passport and visa controls, which only began to be haltingly experimented with in the Hijaz in the early 1880s, there were Muslim migrants from India, Central Asia, and elsewhere who had been born in the Hijaz or had been settled there for decades, sometimes even centuries.[33] These individuals often lived as de facto Ottoman subjects without ever being forced to produce evidence of their nationality.[34] There were

Citizenship, ed. Willem Maas (Philadelphia: University of Pennsylvania Press, 2013), 89–109; Karen M. Kern, *Imperial Citizens, Marriage and Citizenship in the Ottoman Frontier Provinces of Iraq* (Syracuse: Syracuse University Press, 2011); James H. Meyer, "Immigration, Return, and the Politics of Citizenship: Russian Muslims in the Ottoman Empire, 1860–1914," *International Journal of Middle East Studies* 39, no. 1 (2007): 15–32.

31. See Will Hanley, "What Ottoman Nationality Was and Was Not," in this volume.

32. Deringil, *Conversion and Apostasy in the Late Ottoman Empire*, 181–82.

33. The Ottoman state did not attempt to enforce its passport laws on pilgrims until 1880–84. The National Archives, United Kingdom (hereafter TNA): Foreign Office (hereafter FO) 195/1451, 17 April 1883; 13 May 1883; BOA, A. DVN. MKL, 25/25 (15 R 1301/14 Jan. 1884).

34. Can, "The Protection Question."

Indians carrying British Indian identity and travel documents, who nevertheless claimed and maintained Ottoman nationality. There were Ottoman subjects, who claimed Ottoman nationality, but still sailed vessels under British flags and conducted their commercial and financial lives under British consular protection. However, after the passage of the 1869 Nationality Law, anyone living in Ottoman territory would be considered an Ottoman subject until documentary proof of foreign nationality was produced. The Hijaz's diasporic communities were theoretically forced to choose whether to accept Ottoman nationality or to secure evidence of foreign nationality.[35]

Despite this tightening of Ottoman naturalization processes, the Hijaz province and Sharifate of Mecca's ambiguous semi-autonomous statuses and layered sovereignty provided perfect breeding grounds for the proliferation of foreign nationals adept at leveraging this extraterritorial system of "negotiated" or "manipulated" identities to maximize rights and privileges. These individuals were "borderlanders par excellence."[36] More often than not, the complicated identities juggled by these expert "identity freelancers" confounded both European and Ottoman authorities.[37] However, as we shall see, the Ottoman state fought hard to prohibit this kind of affiliation switching and forum shopping, creating a new level of legal uncertainty for non-Ottoman Muslims in the Hijaz.[38] On the other hand, despite determined resistance from both Hijazi locals and the Ottoman state, attempts to turn back the clock on European consular authority proved impossible. Instead, the Hijaz would become a new kind of inter-imperial battleground for influence and allegiance.

The Union Jack over Mecca: The Advent of the Muslim Vice-Consulate

From the 1860s onward, the forces unleashed by both European imperialism and the age of steam brought the hajj and the Hijaz under the scrutiny of non-Muslim empires.[39] With the development of regular steamship routes from

---

35. On the requirement to produce proof of foreign nationality, see Article 9 of the Ottoman Nationality Law in *Sâlnâme-i Nezâret-i Umûr-ı Hâriciyye: Osmanlı Dışişleri Bakanlığı Yıllığı, 1320/1902* (Istanbul: İşaret Yayınları, 2003), 166–67.
36. Ziad Fahmy, "Jurisdictional Borderlands: Extraterritoriality and 'Legal Chameleons' in Precolonial Alexandria, 1840–1870," *Comparative Studies in Society and History* 55, no. 2 (2013): 305–29.
37. James Meyer, *Turks Across Empires. Marketing Muslim Identity in the Russian-Ottoman Borderlands, 1856–1914* (Oxford: Oxford University Press, 2014), 1–47.
38. See Can, "The Protection Question"; Julia Stephens, "An Uncertain Inheritance: The Imperial Travels of Legal Migrants, from British India to Ottoman Iraq," in this volume.
39. On the colonial hajj, see Slight, *The British Empire and the Hajj*; Eric Tagliacozzo, *The Longest Journey: Southeast Asians and the Pilgrimage to Mecca* (Oxford: Oxford University Press, 2013); Eileen Kane, *Russian Hajj: Empire and the Pilgrimage to Mecca* (Ithaca: Cornell University Press, 2015).

the 1830s to the 1860s and the eventual opening of the Suez Canal, the number of oceangoing pilgrims exploded. British officials serving in Jidda, Aden, and India all came to view the Hijaz and the trans-oceanic hajj as liminal spaces of anti-colonial disorder, dangerous mobilities, and conduits for the spread of epidemic disease.[40] Neither Indian exiles nor the pilgrims with whom they came into contact could be left unmonitored.[41]

With the souring of Anglo-Ottoman relations following the Russo-Ottoman War of 1877–78 and the British occupation of Egypt in 1882, fears of a radicalized anti-colonial Indian diaspora in the Hijaz became comingled with a wider diplomatic and colonial paranoia, which imagined potential Pan-Islamic conspiracies hatched by Abdülhamid II himself.[42] As a result of this Pan-Islamic panic and the repeated threat of epidemic cholera outbreaks carried by the Indian Ocean hajj, by the early 1880s British officials had begun to outline more systematic intelligence gathering operations.

While the British Raj could control much of the legal and regulatory framework of the industrializing Indian Ocean pilgrimage services industry, their ability to monitor the hajj did not extend past the port city of Jidda. In 1837, Britain had been the first European state to open a consulate in Jidda, but was eventually followed by France, the Netherlands, Austria, and Russia. While European colonial powers accepted that their Christian consuls were confined to Jidda, they sought to provide consular protection for their colonial subjects by appointing Muslim agents or vice-consuls to act on their behalf in Mecca and Medina. The Ottoman government opposed this scheme and denied Muslim colonial agents the full standing afforded European Christian consuls. It also prevented these officials from residing permanently in Mecca. Nonetheless, between the 1850s and World War I European consular officials became increasingly enmeshed in the affairs of the Hijaz. This emerging system of consular and commercial representation often involved mundane issues surrounding the protection of pilgrims and European protégés in their commercial and real estate dealings, in cases of robbery, tribal raids, disputes over ship registration, and the repatriation of remains or property of deceased subjects.[43]

---

40. On the age of steam, see James Gelvin and Nile Green, eds., *Global Muslims in the Age of Steam and Print* (Berkeley: University of California Press, 2014); Nile Green, "Spacetime and the Industrial Journey West: Industrial Communications and the Making of the 'Muslim World'," *American Historical Review* 118, no. 2 (2013): 401–29; Valeska Huber, *Channelling Mobilities: Migration and Globalisation in the Suez Canal Region and Beyond, 1869–1914* (Cambridge, UK: Cambridge University Press, 2013).
41. On Indian exiles in the Hijaz, see Seema Alavi, *Muslim Cosmopolitanism in the Age of Empire* (Cambridge, MA: Harvard University Press, 2015).
42. Karpat, *The Politicization of Islam*, 136–54, 208–22, 241–75.
43. Ulrike Freitag, "Helpless Representatives of the Great Powers? Western Consuls in Jeddah, 1830s to 1914," *The Journal of Imperial and Commonwealth History* 40, no. 3 (2012): 357–81.

Despite the political and epidemiological threats now associated with it, officials deemed it too risky to overtly discourage Muslims from the hajj. Instead, they opted for a strategy of increased surveillance. In 1879, the British consul in Jidda, James Napoleon Zohrab, proposed that a confidential agent be sent on behalf of the Jidda consulate in order to monitor the hajj. Similarly, in 1880, Austen Henry Layard, the British ambassador in Istanbul, proposed that the Indian government employ Muslim secret agents to infiltrate the holy cities. Again, in 1881, Lord Dufferin revived Layard's suggestions, arguing for the appointment of a "secret paid agent residing in Mecca." As it turned out, the perfect spy was already at work monitoring the region's public health. In 1878, the government of India attached Dr. Abdur Razzack, assistant surgeon of the Bengal Medical Service, to accompany that year's pilgrimage from India. Owing to his previous experience, in 1882, he was chosen as the best candidate for the job. His primary duties were to assist Britain's Muslim subjects, monitor the health of the pilgrims, and protect them in their dealings with Ottoman officialdom. He was also instructed that he might also be expected to obtain intelligence on current affairs and public opinion in Mecca.[44]

Abdur Razzack would not remain a covert agent. In 1882, he was appointed as Jidda's first Indian Muslim vice-consul. Since Christians were unable to travel beyond Jidda, Abdur Razzack's status as a Muslim was meant to circumvent Ottoman objections to the extension of British consular representation to Mecca. This way he could openly attend to public health questions, while also gathering intelligence and securing greater British influence in Mecca. British authorities also hoped to secure Ottoman permission for the consulate's translator, Yusuf Kudzi, to act as a second consular agent in Mecca.[45]

In February 1881, Kudzi travelled to Mecca at the request of consul Zohrab but was expelled and sent back to Jidda by Sharif 'Abd al-Muttalib, who accused him of attempting to meddle in "matters involving the internal politics" of the emirate.[46] Upon learning of the incident, Zohrab pleaded the vital importance of maintaining the consulate's "right to send Mussulman employees" to Mecca. While he acknowledged that the legal limits of consular authority granted by *ferman* and *berat* only extended to Jidda, he began to sketch out the gray areas of informal precedent through which extraterritorial authority over Mecca might gradually be secured. As he pointed out, up until Kudzi's expulsion, while the sharifate had denied the right of consular jurisdiction within the holy cities, they

44. Michael Christopher Low, "Empire and the Hajj: Pilgrims, Plagues, and Pan-Islam under British Surveillance, 1865–1908," *International Journal of Middle East Studies* 40, no. 2 (2008): 282–83; Slight, *The British Empire and the Hajj*, 105–23.

45. BOA, Y. PRK. UM, 4/72 (5 Za 1298/29 Sept. 1881).

46. BOA, Y. PRK. UM 4/37 (13 Ra 1298/13 Feb. 1881).

had *"permitted it by courtesy."* Thus, it was a question "of whether precedent has not established the right."[47]

This was the crux of the argument that British and Ottoman authorities would continue to circle around through World War I. Fearing that precedent would indeed become a right, Osman Nuri Pasha, the then governor of the Hijaz, heartily supported the sharif's expulsion of Kudzi.[48] He reminded Zohrab that all inquiries related to the interior policy of the sharifate should only be addressed to the Sublime Porte.[49] In an odd twist, Osman Nuri, a strident proponent of Ottoman centralization, fiercely determined to strip the Sharifate of Mecca of as much power as possible, seems to have come to appreciate the utility of defending the "internal" sovereignty of the sharifate as a strategic buffer against the extension of consular protection to Mecca.

Osman Nuri recognized the danger of Muslim consular agents having unfettered access to Mecca. He worried that the prolonged presence of British consular representatives in Mecca would set the stage for the opening of a full-fledged consulate and an ever-expanding threat of British espionage and political subversion.[50] He also emphasized how Abdur Razzack's appointment had agitated local public opinion. As he reported, the locals had taken to saying that once a Muslim consul is allowed in Mecca, inevitably "the flag will be unfurled" (*bayrak açılacak*).[51] While the specter of the Union Jack flying over Mecca might have been hyperbole, the legal consequences would have been all too real. Once the British had established this right all the other European powers would have soon demanded Muslim consular representation in Mecca as well.[52]

"The Consul of the Christians Cannot Help You": Two Indian Ladies, an Illicit Affair, and Public Morality as Jurisdictional Proxy War

During the 1880s, a series of court cases involving Indian Muslims accused of crimes in Mecca placed the legal status of the Hijaz under a new level of inter-imperial scrutiny. As these cases unfolded, the British deployed a patient strategy of stealthily enveloping Mecca within the framework of the Capitulations. The British Foreign Office repeatedly claimed that under Article 42 of the Capitulations, Indian Muslim subjects making the hajj or residing in Mecca had the right

---

47. Emphasis mine. TNA: FO 195/375, 17 Feb. 1881.
48. On Osman Nuri's career in the Hijaz, see Selim Deringil, "'They Live in a State of Nomadism and Savagery': The Late Ottoman Empire and the Post-Colonial Debate," *Comparative Studies in Society and History* 45, no. 2 (2003): 311–42; M. Metin Hülagü, "Topal Osman Nuri Paşa Hayatı ve Faaliyetleri, 1840–1898," *Ankara Üniversitesi Osmanlı Tarihi Araştırma ve Uygulama Merkezi Dergisi* 5 (1994): 145–53.
49. TNA: FO 195/375, English translation of 'Abd al-Muttalib's reply, undated.
50. TNA: FO 195/1415, 9 Nov. 1882.
51. BOA, Y. PRK. UM, 5/80 (25 R 1300/5 March 1883).
52. TNA: FO 195/1415, 9 Nov. 1882.

to trial by a mixed tribunal in the presence of a consular officer or translator. From their perspective, Article 42 applied to the entirety of the Ottoman Empire and contained "no provision to except the Hedjaz or the holy cities from their stipulations."[53]

Even as early as 1861, Istanbul had begun to anticipate this situation. That year the vexed question of consular protection and the status of foreign *mücavirin* was put before the Special Council of Ministers (Meclis-i Mahsus-ı Vükela). As the ministers' response reveals, the highest levels of the Ottoman government understood the intractable nature of the problem. In light of the sacred status of the two holy cities, it was decided that the recognition of "foreign protection" (*himaye-i ecnebiye*) was not "legally permissible." At the same time, however, since the individuals concerned were Indian and Jawi subjects "in light of the requirements of *international law* it would not be feasible to not recognize [their] *nationality* at all." It was recommended that every effort should be made to handle such cases as amicably as possible. However, the council also realized that the autonomous status of the holy cities could be used to deflect and circumvent the internationally binding requirements of the Capitulations and prevent the application of foreign protection beyond Jidda. They argued that since there were no mixed courts in the holy cities all cases involving non-Ottoman *mücavirin* should be handled in the Sharia courts of Mecca and Medina.[54]

In 1883–84, this Ottoman attempt to use the sharifate's autonomy and the Hijaz's multi-layered sovereignty as a shield against consular interference would be put to the test. In March 1883, a British Indian subject named Abdul Aziz was arrested and imprisoned in Mecca. When the consulate made inquiries on his behalf, Osman Nuri argued that the holy cities were excluded from the Capitulations. Therefore, Indian subjects accused of a crime in Mecca could not avail themselves of consular protection, the presence of a translator, or be tried by a mixed tribunal. Here, Osman Nuri echoed the 1861 decision almost verbatim, noting that "all foreigners who are in Mecca the Holy, whatever may be their nationality, and whether they are permanent residents, or stopping there temporarily, on the occasion of any claim made by or against them..." the case would be tried in the Sharia courts.[55]

Eventually, Osman Nuri relented, allowing the consulate to send Yusuf Kudzi to Mecca to assist in the proceedings. Although Osman Nuri and his superiors firmly objected to the practice, they attempted to find a *modus vivendi* through which cases of this nature could be expedited without risking further interference. From the British perspective, however, even this limited form of

53. TNA: FO 424/159, "Correspondence respecting the Interpretation of Article 42 of the English Capitulations of 1675," May 1889, pp. 2, 16–17, 19–20, 22–23.
54. Emphasis mine. BOA, A. MKT. UM, 511/80 (25 R 1278/30 Sept. 1861).
55. TNA: FO 195/1610, 14 Dec. 1888.

cooperation constituted a legal precedent establishing their future right to extend consular protection to Mecca.[56]

This was the prelude to an altogether more explosive affair in 1884. Between September and November 1884, a bizarre case involving a complicated struggle over inheritance, real estate, and power of attorney placed members of the Indian diasporic community in Mecca on opposite sides of the Anglo-Ottoman/ Jidda-Mecca jurisdictional divide. Two decades earlier, a wealthy British Indian subject, Hajji Ibrahim 'Abd al-Sattar, had died in Mecca, leaving behind a wife and daughter. Abdul Wahed Yunis, also a British subject, was entrusted with the management of the family's personal and commercial assets. In addition to being a wealthy merchant, Abdul Wahed Yunis was also a business associate of Governor Osman Nuri.

In 1883, Abdul Wahed traveled to Calcutta, leaving his son, Abdullah, in charge of his and by extension the 'Abd al-Sattar family's affairs. At the time, Abdul Wahed employed four brothers of the Zackaria family, all British Indian subjects. In his father's absence, Abdullah went to Hudayda to check on a branch of the family business. Abdullah had a falling out with the Zackaria brother managing the Hudayda operations. Owing to his influence with Osman Nuri, Abdullah succeeded in having him arrested. As this feud escalated, the other Zackaria brothers resigned from the service of the Yunis family. Two of the brothers remained in the Hijaz, Eyub Zackaria in Mecca and Cassim Zackaria in Jidda.

Meanwhile, the 'Abd al-Sattar women had a disagreement with Abdullah Abdul Wahed Yunis and threatened to withdraw their money from his management. As it happened, the 'Abd al-Sattars rented a flat from Eyub Zackaria and lived on the floor above his family. Allegedly, this connection made Abdullah suspect Eyub Zackaria of influencing the widow 'Abd al-Sattar into transferring her estate to his care. In retaliation, Abdullah accused Eyub Zackaria of carrying on a bizarre sexual affair with the 'Abd al-Sattar women.[57]

As a result of these crude allegations, the governor had forbidden Zackaria from escorting the 'Abd al-Sattar family on hajj, as was his family's custom. He had also ordered Zackaria to discontinue living in the same building. Zackaria complied with the governor's instructions relating to the hajj. However, he refused to move out of his family's residence. As a result, Osman Nuri had him expelled from Mecca. As Zackaria claimed, the governor's "ear had been poisoned against me" by his business associate, Abdullah.[58]

When Eyub Zackaria informed the consulate, Osman Nuri confirmed Zackaria's banishment. According to Osman Nuri, Zackaria stood accused of "maintaining illicit relations with the two ladies, both mother and daughter." As

56. TNA: FO 424/159, May 1889, pp. 16, 19–20.
57. TNA: FO 195/1482, 4 Nov. 1884; TNA: FO 195/1514, 20 March 1885.
58. TNA: FO 195/1514, 22 Oct. 1884.

Consul Jago complained, from the evidence gathered from the Indian Muslim communities in Mecca and Jidda, until this dispute "not a breath of suspicion had ever clouded their fair name." As he noted, even as the case exploded into scandal only the most "foul-mouthed" among the Indian Muslim community "sought to attribute immorality to the mother;" most accusations were made only against the more eligible twenty-four year-old daughter. To support his contention, in a rather humorous (if misogynistic) moment of bemusement, Jago declared that the mother's "age [only 40] and appearance necessarily precluded any such accusation."

If Jago was unprepared to accept the first round of salacious accusations, the second further strained credulity. Upon hearing Eyub Zackaria's plight, the consulate sent Cassim Zackaria to Mecca to retrieve his brother's family and goods from his home. Upon his arrival, however, a policeman promptly ordered him to leave the building. Cassim Zackaria was also accused of "immorality" with the mother and daughter.[59]

As the plot thickened, Osman Nuri, who had previously favored the exile of the 'Abd al-Sattar women from Mecca, reversed his opinion. He explained that the transfer of the two women to Jidda constituted a threat to "peace and morality" on the grounds of their possible contact with the brothers Zackaria.[60] As the consulate complained, at first Osman Nuri had called for the banishment of the women and their departure for India on the first available steamer. However, owing to the influence of Abdullah, Osman Nuri became determined to hold the two women under house arrest until he had secured the consulate's agreement to deport both families to India.[61]

And with that, the 'Abd al-Sattar women found themselves detained in Mecca in a legal no-man's land. According to the consulate, Osman Nuri's determination to hold the women in Mecca was a pointed demonstration of his policy that even those Indians registered with the consulate as British subjects would be considered subject to Ottoman jurisdiction and Sharia-court justice while resident in Mecca.[62] In this environment the financial and sexual coercion of Amna 'Abd al-Sattar and her daughter devolved into a proxy war over Mecca's jurisdictional status.

After her eventual release from Mecca, Amna 'Abd al-Sattar recounted how Abdullah had verbally and physically abused her. When Amna 'Abd al-Sattar forbade him from returning to her home, Abdullah and three other men came back and forced their way in. The men threatened to kidnap and forcibly marry her daughter. As Abdullah left, he taunted: "I will put men at your door and then

---

59. TNA: FO 195/1514, 20 March 1885.
60. Ibid.
61. TNA: FO 195/1482, 4 Nov. 1884.
62. Ibid.

who will help you?" She defiantly replied: "God and the Consul." In response to the widow's invocation of consular protection, Abdullah violently grabbed her and warned: "the Consul of the Christians cannot help you." When 'Abd al-Sattar emphasized that she was a British subject, Abdullah was unfazed: "I have the power and will keep you in Mecca." He then demanded that the widow move into a house near him. When she refused his advance, he said that he would "take" her "by force."[63]

One of the two men sent to threaten the 'Abd al-Sattars was Mohammed Saleh, a British Indian who had recently naturalized as an Ottoman subject. He was the nephew of the widow and a rejected suitor of her daughter. As the consulate theorized, his desire to marry the daughter was merely a ruse to strip them of their property. Had he succeeded, according to the consulate, under Islamic law he would have been entitled to three-fourths of their estate.[64]

When Amna 'Abd al-Sattar stated her intention to seek the protection of the consulate in Jidda, Abdullah petitioned the Sharia courts to prevent their departure. He secured a *fatwa* prohibiting the women from departing Mecca without the protection of a *mahrem* (a legally acceptable male guardian, generally an unmarriageable relative), dramatically narrowing the possibility of their escape. As the situation worsened, the consul hatched a plot to rescue the two women. Jago instructed Yusuf Kudzi to locate a suitable *mahrem*. The only man that Kudzi could find was a cousin, Habib Omar. Although initially on the side of the 'Abd al-Sattar family's captors, Habib Omar was tricked into cooperation. Kudzi held out the false promise that he would be given the disputed power of attorney over the family's assets in the event of their success. With Habib Omar as *mahrem*, Kudzi successfully extricated the women from their persecutors.

Upon their arrival in Jidda, the widow declared her intention to secure a new agent from her relatives in Bombay. However, as the consulate feared, Abdul Wahed and Abdullah Yunis signaled their intention to use Mecca's jurisdictional exceptionalism to hold onto the 'Abd al-Sattars' property. For her part, Amna 'Abd al-Sattar was most aggrieved by the damage done to her and her daughter's reputation, prompting concern that she might commit suicide.[65]

The tragic outcome of this case raised serious questions about the future position of vulnerable British subjects, such as widows and orphans. It was also an indication of the growing determination on the part of the Ottoman state to keep (or pry) the Hijaz's real estate and wealth out of the hands of any non-Ottoman Muslims who might wish to avail themselves of consular protection.

---

63. TNA: FO 195/1482, 9 Nov. 1884.
64. Ibid.
65. TNA: FO 195/1514, 20 March 1885.

Banning the Umma from Owning a Piece of the Holy Land

In 1867, the Ottoman government formally recognized the rights of foreigners to purchase real estate throughout the empire (Tebaa-yı Ecnebiyenin Emlake Mutasarrıf Olmaları Hakkında Kanun).[66] Once again, the law explicitly exempted the Hijaz. While this exemption was obviously meant to prohibit Europeans from owning property in the Hijaz, it carried an ironic twist. After the 1869 Nationality Law redefined non-Ottoman Muslims as foreigners, it also placed real estate purchases by foreign Muslims under greater suspicion.

Against the backdrop of the British occupation of Egypt in 1882 and swirling rumors of British support for an Arab caliphate, Hamidian-era suspicion of the potential dangers posed by non-Ottoman Muslims in the Hijaz gained a new sense of urgency. In 1882, the British consulate estimated that in Mecca alone the Indian colony numbered over 15,000. At that time, Ottoman authorities estimated that at least one-eighth of the Hijaz's real estate was already in the hands of non-Ottoman Muslims, most notably British Indian and Dutch Jawi subjects.[67] As Osman Nuri Pasha lamented, even this estimate told only part of the story. As he pointed out, foreign subjects living in the Hijaz operated in a tax-free environment and enjoyed a virtual monopoly over every sector of productivity and commercial resources in the region.[68] While Osman Nuri's reasons for curtailing the sale of real estate to foreigners was partly couched in terms of fiscal responsibility and economic productivity, as he acknowledges, the other primary motivation for the ban was driven by the constant threat of consular interference.[69]

In response to these anxieties, between 1880 and 1883 the Ottoman state moved to completely ban the sale of land and other real estate to non-Ottoman Muslims, especially subjects of European powers.[70] The ban even placed transactions intended for pious and philanthropic purposes under scrutiny.[71] As the British consulate reported, this policy had been in the works since around 1876. However, it appears that these measures were easily evaded through bribes.[72] Because Sharia court judges and officials counted fees and duties from real estate transactions as a significant source of illegitimate profits, the prohibition was apparently repeatedly overlooked.[73] After 1880, however, judges came un-

---

66. Konan, "Osmanlı Devletinde Yabancıların Kapitülasyonlar Kapsamında Hukuki Durumu," 98–111.
67. BOA, İ. DH, 1295-2/102011 (2 R 1299/21 Feb. 1882).
68. Selçuk Akşin Somel, "Osman Nuri Paşa'nın 17 Temmuz 1885 Tarihli Hicaz Raporu," *Tarih Araştırmaları Dergisi* 18/29 (1996): 13–14.
69. BOA, Y. PRK. UM, 5/57 (21 S 1300/1 Jan. 1883).
70. BOA, Y. EE, 88/67 (11 M 1298/14 Dec. 1880); BOA, Y. PRK. UM, 5/57 (21 S 1300/1 Jan. 1883).
71. Can, "The Protection Question."
72. TNA: FO 539/21, 7 May 1882, p. 110.
73. BOA, İ. DH, 1295-2/102011 (2 R 1299/21 Feb. 1882).

der increasing pressure to refuse official assistance to Indians, Jawis, and other non-Ottoman Muslims unless they produced proof that they had petitioned to seek refuge as Ottoman nationals (*tabiiyet-i sultanat-ı seniyeye dehalet arzu ve istidası*).[74] Owing to the persistence of corruption surrounding the law, in 1882 it was proposed that non-compliant judges be tried and punished and that their replacements be provided with salaries sufficient to ensure that they would not flout the law to pursue illegitimate revenue streams.[75] Again, in 1885, however, Osman Nuri would complain that because the government had not shown the necessary sensitivity in curtailing this corruption and encouraging non-Ottoman Muslims to take up Ottoman nationality, real estate continued to pass into foreigners' hands.[76] In this context, even the prospect of property changing hands through marriages between Ottoman women and non-Ottoman men in the Hijaz came to be viewed as a dangerous loophole.[77]

Osman Nuri's repeated warnings coincided neatly with the Ottoman center's growing concern that the Hijaz's foreign Muslims were destined to become stalking horses for European political subversion and extraterritorial control. In 1882, a memorandum produced by the Council of State (Şura-yı Devlet) warned:

> If we remain indifferent to the accumulation of property by devious means in the hands of foreign Muslims, with the passage of time we may find that much of the Holy Lands have been acquired by the subjects of foreign powers. Then, the foreigners, as is their wont, after lying in waiting for some time, will suddenly be upon us at the slightest opportunity and excuse and will proceed to make the most preposterous claims.[78]

The ban was to remain in force through World War I despite the ongoing problem of actually enforcing it. At face value this law seemed to radically contradict the Hamidian state's attempts to cultivate loyalty to the caliphate among foreign Muslims. It is also clear that the ban did not go unchallenged on religious grounds. As one dissenting opinion submitted to the Council of State in 1903 pointed out, although the fundamental political concerns over Indian and Jawi colonial subjects were reasonable enough, the logic behind singling out these groups was unsustainable. As the author quips, what of the territories recently ceded to Russia, Romania, Greece, and Serbia? Were Muslims from those territories not also foreign subjects? Whatever the possible dangers posed by a few Indians or Jawis, the author reasoned that it could not possibly equal the nega-

74. BOA, Y. EE, 88/67 (11 M 1298/14 Dec. 1880); BOA, İ. DH, 1295-2/102011 (2 R 1299/21 Feb. 1882).

75. BOA, Y. A. RES, 15/38 (17 Ca 1299/6 April 1882).

76. Somel, "Osman Nuri," 13–14.

77. BOA, İ. MMS, 104/4442 (24 Ş 1306/25 April 1889).

78. BOA, Y. A. RES, 15/38 (17 Ca 1299/6 April 1882), quoted in Deringil, *The Well-Protected Domains*, 56.

tive influence of this ban. As he chides, the right to settle (*temekkün*) in the holy cities is guaranteed under Islamic law (*İslam hukuk-i diniyece*). In any case, the vast majority of those who choose to settle in the *haremeyn* seek only "to collect a heavenly reward" and "have no other intention." Without the holy places, he worried that there would no longer be a place for the Islamic world to gather. Moreover, to prohibit settlement in the holy places would almost certainly break their ties to the center of the caliphate. After all, as the author challenges, did the caliph not claim leadership as the spiritual head of all Islam and not just Islam in his own domains regardless of their nationality or subjecthood?[79]

As this dissenting opinion seems to ask, was the prohibition of land sales to foreign Muslims a case of the oft cited, though rarely thoughtfully examined, "paranoia" of the Hamidian era? Had the state conjured an unrealistic demon? If not, what kind of "preposterous claims" did Osman Nuri and the Council of State fear? The petition's indignation at the growing chasm between the religious rhetoric of the caliphate and the Hamidian state's actual exclusionary policies identifies the contradictions inherent in the pursuit of Pan-Islamic universalism and territorial sovereignty at the same time. However, this paradox is an artificial one, an artifact of our insistence on thinking of Pan-Islam as a religious discourse. As the attempt to restrict real estate sales to foreign Muslims underscores, Pan-Islam was, more often than not, a set of policies and discourses defined as much by sovereignty and international legal considerations as by Islamic legitimacy. The loftier foreign-policy objectives of Pan-Islam were constantly being weighed against and frequently subordinated to projects designed to shelter Ottoman sovereignty from the corrosive effects of autonomy, extraterritoriality, international law, and their intersection.

Conclusion: Courteous Procedures Unknown to International Law

The stalemate over protection dragged on until the end of Ottoman rule in Arabia. In 1910, four British subjects were tried and convicted of assault in Mecca. Once again, the British Embassy claimed that Ottoman authorities had knowingly refused consular representation to their subjects in blatant violation of the Capitulations. The embassy communiqué claimed that the authorities at the Sublime Porte "do not hesitate to admit" that no "exception of this sort" has ever been established, "neither through the text of the treaties in question nor through any subsequent agreement." The embassy's complaint pointed out that Istanbul had already "recognized more than one time that British subjects who find themselves in the Holy Cities have the right of protection from the Consulate of His Majesty in Jidda."[80] The document cited precedents from 1884, 1888, and 1896 when the consulate's translator had been permitted to represent British

79. BOA, Y. PRK. ŞD, 3/34 (29 Z 1320/29 March 1903).
80. BOA, HR. HMŞ. İŞO, 200/7 (28 Z 1328/31 Dec. 1910).

subjects held in Mecca.[81] In light of these precedents, the embassy insisted that the enforcement of the Capitulations "ought to apply to the Holy Cities just as the other parts of the Ottoman Empire." And in future cases "a Muslim representative of His Majesty's Consulate in Jidda" should always be invited "to assist in all of the proceedings" and be allowed to act in the "capacity of the Consular Authorities."[82]

The complaint was referred to the Ottoman Office of Legal Counsel (Hukuk Müşavirliği İstişare Odası).[83] The Office of Legal Counsel compiled a report on the status of the "Capitulations in the Hijaz" spelling out what might be regarded as the empire's final position on the matter. As the empire's most senior international legal experts reiterated, although it had long been the practice of the local Ottoman government to assist European consulates in Jidda with questions pertaining to their subjects in Mecca and Medina, such assistance was merely a matter of "courteous procedure" (*muamele-i hatırşinasane*) and was undertaken in a strictly "non-official" (*gayri resmiye*) capacity at the discretion of the provincial government. They acknowledged that it had become customary for some Muslim officials of the consulates to visit Mecca during hajj season in order to attend to the civil and criminal affairs of their respective subjects, but noted that the Ottoman government considered such individuals as acting "in a private capacity" (*suret-i hususiye'de*). Owing to this conceptual distinction, they were not recognized as officially sanctioned consular agents.[84]

More importantly, while the Office of Legal Counsel's interpretations underscored that these "unofficial" communications were carried out in a spirit of cooperation and in the best interests of the pilgrims, they cautioned that these niceties were observed "under conditions *unknown* in international law" and "without being bound by formal international commitments."[85] In short, such communications were not linked to any legally binding "exceptions" (*istisnaat*) or "privilege" (*imtiyaz*).[86]

Taken in isolation, this kind of legal maneuvering might appear to be little more than a minor footnote. However, the British Foreign Office's persistent logic regarding the application of Article 42 provides a fuller context to the predicament that the Capitulations presented for Ottoman sovereignty in the Hijaz.

81. BOA, HR. HMŞ. İŞO, 200/8 (8 C 1329/6 June 1911); BOA, HR. HMŞ. İŞO, 200/11 (27 M 1330/17 Jan. 1912).
82. BOA, HR. HMŞ. İŞO, 200/7 (28 Z 1328/31 Dec. 1910).
83. On the origins and function of the Hukuk Müşavirliği İstişare Odası, see Aimee M. Genell, "The Well-Defended Domains: Eurocentric International Law and the Making of the Ottoman Office of Legal Counsel," in this volume.
84. BOA, HR. HMŞ. İŞO, 200/10 (28 L 1329/22 Oct. 1911).
85. BOA, HR. HMŞ. İŞO, 200/5 (2 N 1332/25 July 1915).
86. BOA, HR. HMŞ. İŞO, 200/10 (28 L 1329/22 Oct. 1911); BOA, HR. HMŞ. İŞO, 201/47 (27 Ca 1329/26 May 1911).

As the Foreign Office's 1889 inquiry into the question of consular protection in Mecca concluded:

> ... as the Capitulations contain no provision to except the Hedjaz or the holy cities from their stipulations, Her Majesty's Government can admit no such exception. The only grounds on which Her Majesty's Government could be justified in renouncing at Mecca the rights of protection conceded by the Capitulations for the Ottoman Empire generally would be a distinct declaration from the Porte that that city had ceased to be (in the language of Article 42) "a portion of the Sultan's sacred dominions," *in which case it would be necessary to make such arrangements as might be possible with the Grand Shareef as an independent authority....*[87]

The stakes of these questions—and thinly veiled threats lurking just behind them—extended well beyond the protection of pilgrims accused of crimes in Mecca. Rather, they are a reflection on how the Capitulations and the internationally binding character of the linkage between the Tanzimat reforms and the Treaty of Paris defined Ottoman sovereignty from Britain's perspective. Fair or not, by this logic, if the Ottomans claimed that they could not enforce the Capitulations in a given territory, then the Ottoman state risked not being considered fully sovereign there. The inability to ensure extraterritorial protections provided a pretext for European intervention or, as the Foreign Office hints, the search for an alternative sovereign. In this case, the independent alternative was the Sharif of Mecca and ultimately a harbinger of things to come.

87. Emphasis mine. TNA: FO 424/159, May 1889, p. 22.

6 The Protection Question: Central Asians and Extraterritoriality in the Late Ottoman Empire[*]

Lâle Can

IN A POPULAR song by the late Turkish folk and pop singer Barış Manço, an imaginary interlocutor repeatedly asks him, "my countryman, what is your country?" (*hemşerim, memleket nire?*), to which he responds, "this world is my country" (*bu dünya benim memleket*). This answer only provokes a more insistent framing of the question—"No, you didn't understand; what is your *real* country?" This, in turn leads Manço to despair of people making "long speeches about brotherhood and equality" whilst preoccupied with difference.[1] Listening to the song as a historian of the late Ottoman Empire, the lyrics are oddly evocative of tensions between the central government's promotion of pan-Islamic politics and its increasing preoccupation with nationality in the last decades of the empire's existence. Despite strident rhetoric about Islamic unity, the question of where Muslims were from—specifically their legal nationality and the state to which they belonged—became increasingly connected to questions of jurisdictional sovereignty.[2] As a consequence of both colonial expansion and the 1869 Ottoman Nationality Law, nationality began to determine the rights and protections to which foreign Muslims (i.e., those from beyond Ottoman territory) were entitled, vis-à-vis both the sultan-caliph and European sovereigns. This was as true for pilgrims on the hajj—a ritual associated with the leveling of differences among

[*] This chapter was originally published in the *International Journal of Middle East Studies* (*IJMES*) 48, no. 4 (2016), 679–99, and is reprinted here with the permission of Cambridge University Press. I wish to express my gratitude to Jeff Culang and the reviewers of *IJMES* for their helpful comments on the original article, as well as to Lauren Benton, Aimee Genell, Will Hanley, Michael Christopher Low, and Will Smiley. I also thank Samuel Dolbee, Chris Gratien, Emily Greble, Susan Gunasti, Adeeb Khalid, Masha Kirasirova, Jessica Marglin, Robert D. McChesney, Eric Schluessel, Joshua M. White, and Seçil Yılmaz for valuable feedback during the writing of this essay.

1. "Hemşerim Memleket Nire" was released on the 1992 album *Mega Mano* by Emre Plak.
2. Throughout this chapter I use "nationality" to mean a type of affiliation with a state that enabled claims to rights, without modern connotations of loyalty or political citizenship. This is in line with Will Smiley's usage, also in the context of negotiations over Russo-Ottoman sovereignty. As Smiley succinctly puts it, "all Russian subjects, when abroad, were Russian 'nationals'—sharing membership of the same state, regardless of their status within that state." See "The Burdens of Subjecthood: The Ottoman State, Russian Fugitives, and Interimperial Law, 1774–1869," *International Journal of Middle East Studies* (*IJMES*) 46, no. 1 (2014): 73–93.

the *umma*—as it was for migrants and merchants.[3] But if Ottoman legitimacy in the late nineteenth century rested on claims to universal Islamic authority, why did the nationality of Muslims in the sultan's domains matter?[4] The story of a Bukharan migrant named Celal bin Hekim sheds light on this question, as well as the broader themes of protection and extraterritoriality that are the focus of this chapter.

Sometime in the early 1860s, Celal left the Emirate of Bukhara and traveled across a vast stretch of the fabled Silk Road before settling in the Red Sea port city of Jidda. Over the course of the next three decades, he worked as a *bedelci*, an agent for people who paid to avoid (or were exempt from) military service.[5] Such a job would involve large outlays of money, extensive travel, and strong local and regional connections. During his residence in the empire, Celal "benefited from all the rights of Ottoman nationality"—making it all the more galling for Ottoman authorities when, after getting into trouble with the law, he asserted that he was a Russian subject and exempt from Ottoman jurisdiction. Unsure how to proceed, provincial officials forwarded the case to Istanbul, where the Foreign Ministry would decide whether this Bukharan living as an Ottoman had any valid legal basis for claiming Russian nationality.[6] To paraphrase the lyrics of Manço's song, Ottoman authorities seemed to be asking, "*hemşerim*, what is your real nationality (*asıl tabiiyet*)?" The answer had important implications: if he were an Ottoman, Celal would be subject to Sharia law; if Russian, he would be exempt from detention or trial in the Hijaz and placed under tsarist jurisdiction. But what if he was a Bukharan subject? Were subjects of the emir—a Russian vassal—entitled to the same rights and protection as subjects of the tsar? According to legal advisors in the Ottoman Foreign Ministry, the answer was a firm no. Protectorates such as Bukhara, they countered, were semisovereign and their subjects were ineligible for European capitulatory privileges or protections.

Central Asian Muslims living in the empire had historically been subject to Ottoman law and enjoyed the rights of the sultan's subjects. However, the con-

---

3. According to Victor Turner, communitas was an intense form of brotherhood and equality experienced by people during rites of passage such as hajj. It was "a spontaneously generated relationship between leveled and equal total and individuated human beings, stripped of all structural attributes." Turner, *Dramas, Fields, and Metaphors: Symbolic Action in Human Society* (Ithaca: Cornell University Press, 1975), 202.
4. On the role of Islam and pan-Islamic ideology in the late Ottoman Empire, see Selim Deringil, *The Well-Protected Domains: Ideology and Legitimation of Power in the Ottoman Empire 1876–1909* (London: I.B. Tauris, 1998); Kemal Karpat, *The Politicization of Islam: Restructuring Identity, State, Faith, and Community in the Late Ottoman State* (Oxford: Oxford University Press, 2001). On the sultan's custodianship of the hajj, see Suraiya Faroqhi, *Pilgrims and Sultans: The Hajj under the Ottomans* (London: I.B. Tauris, 2014).
5. Başbakanlık Osmanlı Arşivi (BOA) HR.HMŞ.İŞO 177/34 (11 July 1892).
6. HR.H 571/27 (2 July 1892) and HR.HMŞ.İŞO 177/34 (11 July 1892).

quest of the region by non-Muslim powers in the nineteenth century changed this equation. To the consternation of the Ottoman central government, in the 1880s Britain and Russia started claiming jurisdiction over Afghans and Bukharans, often through the notion of "protection"—a term that could mean anything from consular patronage of travelers in need to the provision of legal immunity and commercial privileges (*imtiyazat*) that had historically been the purview of European Christians. Collectively referred to as the Capitulations, these sultanic grants dated to the early modern period and "provided non-Muslim foreigners with privileges of safe residence and passage, a variety of tax exemptions and low customs duties, and partial if not complete immunity from the jurisdiction of Ottoman courts."[7] Throughout the nineteenth-century European diplomats worked to render these unilateral and theoretically revocable grants binding legal obligations, by incorporating them into bi- and multilateral treaties.[8] To encourage mercantile relationships and expand their spheres of influence, European consuls also began to grant letters of extraterritorial protection (*berat*) to thousands of Ottoman Christian protégés and, increasingly, to Muslim foreign nationals.[9] This form of protection marked a new phase in the expansion of extraterritoriality—what Turan Kayaoğlu terms the quintessential legal imperialism—and threatened to place Muslims with new claims to foreign nationality and protection beyond the reach of Ottoman justice as well as to further compromise Ottoman sovereignty.[10]

An extensive body of scholarship has detailed the deleterious impact of the Capitulations on the late Ottoman Empire. In recent years this area of research has benefited from an infusion of new perspectives that shed light on how these imperialist instruments also created opportunities for people who were able to

---

7. Umut Özsu, "The Ottoman Empire, the Origins of Extraterritoriality, and International Legal Theory," in *The Oxford Handbook of the Theory of International Law*, ed. Florian Hoffman and Anne Orford (Oxford: Oxford University Press, 2016), 124. For additional background on the Capitulations, see Feroz Ahmad, "Ottoman Perceptions of the Capitulations, 1800–1914," *Journal of Islamic Studies* 11 (2000): 1–20; John T. Spagnolo, "Portents of Empire in Britain's Ottoman Extraterritorial Jurisdiction," *Middle Eastern Studies*, 27 (1991): 256–82.

8. Özsu, "The Ottoman Empire," 129.

9. For studies of how Russia and Britain sought to establish themselves as Muslim powers through patronage of the hajj, see Eileen Kane, *Russian Hajj, Empire and the Pilgrimage to Mecca* (Ithaca: Cornell University Press, 2015); John Slight, *The British Empire and the Hajj, 1865–1956* (Cambridge, MA: Harvard University Press, 2015). On British claims to protect Afghans, see Faiz Ahmed, "The British-Ottoman Cold War, c. 1880–1914: Imperial Struggles over Muslim Mobility and Citizenship from the Suez Canal to the Durand Line," in this volume.

10. Kayaoğlu defines extraterritoriality as "the extension of a state's legal authority into another state and limitation of legal authority of the target state over issues that may affect people, commercial interests, and security of the imperial states." Turan Kayaoğlu, *Legal Imperialism: Sovereignty and Extraterritoriality in Japan, the Ottoman Empire, and China* (Cambridge, UK: Cambridge University Press, 2010), 6.

become European protégés or protected persons. Historians bridging imperial and legal history and working at multiple levels of analysis have explored how diverse actors in cosmopolitan cities and borderland settings exploited competition over foreign protection, legal jurisdiction, and spheres of sovereignty.[11] The growth of European consular courts, for example, made practices such as affiliation switching and forum shopping—when individuals within legally pluralist systems switched legal identities and forums in order to maximize benefits—increasingly common.[12] Yet for all of the individuals who achieved favorable results in the legally plural order, there were many others who faced dead ends and what Julia Stephens describes in her contribution to this volume as uncertain outcomes.[13] This was especially true among Central Asian migrants like Celal whom the Ottoman central government did not consider "real" colonial subjects with the same rights as British Indians or French Algerians.

As recent studies on intersections between mobility, sovereignty, and legal imperialism make clear, Ottoman engagement with the question of protection was part of a complex story unfolding worldwide.[14] However, the Ottoman ver-

11. This scholarship is too extensive to cite in its entirety, particularly on the Capitulations, which are discussed in most works on the late Ottoman Empire. In addition to Ahmad, "Ottoman Perceptions" and Spagnolo, "Portents of Empire," see Maurits Van den Boogert, *The Capitulations and the Ottoman Legal System: Qadis, Consuls, and Beratlıs in the 18th Century* (Leiden: Brill, 2005). On legal pluralism in the Ottoman Empire, see Karen Barkey, "Aspects of Legal Pluralism in the Ottoman Empire," in *Legal Pluralism and Empires,1500–1850*, ed. Lauren Benton and Richard Ross (New York: New York University Press, 2013). Studies by Julia Clancy Smith and Mary Dewhurst Lewis have been particularly influential for reconceptualizing the possibilities and problems ushered in by legal imperialism and legal pluralism. Clancy-Smith, *Mediterraneans: North Africa and Europe in an Age of Migration, c. 1800–1900* (Berkeley: University of California Press, 2012); Lewis, "The Geographies of Power: The Tunisian Civic Order, Jurisdictional Politics, and Imperial Rivalry in the Mediterranean, 1881–1935," *Journal of Modern History* 80 (2008): 791–830. On the protégé system, see Salahi R. Sonyel, "The Protégé' System in the Ottoman Empire," *Journal of Islamic Studies* 2 (1991): 56–66. Other works of note on nationality, sovereignty, legal pluralism, and protection include Will Hanley, *Identifying with Nationality, Europeans, Ottomans, and Egyptians in Alexandria* (New York: Columbia University Press, 2017); Eric Beverly, *Hyderabad, British India, and the World: Muslim Networks and Minor Sovereignty* (Cambridge, UK: Cambridge University Press, 2015); Jessica M. Marglin "The Two Lives of Mas'ud Amoyal: Pseudo-Algerians in Morocco, 1830–1912," *IJMES* 44, no. 4 (2012): 651–70; Sarah Abrevaya Stein, "Protected Persons? The Baghdadi Jewish Diaspora, the British State, and the Persistence of Empire," *American Historical Review* 116 (2011): 80–108.

12. Lewis, "The Geographies of Power," 180.

13. On the uncertainties of colonial law and legal pluralism, see Sally Engle Merry, "Colonial Law and Its Uncertainties," *Law and History Review* 28 (2010): 1067–71; Julia Stephens "An Uncertain Inheritance: The Imperial Travels of Legal Migrants, from British India to Ottoman Iraq," in this volume.

14. For these studies, see n. 11. I am influenced here by Clancy-Smith, who writes, "the legal quagmire created by conflicts involving the subjects of local rulers, recognized protégés, resident expatriates, recent immigrants, or familiar strangers under shifting or uncertain juris-

sion of this story had important plot twists that have not received adequate attention and that stemmed from its unique position as both sultanate and caliphate. Joining a small body of research on the empire's vexed position vis-à-vis Muslims from beyond its borders, this chapter argues that the threat of expanding Russian and British jurisdiction prompted the emergence of a "protection question": whether Afghans, Bukharans, and Chinese Muslims in Ottoman lands had legitimate claims to Russian and British legal nationality and, by extension, capitulatory privileges.[15] In contrast to the focus on identity, ethnic kinship, and loyalty that has informed studies of Ottoman–Central Asian relations, this chapter follows Ottoman statesmen down alternate paths—namely, their engagement with international law (*hukuk-ı düvel*) and differentiated forms of colonial rule.[16] By showing how the Ottoman government developed policies toward Asian peoples based on the type of polities from which they originated rather than their ethnicity, it challenges ahistorical assumptions about the role of Turkic kinship in Ottoman history. It also reveals new perspectives on the instrumentalization of the caliphate by examining how the Sublime Porte (the central government in Istanbul) fused international legal norms and novel pan-Islamic claims to deny foreign nationality rights to Muslim colonial subjects.[17] I argue that the assertion that Bukharans and other Central Asians were protected by the sultan-caliph had little to do with Muslim universalism or ethnic kinship; rather, it was primarily a strategy to curtail the expansion of consular protections to people taking on "borrowed nationalities."[18] The Ottomans did not have the power to dismantle

dictions was presented as an episode in modern Middle Eastern history, not as one chapter in larger struggles unfolding across the world in much the same manner and period. Conflicting jurisdictions are universal phenomena, which haunt our world, ever more today due to high-intensity 'globalization.'" Clancy-Smith, *Mediterraneans*, 200.

15. On the Porte's views of foreign Muslims, see Selim Deringil, "The Ottoman Empire and Russian Muslims: Brothers or Rivals?," *Central Asian Survey* 13 (1994): 409–16; Michael Christopher Low, "The Mechanics of Mecca: The Technopolitics of the Late Ottoman Hijaz and the Colonial Hajj" (PhD diss., Columbia University, 2015).

16. Kemal Karpat analyzes Ottoman-Central Asian relations through the lens of ethnic kinship and brotherhood in *The Politicization of Islam*. In another influential but problematic study, Mehmet Saray considers kinship and loyalty as crucial to Ottoman-Central Asian political relations. Saray, *The Russian, British, Chinese and Ottoman Rivalry in Turkestan: Four Studies on the History of Central Asia* (Ankara: Turkish Historical Society Printing House, 2003). Michael A. Reynolds offers a critique of pan-Turkism and pan-Islam as categories of analysis in "Buffers, Not Brethren: Young Turk Military Policy in the First World War and the Myth of Panturanism," *Past and Present* 203 (2009): 137–79.

17. International law emerged as a Eurocentric framework for the practice of international relations by diplomats, based on treaty and customary law and, increasingly, the Capitulations.

18. These were colonial subjects who had no connections to the legal nationalities they acquired and who, according to colonial authorities, employed various ruses solely for the purpose of obtaining rights and protections. Lewis uses the term "borrowed nationalities" to describe how French authorities in Tunisia viewed non-European protégés such as Algerians. Lewis,

the system of extraterritoriality, but they could limit its reach by staking a claim to Central Asians within the empire.

In telling this multilayered story, the chapter first considers Celal's failed attempt to become a Russian national within the context of late nineteenth-century legal and political developments at the local and transregional level. In the next section, I draw on case studies involving Afghans who tried to become British nationals, in order to trace how the Porte arrived at the position that "protected people" (*mahmi*) were under the exclusive protection of the caliphate (*taht-ı himaye-yi halife-i islamiye*). This entailed distinguishing between "real" (*asıl, sahih*) European subjects and informally colonized peoples. This latter category comprised a vast group of Muslims from informally colonized lands such as Bukhara, Afghanistan, and Chinese Turkestan (today's Xinjiang Uyghur Autonomous Region). While this group defies contemporary area studies models, I refer to those it includes as "Central Asians" both for simplicity and based on how the Ottoman Foreign Ministry categorized people in cases involving protection. In the last section, I examine the challenges the central government faced in formulating policies with which provincial authorities would comply (particularly in the Hijaz), and that European powers would accept as law.

In addition to highlighting the range of views within the empire regarding who was a foreign Muslim, the chapter suggests that the Porte was in a tenuous position due to its pursuit of two parallel but somewhat incongruous goals: seeking legitimacy through the caliphate—an institution that in theory did not recognize divisions among the *umma*—while trying to legally differentiate among the very same community of global Muslims. Although my focus is on the latter objective, it is clear that the tensions inherent in these endeavors ended up limiting both the government's and foreign Muslims' range of action. As the chapter demonstrates, the central government often was unable to fully implement reforms designed to protect its sovereignty, and Central Asians who were denied both Ottoman and European legal nationality faced a narrowing of choices. Those who wanted to enjoy the rights of Ottomans (such as landholding) had to officially renounce their foreign nationality and become Ottoman subjects. Yet, given the reluctance of foreign powers such as Russia to relinquish subjects, attempts at Ottoman naturalization could result in a protracted state of liminality that paralleled the pilgrimage but was a product of larger geopolitical struggles.

Becoming Ottoman, Foreign, and Protected

Like many nineteenth-century residents of Jidda, Celal was originally from someplace else. During his three decades in the bustling hajj hub, the world

Divided Rule: Sovereignty and Empire in French Tunisia, 1881–1938 (Berkeley: University of California Press, 2014), 61.

around him had changed extensively, as had the status of Central Asians in the empire. In the 1860s and 1870s, Transoxiana, the Ferghana Valley, and the "six cities" (Altishahr) of the Tarim Basin region were conquered by Russia and China.[19] The emir of Bukhara and the khan of Khiva retained independence over their domestic affairs, but their territories became Russian protectorates, while Khoqand and its people were integrated into the new colony of Russian Turkestan. Farther east, the short-lived Emirate of Kashgar (1864–77), whose ruler Yaqub Beg had successfully courted Ottoman support, was reconquered by Qing China (which did not have diplomatic relations with the Ottomans).[20] In Afghanistan, the British took control of Kabul's foreign affairs after the Second Anglo-Afghan War (1878–80) and established a protected state.[21] This expansion of colonial power also inaugurated a revolution in mobility, and thousands of Central Asians began arriving in the Hijaz on steamships each hajj season. Unlike when he had first arrived, Celal's countrymen were everywhere, with many staying on long after completing the pilgrimage.

This colonial expansion and concomitant revolution in mobility coincided with an extensive period of Ottoman political and administrative "restructuring" known as the Tanzimat (1839–76), during which the Porte sought to secure territorial integrity against nationalist movements and European intervention. Two major reform decrees, the 1839 Rescript of Gülhane and the 1856 Reform Edict, outlined centralizing measures and promised all Ottoman subjects equal rights and protections under the law. The reforms undermined centuries of legal distinctions between Muslim subjects and Christians and Jews, and introduced

19. Rian Thum makes the case for referring to this region as "Altishahr," using the designation that people in the region used historically. Thum, *The Sacred Routes of Uyghur History* (Cambridge, MA: Harvard University Press, 2014).

20. On the Russian Empire in Central Asia, see Seymour Becker, *Russia's Protectorates in Central Asia: Bukhara and Khiva, 1865–1914* (Cambridge, MA: Harvard University Press, 1968); Jeff Sahadeo, *Russian Colonial Society in Tashkent: 1865–1923* (Bloomington: Indiana University Press, 2007); Alexander Morrison, *Russian Rule in Samarkand, 1868–1910: A Comparison with British India* (Oxford: Oxford University Press, 2008). On Chinese Turkestan, see Hodong Kim, *Holy War in China: The Muslim Rebellion and State in Chinese Central Asia, 1864–1877* (Stanford: Stanford University Press, 2004). The meaning of the terms "protectorate" and "protected states" as used in this chapter is not synonymous with post-World War I Mandates. In the Russian protectorates of Khiva and Bukhara, the khan and the emir were Russian vassals who were granted local autonomy but no control over foreign policy. While their territories were neither fully annexed (although parts of Bukhara were annexed to the Russian colony in Turkestan) nor subject to settler colonialism, they were internationally recognized as part of the Russian Empire. In Afghanistan, the emir technically retained independence as the head of a "protected state." The country was never officially part of the British Empire, and the emir controlled internal affairs. But as in the case of the Bukharan protectorate, the British controlled Afghanistan's foreign policy.

21. On British involvement in Afghanistan, see Thomas Barfield, *Afghanistan: A Cultural and Political History* (Princeton: Princeton University Press, 2010).

the legal category "Ottoman" that included subjects of all faiths. The reforms also sought to cultivate an imperial identity among the empire's heterogeneous population, institute more direct forms of control over the nascent citizenry, and curb the proliferation of *berats* among Ottoman Christians by granting them equal rights and opportunities. The 1839 and 1856 decrees were soon supplemented by legislation that formalized naturalization procedures. According to the 1869 Ottoman Nationality Law (Tabiiyet-i Osmaniye Kanunnamesi), any person born to an Ottoman father was a subject, but one could also become an Ottoman through residence. Those born in the empire to foreign parents could become naturalized within three years of reaching an unspecified age of majority (Article 2), and foreign nationals could become naturalized after fulfilling a five-year residency requirement (Article 3). The fourth article allowed for Ottoman nationality to be granted to exceptional individuals who had not fulfilled the terms listed in Articles 2 and 3, and were deemed "worthy of special permission." The final, ninth article stated that each individual living in the empire was considered an Ottoman and subject to Ottoman law, and that anyone claiming to be a foreign national had to provide evidence to this effect.[22]

As Will Hanley argues in his contribution, the law built on an 1863 regulation that forced protégés to choose to naturalize as foreign subjects or submit to Ottoman territorial jurisdiction. When many protégés responded by naturalizing with a foreign state *and* retaining their Ottoman residency and nationality, the Porte sought to resolve this by enacting stricter laws.[23] Per the 1869 law, all non-Ottomans—Muslim and non-Muslim alike—were excluded from the nascent citizenry and legally categorized as foreigners (*ecanib*, sing. *ecnebi*). The word *ecnebi*'s historical association with Christians, however, led Ottoman officials to distinguish non-Ottoman Muslims and refer to them as *ecanib-i müslimin*.[24] "Foreign Muslim" became an unofficial but capacious subcategory that included migrants and travelers from colonies, protectorates, and European spheres or zones of influence in Asia and Africa, as well as pilgrims and long-term pious residents of the holy cities (*mücavirin*).

While the Tanzimat reforms did not have an immediate impact on Celal's everyday life, more consistent implementation of an 1867 law prohibiting foreign Muslims from acquiring property in the Hijaz may have given him incentive to become legally naturalized. Since there was no cadastral survey, taxation, or

22. For a file that summarizes five decades of Ottoman and citizenship- and nationality-related problems and provides the 1869 law in full, see HR.HMŞ.İŞO 221/1 (5 Nov. 1919). For an English translation of the law, see Richard Flournoy and Manley Hudson, eds., *A Collection of Nationality Law of Various Countries as Contained in Constitutions, Statutes and Treaties* (New York: Oxford University Press, 1929).
23. Will Hanley, "What Ottoman Nationality Was and Was Not," in this volume.
24. Prior to the Tanzimat, *ecnebi* was primarily used as a term to describe people from Christian lands.

conscription in the Hijaz, there were few drawbacks to becoming an Ottoman subject.[25] And Celal was probably cognizant that doing so would not foreclose the possibility of later claiming foreign nationality. Many Muslim migrants from North Africa, Bukhara, and Afghanistan with whom he may have done business or met while traveling through Alexandria and Istanbul had managed to secure French, Russian, or British nationality or protégé status and were now enjoying the attendant legal and financial advantages. In the Hijaz, many migrants had previously become Ottomans in order to buy land. Perhaps sensing that he might one day benefit from holding a Russian passport, Celal decided to register at the Russian Consulate-General in Istanbul during a trip to the city in 1890. When he was detained the next year for a legal matter involving a slave (*bir esir köle maddesi*), his decision seemed prescient. The recently established Russian consulate in Jidda was eager to support his assertion of immunity from Ottoman jurisdiction and to protest his detention. What Celal did not anticipate, however, was that a decade of similar attempts had prompted the Ottoman Foreign Ministry to formulate policies regarding the rights of Bukharans and Afghans to Russian and British protection that would prevent him from evading Ottoman justice.

When the Hijaz governor learned of Celal's assertion, he wrote to Istanbul for direction on how to proceed. His query was forwarded to the Ministry of Foreign Affairs, which quickly rejected the proof furnished by the Russian consulate to substantiate its claim of jurisdiction: a copy of an 1890 certificate stating that the fifty-seven-year-old, hazel-eyed Bukharan of average height was born in Russia.[26] In their communications with the Hijaz, the contempt of the Ottoman authorities in Istanbul nearly leapt off the page. They pointed out that not only had Celal left Bukhara long before it became a protectorate, but he had also happily taken advantage of being an Ottoman for thirty years and benefited from all the rights this entailed. Adding that even if he were originally from parts of Bukhara that had been formally annexed to Russia—which would have rendered him a colonial subject rather than a *mahmi*—he had no valid claim to Russian nationality, since he had left when the emirate was still completely independent. Celal's scheme had failed.

In a subsequent note to the Russian consul, the Ottoman Foreign Ministry politely asked him to refrain from further interference since the case was outside his purview. While it is not clear whether the consul acquiesced, he and his successors continued to actively offer their services to people like Celal well into the

---

25. DH.SN.THR 54/45 (3 Aug. 1914). On the government's decision not to implement the Tanzimat reforms in Yemen and other "exceptional provinces," see Thomas Kuehn, *Empire, Islam, and Politics of Difference: Ottoman Rule in Yemen, 1849–1919* (Leiden: Brill, 2011).
26. HR.H 571/27 (2 July 1892); HR.HMŞ.İŞO 177/34 (11 July 1892). On the consular system in Jidda, see Ulrike Freitag, "Helpless Representatives of the Great Powers? Western Consuls in Jeddah, 1830s to 1914," *Journal of Imperial and Commonwealth History* 40 (2012): 357–81.

1910s. Similar to Great Britain, imperial Russia was trying to foster loyalty among colonial Muslim subjects and to establish a foothold in the Hijaz. That Russian authorities differentiated among colonial subjects within Russia's imperial territories—and would have been loath to recognize Bukharans as Russian nationals in the metropole—did not deter them from ignoring these differences when the subjects in question were in Ottoman lands.[27] As Eileen Kane has argued, the conferral of consular protection was part of a broader strategy of extending tsarist power along the pilgrimage routes and into Greater Syria and the Hijaz, and exploiting hajj networks and patronage for political capital and legitimacy.[28] This was not always a cynical move, and many Russian subjects abroad and within the empire (in the case of heirs to the estates of relatives who died while traveling or on the hajj) benefited from tsarist patronage. Many so-called pauper pilgrims, for example, relied on this form of protection to complete what was still a long, costly, and dangerous journey.[29] But as Ottoman statesmen feared, tsarist benevolence was primarily strategic; mobile Muslim migrants and pilgrims constituted a promising path for Russia to project authority into Arabia, which constituted a holy landscape for the empire's large population of Muslim subjects. To borrow a term from Lauren Benton's work on the Atlantic world, ongoing consular support of claims to Russian nationality and the conferral of protection was a means of casting "shadows of sovereignty" into lands beyond Russia's territorial borders.[30]

27. According to Daniel Brower, "tsardom had become the patron of [Central Asian pilgrims]" as a consequence of attempts to regulate the hajj. Brower, *Turkestan and the Fate of the Russian Empire* (London: Routledge Curzon, 2003). As Alexander Morrison argues, even if Russian colonial administrators claimed that inhabitants of Tashkent, Samarqand, and other cities were "considered to be as much Russian citizens as those of Moscow," this claim was patently false because "they were not accorded equal rights with the population of European Russia." Morrison, "Metropole, Colony, and Imperial Citizenship in the Russian Empire," *Kritika* 13 (2012): 327–64. According to Eric Lohr, "the emirates of Bukhara and Khiva (formally acquired by Russia and given protectorate status in 1867 and 1873, respectively) retained their own subjecthood and their subjects were treated as foreigners in nearly all respects when they crossed the border between the emirates and the empire proper." Their status was different from that of subjects of "parts of Central Asia that were annexed and fully incorporated directly" and "ascribed subjecthood on a full *jus soli* [right of the soil] basis." Lohr, *Russian Citizenship: From Empire to Soviet Union* (Cambridge, MA: Harvard University Press, 2012), 32–33.
28. Kane, *Russian Hajj*, especially chapters 1 and 2.
29. For an extensive exploration of Ottoman and Russian patronage of Central Asian pilgrims, see Lâle Can, *Spiritual Subjects: Central Asian Pilgrims and the Ottoman Hajj at the End of Empire* (Stanford: Stanford University Press, 2020).
30. Lauren Benton, "Shadows of Sovereignty: Legal Encounters and the Politics of Protection in the Atlantic World," in *Encounters Old and New in World History: Essays Inspired by Jerry H. Bentley*, ed. A. L. Karras, L. J. Mitchell, and J. H. Bentley (Honolulu: University of Hawaii Press, 2017).

Real Nationals, Legal Fictions, and the Protection Question

The emergence of an international legal order privileging the laws of "civilized" nations (over those of "barbaric" and "quasicivilized" ones) pressed authorities in polities as varied as China, Japan, and French Tunisia to find ways to limit the power of foreign consuls and extraterritorial courts and to rein in the privileges of European protégés.[31] Just as the French balked at recognizing colonial Algerian subjects as French nationals when they crossed the border into Tunisia, Ottoman officials were frustrated by exempting foreign Muslims from Ottoman jurisdiction, particularly when many of them originated from colonies where they would be subject to Sharia law. The Ottoman Foreign Ministry was keenly aware that Central Asians did not have recourse to the types of rights and protections in St. Petersburg and London that they had started seeking in Ottoman Iraq and Arabia, and that it would have been unimaginable for Russian authorities to intervene on Celal's behalf in Bukhara. Thus, like contemporary authorities in French Tunisia and Morocco, they sought to curtail the expansion of extraterritorial privileges to individuals with borrowed nationalities and to end the abuse of treaties that were never meant to protect Muslims. Faced with attacks on jurisdictional sovereignty throughout the empire, and still recovering from the disastrous 1877–78 Russo-Ottoman War (which ended in major Ottoman territorial losses in the Balkans), the Foreign Ministry embraced the fiction that protectorates such as Bukhara and Afghanistan were autonomous or semi-sovereign, and countered that even if subjects of these polities were not Ottoman nationals, they were still protected by the caliphate.

The path to this decision is outlined in an 1886 case involving an Afghan migrant in Baghdad, who, after thirty-five years of living as an Ottoman, had tried to become a British national. A few years prior to Celal's unsuccessful experiment with affiliation switching, Hacı Habib had tried something similar in Ottoman Iraq, a province where the British held sway over an extensive system of extraterritorial courts that served mostly Indian pilgrims to Shi'i shrines and the diasporic communities that had formed in the vicinity of these holy sites. Britain's readiness to extend jurisdiction to another group of Muslims—the large community of Afghans in this frontier province—was a worrisome development for the Porte, and prompted it to try to definitively quash this trend.[32] The task of

31. For a comparative study of legal imperialism, see Kayaoğlu, *Legal Imperialism*. Lewis's work on French North Africa is indispensable for understanding the complexity of overlapping and divided sovereignty. Lewis, *Divided Rule*. Also see works cited in n. 11; Lauren Benton, *Law and Colonial Cultures: Legal Regimes in World History, 1400–1900* (Cambridge, UK: Cambridge University Press, 2002); Benton and Ross, *Legal Pluralism and Empires*.

32. HR.TO 369/98, 1 March 1886. On British Indians and consular courts in Iraq, see Stephens, "An Uncertain Inheritance"; Gökhan Çetinsaya, "The Ottoman View of British Presence in Iraq and the Gulf: The Era of Abdülhamid II," *Middle Eastern Studies* 39, no. 2 (2003): 194–203.

figuring out how was given to legal advisors in the Office of Legal Counsel (Hukuk Müşavirliği İstişare Odası), a bureau within the Foreign Ministry staffed by senior legal experts who advised the government on matters related to international law. As Aimee Genell details in her work on the bureau, from its inception circa 1883, it considered a host of complex issues related to extraterritoriality and issued legal opinions that informed policymaking in other organs of government such as the Council of State.[33]

After researching customary law and dominant international legal norms, Ottoman legal advisors maintained that Afghans who had left their country prior to its "annexation" could not claim British nationality ex post facto, and that these migrants preserved their "original" or "real" nationality (*muhaciret halinde ahali-i merkume tabiiyet-i asliyelerini muhafaza ederler*). In formulating this opinion, they drew on a landmark 1881 Foreign Ministry decision that stated explicitly that "Bukharan and Afghan migrants living and traveling in the empire cannot be considered Russian or British subjects if they are not from *nevahi* [administrative units] annexed to Russian Turkestan or India," and that the only protection to which these peoples were entitled was that of the Ottoman state (*Devlet-i Aliyye himayesi tahtında bulunmaları lazım gelir*).[34] While this ostensibly settled the case in question, the bureau issued a more general opinion regarding Muslims who had left their countries long before annexation and settled in the Ottoman Empire. After years of residence as de facto Ottomans, these migrants were subject to Article 9 of the 1869 Ottoman Nationality Law, and, as such, had "absolutely no right to the protection of a foreign state." What this meant for Hacı Habib was that he could not claim British protection, for he had left Afghanistan when it was completely independent and established permanent residence in Iraq.[35]

The bureau next considered whether foreign Muslims who were *not* Ottomans (naturalized, or in accordance with Article 9) and who "originated from

Although the archival record does not reveal why Hacı Habib tried to become a British national, he may have been motivated to do so if he had sons who faced conscription. Cases involving migrants in Iraq and Greater Syria suggest that while first-generation migrants were exempt from serving in the military, their children were not. On conscription, see Mehmet Beşikci, *The Ottoman Mobilization of Manpower in the First World War: Between Voluntarism and Resistance* (Leiden: Brill, 2012). Karen Kern explores citizenship, marriage, and conscription in Iraq. Kern, *Imperial Citizens: Marriage and Citizenship in the Ottoman Frontier Provinces of Iraq* (Syracuse: Syracuse University Press, 2011).

33. On the training and composition of the legal advisors in the Hukuk Müşavirliği, see Aimee Genell, "The Well-Defended Domains: Eurocentric Law and the Making of the Ottoman Office of Legal Counsel," in this volume. For additional background, see *BOA Rehberi* (Istanbul: Başbakanlık Devlet Arşivleri Genel Müdürlüğü, 2010), 381–82.

34. HR.TO 365/86, 27 Jan. 1881.

35. HR.TO 369/98, 1 March 1886.

states and tribes that, while under Russian and British protection, more or less retained their independence and autonomy," could claim the nationality or protection of either empire.[36] Not surprisingly, the answer was again no. Engaging contemporary international law, the bureau held that protectorates were semiautonomous states, and that their subjects were *mahmi*. All existing treaties and capitulatory privileges applied exclusively to "real" European nationals, and not to these protected peoples, who, as the bureau noted, were not to be confused with European protégés.[37] The Hukuk Müşavirliği held that since the 1869 Nationality Law had started to diminish the numbers of Christian protégés, the Porte would not tolerate the rise of a new innovation in the form of Muslims claiming protégé status.

Hacı Habib, like Celal, got nowhere with his claim. The Foreign Ministry would not allow Habib to switch roles and perform as an Englishman on the Ottoman stage. But he had prompted the articulation of a major Ottoman legal decision: Afghans and Bukharans (and later subjects of Chinese Turkestan) were prohibited from claiming rights in the Ottoman Empire that they could not enjoy at home—whether "home" was an emirate they had left prior to its annexation, or an imperial protectorate or territory where the local population did not have the rights of imperial citizens. The idea that protectorates were independent—which the French employed to maintain their rule in Tunisia—served as the scaffolding for the Porte's position that Bukharans and Afghans were not entitled to the same rights as Russian and British nationals, as well as colonial subjects of Russian Turkestan and British India. While it would prove difficult to enforce, this differentiation informed Ottoman policy through World War I. But despite the nomenclature employed by the Ottoman government, "the protected" were not so protected. First the 1869 law had categorized them as foreigners and excluded them from enjoying certain rights that had previously been customary among Sunni Muslims, and now the Porte did not recognize them as nationals of any state other than the protectorates from which they originated. However, these polities—Afghanistan, Bukhara, and Chinese Turkestan—had no power to independently conduct foreign policy or negotiate international agreements.[38] And while the bureau was adamant that Habib had no rights as a foreign national, it did not elaborate what it meant to be a foreign Muslim "under the exclusive protection of the Ottoman caliphate" or how this argument fit into the framework of international law.

36. The reference to tribes here should be understood in the context of Russian subjecthood/extraterritoriality, where prominent tribal and clan leaders were sometimes given subjecthood rights in negotiations for colonial expansion.

37. HR.TO 369/98, 1 March 1886.

38. In the case of Afghanistan, the British had made this very clear by sending the Porte a copy of the agreement signed with the emir. For example, see HR.TO 264/51, 8 Sept. 1890.

Despite the intended finality of the decision, Russian and British consuls and their subjects continued to press the issue of extraterritoriality. Like the Ottomans, the Russian government also tried (unsuccessfully) to establish a precedent that would put an end to the continual diplomatic contestation arising from individual incidents. For example, in 1895—and again in 1911—the Russian ambassador to Istanbul notified the Ottoman Foreign Ministry that the Bukharan emir wanted his subjects to enjoy Russian protection abroad, and that henceforth Bukharans would "enjoy the protection of Russian consuls" and "the protection assured by international law," that is, the Capitulations.[39] The note presented the issue as a *fait accompli* and did not provide an explanation as to why the emir's purported request should entail the extension of capitulatory rights to all Bukharans in the empire. Was there a valid legal basis for the extension of these privileges? Had other great powers (*düvel-i muazzama*) been notified?

The Foreign Ministry posed these questions to diplomats in St. Petersburg, Paris, Berlin, London, Rome, and Vienna in a series of missives in 1895. The responses made clear that Russia had notified only the Porte, reaffirming its concerns about the dangers of budging on the question of Bukharans' rights to foreign protection. While the Foreign Ministry did not oppose the provisioning of financial or logistical consular patronage to pilgrims and travelers in need, and was generally silent when Russian consuls paid for pilgrims' steamship tickets back home, it did not want to establish any legal precedent for allowing Muslim colonial subjects to benefit from the Capitulations. Ultimately, the Foreign Ministry concluded that Bukharans were not "real subjects" (*veritable sujets*), reaffirming the Hukuk Müşavirliği's differentiation between real subjects and *mahmi*. The investigation also confirmed that the "protection question"—as the archival dossier was labeled—had crystallized as a major issue.

However, as evidenced by Russia's second attempt in 1911 to formalize the tsar's protection of Bukharans, the Porte was not able to put the question to rest. It is also worth noting that the Ottoman Foreign Ministry explicitly expressed its lack of geopolitical interest in Central Asia and made clear that its assertion of caliphal protection was only in response to Russia's claims. As one statesman bluntly put it in 1895, the region had never been central to Ottoman interests or under the empire's sphere of influence.[40] And, in his correspondence to Osman Nejami Pasha (a diplomat posted in Berlin) in 1911, the legal advisor Hakkı Pasha expressed his frustration with Russia's continuing attempts to expand its power through Bukharans. In a pointed comment about international law that also captured how some Ottoman statesmen regarded these colonial subjects, he wrote:

39. HR.SYS 1304, Gömlek 2, June 1895.
40. See, for example, HR. SYS 1304, Gömlek 2, for a 15 Oct. 1895 memorandum issued by the Hukuk Müşavirliği.

"Great Britain has many subjects in Africa—are the Germans to accept that the negroes should enjoy the prerogatives of British subjects in Germany?"[41]

The Protection Question in the Hijaz

Not all Ottoman government officials thought like Hakkı Pasha. This was especially true in the Hijaz, where resolution of the protection question was particularly fraught. Home to the holy cities of Mecca and Medina, the province had been key to legitimizing the government's Islamic credentials since the early sixteenth century. During the Hamidian period (1876–1909), it became the linchpin of the sultan's claims to a diffuse form of universal religio-political and "spiritual" authority.[42] But the sultan-caliph's actual power in the province was tenuous and sovereignty was shared with the sharif of Mecca. As Michael C. Low's chapter on extraterritoriality in the Hijaz makes clear, the Porte had good reason to fear foreign interventions. Britain's continual insistence that the Porte honor the Capitulations in Mecca and Medina and schemes to prop up the sharif as an alternate sovereign, were fundamentally at odds with its pledges to guarantee Ottoman sovereignty at the 1856 Treaty of Paris.[43] With the threat of the Capitulations reaching the gates of Mecca and Medina and fears that wealthy foreigners could act as a fifth column on behalf of European colonial powers, the Porte began to take steps to prevent non-Ottoman subjects from amassing more power.[44]

One of the earliest fields in which the government sought to limit the rights of non-Ottomans was property holding. As Selim Deringil has argued, Ottoman statesmen began to voice concerns about foreign Muslims' accumulation of property in the Hijaz in the 1860s.[45] As early as 1861, the Council of Ministers

41. HR.SYS 1304, Gömlek 2, 16 Dec. 1911.

42. Deringil, *The Well-Protected Domains*. On Ottoman rule in the Hijaz, see William Ochsenwald, *Religion, Society, and the State in Arabia: The Hijaz under Ottoman Control, 1840–1908* (Columbus: Ohio State University Press, 1984). The claim to "spiritual authority" dated to the 1774 Treaty of Küçük Kaynarca, which the Ottomans signed with Russia after the loss of the Crimea. The treaty recognized the tsar as the protector of Orthodox Christians in Ottoman lands and the sultan-caliph's authority over Russian Muslims. For a discussion of the sultan's claims to spiritual authority, see Can, *Spiritual Subjects*.

43. In addition to Low's chapter in this volume, a growing body of research explores how engagement with international law informed Ottoman governance in autonomous and "exceptional" provinces. Two important examples include Aimee Genell, "'Empire by Law': Ottoman Sovereignty and the British Occupation of Egypt, 1882–1923" (PhD diss., Columbia University, 2013); Mostafa Minawi, *The Ottoman Scramble for Africa: Empire and Diplomacy in the Sahara and the Hijaz* (Stanford: Stanford University Press, 2016).

44. Low elaborates that the Council used the autonomous status of the holy cities "to deflect and circumvent the internationally binding requirements of the Capitulations and prevent the application of foreign protection beyond Jidda." Low, "Unfurling the Flag of Extraterritoriality," 314.

45. Deringil, *The Well-Protected Domains*, 53–63.

in Istanbul warned the emir of Mecca and the governor of Jidda that long-term pious residents of the holy cities (*mücavirin*) should not be permitted foreign protection and that Javanese and Indian Muslims should only be allowed to settle in the cities if they agreed to abide by Sharia law.[46] These warnings took the shape of legislation in 1867, when the Porte prohibited foreigners from buying immoveable property in the Hijaz. The Law on the Rights of Foreign Citizens to Own Land (Tebaa-yı Ecnebiyenin Emlake Mutasarrıf Olmaları Hakkında Kanun) had actually formalized the rights of foreigners to purchase real estate throughout the empire, but made an exception for the Hijaz due to sensitivities about foreign intervention.[47]

Over the next three decades, the central government sent a series of decrees directing authorities in Mecca, Medina, and Jidda to enforce prohibitions on land sales and regulations on naturalization. However, these efforts met with continual resistance. Provincial authorities contended that honorable men—some who had been treated as Ottoman subjects for centuries, and many others who were deeply entangled in the religious and economic life of Mecca and Medina—were not foreigners.[48] The "state" was not united in the view that Bukharans and Chinese Muslims could become "stalking horses for European political subversion and extraterritorial control."[49] As a result, Central Asians continued to purchase and endow land with the aid of local judges and officials, who allowed them to act through guarantors and legal proxies who were prominent members of local communities. To the Porte's dismay, between 1877 and 1879 the Medina com-

46. For the 1861 decision, see A.}MKT.UM 511/80 (25 R 1278/30 Sept. 1861). Low also quotes this ruling in "The Mechanics of Mecca," 136–37.

47. For the law in its entirety and a summary of foreigners' property rights and the central government's concerns about the extension of capitulations, see BEO 4338/325334 (17 Jan. 1915). To preempt European intervention, the law stipulated that any future disputes or legal matters involving property would be subject to Ottoman legal jurisdiction alone. It also required states to sign separate protocols in order for their subjects to benefit from the law. Though selectively enforced, this stipulation could be used to prevent *mahmi* from acquiring real estate, since their home countries could not independently sign such international agreements.

48. It is common to come across phrases in these sources that acknowledge that Central Asians had "until recently" (at various points between the 1880s and 1910s) been treated as Ottomans. An 1887 Meclis-i Vükela decision, for example, begins by stating that, "even though Central Asians residing in the empire have until recently been treated as Ottomans..." MV 17/38 (30 Ca 1304/24 February 1887).

49. Deringil's analysis draws on a source in the YA.RES 15/38 file, which states that, "If we remain indifferent to the accumulation of property by devious means in the hands of foreign Muslims, with the passage of time we may find that much of the Holy Lands have been acquired by the subjects of foreign powers. Then, the foreigners, as is their wont, after lying in waiting for some time, will suddenly be upon us at the slightest opportunity and excuse and will proceed to make the most preposterous claims." This citation accurately reflects the Şura-yı Devlet's position but, I argue, does not fully represent debates within the government. Deringil, *The Well-Protected Domains*, 60.

mander approved the sale of twenty-four houses and one mill, and Meccan officials authorized the sale of ninety houses and 290 parcels of land to foreigners.[50] An ensuing investigation placed the blame on Sharia court judges and other officials who derived income from fees associated with transferring and endowing real estate. The Council of State issued a strong statement reiterating the need for the prohibition and calling for the punishment of officials who flouted the law. They did not, however, order the confiscation of the illegally acquired properties because, as they put it, doing so would not "suit the glory of the exalted caliphate." Instead, the council asked for a register of all of the properties in question and recommended further deliberation on the proper course of action. There is no evidence that they were ever seized.[51] The council's admission is an important example of how the need to maintain Islamic legitimacy hampered effective enforcement of the law.

As Will Hanley observes in the Egyptian context, legal nationality needed time to take root. Imperial statesmen and bureaucrats had difficulty imposing their view of what it meant to be an Ottoman or a foreigner, and in replacing local (*mahalli, yerli*) forms of belonging with imperial or national ones.[52] Where local authorities saw pious Muslims engaged in everyday life, the Porte saw potential chinks in their armor against the Capitulations. Moreover, the Porte's position that some foreign Muslims were exclusively protected by the caliphate—with no clear explication of what this meant in legal terms—may have reinforced the notion that being a Sunni Muslim was still integral to membership in the Ottoman Empire. However the Porte chose to classify Muslims from outside the empire, many Ottoman subjects still considered Central Asians locals, and imperial legislation and legal decisions emanating from Istanbul had limited success in convincing provincial authorities that they should be treated otherwise.

The prohibition on land sales also proved difficult to implement due to the historical role that foreign Muslims played in building housing and renting it to their compatriots. If Central Asians could no longer buy land or property, who was going to meet the housing needs of the thousands of people traveling to Arabia each year? This was the question the Hijaz Provincial Assembly posed to Istanbul in early 1882 when a wealthy Kashgari named Abdurresul Efendi was prevented from building a philanthropic foundation in Medina that would provide lodging to pilgrims.[53] The 1867 law had banned sales of land and immoveable

50. YA.RES 15/38 (5 C 1299/24 April 1882). Cezmi Eraslan cites similar numbers in *II. Abdülhamid ve İslam Birliği: Osmanlı Devleti'nin İslam Siyaseti, 1856–1908* (Istanbul: Ötüken, 1991), 31.
51. YA.RES 15/38.
52. In his work on Alexandria, Hanley argues that administrators and bureaucrats met with extensive difficulty in replacing local (*mahalli, yerli*) as a focal point of identity. See *Identifying with Nationality*.
53. YA.RES 15/38, 24 S 1299 (15 January 1882).

property not only for commercial or private use but also for Islamic endowments. In correspondence with Istanbul, the members of the assembly proposed an interim measure that would permit Kashgaris to buy and sell land acquired within the last two years. More importantly, they reiterated that subjects of a Muslim sovereign should not be deprived of rights to landholding. Although Kashgar was no longer ruled by Yaqub Beg (r. 1865–77)—who had recognized the sultan as his sovereign, and minted coins and read the Friday sermon in his name—they contended that people from the city and its environs did not have relations with or citizenship in "a foreign state."[54] This suggests that they equated foreign rule primarily with Christian Europe or that they thought Kashgar was still under Muslim rule.

Local attempts at negotiation with the central government largely fell on deaf ears. Instead of complying with the spirit of the law, officials in the Hijaz continued to sell land, but added window dressing that they believed would nominally satisfy the Porte's demands. This is apparent in a 1902 case involving irregular naturalization attempts and involvement of local agents, which came to the attention of the Interior Ministry via the Medina garrison commander. Two Bukharans (Hoca Abdülhadi and Molla Ustan) had purchased land in Mecca worth 4,150 lira and then endowed it as waqf, acting on behalf of the alleged shaykh al-Islam of Bukhara, Mir Bedreddin bin Sadreddin. The act triggered concern that highly placed foreign Muslims such as Mir Bedreddin could evade the law, leading to an investigation that pointed to a cover-up.[55] The Hijaz governor said the shaykh had been given Ottoman identity papers (tezkire-i osmaniye) on 17 April 1901, but there was no record of his naturalization in the Citizenship Affairs Bureau. The Interior Ministry next inquired on what basis the shaykh had been given the said papers. This time, Hijaz authorities responded that Mir Bedreddin was a mücavir, and that his request for a tezkire had been approved "in the recognized way"—that is, through the provision of an oath and guarantee by an honorable member of the community (the Bukharan pilgrimage leader

54. Until the early 1880s, Kashgar was technically under Ottoman suzerainty. Kim, Holy War in China; Kemal Karpat, "Yakub Bey's Relations with the Ottoman Sultans: A Reinterpretation," Cahiers du Monde russe et soviétique 32 (1991): 17–32.

55. DH.MKT 543/13, 18 July 1902. The question of Mir Bedreddin's identity is thorny. He may have been the son of the chief kadı (qazi al-quzat) of Bukhara, Mulla Mir Sadr al-Din Khuttalani, but there is no evidence that this individual ever went to the Hijaz. According to Robert D. McChesney, he may have had a surrogate acting in his name, or—in a twist on Martin Guerre—the Mir Bedreddin in this case may have been an impostor adopting a well-known but not easily verifiable identity. On the chief kadı and his son, see Edward Allworth et al., eds., The Personal History of a Bukharan Intellectual: The Diary of Muhammad-Sharif-i Sadr- Ziya (Leiden: Brill, 2004), esp. 97 n50.

Şeyh Ahmed).[56] The Hijaz governor's office also claimed they had no knowledge of Mir Bedreddin's position—which given Şeyh Ahmed's involvement seemed unlikely—and that he had since left Mecca and died. As the inquiry progressed, the details became even more confusing. It seemed that Mir Bedreddin had never been naturalized and that his agents had obtained the identity papers of another Bukharan with the same name and then used them to purchase the land. Every reported method of legalizing the sale had been unlawful. But given the Porte's sensitivity to its prestige, it did not risk compromising the "glory of the caliphate" by annulling the transaction. Given that Mir Bedreddin had died, it was fortuitous that he had endowed the land, since the Russian consul was less likely to demand the right to adjudicate the shaykh's estate.

The central problem with land sales to Bukharans was that European authorities often did not recognize the naturalization of their subjects, particularly when there were large estates involved. Even when Ottoman authorities provided proof of Ottoman nationality, Russian authorities challenged the legality of what we might term Central Asian citizenship or nationality conversions (*tebdil-i tabiiyet*). As Eric Lohr and James H. Meyer have shown, tsarist officials insisted that their subjects had to first renounce their citizenship in Russia before obtaining Ottoman nationality. This meant that people who decided to naturalize after arriving in the sultan's domains had to travel to distant Russian cities and file expensive paperwork in order to "legally" become Ottomans—a costly and laborious enterprise that few were likely to undertake.[57] Effectively, these would-be Ottomans were unable to break free of the bonds of their Russian subjecthood. This was true even in death, and especially if they had amassed property in the Ottoman Empire.[58] While a full discussion of Russia's insistence on preserving subjects falls outside the scope of this chapter, the salient point is that Russian reluctance to accept Ottoman naturalization rendered the Porte increasingly cautious about allowing Central Asians to buy land and to obtain Ottoman identity papers without prior approval from Russian consular officials.

The insistence of European consuls in Jidda (and beyond) on the right to regulate the legal affairs of their subjects was not only about protecting the interests of heirs of deceased men and women under their jurisdiction. In the 1900s,

---

56. The Bukharan pilgrimage leader provided the guarantee (*kefalet*). This was an official appointed by the sharif of Mecca and a member of the most important guilds in the Hijaz.

57. Lohr argues that a defining feature of citizenship policy through 1914 was an "attract and hold" approach that sought to counter "a persistent shortage of people and a sense that immigration and naturalization helped expand the economic power of the empire, while emigration and denaturalization were to be avoided for the same reason." Lohr, *Russian Citizenship*, 5 and Ch. 4. James H. Meyer makes a similar argument in "Immigration, Return and the Politics of Citizenship: Russian Muslims in the Ottoman Empire, 1860–1914," *IJMES* 39, no. 1 (2007): 15–32.

58. Smiley, "The Burdens of Subjecthood."

the British and the Russians also tried to extend their protection to Muslims from Chinese Turkestan, making clear that the zeal to protect the dead was motivated in no small part by broader imperial ambitions. In 1908, for example, the Russian consul in Jidda claimed the authority to settle the affairs of a deceased pilgrim from Kashgar.[59] In a letter to Istanbul, the Hijaz provincial commander Mehmed Kazım Pasha explained that when the man died, local authorities followed customary Ottoman practices from "days of old" and absorbed his estate into the treasury. But the Russian consul objected, claiming that the pilgrim was under Russian protection (*taht-ı himaye*).[60] In a clear-cut yet misguided instance of "speaking shari'a" to Ottoman authorities,[61] he berated them for acting against Islamic law and insinuated that the heirs of the deceased man included orphaned children—perhaps thinking he was bolstering his argument by emphasizing the special status of orphans in Islamic law. "It might be the case that when their father died," he wrote, "far from home (*diyar-ı gurbet*) and in the path of God . . . orphans back home were suffering and in need."[62]

That might very well have been the case. But Mehmed Kazim Pasha was not moved. Nor were the legal advisors in Istanbul, who determined that the Russian consulate "had no right to seize the estate in order to send it to the heirs of the Chinese hajji who died in Jidda," and "no authority to intervene in the affairs of Kashgaris or Afghans." They advised the government to find another way to regulate these types of estates so as not to invite continual foreign intervention. The pasha was directed to transfer such estates to the Porte in the future.[63] More importantly, the Hukuk Müşavirliği now argued that Muslims from China—like Afghans and Bukharans—were exclusively under the protection of the Ottoman caliphate. This endeavor to stake a claim to an "unprotected" population, however, left Muslims from Chinese Turkestan with no recourse to foreign consular support and no clear sense of what it meant to be under Ottoman protection. The Hukuk Müşavirliği had still not elaborated what caliphal protection meant in

---

59. According to a 1908 report from Jidda, the Russian consul there reported that Chinese Muslims claimed Russian protection when it suited them, and suggested to the central government that it would make sense to formally assume responsibility over Kashgaris. *Fond* 143, *opis* 491, *delo* 2305, Chinese in Turkey. I thank David Brophy for sharing this source with me.
60. DH. MKT 2736/37, 10 Feb. 1909; DH.MKT 2691/30, 24 Dec. 1908. Also, in 1908, the Ministry of Foreign Affairs stated that Kashgaris were under the protection of the *hilafet-i mukaddese-i islamiye* (holy Islamic caliphate), but did not engage at all with tsarist arguments about Sharia. HR.HMŞ.İŞO 194/68 (30 Dec. 1908); DH.MKT 2691/30 (24 Dec. 1908).
61. Adapting Stephen Kotkin's idea of "speaking Bolshevik" (*Magnetic Mountain: Stalinism as a Civilization* [Berkeley: University of California Press, 1995]), Meyer uses the term "speaking shari'a" to show how Russia and Russian Muslims articulated social, economic, and political conflicts. Meyer, "Speaking Sharia to the State: Muslim Protesters, Tsarist Officials, and the Islamic Discourses of Late Imperial Russia," *Kritika* 14 (2013): 485–505.
62. DH.MKT 2691/30, 24 Dec. 1908; DH.MKT 2736/37, 10 Feb. 1909.
63. HR.HMŞ.İŞO 194/68, 30 Dec. 1908; DH.MKT 2736/37, 10 Feb. 1909.

the legal and diplomatic sense, and in the framework of international law. This ambiguity may have been an intentional strategy for leaving the door open to a future articulation of the caliph's authority.

Many long-term residents of Mecca and Medina, it seemed, could not opt out of being foreign Muslims or become naturalized Ottoman subjects, leaving them stuck in a sort of legal limbo. This is clear in a 1913 incident during which the Medina garrison commander lamented that he had been waiting for a response from the Jidda Russian consul for over a year about a Central Asian resident who wanted to become an Ottoman subject. The commander voiced his frustration that Russian consular officials did not recognize Ottoman naturalization procedures, and explained that, as a result, local Muslims were complaining about delayed real estate deals and housing problems. Their attempts at becoming Ottomans were also blocked by the Porte's insistence that they furnish proof that Russia had relinquished them as subjects.[64] As in the 1882 case involving Abdurresul Efendi of Kashgar, the view from Medina was that Bukharans and other Central Asians who had resided in the empire since "days of old" were locals and should be permitted to buy land. The garrison commander cited the practice of allowing Tunisians to do so, contingent upon swearing oaths that they would not seek foreign protection in any future disputes, and that failure to abide by these oaths would result in confiscation of their property and immediate exile.[65] But his letter suggested that even these measures were unnecessary, and that resolving the matter was urgent for the local population, public improvements, and nothing less than the progress of the country.[66] The Porte, however, did not agree.

Later that year, the secretary to the minister of foreign affairs communicated to the Interior Ministry that certain pilgrims and *mücavirin* were trying to revert to their original nationality to claim foreign protections. He admonished his colleagues to enact strict precautions in granting Ottoman nationality in order to avoid "serious dangers."[67] The measures he prescribed, however, were not markedly different from procedures laid out in the 1867 regulations on foreigners' property rights, the 1869 Ottoman Nationality Law, or numerous legal opinions and decrees that had been issued since the 1880s. This was, in effect, old news. It was now the Foreign Ministry that lamented its situation. Authorities held that each country should be able to determine independently who could become a subject, and that the Ottomans had never recognized Russian procedural

64. DH.SN.THR 54/45, document dated 5 Ca 1331 (22 April 1913).
65. DH.SNTHR 54/45, copy of letter from Medine Muhafiz ve Kumandanlığı 15 Ca [1]331.
66. DH.SN.THR 54/45 nos. 14 and 16, correspondence between Foreign Ministry and Medine Muhafız. Officials in Medina and the province at large repeatedly advocated on behalf of the needs of long-term residents, raising questions about relationships among the Central Asian community, the guild of pilgrimage guides, and the sharif. This might suggest a type of patron–protégé relationship with mutual economic benefit.
67. DH.SN.THR 54/15, Hicaz Vilayet to Dahiliye, 2 Şubat [1]329.

requirements in this regard. But the point was moot: tsarist consuls continued to intervene on behalf of Muslims they considered their subjects, and for over three decades the ministry had not been able to effectively challenge their claims.[68] With the possibility of another war with Russia on the horizon, the Council of State reiterated its concerns that allowing foreign Muslims to purchase property could cause them to act against Ottoman interests.[69]

And yet despite the council's insistence, authorities in the Hijaz continued to push back. They pledged to follow the decree, while actively questioning its logic and insisting that Central Asians, particularly *mücavirin*, were not foreign. "Whether they themselves or their father and grandfathers married and established families here," wrote the Medina commander, "they had become part of the *ahali* [the people]." In earlier times, he wrote, these Muslims had been able to purchase land and real estate; there was "no reason" that they should be exempt now.[70] Protection and nationality had become as much intraempire issues as international ones, as local communities asserted their own understandings of belonging and what it meant to be a foreigner against those of the metropole. As a result, the Porte struggled to implement policies that limited the rights of "protected peoples" and was left continually vulnerable to Russian and British infringements on Ottoman sovereignty.

Conclusion, or the Limits of Protection

As recent scholarship has shown, revolutions in steam and print technology and the expansion of global markets, particularly after the opening of the Suez Canal in 1869, led to unprecedented flows of people, goods, and ideas across the Muslim world.[71] But, as Valeska Huber argues, this era of heightened connections was marked as much by the deceleration of certain types of movement as it was by acceleration. Biopolitical controls such as quarantine and passports, and the hardening of political boundaries and identities, created new chokepoints that slowed down many migrants and travelers.[72] Huber's analysis of the tensions inherent in globalization and attention to how "distinction[s] between categories of movement became a central instrument to speed up the movement of some of

---

68. DH.SN.THR 54/45, Hariciye to Dahiliye, 16 L 1331.
69. DH.SN.THR 54/45, Hariciye to Dahiliye, 19 S 1332.
70. Ibid.
71. Notable works on this broad topic include James Gelvin and Nile Green, eds., *Global Muslims in the Age of Steam and Print* (Berkeley: University of California Press, 2014); Nile Green, "Spacetime and the Industrial Journey West: Industrial Communications and the Making of the 'Muslim World,'" *American Historical Review* 118, no. 2 (2013): 401–29; Eric Tagliacozzo, *The Longest Journey: Southeast Asians and the Pilgrimage to Mecca* (Oxford: Oxford University Press, 2013).
72. Valeska Huber, *Channelling Mobilities: Migration and Globalisation in the Suez Canal Region and Beyond, 1869–1914* (Cambridge, UK: Cambridge University Press, 2013).

them, such as troops and colonial travelers, and develop a bureaucratic apparatus to control and if necessary detain or repatriate others," is instructive for thinking about evolving dynamics between the late Ottoman state and significant segments of the *umma*.[73] Even as conceptions of time and space shrank, new hajj hubs emerged, and Muslims from so-called peripheries became more connected to the central Islamic lands, non-Ottoman Muslims in the last Islamic empire were concurrently becoming legal outsiders. If 1869 represented a watershed for transregional mobility, as this chapter has shown, it also marked a major legal rupture. While the notion of foreignness was subject to multiple and conflicting interpretations that informed praxis and experience, nationality as a legal category was incontrovertibly becoming a defining feature of Muslims' status in the empire.

This shift was a consequence of the Tanzimat reforms, which began to create a citizenship boundary—"the line between members and nonmembers" of the polity—that fundamentally challenged the structure of Ottoman society.[74] The reforms also altered the relationship between the sultan and what I term his spiritual subjects, the Muslims over whom the Ottoman state claimed to wield an imprecisely defined spiritual and political authority. In a sense, the Tanzimat reforms began to sever the link between the constituency of the sultanate and that of the caliphate: the sultan was now the sovereign of a territorially bounded empire where religious distinctions among Ottoman subjects were theoretically leveled, while the caliph claimed to have authority that extended beyond Ottoman subjects to foreign Muslims. However, in reality there was no separation within the Ottoman government reflecting this division. Moreover, despite the pan-Islamic rhetoric associated with this period—as well as the position detailed here that certain *ecanib-i müslimin* were protected only by the caliphate—religion and religious identities did not dictate *realpolitik* and the caliph's protection had very real limits. Even as authorities in Mecca and Medina offered plausible reasons why Central Asians should not be considered foreigners, the Porte maintained that they could not enjoy rights in the empire simply by dint of being Sunni Muslims. As distances across the Muslim world were shrinking, the Ottoman central government was introducing new distinctions among Muslim colonial subjects to combat the expansion of a legal order that threatened the empire's sovereignty. These distinctions, in turn, had important repercussions for Central Asians.

The changes brought on by mass pilgrimage, concurrent processes of exclusion and inclusion, and the expansion of extraterritoriality and the protégé

---

73. Ibid., 6
74. In his analysis of naturalization and migration policies aimed at Russian and Soviet citizens, Lohr defines the citizenship boundary as "the line between members and nonmembers, on the rules and practices that define the boundary, and on the various ways citizenship was acquired, lost, ascribed, or removed." Lohr, *Russian Citizenship*, 3.

system necessitated a steep learning curve for people traveling across empires, whether they were permanent migrants or pilgrims. The literature on the resulting legal pluralism has commonly understood these processes as demonstrating how ordinary people navigated, negotiated, and manipulated flexible identities, and how they pursued strategies to maximize subjecthood rights. Without a doubt, contested and overlapping spheres of sovereignty enabled many people with one foot in two or more empires to maximize economic and political gain.[75] But this is only part of the picture. Although many migrants quickly learned to work within the interstices of imperial mobility regulations and to live as dual nationals in Ottoman and Russian territories, these strategies were not uniformly available to all Muslims, and particularly not to those from protectorates or empires that did not have diplomatic relations with the Ottoman Empire. Rather than overstate the potential for negotiation in a search for subaltern agency (which implies that the parties were on equal footing), this chapter's exploration of Central Asians in the Ottoman Empire cautions us to recognize how plural legal orders also constrained rights and opportunities.[76] The Porte's view that Bukharans were not real Russian subjects, coupled with the fact that Afghans or Turkic peoples from Qing China lacked a recognized foreign nationality, impels us to recognize that these liminal subjects could not benefit from extraterritorial rights and battles over jurisdiction without recourse to various ruses.[77] The stories of Celal and Hacı Habib attest to the limits of their power to negotiate or exploit Russo- and Anglo-Ottoman legal and jurisdictional ambiguities. This limitation also applied to the men and women who could not renounce their Russian subjecthood, as well as to those whom Ottoman statesmen did not recognize as legal nationals of any empire—Russian, British, or Ottoman. Central Asian "protected peoples" were effectively doubly excluded in legal terms: first

---

75. James Meyer shows how Russian Muslims held onto their Russian nationality in Ottoman lands, and how they utilized borrowed (or purchased) identity papers to pass as Ottomans. Meyer, *Turks across Empires: Marketing Muslim Identity in the Russian-Ottoman Borderlands, 1856–1915* (Oxford: Oxford University Press, 2014). In an article on Alexandria, Ziad Fahmy describes consular agents as "borderlanders par excellence" and "legal chameleons" who "used the capitulatory system to manipulate their official identities, juggling at times two or three 'nationalities.'" Fahmy, "Jurisdictional Borderlands: Extraterritoriality and 'Legal Chameleons' in Precolonial Alexandria, 1840–1870," *Comparative Studies in Society and History* 55 (2013): 305–29.

76. This supports Smiley's argument that interimperial mobility regulations "hardened the empires' human and geographic boundaries," and could result in foreign subjecthood becoming a liability. Smiley, "The Burdens of Subjecthood," 73.

77. On liminal subjects in other settings, see Erin G. Carlston, *Double Agents: Espionage, Literature, and Liminal Citizens* (New York: Columbia University Press, 2013); Anne Haour, *Outsiders and Strangers: An Archaeology of Liminality in West Africa* (Oxford: Oxford University Press, 2013); Andrew Arsan, *Interlopers of Empire: The Lebanese Diaspora in Colonial French West Africa* (New York: Oxford University Press, 2014).

designated as non-Ottomans by the state, then labeled *mahmis* who did not bear the rights of European nationals or protégés, including capitulatory rights. The claim of being protected by the caliphate could even result in the denial of rights via Islamic law; in the 1908 dispute over the deceased Kashgari pilgrim's estate, for example, the man's legal heirs—who may or may not have included orphans— would never receive their share of his wealth.

Nationality slowly started to occupy a more important place in people's lives, and became a major preoccupation for the Ottomans. Legal advisors approached each protection case that came before them with the question "My countryman, what is your real nationality?" But like Manço's interlocutor, they were often dissatisfied with the answers they received. Despite decades of trying to defend Ottoman sovereignty by working within the system of international law, the Porte met with only limited success in preventing the expansion of extraterritoriality and protection. And even as nationality seemed to be the question on everyone's lips, it was by no means universally clear what this term meant. For the *mücavirin* waiting throughout 1913 to become Ottomans, nationality was about settling down, buying land, and, possibly, living a pious life in Medina. For officials at the Porte it was a legal status tied to concerns about jurisdictional sovereignty. For people desiring to transact real estate deals or judges and provincial administrators in the Hijaz, it was not always apparent what was at issue: why were people from Bukhara, Afghanistan, and Kashgar not able to enjoy rights their forefathers had—especially if they were under the protection of the caliph? Contestation, confusion, and diplomatic struggles had resulted in a type of legal limbo in which many "protected peoples" bore the burdens of colonial pressures and jurisdictional disputes. As the Central Asians in Medina waited for their naturalization to be approved, they had no national identity to use to their advantage in any legal forum, and no clear sense of what it meant to be protected by the caliph. Was there a passport or a consul that would serve them? If asked where they were from, they would likely have said "Bukhara the Noble" or the "City of the Prophet" (*medīnat al-nabī*), inspiring intense frustration among Ottoman legal advisors in Istanbul who were interested in their legal nationality. In trying to navigate the international legal order, foreign Muslims and Ottoman statesmen alike were joined in an increasingly arduous pursuit that often led to one dead end after another.

7 An Uncertain Inheritance: The Imperial Travels of Legal Migrants, from British India to Ottoman Iraq[*]

Julia Stephens

LIKE MANY NINETEENTH-CENTURY travelers, Iqbal al-Daulah, a cousin of the nawab of the Indian princely state of Awadh, navigated multiple legal systems as he migrated across Asia, Europe, and the Middle East. Living through the absorption of Awadh into the expanding British Empire, he eventually joined a community of Indian Shias in Ottoman Iraq, which regularly used British consular courts. While still in India, Iqbal al-Daulah composed a tribute in Persian and English to British justice. He described British courts in the following laudatory terms: "What Ease is afforded to Petitioners! The Doors of the numerous Courts being open, if any by reason of his dark fate, should be disappointed in the attainment of his desire, in one Court, in another he may obtain the Victory and Succeed."[1] Indeed, Iqbal al-Daulah secured a sizeable pension and knighthood from the British government. Yet, at the end of his life he had lost faith in British courts. In his will he lamented: "British courts are uncertain, stock in trade of bribery, wrong, delay...the seekers of redress, are captives of the paw of the Court officials; and business goes on by bribery not to be counted or described."[2] Despite Iqbal al-Daulah's words of caution, his friends and relatives became enmeshed in legal battles over his inheritance in British courts in India and Ottoman Iraq. In doing so, they joined the crowds of British colonial subjects which flooded the courts, enduring expense and annoyance despite the prospect of uncertain outcomes.

Iqbal al-Daulah's musings on British colonial law were shaped by his experience living in the frontier zones of multiple systems of imperial law. While

[*]This chapter was originally published in *Law and History Review* 32, no. 4 (2014): 749–72, and it is reprinted here with the kind permission of Cambridge University Press. I am grateful to Fahad Bishara, Rohit De, Iza Hussin, Riyad Koya, Johan Mathew, Renisa Mawani, Emma Rothschild, the editor and reviewers of the *Law & History Review* for their helpful comments on drafts of the original article, and to Lâle Can and Michael Christopher Low for the invitation to revisit these themes from the perspective of Ottoman legal encounters.
1. Iqbal al-Daulah, *Iqbal-i Farang: Dar Shamma-yi Siyar-i Ahl-i Farang ba Farhang* (Calcutta: Matba-yi Tabi, 1249 AH), 45–47.
2. Translation of Will of Late Nawab Sir Ikbal-ud-Daula, 21, in National Archives of India (hereafter NAI)/Foreign/Internal A/June 1888/Nos. 216–40.

The Subjects of Ottoman International Law (2020): 124–145
DOI: 10.2979/subjectsottomaninternationallaw.0.0.08

the contributions to this volume primarily focus on Ottoman legal worlds, this chapter explores how the Ottoman Empire served as a transnational legal laboratory, in which shifting conceptions of sovereignty, territoriality, and nationality were simultaneously made and remade by multiple empires and the mobile subjects, like Iqbal al-Daulah, who navigated between them. Viewing imperial legal regimes from the perspective of these mobile subjects as they traversed frontier spaces provides a strikingly different perspective on law's logics than those presented in legal treatises written from the centers of empire.

For example, Iqbal al-Daulah emphasized the flexibility of British law, although his earlier faith in the opportunities this malleability presented faded into frustration with its uncertainty and corruption. This picture of British justice stood in stark contrast to official visions of British colonial law. James Mill succinctly captured the goal of colonial law when he argued that it must deliver justice with "Clearness, certainty, promptitude, cheapness...."[3] For Utilitarian reformers like Mill one of the greatest gifts Britain could bestow on its colonies was an ordered and efficient legal system that would direct human behavior towards social goods. British officials believed that certainty was particularly important in colonial legal systems, like India, that catered to diverse populations and thus relied on multiple sources of law. As Thomas Macaulay, the first president of the Indian Law Commission, argued, "Our principle is simply this: uniformity where you can have it; diversity where you must have it; but in all cases certainty."[4] Thus, where a single unified system was not possible, colonial law strengthened legal hierarchies and divisions to deliver predictable results. The promised benefits of legal certainty powered the globalization of European law, both through the formal spread of empire and through the modernizing legal reforms non-European powers pursued to stave off colonization. Along with maps, censuses, and dictionaries, law codes recorded cultural and religious differences while disciplining them to conform to modern legal rationality.

Yet, echoing Iqbal al-Daulah's observations, scholars in recent years have emphasized the ambiguity and flexibility of colonial law, unsettling a simplistic picture of the totalizing power of colonial knowledge. This shifting analysis has often placed greater emphasis on studying actual legal cases, revealing that the workings of colonial courts were more complex and varied than was apparent from studying legislation and legal texts alone. This scholarship has highlighted the agency of colonial subjects and challenged simplistic narratives of top-down

---

3. James Mill, *The History of British India*, 2nd ed., vol. 5 (London: Baldwin, Cradock, and Joy, 1820), 474.
4. Thomas Babington Macaulay, "Government of India," in *The Complete Works of Thomas Babington Macaulay: Speeches and Legal Studies*, University ed. (New York: Sully and Kleinteich, 1900), 164.

colonial domination.[5] Iqbal al-Daulah's comments support this line of argument, suggesting that uncertainty, as much as knowledge, shaped colonial legal encounters.[6] His deathbed lamentations, however, caution against framing these histories of uncertainty as a triumph of subaltern agency or a weakening of colonial domination. While historians have often seen the ambiguity of colonial law as opening up opportunities for subaltern resistance, for Iqbal al-Daulah, the uncertainties of the law frustrated colonial litigants, as much as they foiled the objectives of imperial officials. Yet, despite its failings, colonial law did not wither away, nor did litigants like Iqbal al-Daulah's relatives abandon the colonial courts. Faced with unpredictable outcomes, litigants brought cases in multiple jurisdictions to maximize their chances of success, and officials drafted new laws to clarify unclear cases. Uncertainty therefore often fueled more, rather than less, legal activity, and the persistence of uncertainty, far from undermining the workings of colonial law, powered its ongoing expansion.[7] This chapter explores how these dynamics of uncertainty functioned alongside colonial law's emphasis on certainty through a close study of the legal disputes over the estates of Iqbal al-Daulah and one of his distant relatives, Taj Mahal Begam. A dancing girl who married the nawab of Awadh, Taj Mahal, like Iqbal al-Daulah, later migrated and died in Ottoman Iraq, where an intense struggle ensued over her estate.[8]

Tracing the history of these cases requires working at multiple geographical and analytical scales, in order to understand both the broad legal terrain through which the cases traveled as well as the complex local and global negotiations that the inheritance disputes inspired. The cases unfolded between the heart of Britain's empire in colonial India and one of its Indian Ocean frontiers, Ottoman Iraq, where Britain exercised a range of informal forms of control, including operating a system of extraterritorial courts. The chapter begins by surveying this landscape, highlighting the ways in which law worked to integrate varied imperial geographies through overlapping legal vocabularies.[9] In both India and the Ottoman Empire, Britain deployed the twinned concepts of territorial and personal law to assert British paramountcy. A substantial body of scholarship has charted the rising influence of territoriality during the nineteenth century, as

---

5. The pioneering work in this field is Lauren A. Benton's *Law and Colonial Cultures: Legal Regimes in World History, 1400–1900* (Cambridge, UK: Cambridge University Press, 2002).

6. For another account emphasizing the uncertainties of colonial law, see Sally Engle Merry, "Colonial Law and Its Uncertainties," *Law and History Review* 28 (2010): 1067–71.

7. On uncertainty in other colonial contexts, see Ann Laura Stoler, *Along the Archival Grain: Epistemic Anxieties and Colonial Common Sense* (Princeton: Princeton University Press, 2009); Renisa Mawani, *Colonial Proximities: Crossracial Encounters and Juridical Truths in British Columbia, 1871–1921* (Vancouver: UBC Press, 2009), esp. 14–15, 209.

8. K. S. Santha, *Begums of Awadh* (Varanasi: Bharati Prakashan, 1980), 283–85.

9. On such legal connections, see Thomas R. Metcalf, *Imperial Connections: India in the Indian Ocean Arena, 1860–1920* (Berkeley: University of California Press, 2007), 17–32.

European nations at home and in their empires centralized law within geographically bounded spaces, displacing the more plural legal orders that had dominated the early-modern world.[10] Far less attention, however, has been paid to how these new discourses of territoriality relied on juxtaposing European territorial sovereignty against the supposed personal sovereignty of non-European powers. Where a single uniform legal system was impossible, Britain relied on the distinction between territorial and personal law to reorder the overlapping legal jurisdictions they inherited from the Mughals and Ottomans into clear hierarchies and divisions. By promising that these newly ordered legal systems would deliver certainty in the place of arbitrary "Oriental" justice, Britain justified increasingly aggressive legal interventions in its colonies and informal spheres of influence.

Yet, as the legal disputes over the Awadh inheritances make clear, when we shift from a birds-eye perspective of this legal landscape to an in-depth analysis of how cases unfolded in practice, this vision of certainty unravels into dynamics of uncertainty. Consular courts in Iraq and courts in India competed for jurisdiction over the estates, while Ottoman and British officials squabbled over who was responsible for administering the property. Because both Iqbal al-Daulah and Taj Mahal Begam received large government pensions, officials were unwilling to leave the cases entirely to the courts, and instead intervened in speculations about illegitimate children and invalid bequeaths. These jurisdictional quarrels left behind reams of correspondence that documented in great detail the struggles that unfolded inside and outside the courts for control over the estates. These records provide insight into how colonial litigants financed exorbitant legal fees, and how networks of intimidation outside the courts influenced legal outcomes, details rarely included in published legal decisions. Ironically, the exceptional nature of the Awadh case therefore provides a rare window into the quotidian workings of colonial justice. The cases suggest that uncertainty deeply shaped how colonial subjects, whether former princes or more humble litigants, interacted with British courts, spurring diverse mechanisms for managing unpredictable outcomes.

Following the lives, and legal afterlives, of imperial migrants like Iqbal al-Daulah and Taj Mahal Begam therefore brings into dialogue scales and methods of studying colonial law that often remained isolated from each other. The geographical reach of their lives challenges us to think about how colonial law worked at imperial scales—ordering diverse political landscapes into increasingly interconnected legal spheres. The depth of the historical record that their cases left behind draws us deep into the workings of colonial justice, document-

10. Charles S. Maier, "Consigning the Twentieth Century to History: Alternative Narratives for the Modern Era," *American Historical Review* 105, no. 3 (2000): 807–31. On legal territoriality, see Benton, *Law and Colonial Cultures*; Lisa Ford, *Settler Sovereignty: Jurisdiction and Indigenous People in America and Australia, 1788–1836* (Cambridge, MA: Harvard University Press, 2010).

ing outcomes that were contingent and unpredictable. As a result the inheritance cases present a challenging picture of colonial law in which certainty and uncertainty, global connections and local machinations, legal discourse and practice coexisted, even if they at times seemingly pulled in different directions. Taking the inheritances cases as a point of departure, the chapter outlines some preliminary thoughts on how historians can bring these perspectives into greater dialogue, tracing mechanisms through which certainty and uncertainty both fueled the imperial travels of law.

Ordering Imperial Legal Landscapes

Iqbal al-Daulah and Taj Mahal's lives were deeply entangled with the territorial growth of Britain's Indian and Indian Ocean empire. Both early on recognized the growing influence that the British exercised over the theoretically independent Awadh dynasty. Iqbal al-Daulah traveled to London in the late 1830s to petition the British government to intercede on his behalf in a dispute over succession to the Awadh throne.[11] Taj Mahal asked the British resident, who represented British interests at the Awadh court, to prevent her husband's family from placing guards on her house due to her supposed sexual improprieties.[12] While neither effort was successful, Iqbal al-Daulah and Taj Mahal's lives were nonetheless deeply shaped by Britain's imperial ambitions. Taj Mahal was one of the beneficiaries of a loan agreement between the East India Company and the nawab, which linked the Awadh dynasty's financial fortunes to the capital needs of the expanding British Empire.[13] In exchange for low-interest loans, the British paid pensions to members of the nawab's family and their heirs.[14] Having already raided the nawab's coffers, the British annexed Awadh in 1856. Iqbal al-Daulah and Taj Mahal's fates were thus overtly influenced by the physical expansion of Britain's colonial territories. Yet their lives, and particularly their legal afterlives, also testify to how Britain deployed the concept of territoriality much more broadly. Like a surveyor's map, the concept of territoriality rendered a diverse range of legal arrangements into a single mode of representation that emphasized Britain's mastery over the landscape caught within its frame.

Britain ultimately extended this legal map from its formal territories in India outwards into the Indian Ocean rim, establishing a network of "protected states," where native rulers operated under British supervision, and across an even wider

11. Michael Herbert Fisher, *Counterflows to Colonialism: Indian Travellers and Settlers in Britain, 1600–1857* (Delhi: Permanent Black, 2004), 271.
12. Santha, *Begums of Awadh*, 284.
13. Charles Umpherston Aitchison, ed., *A Collection of Treaties, Engagements, and Sanads Relating to India and Neighbouring Countries*, 12 vol. (Calcutta: Office of the Superintendent of Government Printing, India, 1892), 2:140–42.
14. Michael Herbert Fisher, *A Clash of Cultures: Awadh, the British, and the Mughals* (New Delhi: Manohar, 1987), 181–87.

indistinct sphere of informal influence. In this third sphere, which included Ottoman Iraq, or what the British referred to as Turkish Arabia, Britain claimed special legal privileges, asserting the right to protect its own subjects from laws it deemed uncivilized. Britain claimed such jurisdiction over a large community of Indians who traveled on pilgrimage to Shia shrines, some of whom, like the Iqbal al-Daulah and Taj Mahal, settled permanently in the region. Indians, including the Awadh royal family, also made significant financial gifts to shrines and scholars in the region.[15] Citing the steady flow of Indian pilgrims and capital, as well as Britain's trading interests in the Persian Gulf, the British jealously guarded their right to maintain a large consular bureaucracy in Iraq.[16] For Indians such as Iqbal al-Daulah and Taj Mahal, Ottoman Iraq could at times feel distinctly British. Iqbal al-Daulah became a trusted ally of local British officials, lending them support during the Anglo-Persian war and aiding in the management of the Awadh Bequest, a large religious endowment funded by interest on the Awadh loans. In return the British paid Iqbal al-Daulah a sizeable pension and awarded him a knighthood.[17] When Iqbal al-Daulah and Taj Mahal died, the British consul in Iraq asserted jurisdiction over their estates.

The laws that the consular courts in Iraq actually used to decide such inheritance disputes were Indian religious laws, often called personal laws, adding yet another layer of complexity to the legal landscape. British consular courts, like courts in India, administered a range of personal laws in cases involving domestic or religious disputes, including marriage, inheritance, or ritual concerns. Even as British officials worked to streamline colonial law, they widely believed that religious differences among colonial subjects and between colonial subjects and their British rulers necessitated special legal accommodations. Outside of Europe, the perceived cultural divide between Christian and non-Christian, and civilized and uncivilized peoples thus checked the push to standardize law within geographically defined units, leading to a range of different legal exceptions.[18]

Yet, as the Indian and Ottoman cases make clear, British officials managed to incorporate these legal exceptions into a reformulated concept of territoriality, and thus brought diverse legal arrangements into a singular system of legal mapping. Across its colonies, protectorates, and informal spheres of influence, Britain defined its own judicial authority as territorial while classifying non-European

15. Juan R.I. Cole, "'Indian Money' and the Shi'i Shrine Cities of Iraq, 1786–1850," *Middle Eastern Studies* 22, no. 4 (1986): 461–80.
16. Gökhan Çetinsaya, "The Ottoman View of British Presence in Iraq and the Gulf: The Era of Abdulhamid II," *Middle Eastern Studies* 39, no. 2 (2003): 194–203.
17. Jerome A. Saldanha, *The Persian Gulf Précis,* 8 vol. (Gerrards Cross: Archive Editions, 1986), 6:295–96; Meir Litvak, "Money, Religion, and Politics: The Oudh Bequest in Najaf and Karbala, 1850–1903," *International Journal of Middle East Studies* 33, no. 1 (2001): 6–7.
18. Lauren A. Benton, *A Search for Sovereignty: Law and Geography in European Empires, 1400–1900* (Cambridge, UK: Cambridge University Press, 2010).

laws as personal, a rubric that promised to discipline plural legal regimes into clear and consistent hierarchies. This terminology drew on an emerging body of scholarship on the historical development of European law. One of the most influential scholars in this field, Friedrich von Savigny, argued that after the fall of the Roman Empire the Germanic tribes that invaded Europe allowed the inhabitants to retain their own laws, fostering a system in which laws attached to persons, rather than to territory.[19] In Europe, according to von Savigny, territorial law gradually replaced personal law due to increasing interaction between different peoples and the unifying force of Christianity, which had "thrown their characteristic differences more and more into the background."[20] In contrast legal historicists such as von Savigny often cited the Ottoman Empire and India, where different communities enjoyed a considerable degree of legal autonomy, as contemporary examples of personal law.[21] Projecting Europe's past onto the non-Western world fueled historicist hierarchies in which Europe's modernity was cast against the supposed legal backwardness of the rest of the world.

The British increasingly used this distinction between territorial and personal law to reorder plural legal landscapes according to hierarchies that subordinated non-European laws. In the middle decades of the nineteenth century British law, rooted in territorial claims, was increasingly portrayed as secular and universal, and therefore capable of providing neutral and efficient justice to a broad range of different peoples. In contrast British officials labeled non-European legal systems as personal laws, limiting their scope by defining them as familial and religious, and denigrating them as irrational, arbitrary, and resistant to change. In its overseas empire, this twinned vocabulary of territoriality and personality allowed Britain to portray its own sovereign claims as supreme, and therefore unified and uncontested, even as it accommodated legal diversity. By replacing overlap with clear divisions and hierarchies, Britain promised, at least in theory, to deliver certain results.

During their lives Iqbal al-Daulah and Taj Mahal witnessed the British redraw maps of political power in Asia through these new legal hierarchies. In the second quarter of the nineteenth century the East India Company annexed a large number of Indian princely states, including Awadh. The company legally justified these acts on the grounds that as the paramount power in India it had the right to intercede when native rulers were incompetent, disloyal, indebted,

---

19. Michael H. Hoeflich, "Savigny and His Anglo-American Disciples," *The American Journal of Comparative Law* 37, no. 1 (1989): 17–37.

20. Friedrich Carl von Savigny, *Private International Law, and the Retrospective Operation of Statutes: A Treatise on the Conflict of Laws, and the Limits of Their Operation in Respect of Place and Time*, trans. William Guthrie, 2nd ed. (Edinburgh: T. & T. Clark, 1880), 59.

21. Ibid., 58–62.

or lacked a direct heir, a policy known as the "doctrine of lapse."[22] In asserting its paramountcy the company effectively created a hierarchy of sovereignty that "personalized" the authority of native states.[23] The doctrine of lapse circumscribed Indian dynasties to a narrowly conceived family unit, ignoring the flexible modes of incorporation Indian states used to recruit and sustain political leadership.[24] In the case of Awadh the British justified annexation due to the nawab's supposed personal incompetency, emphasizing the benefits that systematic and efficient British administration would offer over the erratic whims of its princely ruler.[25] By "personalizing" Indian sovereignty Britain built its empire on the cheap, using treaties and international law in the place of costly military conquests.

Britain also employed the distinction between territorial and personal sovereignty in cases where it chose not to eliminate non-European sources of law, as in Awadh, but to subordinate them to British legal hegemony. Britain used similar legal vocabulary to limit the scope of religious laws in India and to expand its consular jurisdiction in Ottoman territories. Britain's legal positions in the two countries were essentially mirror opposites. In India the British presided over a plural system of different legal jurisdictions, many of which they had inherited from the Mughal Empire. In contrast in the Ottoman territories, Britain participated in a plural system, under the overarching authority, at least from the perspective of the Ottomans, of the Sublime Porte. While in the eighteenth century Britain often worked within these flexible and overlapping systems of sovereignty, by the 1830s officials saw such legal ambiguities as inconsistent with the increasing emphasis European legal thought placed on centralized and certain justice.

In both contexts officials underlined the benefits of more aggressive British legal interventions by decrying the uncertainty generated by ongoing entanglement with Muslim legal systems that were derided as arbitrary and fanatical. For example the British consul in Egypt in the 1830s described: "a country where the total want of written law, renders every sentence the expression of the caprice of the magistrate who awards it, and where the Turkish magistrates, who are invariably selected among the religious people, are imbued with prejudice and hatred

---

22. Sri Nandan Prasad, *Paramountcy under Dalhousie* (Delhi: Ranjit Printers & Publishers, 1964).
23. On the "personalization" of princely authority in the second half of the nineteenth century, see Mridu Rai, *Hindu Rulers, Muslim Subjects: Islam, Rights, and the History of Kashmir* (Princeton: Princeton University Press, 2004), 81–127.
24. Indrani Chatterjee, *Gender, Slavery, and Law in Colonial India* (Oxford: Oxford University Press, 1999), esp. 28–31.
25. Partha Chatterjee, *The Black Hole of Empire: History of a Global Practice of Power* (Princeton: Princeton University Press, 2012), 185–221.

against Christians."[26] While such portraits of Oriental despotism were a staple of European commentary, British officials in India had at times portrayed Indo-Islamic legal traditions in a more positive light, treating them as well suited to local conditions.[27] As late as the 1820s some colonial commentators insisted that Islamic law as administered by the Mughals was the territorial law of British India, since it had never been formally replaced by English law.[28] In the 1840s, however, the India Law Commission soundly rejected this argument on the grounds that Islamic law was incapable of serving as territorial law because it was intolerant of religious differences. They argued that Muslim jurists neither allowed a Muslim conqueror to retain laws that were incompatible with Islam nor recognized the right of a non-Muslim conqueror to change the laws of a Muslim territory. In contrast the Indian law commissioners argued that, "The English law, as it does not profess to be a revelation from God, may be changed by Parliament in the way of legislation, and by the Courts of law...."[29]

These concerns culminated in a series of influential reports written in the 1840s that embraced the language of territoriality to justify sweeping reforms that strengthened and centralized British legal authority abroad. In one of its earliest reports, widely known as the Lex Loci Report, the Indian Law Commission recommended that English law should be officially declared India's territorial law. In contrast the commission described Hindu and Islamic law as "religious and personal Laws," which British courts should only apply in cases involving a limited community of fellow believers.[30] While the Lex Loci Report's recommendations were never legislatively enacted, they cleared the way for successive Indian Law Commissions to overhaul the Indian legal system with a series of reforms that limited religious laws to a small range of domestic and ritual matters.[31]

After a similar report on the Ottoman legal conundrum, Parliament passed the Foreign Jurisdiction Act of 1843, which spurred the development of a global network of British consular courts that eventually extended across large areas

26. "Report from the Select Committee on Consular Establishment," 177, House of Commons Parliamentary Papers, 1835 (499) VI.149.
27. Robert Travers, *Ideology and Empire in Eighteenth-Century India: The British in Bengal* (Cambridge, UK: Cambridge University Press, 2007).
28. In reviewing this argument the Indian Law Commission referenced the writings of Archibald Galloway, a former colonial officer in Bengal and a director of the East India Company. *Observations on the Law and Constitution of India...* (London: Kingsbury, Parbury, and Allen, 1825), 262–63. Although Galloway published the first edition anonymously, he included his name in the 1832 edition.
29. Indian Law Commissioners to Governor General, 31 Oct. 1840, Indian Legislative Consultations, 11 Jan. 1841, no. 16, 13, India Office Records [hereafter IOR]/P/207/14.
30. Minute by Charles Hay Cameron, 1 Aug. 1845, Indian Legislative Consultations, 2 Aug. 1845, no. 35, IOR/P/207/36.
31. Julia Stephens, *Governing Islam: Law, Empire, and Secularism in South Asia* (Cambridge, UK: Cambridge University Press, 2018).

of the non-Western world.[32] The act specified that the legal authority that the Crown exercised in foreign jurisdictions such as the Ottoman territories had the same force "as if Her Majesty had acquired such power or jurisdiction by the cession or conquest of territory."[33] According to any normal logic, the British in Ottoman territories administered a form of personal law to their own subjects. Yet defining British jurisdiction as a form of personal law would have entailed acknowledging that consuls acted in part as "delegates of the Porte," an overlapping sovereignty that the British found unacceptable.[34] The Foreign Jurisdiction Act therefore instead translated extra-territorial jurisdiction into the language of territoriality to construct a singular chain of authority between Britain and its overseas courts.

The Uncertain Legal Afterlives of Imperial Migrants

Interventions such as the Lex Loci Report and Foreign Jurisdiction Act paved the way for Britain to implement wide-ranging legal reforms across its formal and informal empires in the middle decades of the nineteenth century. In theory these reforms reduced uncertainties about where, how, and according to which laws, cases would be decided by putting in place increasingly formalized and centralized judicial systems.[35] Yet in practice significant areas of ambiguity remained, creating uncertainties that became particularly apparent when imperial subjects traveled across jurisdictions. When Iqbal al-Daulah and Taj Mahal died leaving property in Iraq and India, and relatives and friends spread between the two, it was unclear whether their scattered assets fell under the jurisdiction of British consular courts, Ottoman authorities, or Indian colonial courts. In theory all the relevant courts would administer the estates according to Islamic law. Yet, the bitter disputes that ensued over where the cases should be adjudicated revealed the considerable differences in how Islamic law was interpreted in different jurisdictions. Adding another layer of complexity, political interventions by the government significantly influenced where the cases were decided, complicating any easy division between executive and judicial authorities. Underlining the unpredictability of imperial justice, the dispute over Taj Mahal's inheritance was decided by a court in Lucknow while Iqbal al-Daulah's relatives and executors reached a settlement in the Supreme Consular Court in Constan-

32. Turan Kayaoğlu, *Legal Imperialism: Sovereignty and Extraterritoriality in Japan, the Ottoman Empire, and China* (Cambridge, UK: Cambridge University Press, 2010).
33. *Statutes of the Realm*, 6 & 7 Vict., c. 94, para. 1.
34. James R. Hope, "Report on British Jurisdiction in Foreign States," in *Law Officers' Opinions to the Foreign Office, 1793–1860*, vol. 89, ed. Clive Parry (Westmead: Gregg International Publishers, 1970), 241.
35. Rachel Sturman, *The Government of Social Life in Colonial India: Liberalism, Religious Law, and Women's Rights* (Cambridge, UK: Cambridge University Press, 2012), 16–17; Kayaoğlu, *Legal Imperialism*, 124.

tinople. While the Awadh inheritance cases traversed an unusual number of different jurisdictional boundaries, the rich records these legal travels left in their wake provide insight into how uncertainty more generally shaped colonial legal cultures.

Soon after the British annexation of Awadh and the Indian Rebellion of 1857, Taj Mahal fled both her personal difficulties and political turmoil in Lucknow, traveling to Karbala with her second husband, Kalb Hussain. After the death of her first husband, the nawab, in 1837, Taj Mahal was increasingly shadowed by speculation that she had given birth to an illegitimate child. During the legal dispute over her estate, some of Taj Mahal's relatives claimed that this child was the lawful offspring of a secret marriage with Kalb Hussain, which she had kept hidden from the nawab's family because they disapproved of her remarrying.[36] When Taj Mahal died in July 1875, she left behind a large estate consisting of her pension, jewelry, and household goods in Baghdad, properties in Kanpur and Lucknow, and a government promissory note deposited in Bombay.[37] She also left behind unresolved questions about her marriages, and in the years after her death individuals claiming to be her brother, nephews, granddaughter, and wife of her deceased husband made claims against the estate in Baghdad, Lucknow, Calcutta, and Bombay.

In February 1876 the British consul in Baghdad declared Taj Mahal's brother, Ramzan Ali Khan, her rightful heir. After interviewing just three witnesses he awarded the entire estate to Ramzan Ali on the grounds that he was the nearest male relative.[38] The consul claimed jurisdiction over the estate on the grounds that Taj Mahal was a British subject living in Iraq and, therefore, subject to the consul's extra-territorial jurisdiction. In contrast Indian officials wanted the case to be decided in India, claiming that the Indian courts were better versed in the relevant religious laws. The Foreign Department of the Government of India complained that the consul was "potter[ing] about the case in a bungling sort of way," and speculated that he did not understand the distinction between Sunni and Shia laws of inheritance, according to which Taj Mahal's granddaughter, Kulsumnissa, rather than her brother, was entitled to the estate.[39] Since both the consular and Indian courts decided inheritance cases according to personal laws, which depended on the litigants' religious identity rather than their territorial location, theoretically the outcome in both courts should have been the same. Yet, as the dispute over jurisdiction made apparent, in practice the distinction

36. In the Court of the District Judge, Lucknow, Taj Mahal's Pension, in NAI/Foreign/A General G/August 1883/Nos. 50–57.

37. Petition of Moulvie Syud Mehndee Hossein to the Governor-General of India, 4–5, in NAI/Foreign/General A/June 1877/Nos. 17–114; Exhibit C in the High Court of Indicature at Fort William in Bengal, 8, in NAI/Foreign/General A/Oct. 1879/Nos. 12–24.

38. At the Court of the Consul-General and Political Agent, Baghdad, 32-34, in NAI/Foreign/General A/June 1877/Nos. 17–114.

39. Keep With [hereafter K.W.], No. 2, 10, in NAI/Foreign/General A/June 1877/Nos. 17–114.

between personal and territorial jurisdiction was not so clear. Courts in different parts of the British Empire, and even individual judges, interpreted religious laws in varied ways, and, therefore, the location of a trial could be decisive.[40] While in Taj Mahal's case officials in India blamed these diverging interpretations on the consul's incompetence, conflicting rulings were common within India as well. In theory colonial courts administered stable bodies of religious tradition in cases that came under the jurisdiction of personal law. During the course of the nineteenth century, however, colonial courts continually grappled with differing interpretations of religious laws. They also struggled with increasing awareness of local and sectarian customs that deviated from orthodox Sunni norms, and courts in different parts of India and in the wider British Empire recognized these alternative practices to varying extents.[41] Far from delivering the certainty reformers like Mill and Macaulay promised, the British administration of religious personal laws fueled ongoing uncertainty.

In the years following Taj Mahal's death, these uncertainties encouraged her relatives to pursue their competing claims in different jurisdictions. While Ramzan Ali brought his case in Baghdad, Kulsumnissa's relatives pursued her claims in Lucknow. Mehdi Hussain, who claimed to be Kulsumnissa's uncle and stepfather, was granted guardianship and the power to administer Kulsumnissa's property in September 1875.[42] When he attempted to collect Taj Mahal's pension on Kulsumnissa's behalf, however, Ramzan Ali's representatives in Lucknow lodged a counter claim and the dispute was referred to the Lucknow Civil Court. While Ramzan Ali disputed the court's jurisdiction over the case, the judge found that Taj Mahal had never officially changed her place of domicile, and, therefore, her estate fell under Indian jurisdiction.[43] Complicating matters further, another woman claiming to be Kalb Hussain's first wife disputed Taj Mahal's claim to his estate, and instituted a suit against Kulsumnissa in the Calcutta High Court. She argued that Taj Mahal's marriage with Kalb Hussain was invalid because the nawab's widows were forbidden from remarrying.[44] Eventually the former nawab

40. Mitra Sharafi, "The Marital Patchwork of Colonial South Asia: Forum Shopping from Britain to Baroda," *Law and History Review* 28, no. 4 (2010): 979–1009.
41. Ayesha Jalal, *Self and Sovereignty: Individual and Community in South Asian Islam since 1850* (New York: Routledge, 2000), 139–53.
42. Judgment, 41, in NAI/Foreign/General A/June 1877/Nos. 17–114. Mehdi Hussain married Kulsumnissa's mother after his brother, her first husband and the father of Kulsumnissa, passed away.
43. In the Court of the Civil Judge of Lucknow, 51–53; No. 250 of Appeal Civil Court, 66–68, in NAI/Foreign/General A/June 1877/Nos. 17–114.
44. Suit on the Ordinary Original Civil Side of the High Court of Judicature at Fort William in Bengal, 3–5, in NAI/Foreign/General A/Oct. 1879/Nos. 12–24.

himself, also based in Calcutta, wrote to the government to claim Taj Mahal's pension.[45]

As her legal battles dragged on, Kulsumnissa amassed a staggering pile of debt. Given the uncertainty of her claim to the estate, she was forced to pay annual interest rates of twenty-four percent.[46] While Mehdi Hussain initially pursued Kulsumnissa's claim through the Indian courts, after arriving in Iraq he pressed for the case to be settled by the consular courts, frustrated by the Indian government's delay. In a memo to the government his legal counsel insisted that Kulsumnissa "is certainly not resident within the limits of the jurisdiction of any Indian Court of Justice…She is simply a creditor, having claim against the Indian revenues."[47] The government of India, however, had far greater political power than a typical debtor and wanted to ensure that it was not held liable for multiple claims on the estate in different jurisdictions. It therefore passed special legislation in 1881 that tasked the District Court of Lucknow with determining Taj Mahal's legal heir and indemnified the government from any obligation to pay other claimants.[48] In January 1883 the District Court declared Kulsumnissa the heir.[49]

A few years later Iqbal al-Daulah passed away in Ottoman Iraq, provoking another flurry of legal activity. Outliving his wife and children, Iqbal al-Daulah had deposited a will with the British political resident in Baghdad in the late 1840s and asked him to serve as its executor. When the resident opened Iqbal al-Daulah's will after his death, he found an elaborate Persian document. As the resident noted: "A vein of eccentricity certainly runs through the Will. To the last the author of it considered himself a 'Royalty,' and parts of it read as if he had lost sight of the essential difference between Turkish Arabia at the present time and Lucknow in the palmiest days of its Nawab Vazirs."[50] In his will Iqbal al-Daulah dedicated his property in Iraq to the upkeep of his tomb. Going into exquisite detail about the decorations he wanted at the tomb, Iqbal al-Daulah declared that, "From the fittings of my tomb let it appear as if I were not dead but living, and only gone to sleep."[51] He left his property in India for the maintenance of the tombs of his parents, with any remaining amount going to his nephews in India.

45. From Agent, Governor-General with the King of Oudh to Secretary to Government of India, Foreign Department, 8 May 1877, 62–63, in NAI/Foreign/General A/June 1877/Nos. 17–114.
46. Opinion, in "Regarding the Claim of Kulsooman Nisa Begam…," 1875–1883, Uttar Pradesh State Archives, Miscellaneous Papers, List No. 4, Sl. No. 1, Packet No. 1, Boxes Nos. 1–3, 713.
47. Ibid., 707.
48. Taj Mahal's Pension Act, in *The Legislative Acts of the Governor General of India in Council of 1881* (Calcutta: Thacker, Spink and Co., 1882), 1–6.
49. In the Court of the District Judge, Lucknow, Taj Mahal's Pension.
50. From Colonel W. Tweedie to Secretary to the Government of India, Foreign Department, 6 Jan. 1888, 3, in NAI/Foreign/Internal A/June 1888/Nos. 216–40.
51. Translation of Will of late Nawab Sir Ikbal-ud-Daula, 18.

Iqbal al-Daulah felt he was being more than generous. Yet he clearly anticipated that his relatives in India might not agree, and warned that if they attempted to claim his Iraqi estate, the resident should "drive them like dogs from door."[52]

On opening the will the resident recognized that it would cause him a host of headaches. He wrote to his superiors in Constantinople that the will "can hardly fail to give offence to Ottoman Government, to more than one large community and to individuals."[53] Iqbal al-Daulah's friends and servants who he had named as co-executors were also less than enthused. Two of them informed the resident that they were disinclined "to risk their money in setting up litigation."[54] The concerns of the resident and co-executors were well founded; in August 1889 members of Iqbal al-Daulah's family instituted proceedings in Calcutta to claim the estate.[55] Meanwhile the vali of Baghdad, the Ottoman provincial governor, demanded that the resident hand over Iqbal al-Daulah's landed property, claiming territorial jurisdiction over the immoveable estate. The vali insisted that under Ottoman law the estate devolved to the government since no legitimate heirs had applied to the Ottomans courts, and the will was not drawn up in accordance with the Sharia, which only allowed one-third of an estate to be willed away.[56] In response, the legal counsel employed by Iqbal al-Daulah's executors insisted that although the estate should be administered according to the Sharia, "that law has to be administered and interpreted by the British and not by the Native Court." He further argued that although Iqbal al-Daulah's immoveable property was subject to Ottoman law, it was the consular courts that should administer that law, in essence subordinating Ottoman territorial claims to British extra-territorial jurisdiction.[57]

Ultimately the dispute over Iqbal al-Daulah's estate was resolved relatively quickly because the parties were anxious to bring the case to a conclusion and avoid further Ottoman involvement. Although the judge of the Supreme Consular Court in Constantinople believed that the case fell within his jurisdiction, he wanted to avoid a situation in which "two English Courts, with the same Court for Appeal, would be trying the same case," fearing that the result would be "a ru-

52. Ibid., 22.
53. From Colonel W. Tweedie to Consul-General and Judge, Constantinople, 9 Jan. 1887, 2, in NAI/Foreign/Internal A/June1888/Nos. 216–40.
54. Extract from the Diary of the Political Resident Turkish Arabia, 19 Oct. 1889, 55, in NAI/Foreign/Internal A/March 1890/Nos. 58–92.
55. In the High Court of Judicature at Fort William in Bengal, 57–59, in NAI/Foreign/Internal A/March 1890/Nos. 58–92.
56. From the Wali of Baghdad to Consul-General Baghdad, 22 Oct. 1889, 55–56, in NAI/Foreign/Internal A/March 1890/Nos. 58–92.
57. From E. Pears to Consul-General and Judge, Constantinople, 16 Jan. 1890, 1–2, in NAI/Foreign/Internal A/April 1890/Nos. 81–87.

inous expence to the estate."[58] The judge felt that he could not formally renounce jurisdiction over the case, but agreed to postpone proceedings until the case was decided in Calcutta.[59] Ultimately, however, Iqbal al-Daulah's relatives and executors decided that the case could be more quickly settled in the consular courts. Referencing their concern that the Ottomans might seize the estate, or that the relatives "being elderly people might die before the litigation was concluded," the parties signed a settlement in August 1891.[60] Two-thirds of the estate went to Iqbal al-Daulah's relatives, and one-third was dedicated to his tomb. Iqbal al-Daulah would probably have been disappointed with the result.

Mobile subjects such as the Awadh royals thus revealed ambiguities in the boundary between territorial and personal law and ongoing contests between local and British officials about the scope of extra-territorial jurisdiction. The cases also show how colonial officials while in theory praising the benefits of legal certainty, in practice often interpreted the "rule of law" in flexible ways to accommodate shifting imperial needs. While exceptional in the number of different causes that fueled uncertainty, the Awadh cases thus reflected more pervasive sources of ambiguity in colonial law. Parties to the disputes responded to this uncertainty by pursuing claims through multiple legal and extra-legal avenues. In many colonial legal records, which focus on final decisions and official outcomes, such efforts to navigate shifting legal terrain remain frustratingly obscured from view. Yet because officials were intensely preoccupied with the outcome in the Awadh disputes, the cases offer a tantalizing glimpse into how colonial litigants and officials managed unpredictable legal outcomes.

Uncertain about what laws the courts would use to decide the cases, the Awadh litigants supported their claims with citations to multiple sources of law. For example in the dispute over the guardianship of Kulsumnissa, Mehdi Hussain argued that Taj Mahal's brother, Ramzan Ali, as a rival claimant to the estate, "cannot be deemed worthy to be the guardian of the minor, either according to the Mahomedan law, or any other law, or rules of justice."[61] Parties to the disputes also worked through both legal and political channels, simultaneously defending their cases in courts and petitioning colonial officials. Mehdi Hussain flooded officials in Iraq and India with requests on Kulsumnissa's behalf, leading one official to describe him as "a perfect master of petition-writing and of wire-pulling."[62] The resident in Baghdad complained that Iqbal al-Daulah was

58. From Consul-General and Judge, Constantinople to Foreign Office, 20 Feb. 1890, 2, in NAI/Foreign/Internal A/Aug. 1890/Nos. 96–116.

59. Ibid., 2–3.

60. In Her Britannic Majesty's Supreme Consular Court at Constantinople, in Probate in the Matter of the Estate of the Late Nawab Sir Iqbal-ul-Dowlah, 5, in NAI/Foreign Department/Internal A/June 1892/Nos. 20–58.

61. Petition of Moulvie Syud Mehndee Hossein, 4.

62. K.W. No. 1, 2, in NAI/Foreign/A General G/Jan. 1883/Nos. 1–11.

attempting to subvert normal legal channels by directly involving British officials in the administration of his property. The resident dismissively declared
that Iqbal al-Daulah was "Utterly ignorant of the forms of English law, and relying confidently upon the favour and protection of the English Government, but
unable to discriminate the powers and obligations of the one from those of the
other..."[63] While the resident scoffed at Iqbal al-Daulah's conflation of executive
and judicial authority, there was a considerable amount of truth to his understanding. While British officials largely left the administration of his estate to
the courts, they interceded in Taj Mahal's case, where they had a greater vested
interest. Not only did the Indian government pass the 1881 Act, officials considered replacing the district judge when they thought that he was taking too long
to decide the case.[64]

While litigants, unlike officials, did not have the power to rewrite laws, they
also pursued extra-judicial strategies. Hints of informal mechanisms for influencing cases seep through the cracks of the official archive. While there is little
indication of how a settlement was reached in Iqbal al-Daulah's case, there are
suggestions that interactions between Taj Mahal's relatives outside of court influenced the course of events. When Mehdi Hussain arrived in Iraq with a certificate of guardianship for Kulsumnissa, a disturbance ensued between him and
Ramzan Ali. Mehdi Hussain enlisted the help of Ramzan Ali's nephew in con-
fronting his uncle, and the resident reported that, "Subsequently Ramzan Ali
Khan made a complaint against his nephew for his conduct, but this dispute was
settled among the parties concerned."[65] As these oblique references suggest, parties to legal disputes exercised forms of social coercion that were often as powerful as those of the state.

The uncertainty surrounding the outcome in legal cases also encouraged
third parties to "speculate" on legal cases, buying shares in legal cases in exchange for financial resources to fund legal fees. Parties in both Taj Mahal and
Iqbal al-Daulah's case sold all or part of their claims to third parties.[66] Common-
law doctrines prohibiting champerty, or the participation of a third party in a
lawsuit in exchange for a financial share in the final award, made it more difficult
to sell legal claims in England. Indian courts, however, forbid the sale of shares
in litigation only when they were extortionate or otherwise morally suspect.[67]

63. From Colonel W. Tweedie to Secretary to the Government of India, Foreign Department,
10 Jan. 1888, 2, in NAI/Foreign Department/Internal A/June 1888/Nos. 216–40.
64. K.W. No. 2, 3, in NAI/Foreign/A General G/Jan. 1883/Nos. 1–11.
65. From Political Resident in Turkish Arabia to Officiating Secretary to the Government of
India, Foreign Department, 7 Aug. 1876, 11, in NAI/Foreign/General A/June 1877/Nos 17–114.
66. In the Court of the District Judge, Lucknow, Taj Mahal's Pension, 26; Note, 41, in NAI/
Foreign/Internal A/June 1892/Nos. 20–58.
67. For the Privy Council decision upholding this interpretation, see *Ram Coomar Coondoo
and Another v. Chunder Canto Mookerjee*, The Law Reports. Indian Appeals: Being Cases in

This method of financing legal cases in colonial India deserves further study and may help provide a more economic explanation for the cultural stereotype of the "litigious Indian."

While Iqbal al-Daulah and Taj Mahal's cases were certainly exceptional, the strategies that their relatives used to manage uncertainty were not unique. Historians of colonial law working in multiple locations have documented how litigants strategically maneuvered between different legal forums in order to maximize their chances of success, a strategy that is often described as "forum shopping."[68] While evidence of extra-legal networks and coercion are often difficult to locate in official legal records, contemporary ethnographic research has richly documented the dynamic relationship between formal and informal spheres of legal adjudication.[69] One scholar has compared these strategies of managing uncertain outcomes to gambling in a "legal lottery."[70] This metaphor is particularly useful because it underlies the power imbalances involved. Litigants worked to maximize their chances of winning cases in an environment weighted against them. Their own chances of profiting were often relatively small, given that the cost of pursing a legal dispute could significantly cut into any financial benefits. Yet, groups with greater access to political, social, or financial capital were able to hedge their bets by pursuing multiple legal strategies and outlasting their opponents in court. Meanwhile the government could game the system, mitigating unpredictable outcomes by writing new laws and pushing courts in certain directions.

Entangled Histories of Certainty and Uncertainty

Iqbal al-Daulah and Taj Mahal's cases therefore provide a double vision of colonial law. They lead us through a landscape in which the jurisdictional expansion of British law was fueled by the promised benefits of delivering certain justice but then draw us deep into legal negotiations that were governed more by pervasive dynamics of uncertainty. In the process the cases bring into a common frame of analysis two approaches to colonial law that are often developed

---

the Privy Council on Appeal 4 East Indies, 23 (1876).

68. Sharafi, "The Marital Patchwork of Colonial South Asia;" Paolo Sartori and Ido Shahar, "Legal Pluralism in Muslim-Majority Colonies: Mapping the Terrain," *Journal of the Economic and Social History of the Orient* 55, nos. 4–5 (2012): 653.

69. For a rare historical account of these interactions, see Niels Brimnes, "Beyond Colonial Law: Indigenous Litigation and the Contestation of Property in the Mayor's Court in Late Eighteenth-Century Madras," *Modern Asian Studies* 37, no. 3 (2003): 513–50. Scholars working on contemporary legal culture have studied this topic in more depth. Erin Moore, *Gender, Law, and Resistance in India* (Tucson: University of Arizona Press, 1998); Gopika Solanki, *Adjudication in Religious Family Laws: Cultural Accommodation, Legal Pluralism, and Gender Equality in India* (Cambridge, UK: Cambridge University Press, 2011).

70. Sharafi, "The Marital Patchwork of Colonial South Asia," 980, 982, 1009.

in isolation, or at times, in opposition to each other. The first has focused on how law produced discourses on imperial justice and sovereignty that legitimated colonial rule. These studies have used legal treatises, legislation, and historic trials to trace the genealogy of legal concepts and their connection to colonial governance. This literature explores the intimate ties between colonial knowledge and imperial domination, and thus emphasizes how discourses such as legal certainty empowered the colonial state.[71] The second approach, which has often prioritized studying legal practice as opposed to theory, has been more attuned to dynamics of uncertainty. Scholars embracing this approach have emphasized the limits of colonial knowledge, and in turn, the contingent nature of colonial power. Drawing in particular on the work of Lauren Benton, historians have emphasized the complexity of colonial legal cultures and the role that indigenous agents played in their formation.[72] In practice many scholars combine elements of both these approaches, as this article has attempted. Yet, despite this productive cross-fertilization, historians favoring one approach over the other have often presented diverging pictures of colonialism.[73] The first approach has emphasized the constraining force of legal subjectivities and their role in the exercise of colonial domination. In contrast the second approach has often portrayed colonial law as a more open field of negotiation.

The Awadh inheritance cases encourage us to think about how these two seemingly contradictory images of colonial law might be brought into greater dialogue through histories that attend to both the role of certainty and uncertainty, and most critically, the relationship between them. The cases demonstrate how uncertainty and certainty were mutually generative when one of the key purposes of colonial law was to impose order on populations that were widely believed to be both diverse and disorderly. Cases in which the law was ambiguous and the subject of litigation was unclear resulted in lengthy trials and judicial appeals, providing law with some of its most productive material. When courts failed to deliver clear and consistent outcomes, legislatures often stepped in. While courts and legislatures claimed to replace confusion with clarity, in

71. Some exemplary examples of this approach include: Nasser Hussain, *The Jurisprudence of Emergency: Colonialism and the Rule of Law* (Ann Arbor: University of Michigan Press, 2003); Mithi Mukherjee, *India in the Shadows of Empire: a Legal and Political History, 1774–1950* (New Delhi: Oxford University Press, 2010).

72. Some excellent examples of this approach appeared in the special forum "Maneuvering the Personal Law System in Colonial India," *Law and History Review* 28, no. 4 (2010): 973–1071. For another noteworthy example, see Nandini Chatterjee, "Muslim or Christian? Family Quarrels and Religious Diagnosis in a Colonial Court," *American Historical Review* 117, no. 4 (2012): 1101–22.

73. For an account underlining differences between these two approaches, see Kunal M. Parker, "The Historiography of Difference," and Elizabeth Kolsky, "A Note on the Study of Indian Legal History," *Law and History Review* 23, no. 3 (2005): 685–95, 703–06.

practice this promise was often an ever-receding goal rather than a definitive accomplishment. Thus, rather than undermining the power of the law, the persistence of uncertainty kept the wheels of justice spinning. For example in Taj Mahal's case officials justified legislative intervention because of "the existence of grave doubts."[74] Yet just a few years after the 1881 act and the conclusion of Taj Mahal's case, officials expressed concerns that the act had raised new questions about whether other Awadh pensions could be litigated. The normal procedure was for officials, rather than the courts, to decide who were the rightful heirs to the pensions. Officials were therefore concerned that by involving the courts in Taj Mahal's case, they had exposed the government to the threat of "endless litigation and great expense."[75] The government passed additional legislation in 1886, clarifying that the Awadh pensions could only be litigated with the permission of the administration. Yet far from eliminating uncertainty, the Awadh pensions, which the Indian government continues to pay out today, continued to spawn ongoing legislative, judicial, and bureaucratic interventions.[76] Straddling different systems of past and present sovereignty, the Awadh pensions have provided seemingly limitless fuel for legal activity.

Subjects, like the Awadh royal family, who traversed legal boundaries, whether religious, political, or territorial, thus often facilitated the law's expansion by highlighting new areas of uncertainty that the law could bring within its grasp. These subjects, often unwittingly, fueled the expansion of colonial bureaucracies that promised to deliver more predictable and precise legal outcomes. Looking back to earlier discussions of legal reform in the 1840s, border-crossing subjects played a critical role in fueling efforts to "territorialize" British law in India and the Ottoman Empire. The initial impetus for the Lex Loci Report was a petition submitted by a group of Indian Christians and Armenians complaining of their uncertain civil status and their subjection to Islamic criminal law.[77] Indian converts to Christianity crossed religious and racial boundaries, while Armenians, with their global trading networks, occupied an uneasy position between Asian subjects and European colonists. Anxieties about anomalous minorities fueled efforts to clarify ambiguities surrounding the relationship between colonial law and Indian religious laws. In a similar fashion, concern about the legal position of Maltese and Ionian migrants in Ottoman territories helped spark debates that eventually led to the passage of the Foreign Jurisdiction Act of 1843. A series of sensational criminal cases involving these often lower-class migrants raised

---

74. K.W., 2, in NAI/Legislative A/Oct. 1886/Nos. 153–88.

75. From Wasika Officer of Lucknow to Secretary to the Government, N.W. Provinces and Oudh, Financial Department, 16 Dec. 1884, 66, in NAI/Legislative A/Oct. 1886/Nos. 153–88.

76. The pensions are still administered through the Wasika Office located in Lucknow. I would like to thank the officers for speaking with me in Jan. 2013.

77. Indian Law Commissioners to Governor General, 31 Oct. 1840, 1.

concerns among both British and Ottoman officials. But as subjects of a British colony, in the case of Malta, and a British protectorate, in the case of the Ionian Islands, it was unclear whether they fell under Ottoman or British jurisdiction.[78] The practical issue of where migrant subjects should be put on trial thus opened up much broader questions about the relationship between territorial, colonial, and extra-territorial jurisdictions. In the process they spurred efforts to clarify these areas of ambiguity through reforms that expanded the reach of British legal powers, but rarely succeeded in eliminating legal uncertainties.

Emphasizing the unpredictable nature of legal outcomes challenges both top-down models of colonial domination and bottom-up assertions of native agency. Colonial law was not a one-sided imposition of power; courts depended on subjects bringing cases. Legislation and judicial rulings often had different effects than officials or judges intended, as in Taj Mahal's case, where legislation that was supposed to end litigation in one case opened up the possibility of new litigation in other cases. On the flipside, law rarely provided straightforward routes for colonial subjects to assert independent agency. Actors that appeared in legal cases were the product of complex hierarchies of power, frustrating any attempt to isolate autonomous agents from broader networks of colonial power. The ability of litigants to enter the courts depended on access to social and financial capital. Unpredictable, and often lengthy, legal proceedings meant that uneven access to resources might easily determine the outcome in a case, depending on which party could hold out the longest. Third parties, whether lawyers or financiers, may have been the actual beneficiaries in many cases, and thus may have been the driving force behind litigation. And finally, by engaging colonial courts, non-European subjects often unwittingly contributed to the expanding power of colonial legal systems. The concept of agency, if framed in terms of autonomy and a link between conscious intentions and outcomes, thus seems poorly suited to understanding the way in which the law operated.[79]

Although the unpredictable nature of legal outcomes often frustrated individual intentions, including those of colonial officials, it nonetheless facilitated the expansion of imperial power more broadly. Legal discourses promising certainty helped justify European expansion, while courts brought colonial power into the everyday lives of colonized subjects. The participatory nature of colonial law facilitated penetrating forms of governance, while the ever-receding promise of certainty contributed to a constantly expanding system of control. These characteristics made colonial law a particularly dynamic and adaptable mode of dom-

78. Richard Pennell, "The Origins of the Foreign Jurisdiction Act and the Extension of British Sovereignty," *Historical Research* 83 (2010): 465–85.
79. Jon E. Wilson, "Subjects and Agents in the History of Imperialism and Resistance," in *Powers of the Secular Modern: Talal Asad and His Interlocutors*, ed. David Scott and Charles Hirschkind (Stanford: Stanford University Press, 2006), 180–205.

ination. While historians have become accustomed to thinking about knowledge as an instrument of power, fine-grained analysis of colonial law pushes us to think more carefully about how uncertainty also facilitated imperial expansion.

If focusing on the relationship between certainty and uncertainty pushes historians to rethink traditional models of colonial power, it also draws attention to the ways in which our own search for certainty in legal archives is at best an imperfect pursuit. While women and other marginalized groups appear with tantalizing frequency in court cases, on close inspection, this picture of subaltern agency often fractures. Although we do not know whether Mehdi Hussain was a benevolent stepfather or a conniving patriarch, there is little doubt that he heavily mediated Kulsumnissa's interactions with the courts. Seemingly captivating narratives of legal agency on closer inspection often unravel into histories and arguments constructed by other parties. Historians of colonial law, as much as colonial litigants and officials, therefore need to creatively engage with this uncertainty, seeing it as the very essence of the law, rather than its undoing.

Conclusion: From Macro to Micro Histories and Back Again

Thinking about how certainty and uncertainty were mutually constitutive brings the double vision of colonial law that emerges from the Awadh inheritance cases into a more unitary frame. In a similar fashion, as micro histories of individuals and legal cases that unfolded across the geographically dispersed space of Britain's Indian Ocean empire, the Awadh disputes bring together divergent scales of analysis. While perhaps counter-intuitive, such macro-micro histories have gained growing traction in recent years as historians have expanded the geographical scope of historical inquiry, whether to imperial, transnational, or global scales. Tracing the histories of a mobile individual, commodity, or text has provided circumscribed paths through transnational history's seemingly infinite archive, and packaged global spaces into human-sized narratives. These macro-micro histories have considerably enriched our understanding of the complexity of global phenomena, adding rich texture to what can otherwise appear as abstract generalizations about large swathes of space and diverse populations.[80] For perhaps not dissimilar reasons legal historians have long been attracted to micro history as a method that brings human depth to histories of law that can, particularly to non-specialists, often seem dry and overly abstract. Micro histories

---

80. Bernhard Struck, Kate Ferris, and Jacques Revel, "Introduction: Space and Scale in Transnational History," *International History Review* 33, no. 4 (2011): 577; Emma Rothschild, *The Inner Life of Empires: An Eighteenth-Century History* (Princeton: Princeton University Press, 2011), 7, 278; Francesca Trivellato, "Is There a Future for Italian Microhistory in the Age of Global History?" *California Italian Studies* 2 (2011); Sebouh David Aslanian, Joyce E. Chaplin, Ann McGrath, and Kristin Mann, "AHR Conversation How Size Matters: The Question of Scale in History," *American Historical Review* 118, no. 5 (2013): 1438–58.

of legal cases, not unlike micro global histories, also allow historians to move beyond the particular and the general, tying together the different scales on which law operates. During a moment in which historians are working at increasingly diverse scales, this approach seems particularly promising, but perhaps will also demand increasingly self-conscious reflection on its own methodological eclecticism. In the field of imperial history, which often intersects with the expanding field of global history, histories that explicitly engage with different scales of analysis offer further advantages. Contextualizing in-depth studies of individual cases in broader patterns of imperial power avoids the pitfalls of de-contextualized narratives of individual agency. For historians of colonial law this approach also promises to connect rich existing bodies of scholarship on law in specific colonial contexts to a broader awareness of how law operated at imperial scales, as precedents and legal models circulated across multiple regional contexts.

In moving between a bird's-eye overview of the legal landscape through which the Awadh cases moved to a zoomed-in study of the detailed records of the cases, this chapter has offered one possible way of self-consciously mixing different scales. In doing so the chapter suggests that mixing macro and micro perspectives, and in the process blurring the distinction between the two, has the added advantage of bringing into dialogue other seemingly desperate trajectories of historical analysis. While the chapter has explored this overlap more deeply in terms of the relationship between certainty and uncertainty, it also suggests the possibility of more interconnected histories of legal theory and practice, agency and structure, and global and local networks. Rather than pitting micro histories against macro arguments, these macro-micro histories explore connections between seemingly divergent phenomena, such as the role native litigants played in the expansion of colonial legal institutions. In doing so the goal is not a seamless integration of different scales and perspectives, but a provocative invitation to think about unexpected links—a process that the travels of Iqbal al-Daulah, Taj Mahal Begam, and their disputed estates, help facilitate.

8   The British-Ottoman Cold War, c. 1880-1914: Imperial Struggles over Muslim Mobility and Citizenship from the Suez Canal to the Durand Line*

Faiz Ahmed

As BOTH A mirror and foil to Vietnam's role in the Second Indochina War (1955–1975), Afghanistan in the 1980s became synonymous with a catastrophic and profoundly costly proxy war between the United States and the USSR. Exactly a century before the 1979 Soviet invasion, however, Afghanistan was a cold war battleground but of a very different kind. While the British and Ottoman Empires did not declare all-out hostilities and come to blows until the autumn of 1914 and the calamities of World War I, imperial rivalries between the Sublime Porte and the British Crown were already playing out between the erstwhile allies in South and Central Asia as early as the 1880s. As a British protectorate since 1879, Afghanistan had relinquished its foreign affairs to the supervision of the Raj's vast military-administrative network in Asia, but internally the Kabul-based emirate was a rare autonomous kingdom in the region not subject to European, Russian, Ottoman, Iranian, or Chinese rule at the time.

Meanwhile in the eastern Mediterranean, Ottoman efforts to "strike back" at the European Capitulations and rein in legal pluralism within the empire through a new vision of Ottomanism in the late nineteenth century have been the subject of a rich scholarly literature. Central to these historiographical contributions has been not only a better understanding of the late Ottoman Empire's legal, administrative, and educational reforms championing centralization, equal citizenship, and a civilizing mission of its own, but the idea that Ottoman officials and their subjects were not passive spectators to European economic and political ascendance in the region—especially when occurring within Ottoman borders.[1]

*This chapter is dedicated to the memory of Professor Saba Mahmood (1962–2018) and to her family. Research for this chapter was made possible by grants from the Social Science Research Council, Council on Library and Information Resources, Council of American Overseas Research Centers, and American Research Institute in Turkey. I am grateful to Indiana University Press for allowing me to reprint an earlier version of this chapter appearing as "Contested

The Subjects of Ottoman International Law (2020): 146–170
DOI: 10.2979/subjectsottomaninternationallaw.0.0.09

Recent years have seen historians of international law, sovereignty, and imperial citizenship advance the study of Ottoman extraterritoriality in global directions. Accessing international archives previously treated in isolation and transgressing conventional area studies divides, their work has pushed us to rethink questions of extraterritoriality as not simply a one or two-sided story of European dominance and Ottoman response in the eastern Mediterranean. Rather, scholars have begun to explore the myriad possibilities for contestation, negotiation, and mobility in a multipolar and increasingly inter-connected late imperial world.[2] Utilizing archival records from Istanbul, Delhi, and London, this chapter contributes to the growing body of literature on Ottoman extraterritoriality, Muslim mobility, and imperial citizenship by focusing on a series of consular and jurisdictional conflicts between the Ottomans and the British. It argues that from the 1880s to the eve of the First World War, the Ottoman government forcefully campaigned for its own extraterritorial privileges—not through overpowering military or economic might, but by persistently waging legal and diplomatic rows with its former ally, the British Crown, over Afghans and Indian Muslims.

While considerable scholarly work has been produced on the Ottoman Capitulations, the Eastern Question, and other related minority "Questions" from the Hamidian era to the rise of the Committee of Union and Progress (CUP), another Anglo-Ottoman arena brewing with contestation in this period has not nearly received as much attention: Afghanistan and its eastern borderlands with India. Exploring the juridical contours of an intensifying imperial rivalry between the British Crown and the Sublime Porte from the eastern Mediterranean

---

Subjects: Ottoman and British Jurisdictional Quarrels in re Afghans and Indian Muslims," *Journal of the Ottoman and Turkish Studies Association* 3, no. 2 (2016): 325–46, and to Chris Low, Lâle Can, Kent Schull, and Robert Zens for their invaluable feedback on improving it.
1. For example, see Selim Deringil, *The Well-Protected Domains: Ideology and the Legitimation of Power in the Ottoman Empire, 1876–1909* (London: I.B. Tauris, 1999); Benjamin C. Fortna, *Imperial Classroom: Islam, the State, and Education in the Late Ottoman Empire* (New York: Oxford University Press, 2002); Christine Philliou, *Biography of an Empire: Governing Ottomans in an Age of Revolution* (Berkeley: University of California Press, 2010).
2. For example, see Turan Kayaoğlu, *Legal Imperialism: Sovereignty and Extraterritoriality in Japan, the Ottoman Empire, and China* (Cambridge, UK: Cambridge University Press, 2010); Lâle Can, "The Protection Question: Central Asians and Extraterritoriality in the Late Ottoman Empire," in this volume; Will Hanley, *Identifying with Nationality: Europeans, Ottomans, and Egyptians in Alexandria* (New York: Columbia University Press, 2017). Other emergent scholarship in this direction not dealt with here concerns religious minorities and how the latter navigated both Ottomanism and European extraterritoriality in increasingly complex ways. See Michelle Campos, *Ottoman Brothers: Muslims, Christians, and Jews in Early 20th Century Palestine* (Stanford: Stanford University Press, 2010); Julia Cohen, *Becoming Ottoman: Sephardi Jews and Imperial Citizenship in the Modern Era* (New York: Oxford University Press, 2014); Sarah Abrevaya Stein, *Extraterritorial Dreams: European Citizenship, Sephardi Jews, and the Ottoman Twentieth Century* (Chicago: University of Chicago Press, 2016).

to southern and central Asia, this chapter is divided into three parts. The first provides a brief historical background for mounting British-Ottoman tensions in the second half of the nineteenth century, contextualizing inter-imperial tensions over Afghans and Indian Muslims who also constitute primary actors in his drama. The second examines cases of disputes between the Sublime Porte and the British Raj over diplomatic privileges in India, especially the sensitive issue of expanding Ottoman consulates from coastal cities to the subcontinent's interior. The final section explores Ottoman and British contestations over itinerant Muslims falling in the nebulous and overlapping categories of Afghans, Indian Pashtuns ("Pakhtuns/Pathans"), and other Indian Muslims. It focuses on Ottoman attempts to exercise jurisdiction over itinerant Afghans and Indian Muslims traveling within the sultan's domains, especially Mesopotamia, Greater Syria, and the Hijaz. During the Hamidian period (1876–1909) in particular, Ottoman and British records reveal several instances of the Porte—mainly through its provincial branches from Jerusalem to Baghdad and Aleppo to Medina—awarding Muslim emigrants from India and Afghanistan with Ottoman nationality, thereby reconstituting these foreign nationals as subjects of the sultan. By considering the Porte's own jurisdictional reach across imperial borders, the study challenges linear and one-dimensional narratives of extraterritoriality in the late Ottoman Empire that focus on the apex of European Capitulations in the nineteenth century and their abolition by the CUP triumverate during World War I. At the same time, it highlights the agency of Afghans and Indian Muslims in capitalizing on the opportunities extraterritoriality could provide, while "pulling in" the aforementioned empires as they pursued their own aims and interests.

Great Games? A New Imperial Rivalry in Eurasia and the Roots of British-Ottoman Mistrust

This study focuses on how consular correspondence and imperial citizenship constituted arenas where British and Ottoman contestations over Afghan and Indian Muslim subjects took place. But the legal and diplomatic spats emerging between London and the Sublime Porte in the late nineteenth century and escalating to the eve of World War I were rooted in a dramatic pair of back-to-back traumas that remade the so-called Eastern Question as the world knew it. These two transformative processes were the Russo-Ottoman war in 1877–78 and the British occupation of Egypt in 1882. The first—with its profound territorial and demographic consequences, including an influx of Muslim refugees from the Balkans and Caucuses, and concurrent flight of Christian refugees from the empire's frontiers—served to reconstitute both territorial boundaries and ethnoreligious demographics of the Ottoman state in ways that led Sultan Abdülhamid

II to emphasize a newfound "Islamic" character to the empire.[3] As for Britain's military occupation of Egypt, it provided London with exclusive control of the Suez Canal, a maritime lifeline to the jewel in the crown of Britain's global empire, India. Britain's de facto control over the Suez rendered the Porte's de jure sovereignty over Egypt even more titular and inconsequential.

The Russo-Ottoman War of 1877–78 signaled a watershed turning point not only in Russo-Ottoman relations, but also between the Sublime Porte and London. Still, the politics of suspicion which characterized British-Ottoman relations from the 1880s until the eve of the Great War should not be essentialized as a static or perennial trait of relations between the English Crown and Istanbul. Though the empires certainly entertained differences of opinion, sometimes vociferous, on matters internal to each other's domains—particularly concerning economic and legal capitulations, as well as the rights of minorities in each empire—for the majority of the nineteenth century the Porte and Crown were allied in curbing Russian ambitions in southern Europe and the Mediterranean.[4] For London, the threat of an expansionist St. Petersburg seeking access to warm-water ports presented a far more ominous threat than upholding Ottoman suzerainty in a strategic region.[5]

Following the dramatic geopolitical shifts of the Russo-Ottoman War and British occupation of Egypt, the new balance of power in Eurasia and the eastern Mediterranean in particular left an indelible impact on British-Ottoman relations. As Istanbul's loss of massive swaths of territory in southeastern Europe brought Russia even closer to the warm waters of the Mediterranean and, most crucially, Britain's occupation of Egypt providing London with unrestricted access to India, it seems the Porte's friendship no longer presented the same geostrategic dividends to London that it once had. Over the course of the 1880s and 1890s, this translated into less British guarantees of protection to the Ottomans at best, an increased criticism of the Porte for treatment of its minority populations

---

3. On the internal transformations and reconstitution of the empire in the Hamidian era, see Deringil, *The Well-Protected Domains.*
4. Neither was the Anglo-Ottoman entente limited to the nineteenth century, with alliances dating to Queen Elizabeth I's (1533–1603) maritime pact with Ottoman Sultan Murad III (1546–95). The latter ties oversaw the chartering of the English Levant Company and the dispatch of England's first ambassador to the Porte, William Harbonne, in 1578. Nabil Matar, *Turks, Moors, and Englishmen in the Age of Discovery* (New York: Columbia University Press, 1999), 9–12. For a detailed account of Elizabethan England's relations with the Ottomans, see Jerry Brotton, *The Sultan and the Queen: The Untold Story of Elizabeth and Islam* (New York: Penguin Books, 2017).
5. For example, the Ottoman sultans enjoyed British support during conflicts with foreign and domestic enemies alike, as against Russia in the Crimean War of 1853–56, and earlier against the Egyptian governor Mehmed Ali's rebellion against the Porte in 1831.

and, at worst, an active policy of dismemberment and distribution of the empire's territories as a permanent solution to the Eastern Question.

In the early 1880s, Istanbul and London increasingly accused each other of two-faced dealings, outright hostility, and malicious intent to undermine the other. Trading accusations was only a symptom, however, of deeper tensions boiling beneath the surface of diplomatic relations between London and the Porte. Before 1877, for example, communications between the Porte and the British Government of India were direct, but after the embarrassment of repeated miscommunications between London and Calcutta concerning the first Ottoman mission to Kabul in 1877–78, upon the Crown's insistence, the British Foreign Office instructed that all communication with the Porte would thereafter be via London.[6] Relations with the Porte assumed an even sharper decline when the Liberal Party administration of William Gladstone ascended to the premiership in 1880.[7] Given the pride and defiance of Hamidian Pan-Islamism, itself a response to shifting policies in London, the British and the Ottomans appeared to be on a course not of civilizational clash, but a parting of imperial visions. The latter divergence concerned the optimal route through which each empire sought to preserve their strategic interests and territorial integrity—visions which had once cemented them in alliance.

That friendly ties between the Porte and London were unraveling was manifest in a series of diplomatic and legal spats emerging in the 1880s. Rooted in diverging imperial interests in the region and the world, rather than an a priori East-West divide, Anglo-Ottoman mistrust surfaced in the increasing number of accusations traded between the Porte and London at this time. The latter was matched by increasingly polarized newspaper coverage in the British and Ottoman Empires.[8] It was at this juncture, coming on the heels of the Russo-Ottoman War of 1877–78, that the Porte was growing increasingly indignant at what they saw as unwelcomed foreign interference in Ottoman internal affairs—from Bulgaria to eastern Anatolia and Mount Lebanon to North Africa. As criticism from European capitals over the Ottoman treatment of Christian minorities mounted, the Porte responded twofold: first, with with tit-for-tat condemnations of Britain's misdeeds in Africa, Asia, and even Ireland; and second, by expanding its outreach to Muslims living under colonial rule, at times bypassing British protocols in the process. In this increasingly polarized atmosphere, we find a brewing controversy over the Ottomans' attempts to press for more consular rights in India.

---

6. Azmi Özcan, *Pan-Islamism: Indian Muslims, the Ottomans and Britain* (Leiden: Brill, 1997), 125.
7. Ibid., 94.
8. Ibid., 121.

Ottoman Consulates in British India

Evidence of Ottoman correspondence with Muslim rulers in India dates to the mid-fifteenth century, but the first consulates in the subcontinent were not established until 1849. The royal *ferman* authorizing the appointments of liaisons to Calcutta and Bombay specified their duties as "executing the affairs of the merchants and our people" and "consulting their interest and ensuring the respect of property and honour."[9] After the termination of the Mughal sultanate in 1857 political ties with the Ottomans largely rested on individual outreach by the semi-autonomous rulers of princely states, such as the begum of Bhopal or nizam of Hyderabad, none of whom had embassies in Istanbul.[10] By the late nineteenth century, with the enhanced mobility that steamships and railroads provided, more Indian Muslims traveled—and emigrated—to Ottoman lands where they met co-religionists from across the world. Such movements and interactions often attracted the attention of British surveillance. It was not uncommon for the British Agency at Constantinople, for example, to report in routine intelligence exchanges with the Raj's Foreign Department that a visiting Indian had "taken a house in Constantinople" where he "sees a good deal of the Turkish notables and of the Mussulman population of the city."[11]

British Apprehension in Bombay

In the last quarter of the century British authorities began to eye the activities of Ottoman consuls in India with increasing concern. During the 1877–78 Russo-Ottoman War, the Porte's consul-general at Bombay, Hüseyin Hasib Efendi, emerged as a prominent social figure in the local Muslim community and frequent commentator in the city's vibrant Urdu press. In scarcely five years Hasib Efendi had galvanized the Muslims of Bombay to several pro-Ottoman projects, including donations to Ottoman relief funds.[12]

While Hasib Efendi's activities in Bombay took place amid a longstanding British-Ottoman alliance against Russian expansion in Asia, the burgeoning popularity of a foreign state's representative on Indian soil discomforted some in the Raj. Indian archival records indicate Hasib Efendi was under close surveil-

---

9. Ibid., 112. On Ottoman diplomacy in India before British rule, see Naimur Rahman Farooqi, *Mughal-Ottoman Relations* (Delhi: Idarih-i Adabiyat, 2009).

10. This chapter employs the terms "Indian Muslim" and "Muslims of India" primarily as geographical referents; they should not be taken to connote a static or homogenous people, obscuring the profound regional and linguistic diversity of the subcontinent's Muslims. On Indian Muslims as a modern legal and political category, see Ayesha Jalal, *Self and Sovereignty: Individual and Community in South Asian Islam since 1850* (New York: Routledge, 2000), 139–86.

11. National Archives of India, New Delhi, India (hereafter NAI), FD/SEC/April 1878/163–164.

12. Özcan, *Pan-Islamism*, 112–13.

lance of British authorities until his departure in the early 1880s. An August 1880 intelligence brief, for example, reported the consul-general moving his Bombay residence from the isolated Chowpatty district on Queen's Road to the city's main "Mahomedan quarter." Citing a local informant, the memorandum proceeded to describe noteworthy occurrences at Friday prayers in the local congregational mosque:

> The Turkish Consul, as representing the Sultan of Turkey, the Khelif of Islam, is present and joins in the public prayers in the mosque. When the Imam concludes the Friday prayer, he offers a thanksgiving to the Almighty, praises the messenger of God, his principal Khelifs, and then comes to praise the Khelif of the time, the Commander of the Faithful, as servant of the two sacred shrines, *viz.*, Abdulhamid Khan, Sultan of Islam and Mussulmen. All this is done in the presence of his direct representative, who is accredited from Constantinople, to the followers of Islam. The hearts of all present are drawn towards him, and this performance affects the minds of the people, not only of the ignorant and bigoted, but also the minds of those who are educated.[13]

Encouraged by Hasib Efendi's influence at Bombay, the Porte sought to expand its diplomatic presence in the subcontinent. From the late 1870s on, the Ottoman government increasingly petitioned their British counterparts for permission to open more consulates on Indian soil, including along the strategic frontier with Afghanistan. By and large, the response was unbending refusal. Because the Porte lacked significant commercial interests in the Indian provinces—or so Raj officials claimed—and Muslim pilgrims could be facilitated through ports at Bombay, Calcutta, and Karachi, the Ottomans had no grounds to open consulates in the Indian interior. In a June 1877 memorandum on the question of a new Ottoman consulate at Peshawar, Under-Secretary of State for India Louis Mallet provided the rationale for denying such requests. "With regard to the proposed Consulate at Peshawar," explained Sir Mallet, "I am directed to observe that it is not the practice to permit a consul to act in any town in India except where the country he represents has important commercial interests, and, further, that up to this time no consul has been appointed to any inland Indian town."[14]

While providing ostensible cause, the Raj's argument became increasingly tenuous in light of the Porte's growing social and economic ties with Indian Muslims, over and above the annual hajj and other pilgrimages supervised by the Ottomans.[15] As Michael Christopher Low and John Slight have emphasized, it

---

13. NAI-FD/SEC/March 1881/92–103.
14. NAI-FD/SEC/March 1878/6–63.
15. It should be noted here that Indian Muslim pilgrims in the Ottoman lands were never limited to the hajj season nor the Hijaz region, but included those performing the minor pilgrimage (*'umra*) as well as visitations of saintly tombs (*ziyārāt*). The latter rites were performed year-round and attracted substantial numbers of Indian Muslims to travel (if not emigrate) to

is important to not divorce the Ottomans' considerable economic and geo-strategic interests from religious considerations underlining the hajj or other forms of "Pan-Islamic" activity. In light of the lucrative trade opportunities connecting the Central Asian and Indian Ocean regions—interlaced, perhaps, with a desire to mirror European diplomatic protocols and projecting its own extraterritorial influence—establishing consuls in new hubs may well have had more to do with expanding mercantile relationships than religious politics.[16]

The Ottoman-Indian Consular Controversy

Ottoman and British archival records from the late nineteenth century reveal continual petitions by the Porte to build regional consulates (*şehbenderlikler*) in India, in addition to their official Consulate General (*başşehbenderlik*) at Bombay. The choice of locales for expansion was not haphazard. Ottoman petitions reflected special interest in Hyderabad, Delhi, Lahore, Karachi, and Peshawar— large cities with significant Muslim populations.[17] In the case of Peshawar—a bustling border town at the base of the Khyber Pass—the city was a hub for profitable textile commerce crisscrossing Khorasan, Turkistan, and the Punjab, and possibly the world's best horse-trading. It was also India's gateway into Afghanistan and the fertile plains of Central Asia, where Turkic vassal states formed a restive southern frontier for the Ottomans' chief nemesis, Russia.

From this perspective it is not surprising that the Ottomans eyed Peshawar for a new consulate in the summer of 1877, precisely when the Porte dispatched

Syria, Mesopotamia, and Egypt, and for Indian Shi'is in particular, to the hallowed *'atabāt* shrines of Iraq. For an 1882 British report on the large community of Indian subjects residing in Najaf and Kerbala, for example, see NAI-FD/GNL/B/April 1882/14.

16. On the emergence of modern bureaucratic, environmental, and public health regimes in the context of the hajj and inter-imperial relations between the late Ottomans, British, and Russians in particular, see Michael Christopher Low, "Ottoman Infrastructures of the Saudi Hydro-State: The Technopolitics of Pilgrimage and Potable Water in the Hijaz," *Comparative Studies in Society and History* 57 (2015): 942–74; idem, "Empire and the Hajj: Pilgrims, Plagues, and Pan-Islam under British Surveillance, 1865–1908," *International Journal of Middle East Studies* 40, no. 2 (2008): 269–90; John Slight, *The British Empire and the Hajj, 1865–1956* (Cambridge, MA: Harvard University Press, 2015); Nile Green, "The Hajj as Its Own Undoing: Infrastructure and Integration on the Muslim Journey to Mecca," *Past and Present* 226 (2015): 193–226; Eileen Kane, *Russian Hajj: Empire and the Pilgrimage to Mecca* (Ithaca: Cornell University Press, 2015).

17. For example, see Başbakanlık Osmanlı Arşivi (hereafter BOA), HR.TO 126/76 (16 May 1877); BOA-Y.A.HUS 211/84 (28 C 1305/11 March 1888); BOA-Y.PRK.PT 15/121 (15 Ra 1315/14 Aug. 1897); BOA-Y.PRK.AZJ 51/72 (1323); BOA-DH.EUM.2.Şb 3/10 (17 M 1333/6 Dec. 1914). On the Porte's embassy in Bombay ("Bombay Başşehbenderliği"), see BOA-Y.A.HUS 207/55 (23 M 1305/11 Oct. 1887). For British Indian perspectives on Ottoman requests to expand interior consuls, see NAI-FD/SEC/March 1878/6–63.

its first official envoy to Kabul. On 8 June, British Ambassador at Constantinople Sir Austen Layard wrote to the British Viceroy of India,

> GRAND VIZIER has asked me whether Her Majesty's Government would object to the Turkish Government naming a consul at Peshawur. I avoided giving an answer to the question, but I understand that it may be repeated to me or to Her Majesty's Government in a more formal manner. The object, it is stated, of the appointment would be to promote Sultan's influence, a good understanding between England and Afghanistan, and to counteract influence of Russia.[18]

Wary of the sultan-caliph's growing influence in Asia, the Foreign Office in London not only declined the Porte's request but urged that extreme caution be exercised when escorting Abdülhamid's envoy to Kabul. In a 28 June 1877 memorandum from then-Secretary of State for India (and later UK Prime Minister) Lord Salisbury, the latter went so far as to prohibit the Ottoman envoy's passage by any towns with large Muslim populations.

> I need hardly call your attention to the probability that, if the envoy is permitted to remain in any of the towns where a powerful Mussulman population exists, popular demonstrations will result, which may involve hazard to the public peace as well as be likely to give a false impression of the intentions of Her Majesty's Government. Your Excellency will best avoid this danger by arranging that the envoy should rest at places where the Mussulman element is not predominant in the population.[19]

That the Foreign Office consistently rejected Ottoman requests to expand its diplomatic representation into the Indian hinterlands revealed trepidation on London's part. Stressing that religious rites were the only basis for the Turkish caliph's extraterritorial influence, London was quick to remind the Porte that Indian Muslims were subjects of the British Crown and no other sovereign. British attempts to limit Abdülhamid's influence to "religious" matters are also evident in their rejecting the Porte's offer to send an envoy to Kabul to mediate a peace during the Second Anglo-Afghan War (1878–80).[20]

Undeterred, Ottoman outreach to Indian Muslims advanced in multiple venues and directions in ensuing decades, including written correspondence, courtly receptions in Istanbul, and financial assistance for émigrés to Ottoman lands.[21] If Porte officials could not go to Indian Muslims, it found ways for Indian Muslims to come to them.

18. NAI-FD/SEC/March 1878/6–63.
19. Ibid.
20. Ibid.; NAI-FD/SEC/E/June 1896/286–290.
21. On British Indian subjects residing in Baghdad, for example, see NAI-FD/GNL/B/April 1882/14. On the Porte's receiving a prominent Indian Muslim fugitive from India, see NAI-FD/

An English Pasha's Proposal

Petitions to expand consular services for Indian pilgrims to the Ottoman lands were hardly a monopoly of the Porte.[22] An example of the lengths to which some British subjects went in this regard was a proposal submitted by the English-born soldier of fortune Sir Stephen Bartlett Lakeman (1823–1900). Knighted by Queen Victoria and christened "Mazar Pasha" by the Porte for his service to the Ottoman Army during the Crimean War (1853–56), Lakeman had previously fought with the French Army in Algeria and served as captain and commander of British forces in South Africa.

On 29 March 1897, Lakeman submitted a formal plea to Her Majesty's Government to expand consular services for Indian Muslims seeking to perform the hajj. In his petition to the Secretary of State for Foreign Affairs in London, Lakeman highlighted the prominent role of Indian Muslims in bolstering Abdülhamid's claims to the caliphate, noting that over eighty percent of foreign Muslims arriving in Constantinople to pay homage to the caliph in the prior seven years were Indian Muslims. "They were for the most part of high rank and no doubt leading men in their part of the world," Lakeman added.[23] The petition concluded with a concrete recommendation: endow a special Indian Affairs Agency at Constantinople. Lakeman was at pains to explain this was not a charitable undertaking. Such an agency, he emphasized, would not only facilitate British political and economic interests in Ottoman territory, but also impress on the millions of Indian Muslim subjects that Britain was the friend of Muslims in India and Turkey alike.

> What I would propose is to create an Agency at Constantinople exclusively for Indian affairs; it would have nothing to do with foreign powers or European questions: it would be exclusively under the control of the Indian Board; and only transact business with British Dependencies; in fact, be a link between Europe and Asia: in the hands of England it would make us more one power than our combined efforts without continuity make us to-day; it would be an invasion of Europe under British guidance, and repeople the Mediterranean. With an Agency, such as I propose, Indian pilgrims would not require Russian aid in any shape; the expense would be very slight. The Sultan would be only too happy to have any participation in the matter to and to give the Agency

SEC/F/November 1884/243–253. On Indo-Ottoman correspondence from the 1880s through the 1900s, for example, see NAI-FD/SEC/March 1881/92–103; NAI-FD/EXTL/B/March 1904/109.

22. As Michael Christopher Low vividly demonstrates in his complimentary study of British-Ottoman consular quarrels in this volume, jurisdictional tensions over Indian pilgrims extended to the Hijaz itself. Low, "Unfurling the Flag of Extraterritoriality."

23. NAI-FD/SEC/E/January 1898/128–129.

one of the empty palaces on the Bosphorus as a residence for the pilgrims when they stay a few days at Stamboul.[24]

Putting aside fanciful calls to "repeople the Mediterranean" with British subjects, at the core of Lakeman's proposal was a more pragmatic initiative: establish a lodge for Indian Muslims in Istanbul, similar to longstanding ones for Uzbek and Afghan pilgrims but under British administration.[25] Here, the English Pasha was keen to justify his proposal in the language of imperium—enhancing British prestige among Asian Muslims, while containing Russia. Like the first Ottoman mission to Afghanistan in 1877–78—a scheme envisaged and facilitated by Raj officials to counter Russian influence in Kabul—Lakeman's proposal is a reminder that British geopolitical strategy must also be considered in any discussion of Pan-Islamic projects during this period.

Citing expenses and a lack of personnel, the Foreign Office rejected the proposal. The Crown's aloofness amid a seemingly golden opportunity to expand its own extraterritorial privileges within the Ottoman domains contrasts with conventional narratives of an onslaught of European Capitulations in the nineteenth century. Had Lakeman's proposal been implemented, it may well have compromised Ottoman sovereignty over its own territory even further, since more Indians in Istanbul could pave the way for British intervention on their behalf. On the other hand, it is possible the Foreign Office interpreted Lakeman's plan as potentially expanding Abdülhamid's influence, rather than Great Britain's. In any case, from the Porte's requests to build more consulates in India to an English Pasha's appeal for an Indian pilgrims' lodge in Istanbul, attempts to expand Indo-Ottoman ties through official British diplomatic channels largely met with closed doors.[26]

Bypassing the British: Independent Contact between the Sublime Porte and Indian Muslims

Among the ironies of British recalcitrance in the face of repeated petitions to build more consulates in India was that it motivated the Porte to bolster its contacts with Indian Muslims through more direct means. By the 1890s, there is evidence to suggest Ottoman officials were already carrying out consular activities

---

24. Ibid.
25. On Afghan lodges in Istanbul, see BOA-A.MKT.MVL 97/73 (5 L 1274/19 May 1858); BOA-Y. PRK.AZJ 47/25 (29 Z 1320/28 March 1903); BOA-Y.MTV 254/114 (17 L 1321/5 Jan. 1904); BOA-ZB 608/57 (1323); BOA-BEO 2787/208952 (25 M 1324/21 March 1906).
26. These were some of the most prominent attempts from the Hamidian period, but not the only ones. For example, see BOA-Y.PRK.EŞA 37/36 (13 L 1318/3 Feb. 1901); BOA-Y.PRK.TKM 28/56 (1310); BOA-HR.SYS 216/9 (18 June 1890); BOA-BEO 1182/88583 (5 R 1316/23 Aug. 1898); BOA-HR.TO 59/24 (5 July 1877). For British perspectives, see NAI/FD/SEC/E/Oct. 1892/39–46; India Office Records, London, UK (hereafter IOR), L/PS/10/196.

in the Indian interior.[27] At the same time, Indian Muslims were also bypassing official diplomatic channels in their outreach to the Porte by forming a number of transnational Muslim associations, or *anjumans* in Persian and Urdu. Founded in the late nineteenth century as literary and philanthropic societies dedicated to preserving Islamicate culture and promoting Muslim interests in India, *anjumans* also served to connect expatriate Indian communities in Europe with their ancestral homes in the subcontinent. But from Lahore to Liverpool, *anjumans* also served another purpose: to bolster ties between Indian Muslims and the sultan-caliph in Istanbul. The activities of *anjumans* were not uni-directional; some were founded in England and inspired local branches in India; others fostered connections with affiliates in Egypt, Afghanistan, or the Ottoman domains. A British Indian intelligence briefing from 1880, for example, describes the founding of a branch of the London Islamic Society in Calcutta, where weekly meetings were held in a prominent Muslim's home and communications were drafted for correspondence with the Ottoman government.[28]

Meanwhile in Istanbul and London, Porte officials were relentless in pressuring their British counterparts to expand the Ottoman diplomatic presence in India—and Afghanistan. As late as 1899, the Porte again offered to send an envoy to Kabul, this time with an invitation to the emir for establishing an Afghan Agency at Constantinople. The subsequent exchange between the Indian Foreign Department and governor-general in Khorasan revealed continuing British unease over unsupervised correspondence between Istanbul and Kabul. "I think we can still only watch the development of this matter," wrote the Foreign Department officer in anticipation. "If the Amir entertains the alleged proposal of the Sultan that an Afghan Consular Agent should be appointed at Constantinople," he continued, "it will doubtless be thought necessary to remind His Highness of the arrangement of 1880, under which he 'can have no political relations with any foreign Power, except with the British Government'."[29]

Even more perturbing to British authorities was the flight of Indian fugitives to Ottoman territories, where they could find political asylum and more. A prominent example was the refuge granted to the Indian Muslim scholar Rahmatullah Kairanwi (1818–91). A leading participant in the 1857 Rebellion, Kairanwi had since fled to Ottoman-administered Yemen and the Hijaz. In 1883 he was

27. For a letter to the "Turkish Consulate at Peshawar," see BOA-İ.HR-335/21534 (21 C 1295/22 June 1878). Ottoman sources also document Muslims of the subcontinent corresponding with consulates outside of Bombay, as with Indian journalist Muhammad Inshaullah's letter to the Ottoman "consulate" (şehbenderlık) at Karachi. BOA-Y.A.HUS 377/4 (1 Ca 1315/27 Sept. 1897).
28. NAI-FD/SEC/Nov. 1881/86. According to British intelligence reports, among the leading members in this organization were Khuda Bakhsh and Syed Amir Ali, who would play leading roles in the Khilafat Movement after World War I. Also see Özcan, *Pan-Islamism*, 97.
29. NAI-FD/SEC/F/Nov. 1899/29–30.

hosted in Istanbul by Sultan Abdülhamid himself.[30] The ability of Kairanwi and others like him to escape British authorities by resettling in the sultan's domains demonstrated how far Anglo-Ottoman relations had drifted.[31] In 1857, the Ottomans displayed their rapport with the British by not only standing aloof from the rebellion, but going as far as to condemn its participants. A quarter-century later, the Sublime Porte was embracing its ringleaders.

Itinerant Afghans and the Right of Protection

Complicating British-Ottoman quarrels over extraterritoriality in the late nineteenth century were the Sublime Porte's efforts to strengthen bilateral ties with the Raj's immediate neighbor to the west, the semi-autonomous Emirate of Afghanistan. Separated from India by a notoriously permeable frontier, Afghanistan was technically a protectorate of the British Empire since the Treaty of Gandamak of 1879 and reinforced in the Durand Line Accord of 1893.[32] Per these agreements, Afghan emirs maintained control over the internal affairs of their country but were enjoined from conducting their own foreign relations, including establishing consulates abroad. This did not stop the Ottomans from reaching out to Afghan officials and vice-versa, however, as scores of documents in Ottoman, Indian, and Afghan archives attest in the decades following the first official mission to Kabul in 1877–78.[33]

This section focuses on an impasse beleaguering relations between the Porte and British Crown over Afghanistan at the turn of the twentieth century: Afghans traveling outside of their domicile country. Ottoman and British administrations clashed over who exercised the right of protection, also known as personal jurisdiction, over said itinerants. Unlike consulates which could be closed or enjoined from construction, the right of protection presented even thornier quandaries because as mobile human beings with competing notions of allegiance, Afghans were often entangled in fluid and pluralistic notions of sovereignty and nationality.

---

30. NAI FD/SEC/F/Nov. 1884/243–253. As Kairanwi continued to live in Mecca until his death in 1891, British officials were dismayed that such a "notorious rebel of Indian Mutiny" would be so well received by Ottoman authorities. On the life, travels, and religious politics of Kairanwi, see Seema Alavi, *Muslim Cosmopolitanism in the Age of Empire* (Cambridge, MA: Harvard University Press, 2015), 169–220; Özcan, *Pan-Islamism*, 18–19.

31. Kairanwi was not the only fugitive from anti-British revolts in India to be welcomed in Ottoman territory. Other prominent examples included Sayyid Fazl (1823–1901) and Haji Imdadullah Makki (1817–99). See Alavi, *Muslim Cosmopolitanism*, 169–221 and 222–66, respectively.

32. The 1893 agreement recommitted Afghanistan and India to non-intervention beyond a demarcated border, the so-called Durand Line. Kabul also ceded the strategic frontier towns of Peshawar and Quetta to India, dividing ancient Pashtun and Baluch homelands into two states and laying the seeds for future irredentist claims and conflict.

33. Faiz Ahmed, "Istanbul and Kabul in Courtly Contact: The Question of Exchange between the Ottoman Empire and Afghanistan in the Late Nineteenth Century," *Journal of Ottoman Studies* 45 (2015): 265–96.

The Law(s) of Jurisdiction: Legal Pluralism and its Discontents

At the root of British-Ottoman disputes over the legal status of itinerant Afghans is the fact that there was no singular, dispositive treaty or universal law of jurisdiction with regard to Afghans and Indian Muslims traveling outside of their domicile countries. On the British side, the Raj claimed jurisdiction over Indian subjects wherever they were, presenting a traditional English common law argument of in personam jurisdiction. In the case of Afghanistan—formally a protectorate of the Raj—treaty agreements stipulated that Afghans could claim British protection when traveling outside of the emirate if they so chose, but as they were not considered British subjects the exigencies of their case depended on the actual territory they were in.

Muddling the legal terrain was an increasingly assertive Abdülhamid II who, in a number of diplomatic tussles with the British from the 1880s on, claimed a form of politico-religious jurisdiction over all Muslims—even those without Ottoman papers—based on claims to the Pan-Islamic caliphate. As with their dismissal of Ottoman requests to build more consulates in India, the British adamantly refused to accept any political rights accruing from the Ottoman caliphate, a solely "religious" office in the eyes of London. Therein lay the seeds of an Anglo-Ottoman struggle over Afghans abroad.

From Istanbul's perspective, Britain and other European powers were engaging in a double-standard with regard to religious minorities. While the Porte was prevented from claiming jurisdiction over Indian Muslims and Afghans living within British imperial domains, such as India, this arrangement was a conspicuous contrast to the legal status of many Christian "protégés" and other protected minorities attached to European embassies. The latter were increasingly successful in claiming foreign subject status within the Ottoman domains itself, particularly in Mediterranean coastal cities, among other locales.[34] While the Porte's attempts to constrict legal pluralism within the empire through a new centralizing and equalizing ideology of Ottomanism have been studied in depth, what has not been given as much attention is how the Ottomans endeavored to level the jurisdictional playing field by claiming authority over non-Ottoman Muslims residing within the sublime domains. As documented in both Turkish and British imperial archives, the Ottoman government did not shy from award-

---

34. Ziad Fahmy, "Jurisdictional Borderlands: Extraterritoriality and 'Legal Chameleons' in Precolonial Alexandria, 1840–1870," *Comparative Studies in Society and History* 55 (2013): 305–29; Will Hanley, "Papers for Going, Papers for Staying: Identification and Subject Formation in the Eastern Mediterranean," in *A Global Middle East: Mobility, Materiality and Culture in the Modern Age, 1880–1940*, ed. Liat Kozma, Avner Wishnitzer, and Cyrus Schayegh, (London: I.B. Tauris, 2014), 177–200; Mary Dewhurst Lewis, "Geographies of Power: The Tunisian Civic Order, Jurisdictional Politics, and Imperial Rivalry in the Mediterranean, 1881–1935," *Journal of Modern History* 80, no. 4 (2008).

ing Muslim emigrants of India, Afghanistan, and Algeria with Ottoman nationality, thereby reconstituting these foreign nationals as subjects of the sultan.[35]

British perspectives on the international legal status of Afghans are summarized in an 1890 Indian Foreign Department memorandum entitled "Protection by the British Government of Afghans in Foreign Countries." The document outlines the three categories for classifying Afghans traveling outside the Emirate of Afghanistan:

> 1. Afghans resident in Persia and Turkish Arabia, who have for years past been recognized as under British protection,—refugees, pensioners, &c.

> 2. Afghans from British territory, particularly Pishin and districts bordering on Afghanistan. This is an increasing class.

> 3. Afghans proper, subjects of the Amir.[36]

Following this tripartite division, the memorandum proceeded to describe the official policy regarding passports for the aforesaid groups. According to the Foreign Department, Afghans traveling outside of Afghanistan were bound by bilateral agreements rendering them reliant on British protection, regardless of which country or territory they enter. The document continued:

> [T]he Amir having placed the conduct of his foreign relations in their [Government of India's] hands, they [Government of India] are bound to act on the behalf of such Afghan subjects as may require the intervention of a foreign

35. For example, see BOA-MVL 1035/131 (10 S 1284/13 June 1867); BOA-DH.MKT 1358/3 (1 Za 1303/1 Aug. 1886); BOA-Y.PRK.BŞK 11/25 (1303); BOA-A.MKT.UM 565/25 (15 Za 1278/14 May 1862); BOA-BEO 459/34377 (17 S 1312/19 Aug. 1894); BOA-BEO 459/34391 (17 S 1312/19 Aug. 1894); BOA-BEO 488/36529 (3 R 1312/2 Oct. 1894); BOA-DH.MKT 2508/121 (23 Za 1319/3 March 1902); BOA-DH.MKT 2501/27 (3 Ra 1319/20 June 1901); BOA-DH.MKT 2505/140 (16 Ra 1319/3 July 1901). For additional perspectives from the India Office and Raj's Foreign Department, see IOR-L/PS/20/42, 406-17, 451-70; NAI-FD/SEC/F/Oct. 1890/10-13. Ottoman grants of nationality to Afghan émigrés were often accompanied by generous stipends for resettling in Ottoman domains. In some cases Ottoman support outlasted the life of the original recipient and extended to descendants, as with Shaykh Musa Efendi, an Afghan émigré resettled in Jerusalem, and Mahmud Tarzi Bey, the son of an influential Afghan exile resettled in Damascus. On the former, see BOA-MVL 1035/131 (10 S 1284/13 June 1867); on the latter, BOA-A.MKT.UM 565/25 (15 Za 1278/14 May 1862); BOA-Y.PRK.BŞK 11/25 (1303); BOA-İ.DH 1278/100575 (12 Za 1309/7 June 1892); BOA-BEO 488/36529 (3 R 1312/2 Oct. 1894); BOA-DH.MKT 2453/39 (1 Za 1318/20 Feb. 1901); BOA-ŞD 2293/4 (5 Za 1318/24 Feb. 1901). National forum-shopping could run in several directions, of course, as with the Pan-Islamist international Jamal al-Din "al-Afghani", who over the course of his lifetime transmuted from Iranian to Afghan to Ottoman to British Indian nationalities. For British-Ottoman quarrels on al-Afghani, see BOA-BEO 176/13184 (8 N 1310/26 March 1893); BOA-İ.HUS 10/1310/N-24 (7 N 1310/25 March 1893); NAI-FD/SEC/E/ March 1896/186-187.

36. NAI-FD/SEC/F/June 1890/157-218.

power when temporarily sojourning in foreign countries; and they cannot, therefore, regard without apprehension any arrangement under which Afghan subjects requiring passports in Persia or in any other foreign country would no longer be dependent for assistance upon British authorities.[37]

While the Indian Foreign Department's statement appears to indicate a uniform rule, in practice itinerant Afghans presented diplomatic quagmires that largely went unresolved, precisely because they involved two sovereign states at loggerheads and with no mechanism other than bilateral negotiations to settle them.

In re *Afghans in India*

Most jurisdictional contests between London and the Porte over itinerant Afghans did not involve high-profile political cases such as that of the Indian exile Rahmatullah Kairanwi or Pan-Islamist activist Jamal al-Din al-Afghani. More often they involved ordinary people entangled in mundane crimes or civil suits. As for cases involving Afghans within the Emirate of Afghanistan—that is, west of the Durand Line—bilateral accords between Emir Abdurrahman Khan and the Raj rendered such cases firmly within the emir's jurisdiction.

Nevertheless, as possibly the most porous border in the world, from its inception the Durand Line was the subject of disputes involving subjects caught in the jurisdictional crosshairs of British India and Afghanistan. Among the most common points of contention between Emir Abdurrahman and the British Raj concerned civil suits by Indians or other foreigners against the emir or other Afghans in British Indian courts, claiming British jurisdiction because Abdurrahman was an "Indian prince." Available evidence suggests British courts almost never accepted jurisdiction in such cases and dismissed them outright.

In one illustrative case from 1892, the mercantile firm of Messrs. Jehangir & Co. applied to British Indian authorities to institute a civil suit against the Emir of Afghanistan. The court rejected the firm's petition on procedural grounds. Sidestepping the merits of the case, the opinion presented a short discussion addressing the question of whether the Indian Civil Procedure Code applied to His Highness the Emir. The court ruled that Emir Abdurrahman was not an Indian prince, but the internally sovereign ruler of a British protectorate. The petition was therefore denied on grounds of lacking jurisdiction.[38]

Conversely, Indian archives from the period cite cases of Emir Abdurrahman claiming jurisdiction over Afghans accused of crimes in Afghanistan but who had since fled to India and were therefore beyond the jurisdiction of the emir's courts of justice. For example, an Indian Foreign Department report from 1893 discusses the proposed arrest in British Indian territory, on application from

---

37. Ibid.
38. NAI-FD/SEC/F/Sept. 1892/727–737.

the Emir of Afghanistan, of two Afghan subjects named Abdurashid and Sher Ali.[39] Officials serving the emir in India suspected said individuals of committing in Afghanistan an offence which would amount to criminal breach of trust under Indian law. The Afghan government then requested British authorities to arrest the men under the terms of the Foreign Jurisdiction and Extradition Act of 1879 (FJEA). As the first body to examine the issue, the Commissioner and Superintendent of the Peshawar Division agreed with the emir and viewed the FJEA as the prevailing law on this issue. As the Peshawar Division explained in a July 1893 memorandum and the earliest opinion penned on the case,

> The Commissioner of Peshawar has directed the Deputy Commissioner to arrest the two men mentioned on the indication of the Amir's Postmaster at Peshawar, and to detain them in custody pending our orders. The persons accused are Afghan subjects, and the offence if committed at all has been committed within the jurisdiction of His Highness the Amir. There is no extradition treaty between us and the Amir of Afghanistan.... It is presumed that there is no provision under law except Act XXI of 1879 (the Foreign Jurisdiction and Extradition Act, 1879) which authorises a Magistrate in British India to arrest a foreigner for an offence committed in a foreign country. And in case the Amir asks for the surrender of the fugitives, we shall probably set in motion the Extradition Act of 1879.[40]

Here, officials writing for the Peshawar Division of the British Indian Government viewed the FJEA as dispositive, allowing for the arrest of Afghans in India accused of crimes committed in Afghan territory. This case was far from over, however. One month later, the British barrister and legislative draftsman Sir John Molesworth Macpherson (1853–1914) weighed in on the manner, challenging the Peshawar Division's earlier decision. Macpherson argued that the FJEA only empowered a magistrate to issue a warrant for the arrest of a person for an extraditable offence if the suspect was within the physical limits of his jurisdiction, or if the magistrate had sufficient evidence to justify the issue of such a warrant if the offence had been committed in his jurisdiction. Furthermore, Macpherson claimed there was no such evidence demonstrated.

> Unless the Magistrate had before him further evidence than appears from these papers, I do not understand how he considered that the evidence in the Amir's letter justified him in issuing a warrant in this case. It is perfectly clear from the last words of that letter that the Amir only *suspects* these men.... [T] he Amir's letter does not disclose any facts which could be deemed to be evidence of the guilt of these men.[41]

39. NAI-FD/FRONT/A/Nov. 1893/1–29.
40. Ibid.
41. Ibid.

This seemingly authoritative reading of the FJEA notwithstanding, two weeks later the Deputy Secretary to the British Indian Foreign Department stepped into the legal fray. He wrote:

> In the absence of an Extradition Treaty, no Foreign State can require us to deliver up its fugitives from justice, but we are not bound to afford them an asylum, and where the act with which they are charged would be an offence against our laws if committed in British India, it is in accordance with the comity of nations to deliver them up.

Here, the Foreign Department asserted its freedom from any obligation to surrender accused individuals or fugitives who were foreign subjects to said foreign state, while at the same time paying respect to political considerations such as "the comity of nations." On 11 October 1893, the Chief Secretary to the Provincial Government of the Punjab offered the final word on the matter, recommending the arrest and capture of the said individuals in order to preserve amicable relations with the Afghan emir.[42] In the end, cross-border politics with Afghanistan trumped the Raj's domestic legalese. It would not be the last time.[43] Still, some of the Raj's prickliest diplomatic rows with the Porte over Afghan subjects concerned those found neither in Afghanistan nor India, but in Ottoman territories.

In re *Afghans in the Ottoman Domains*

As a British protectorate, Afghanistan was internally self-governing but subject to the Raj's control over its foreign affairs. Treaty agreements in 1879 and 1893 prohibited the establishment of Afghan embassies abroad and subjected Kabul's foreign correspondence to pass through Indian authorities. Challenges to British control over Afghanistan's foreign relations came not only from the emir in Kabul, however, but the Sublime Porte in Istanbul. An illustrative example of the unbending British position on guarding Afghanistan's foreign relations from any other sovereign influence is found in an exchange from Sir William Arthur White (1824–91), British ambassador at Constantinople, and Ottoman officials in the summer of 1890. The context of the exchange was an initial request on 9 August by Said Pasha to the British ambassador for a copy of the treaty between Britain and the emir of Afghanistan, "in order that the Sublime Porte may be

---

42. Ibid.
43. Jurisdictional tensions between the Afghan emir and the British Raj were not limited to criminal cases. For example, see the case of Sardar Ahmad Khan, an Afghan employed in India whose civil suit raised the question over whether Indian or Afghan courts exercised jurisdiction. NAI-FP/A/Nov. 1881/54–58.

made properly acquainted with the status of Afghan subjects abroad."[44] On 8 September, White responded via telegram as follows,

> I have the honour to enclose to Your Excellency herewith, under instructions from my Government, copy of a communication addressed to Sardar Abdul Rahman, stating the terms on which Her Majesty's Government recognized His Highness as Amir of Afghanistan in 1880, and which it is declared that the Amir can have no political relations with any foreign Power except the British Government. It is this instrument which regulates the position of His Highness towards Her Majesty's Government, and upon it is based the claim of Her Majesty's Government to extend protection to the subjects of His Highness the Amir of Afghanistan when traveling outside His Highness' dominions.[45]

The exchange provides a glimpse of the legal quandary several Afghans found while traveling abroad. On the one hand, agreements signed by Emir Abdurrahman prevented them from conducting independent foreign relations. On the other hand, after the Porte's 1877–78 mission to Kabul the Ottomans increasingly saw it within their prerogative to conduct free relations with fellow Muslim monarchs and their subjects, even vassals of the British Crown.

That the Ottomans were averse to recognize the Raj's absolute control over Afghan affairs abroad is also evident in the Porte's own correspondence with London and the British Foreign Office's internal deliberations on the matter. An August 1891 memorandum from White to Lord Salisbury entitled "British protection to Afghan subjects in Turkey," for example, states that "the Ottoman Council of Ministers declined to accept the view of Her Majesty's Government as to the protection of Her Majesty's Consular officers over Afghans, subjects of the Amir, and that the Porte was intending to inquire from its Representatives abroad how far the other Powers recognized such protection."[46] Just as the British claimed the right of protection over Afghan subjects, the Porte continued to assert its own view.

Even more remarkable is that the British ultimately relented. An internal memorandum to the Crown's diplomatic corps in the Ottoman domains from White explained that British claims to Afghan subjects in Ottoman territory were not on as firm ground as initially presumed.

> Some misunderstanding has recently arisen with regard to the extent to which persons of Afghan nationality are entitled to British protection in the Ottoman dominions. In order that all doubt on the subject may be removed, I beg to inform you that you are hereby instructed to extend to subjects of the Amir sojourning in the Ottoman Empire your unofficial countenance and protection whenever needed. Such protection would not give them the right to claim

44. NAI-FD/SEC/F/Oct. 1891/116–122.
45. Ibid.
46. Ibid.

the benefit of the capitulations between Great Britain and Turkey, but it would entitle them as British protected persons to receive British passports, and to have the aid and support of Her Majesty's Consular Officers in any difficulties which they might have with the Ottoman authorities.[47]

With a noticeable shift in tone, the British ambassador backtracked on London's earlier position of an absolute right of protection over Afghans in Ottoman lands. Clarifying Her Majesty's position with regard to Afghan nationals in Ottoman territory, White explained that as subjects of a "protected" sovereign (Emir Abdurrahman), Afghans were entitled to diplomatic assistance of the Queen's officers, such as passports or other consular aid, but could not be *obligated* as such. Nor would they receive the full protection of British subjects or those with protected minority status per Ottoman Capitulations. According to this understanding, only purported "Pathans" (Pashtuns residing east of the Durand Line) could claim full privileges as British subjects when traveling in the Ottoman domains. As the ambassador explained, "Those who were originally Afghans by race and are now subjects of the Empress of India will be entitled to the full enjoyment of rights which belong to such subjects in His Majesty the Sultan's dominions and to the full benefit of the capitulations, and the exercise of such rights is distinctly claimed for them."[48] Revealing an uncompromisingly territorial approach to the so-called Pathan Question—the problem of Pashtuns divided by the Durand Line—the British position turned not on an individual's tribe, dialect of Pashtu/Pakhtu spoken, or cross-border ties to Afghanistan, but which sovereign state exercised jurisdiction over them.

The British ambassador's clarification notwithstanding, this quarrel was far from resolved. That the Porte was still not inclined to defer to British posturing on Afghans is evident in an August 1891 telegram from T.H. Sanderson, Under-Secretary of State for Foreign Affairs, to the Undersecretary of State for India, stating "The Porte contends that the communication addressed to the Amir of Afghanistan by the Government of India in July 1880 does not confer on British Consular officers any right to protect Afghans in Turkey."[49] Jurisdictional contests between the British and Ottomans over the legal status of itinerant Afghans continued into subsequent decades, and as Lâle Can has shown, also drew in Russia.[50] The aforesaid exchanges demonstrated how as much as Britain tried to resolve the Afghan/Pathan Question through bilateral agreements with Kabul,

47. NAI-FD/SEC/F/July 1891/128–140.
48. Ibid.
49. NAI-FD/SEC/F/Oct. 1891/116–122.
50. For Afghan cases from the early 1900s, see NAI-FD/SEC/F/May 1904/266–273; NAI-FD/FRONT/A/Feb. 1903/56–57; NAI-FD/FRONT/A/Jan. 1900/56–58; NAI-FD/EXTL/A/July 1904/17–18. For an alternative perspective on Afghan migrants, Ottoman naturalization, and imperial competition, see Can, "The Protection Question." As Can demonstrates in her inci-

by the turn of the twentieth century the Hamidian government had inserted itself into the legal fray enough times to have made it also an *Ottoman* issue.

A Role for Afghan Agency

In 1884, Ottoman officials overseeing the resettlement of foreign refugees in the sultan's domains produced a remarkable dossier. The file describes the arrival of a prominent exile from Kabul and nephew of former Afghan emir Dost Muhammad Khan (1793–1863), Eminül Devlet Han (Amin al-Dowla Khan). The latter fled Afghanistan during the Second Anglo-Afghan War before the British occupied Kabul, journeyed to Istanbul, and took refuge in a lodge built for pilgrims from Central Asia. In four separate documents the file discusses his emigration from Afghanistan to Istanbul, where he applied for permission to build a new home.[51]

Ottoman sources such as the aforementioned dossier on Eminül Devlet Han provide a different portrait of Afghan travelers than most British sources would lead us to believe. Far from helpless subjects beholden to either the queen or emir, Porte records illustrate Afghans applying for Ottoman nationality (*Osmanlı tabiiyyeti*) with the expectation that the sultan's protection extended to Afghans found on Ottoman soil.[52] Taken as a whole, Ottoman records on Afghans in the empire impart few stereotypes or patterns other than the diversity of circumstances driving Afghans to seek Ottoman nationality. Another record from 1895 highlights the naturalization of two Afghans originally from Kabul who had been residing in Baghdad for roughly a quarter century.[53]

Despite multiple cases of Afghans applying for and receiving Ottoman nationality in the late nineteenth century, apparently with little British intervention, London continued to dispute legal interpretations that endowed Abdülhamid II with anything more than religious authority over itinerant Afghans. Arguing that Anglo-Afghan bilateral agreements with the emir were dispositive, the British Foreign Office's attempts to curb Hamidian outreach to Afghans were grounded in assumptions that the Ottoman caliph's bond with Indian and Afghan Muslims was one of "faith, not politics."[54] Still, some Afghans resided with-

---

sive study, some of the Porte's fiercest jurisdictional tussles with Britain and Russia extended to Bukharans as well.

51. BOA-Y.A.RES 25/44 (28 Z 1301/18 Oct. 1884).

52. See, for example, BOA-HR.HMŞ.İŞO 173/20 (6 Ra 1307/31 Oct. 1889); BOA-DH.SN.THR 47/94 (6 S 1332/3 Jan. 1915).

53. BOA-HR.HMŞ.İŞO 183/41 (29 C 1313/16 Dec. 1895).

54. That British attempts to limit the Ottoman sultan's influence to "religious" matters among Indian Muslims rested on shaky grounds is underscored by the few qualms British officials displayed in touting the sultan's support of Britain and condemnation of the rebels during the 1857 Sepoy Rebellion. On Ottoman responses to the revolt, see Özcan, *Pan-Islamism*, 15–17.

in the sultan's domains for so many years that they qualified for the Ottoman state's own internal laws of nationalization.[55]

In any case, the legal conditions of Afghans in the Ottoman Empire cannot be reduced into a simplistic binary of Great Britain claiming jurisdiction on the one hand, versus a reactionary resistance by the Porte on the other. The individual circumstances of Afghan petitioners were more complex than such dichotomies would have it. A memorandum from the Frontier Branch of the Indian Foreign Department in 1900, for example, addresses the case of a certain Muhammad Sharif, purportedly of Peshawar but who had taken up residence in Istanbul. Curiously, the British government refused to exercise jurisdiction in the matter of Sharif's petition for legal aid, and virtually "disowned" the petitioner, stating that Sharif was a subject of the Afghan emir, and not India. The reasoning is significant. Sharif argued in his request for assistance that because he was from Peshawar, he therefore was a subject of British India and could claim Her Majesty's diplomatic protection. Specifically, Sharif sought the aid of British officials in a complaint he filed against Russian officers who allegedly stole from him while traveling through Turkistan. The official response was to deny jurisdiction, stating that Sharif was actually from Bajaur, Afghanistan, and, therefore, not a British subject. The case was closed without offering further assistance.[56]

Sharif's case presents a good example of how British policies of extraterritoriality—or that of any foreign ministry, for that matter—are driven by specific political considerations grounded in history rather than abstract, ideological, or other categorical notions of allegiance. Without a mutually binding treaty or universal law of jurisdiction with regard to Afghans traveling outside of their countries of domicile, such contentious disputes between the Sublime Porte and British Crown were often left to the political and diplomatic fields of ad hoc correspondences, some short-lived agreements, and many more quarrels that simply remained unresolved.

While Afghans often constituted the literal bodies over which late Ottoman and British jurisdictional contests were waged, taken as a whole the cases documented above present Afghans as transborder subjects and historical agents in their own right. Fighting for their right to travel, or litigate in a foreign court of law, some claimed to be subjects of the emir in Kabul by virtue of their birth in the semi-autonomous Emirate of Afghanistan. Others claimed to be subjects of the queen by way of British diplomatic protection afforded to Afghans outside of Afghanistan, and this allowed for many Afghans to file suits in British Indian courts. Yet still, during the 1880s and 1890s, increasing numbers of Afghans were

---

55. See, for example, cases of Afghan itinerants and communities in Baghdad and Jerusalem described by both Ottoman and British officials. IOR-L/PS/20/42 (1914), 406; BOA-HR.HMŞ. İŞO 183/41; BOA-DH.MKT 1358/3.
56. NAI-FD/FRONT/A/Jan. 1900/56–58.

naturalized as subjects of the sultan-caliph in Istanbul. More than just imperial contests, these cases highlight the agency of Afghans in exploiting opportunities legal pluralism provided, pulling in empires to adjudicate the disputes their mobility and citizenship claims created as they pursued their *own* interests from the eastern Mediterranean to the Indo-Afghan borderlands.

Conclusion

This chapter approached an intensifying geopolitical rivalry between the Ottoman and British Empires in the last two decades of the nineteenth century in two areas of diplomatic contestation: the Sublime Porte's consular privileges in British India and the legal status of itinerant Afghans traveling beyond the recognized borders of the Emirate of Afghanistan. As a glimpse into the late Ottoman Empire's own extraterritorial projects, it examined how the Porte worked to expand its consular representation abroad while bolstering its influence among foreign Muslims, including those considered colonized European subjects.

It goes without saying that legal questions, whether domestic or international, do not emerge in a political vacuum. While this chapter focused on consular and jurisdictional questions that formed the axis over which Ottoman and British diplomatic quarrels turned, not explored here are the broader conflicts plaguing British-Ottoman relations from the early Hamidian era to the eve of the Great War. The latter inquiry would have to examine how relations between the Sublime Porte and British Crown—allied sovereigns for the majority of the nineteenth century—degenerated through a succession of transformative events and processes in the Balkans and Eastern Mediterranean that included, *inter alia*, the Russo-Ottoman war of 1877–78, the British occupation of Egypt in 1882, and the Italo-Ottoman War of 1911–12. What has often been overlooked in these macropolitical processes is how Afghans and Indian Muslims became the contested subjects over which larger imperial struggles between the Ottoman and British Empires were waged.

At the heart of these quarrels was not simply an imperial rivalry over papers, property rights, and international prestige, but a more subtle contest over the loyalties and bodies of human beings who did not fit neatly into either Ottoman or British imperial frameworks of subjecthood. While the cases explored in this chapter concerned Afghans and Indian Muslims, the jurisdictional conflicts in which they were entangled reflect a broader web of imperial contests between the Sublime Porte and European powers, from Egypt to Afghanistan. By inverting the extraterritorial gaze, so to speak, these contests push us to consider how just at the time of Eurocentric globalization and a scramble for African and Asiatic colonies, the ties between Ottomans, Afghans, and Indian Muslims were growing stronger than ever before.

One subject still left unaddressed but pertinent to the British-Ottoman Cold War was London's mounting insecurity over pro-Ottoman militant activity by Afghans and Indian Muslims, many of whom were under British surveillance. In particular, during the catastrophic Libyan and Balkan Wars of 1911–13, there is evidence to suggest that anywhere from several scores to several hundred of Afghans and Indian Muslims engaged in a more aggressive form of support for the Ottoman caliph than simply traveling to the latter's domains or claiming Ottoman nationality.[57] Amid British inaction vis-à-vis Italy's 1911 invasion of Tripolitania—an Ottoman province for the preceding four centuries—the war in Libya witnessed an increasing number of Afghans and Indian Muslims volunteering for the Ottoman war effort against Italy. Although the officially neutral British were not among the Porte's adversaries on the battlefields of North Africa or the subsequent Balkan conflict between 1911 and 1913, the rapid and covert movement of armed Muslim warriors crisscrossing between India and the Mediterranean in aid of the besieged Ottoman government put British administrators across the region on edge. It was an uneasy feeling that was not to subside in London, or Calcutta, for the remainder of the Ottoman Empire's duration.

Along these lines, from the last two decades of the nineteenth century to the first two decades of the twentieth, British colonial anxieties over Muslim mobility in the Balkans-to-Bengal region was matched by Ottoman opportunism in exploiting those anxieties to further the Porte's strategic interests, including exerting a novel form of imperial citizenship over Afghans and Indian Muslims during the same period. With the benefit of hindsight, we now know that British-Ottoman tensions were to reach a devastating climax with the breakout of World War I.[58] Most dramatically, in the summer of 1915 the Ottomans and Germans, as wartime allies, dispatched a secret mission to Kabul with an audacious mission. Reaching the Afghan capital in early autumn, representatives of the Porte and Berlin appealed to the semi-autonomous emir of Afghanistan, Habibullah Khan, to join the Central Powers so they could together invade India, overwhelm and

---

57. For example, see NAI-FD/EXTL/B April 1913 301–302, where British intelligence officers in Jaffa and Jerusalem reported some seventy-three Afghans leaving Palestine for the Libyan front as volunteers for the Ottomans.

58. This is not to suggest that Ottoman entry into World War I was a foregone conclusion, or the Porte's joining the side of the Central Powers for that matter. As Mustafa Aksakal has shown, the CUP's fateful decision to enter the war in late 1914 by allying with Germany was riddled with historical contingency, complexity, and contradictions, as ever. Mustafa Aksakal, *The Ottoman Road to War in 1914: The Ottoman Empire and the First World War* (New York: Cambridge University Press, 2010).

smash the Raj, and permanently expel the British from the subcontinent.[59] But by that time, the British-Ottoman Cold War was already over.

59. On the 1915 Ottoman-German mission to Kabul, see Faiz Ahmed, *Afghanistan Rising: Islamic Law and Statecraft between the Ottoman and British Empires* (Cambridge, MA: Harvard University Press, 2017), 138–50; Thomas L. Hughes, "The German Mission to Afghanistan, 1915–1916," *German Studies Review* 25 (2002): 447–76.

9   Pan-Islamic Propagandists or Professional Diplomats?: The Ottoman Consular Establishment in the Colonial Indian Ocean

Jeffery Dyer

OVER THE COURSE of the late nineteenth century, Muslim territories through-out the Indian Ocean were forced to adapt to rapid and dramatic changes brought on by the introduction of new technologies and the expansion of European colonial power. From Bombay to Batavia and Java, the spread of direct and indirect colonial rule reconfigured regional social, political, and economic relations. But they also had an impact on this vast region's ties to the distant Ottoman state, the sole remaining Islamic empire and a member of the Concert of Europe. Between 1870 and 1914, the sultan's government in Istanbul began to employ new strategies to protect Ottoman interests in the region. Through new consular agents, engagement with international law and diplomacy, and the promotion of global Pan-Islamic discourse, the Sublime Porte (the central government in Istanbul) adapted to the changing currents of commercial and political power relations in the Indian Ocean world.

While the Ottomans had long maintained a variety of official contacts with rulers and populations throughout South and Southeast Asia, the appointment of Hüseyin Hasib Efendi as Ottoman consul-general (*başşehbender*) to Bombay in 1870 marked a watershed moment.[1] This was the first time that the Sublime Porte dispatched an official to reside in the region as a full-time representative of the government's interests in India and the broader region.[2] From 1870 through

---

1. For more on Hüseyin Hasib and his role in fostering Ottoman ties to Indian Muslims, see Faiz Ahmed, "The British-Ottoman Cold War, c. 1880-1914: Imperial Struggles over Muslim Mobility and Citizenship from the Suez Canal to the Durand Line" in this volume.
2. In Turkish-language correspondence, the Ottoman government most often referred to their own consuls as *şehbender* while reserving the cognate *konsolos* for consuls of foreign governments. In their French correspondence, both terms were translated into the French term *consuls*. The use of the term *şehbender*—derived from the Persian *shah-i bandar*, or "king of the port"—evolved from its use in the sixteenth-century Indian Ocean to refer to a foreign community's trade representative through its adoption by the Ottoman Foreign Ministry in the late eighteenth century for its consular officers. See W.H. Moreland, "The Shahbandar in the Eastern Seas," *Journal of the Royal Asiatic Society of Great Britain and Ireland* 4 (1920): 517–33; Nelly Hanna *Making Big Money in 1600: The Life and Times of Ismail Abu Taqiyya, Egyptian*

The Subjects of Ottoman International Law (2020): 171–195
DOI: 10.2979/subjectsottomaninternationallaw.0.0.10

the outbreak of the First World War, the Porte would send nearly two dozen consular representatives to manage Istanbul's affairs in Bombay and other prominent Indian Ocean cities like Batavia, Singapore, and Karachi. Located primarily in major centers of British and Dutch colonial administration and in territories with large Muslim populations, these consulates sparked a mixture of wariness and cautious engagement among European colonial powers, who feared a thinly veiled agenda to expand Ottoman religious prestige at their expense. The British and Dutch governments harbored deep suspicions that these consulates were responsible for spreading Pan-Islamic propaganda. Their speculation, however, was misguided. As this chapter demonstrates, the consuls' activities and their government's broader imperial goals were not altogether different from European powers seeking to extend their influence across the Indian Ocean world.[3]

Departing from the conventional historiographic focus on the empire's alleged pan-Islamic goals,[4] this essay argues that Ottoman foreign policy in the last decades of the nineteenth century increasingly relied on international legal and diplomatic foundations and was aimed at protecting the Porte's growing interests in colonized territories around the Indian Ocean. These policies engaged both European governments and local Muslims in strategic outposts in Asia and Africa. In this new theater of diplomacy, the Ottomans sought to bolster their legitimacy as an active participant in global affairs well beyond the empire's more traditional spheres of interest in the Mediterranean and wider Middle East.

During the Hamidian period (1876–1909), the expansion of salaried consular representatives was a means of expanding the Porte's influence in recently

Merchant (Syracuse: Syracuse University Press, 1998) 36–39; Christine Philliou, *Biography of an Empire: Governing Ottomans in an Age of Revolution* (Berkeley: University of California Press, 2011); Bruce Masters, "The Sultan's Entrepreneurs: The Avrupa Tuccaris and the Hayriye Tuccaris in Syria," *International Journal of Middle East Studies* 24, no. 4 (1992): 586; Carter V. Findley, *Bureaucratic Reform in the Ottoman Empire: The Sublime Porte 1789–1922* (Princeton: Princeton University Press, 1989), 127–28.

3. For examples of British Indian officials' suspicions, see Azmi Özcan, *Pan-Islamism: Indian Muslims, the Ottomans and Britain, 1877–1924* (Leiden: Brill, 1997), 112–13. Also see Ahmed, "The British-Ottoman Cold War."

4. For examples of how the historiography has traditionally addressed Pan-Islamic concerns, see Jacob Landau, *The Politics of Pan-Islam: Ideology and Organization* (Oxford: Clarendon Press, 1990); Kemal Karpat, *The Politicization of Islam: Reconstructing Identity, State, Faith, and Community in the Late Ottoman Empire* (New York: Oxford University Press, 2001); Anthony Reid, "Nineteenth Century Pan-Islam in Indonesia and Malaysia," *The Journal of Asian Studies* 26, no. 2 (1967): 267–83. For more recent reassessments, see Selim Deringil, "Legitimacy Structures in the Ottoman State: The Reign of Abdülhamid II (1876–1909)," *International Journal of Middle East Studies* 23, no. 3 (1991): 345–59; Cemil Aydın, *The Politics of Anti-Westernism in Asia: Visions of World Order in Pan-Islamic and Pan-Asian Thought* (New York: Columbia University Press, 2007); idem, *The Idea of the Muslim World: A Global Intellectual History* (Cambridge, MA: Harvard University Press, 2017); Seema Alavi, *Muslim Cosmopolitanism in the Age of Empire* (Cambridge, MA: Harvard University Press, 2015).

colonized Muslim-majority territories bordering the Indian Ocean.[5] Consulates were particularly well-suited to establishing Ottoman power in the Indian Ocean due to the increasing importance of formal diplomacy among European powers. Consuls were recognized as representatives of their governments abroad and their authority derived from bilateral legal agreements.[6] These consulates were primarily located in coastal urban centers of British and Dutch territories in India and Southeast Asia. As this essay demonstrates, the government in Istanbul hoped to establish a consular presence in these cosmopolitan trade entrepôts, many of which were also growing hajj hubs during the steamship-era. By enhancing its presence in the region, the Porte hoped to assert its right to provide extraterritorial protections to Ottoman subjects and protected persons in the increasingly mobile world that took shape after the construction of the Suez Canal in 1869. Consuls were charged with duties not unlike their European counterparts, which included "the promotion and facilitation of particular trade flows to the assistance of individual citizens living or traveling overseas."[7] The extensive overlap between the economic and diplomatic spheres, however, often ruffled feathers among the British and Dutch, who wanted to limit their interventions to narrower commercial interests due to their fear of Pan-Islamic "agitation." [8]

While the Ottomans began to establish consulates in European capitals in the late eighteenth century, the path to doing so in colonial territories was more challenging. Due to colonial administrators' fears over the impact that Pan-Islamic agitation could have on the Muslim populations within their colonies, the Porte often faced stiff opposition in places like the Dutch East Indies or Sin-

---

5. Due in part to the use of consulates as a framing device, this essay focuses primarily on the British and Dutch colonial territories in South and Southeast Asia where those consulates were located. Although the Ottomans also operated consulates in British South Africa, they did not have as much contact with the consulates further north. In part this was likely due to distance and the relative infrequency of population movements between the colonial territories in South Africa and Ottoman domains in the Arabian Peninsula. Territories like Zanzibar or the Somali coastline in East Africa feature enough thematic crossovers that they would make a valid comparison, but for a variety of reasons, ranging from budget to lack of desire to acknowledge their dependence on colonial control, no consulates were opened in East Africa until the Habeşistan (Ethiopia) consulate was opened in Harar in 1912. See Başbakanlık Osmanlı Arşivi (hereafter BOA), İ. HR. 428/37 (15 Ra 1330/3 March 1912). In any event, the Habeşistan consulate does not appear to have operated for very long.
6. Halvard Leira and Iver B. Neumann, "The Many Past Lives of the Consul," in *Consular Affairs and Diplomacy*, ed. Jan Melissen et.al. (Leiden: Martinus Neijhoff Publishers, 2011), 240.
7. Jan Melissen, "The Consular Dimension of Diplomacy," in *Consular Affairs and Diplomacy*, 1.
8. In one case in Batavia, Dutch administrators claimed that the Ottoman consuls "had only been accepted as 'commercial agents' (*handelsagenten*) without diplomatic status." Jan Schmidt, "Pan-Islamism between the Porte, the Hague, and Buitenzorg," in *Through the Legation Window 1876–1926: Four Essays on Dutch, Dutch-Indian and Ottoman History* (Istanbul: Nederlands Historisch-Archaeologisch Instituut, 1992), 86.

gapore. European consular officials in Bombay and Batavia, for example, were concerned that Ottoman officials in predominantly Muslim territories sought to boost their prestige through association with the religious authority of the sultan-caliph.[9] And yet, this one aspect of their activities has received a disproportionate amount of attention in the literature on Ottoman diplomatic interests in the Indian Ocean. The fact that Ottoman consuls were also career Foreign Ministry officials, operating within clearly defined parameters, and under the close scrutiny of colonial officials, is often overlooked.

Shifting the focus away from sentiment and discourse, this essay argues that the Hamidian Foreign Ministry utilized the nascent international legal bureaucracy in Istanbul to leverage existing consular agreements with their British and Dutch counterparts. It shows how the government sought to establish a foothold in the colonial Indian Ocean world via civil servants dispatched from the ranks of the Porte's diplomatic cadre. At the same time, the consuls in the colonial Indian Ocean were part of a larger body of diplomatic officials that spanned the globe and were subject to the same bureaucratic reforms that were being put in place to regulate the activities of their fellow consuls from the Foreign Ministry, and who were operating in quite different circumstances throughout Europe and the Americas. These aspects of their authority and activities defined the Ottoman consuls in the colonial Indian Ocean as much, if not more than, their alleged ties to the Pan-Islamic sympathies of a variety of Ottoman and foreign Muslims.

In the first section of this chapter, I consider how the changing political-economy of the Indian Ocean and increased regional mobility spurred the Porte's interest in reforming and expanding their consular representation in strategic centers of the colonial Indian Ocean. Next, I examine the Foreign Ministry reforms aimed at standardizing consular duties and responsibilities, and their impact on the development of the Indian Ocean consulates. These developments inform the third section's examination of how the Foreign Ministry's jurists used international law to challenge European opposition to the expanding Ottoman consular presence in South and Southeast Asia. The final section examines how consular activities and the Porte's plans for further expansion in the region were influenced by issues of extraterritorial rights and attempts to control the increased mobility of Ottoman and foreign populations in Ottoman territories in the Arabian Peninsula and the Persian Gulf. In so doing, I attempt to recast the Ottoman consuls of the colonial Indian Ocean in the late nineteenth century as career Foreign Ministry officials whose statements in support of the global authority of the caliph or the potential benefits of Pan-Islamic solidarity should not overshadow their position as diplomats and government officials whose re-

9. For two great examples of consuls emphasizing the role of the caliphate and Islamic ties in their reports, see BOA, Y.EE. 148/7 (21 Ca 1306/22 Jan. 1889) and Y.EE. 148/8 (25 Ca 1306/26 Jan. 1889).

sponsibilities were rooted in extensive bureaucratic regulations and bilateral international legal agreements with European imperial powers.

Ottomans East of Suez?: Indian Ocean Mobility and the Rise of Ottoman Consular Interests in the Indian Ocean

By the last quarter of the nineteenth century the Ottoman government was faced with mounting political crises in southeastern Europe, North Africa, the Levant, and eastern Anatolia. These troubles were compounded by budgetary problems that forced Ottoman officials to operate under severe financial constraints. Yet, throughout this period, the Foreign Ministry set aside funds from an already stretched budget to dispatch consular representatives to the Indian subcontinent and Southeast Asia who would support Ottomans living or traveling abroad and help manage the increasing volume of commercial and passenger traffic moving through the Ottoman Empire's porous southern frontiers.[10] The diversion of critical resources to this region was a response to rapidly changing inter-imperial dynamics between Ottoman territories bordering the Red Sea and Persian Gulf in the west and the colonial territories of the Indian Ocean further east driven by the opening of the Suez Canal.[11] Increased traffic through the canal spurred the proliferation of commercial and passenger lines linking major Indian Ocean port cities.[12] By the 1880s, these developments increased the Porte's interest in cities like Karachi, Bombay, and Singapore, all of which were commercially active maritime transportation hubs with direct connections to Ottoman ports like Basra and Jidda and transit points for the growing numbers of pilgrims traveling to the Arabian Peninsula.[13]

10. For an excellent survey of some of the geopolitical crises faced by the Porte, see M. Şükrü Hanioğlu, *A Brief History of the Late Ottoman Empire* (Princeton: Princeton University Press, 2008) 109–35. For Ottoman administrators' concerns about distant consulates' impact on their budget, see BOA, İ. HR. 289/18146 (04 C 1300), doc. 2 for Batavia and BOA, HR. SFR (3) 335/78 (17 Aug. 1887), doc. 2 for additional Indian consulates outside Bombay.
11. On the Suez Canal's impact on mobility in the Red Sea and beyond, see Valeska Huber, *Channelling Mobilities: Migration and Globalisation in the Suez Canal Region and Beyond, 1869–1914* (Cambridge, UK: Cambridge University Press, 2013); On Barak, *On Time: Technology and Temporality in Modern Egypt* (Berkeley: University of California Press, 2013); D.A. Farnie, *East and West of Suez: The Suez Canal in History 1854–1956* (Oxford: Oxford University Press, 1969). For an Ottoman perspective on the Suez Canal, see Sevda Özkaya, *Süveyş Kanalı: XIX. Yüzyılda Doğu Akdeniz'de Bir Rekabet Unsuru (Osmanlı Arşivi Göre)* (Istanbul: Bilge Kultur Sanat, 2015).
12. For the coeval development of steamship technologies and increased access to Red Sea ports via Suez, see Colette Dubois, "The Red Sea Ports During the Revolution in Transportation, 1800–1914," in *Modernity and Culture: From the Mediterranean to the Indian Ocean*, ed. Leila Tarazi Fawaz and C.A. Bayly (New York: Columbia University Press, 2002).
13. On the steamship-era hajj in the Indian Ocean, see Michael Christopher Low, "Empire and the Hajj: Pilgrims, Plagues, and Pan-Islam under British Surveillance, 1865–1908," *Interna-*

Imperial decrees (*iradeler*) announcing the opening of new consular offices reveal how Ottoman interests evolved in the second half of the nineteenth century. In the decades prior to the opening of the canal, the importance of cities like Bombay was connected to the passage of sailing ships between target cities and ports within or in close proximity to Ottoman jurisdiction in the Arabian Peninsula.[14] By the time the first salaried consul was being considered for Bombay in 1869–70, however, the Porte's focus narrowed to Bombay's role as an essential link in the "commercial affairs of the people of Iraq," even though it was still broadly concerned with maritime frontiers between the subcontinent and the Persian Gulf.[15] By 1887–88, correspondence between the Bombay consul-general and the director of consular affairs in Istanbul suggest that the Porte's interests had shifted again and were increasingly centered on the growing steamship traffic that passed through the Suez Canal and linked Ottoman Red Sea and Persian Gulf ports to markets in India and Central Asia, Southeast Asia, and East and South Africa.[16] In one example, Bombay Consul-General Ismail Zühdü Bey argued for renewed consular activity in Karachi, Madras, Colombo, and Calcutta by referencing the revenues that the Bombay Consulate-General accrued from

---

tional Journal of Middle East Studies 40, no. 2 (2008): 269–90; Nile Green, "The Hajj as its Own Undoing: Infrastructure and Integration on the Muslim Journey to Mecca," Past & Present 226, no. 1 (2015): 193–226; Eric Tagliacozzo, The Longest Journey: Southeast Asians and the Pilgrimage to Mecca (Oxford: Oxford University Press, 2013); John Slight, The British Empire and the Hajj, 1865–1956 (Cambridge, MA: Harvard University Press, 2015). For parallel questions related to the management of the hajj along the Ottoman-Russian frontier, see Eileen Kane, Russian Hajj: Empire and the Pilgrimage to Mecca (Ithaca: Cornell University Press, 2015); Lâle Can, "The Protection Question: Central Asians and Extraterritoriality in the Late Ottoman Empire," in this volume.

14. BOA, İ. HR. 327/21160 (19 R 1269/30 Jan. 1853). In these documents there is a clear association between Bombay and Ottoman interests in Jidda, Yemen, Basra, Kuwait, Bahrain, Muscat, and Ethiopia (Habeşistan). For further evidence of an emerging Indian Ocean frontier along the Ottoman Persian Gulf and Red Sea, see Frederick F. Anscombe, The Ottoman Gulf: The Creation of Kuwait, Saudi Arabia, and Qatar (New York: Columbia University Press, 1997); Yeniçeşmeli Hâfız Fâik Efendi, İstanbul'dan Bombay'a bir Osmanlı Fırkateyni'nin Keşif Seyahati, ed. Ali Ergun Çınar (Istanbul: Kitabevi, 2014).

15. BOA, İ. HR 242/14354 (27 L 1246/10 April 1831); BOA, İ. HR. 246/14630 (3 B 1287/29 Sept. 1870).

16. Although this essay focuses primarily on the Porte's engagement with South and Southeast Asia, the Ottoman government utilized a variety of strategies to protect their interests throughout Africa, particularly in strategic parts of East and South Africa. For Ottoman activities in various parts of Africa, see Mostafa Minawi, The Ottoman Scramble for Africa: Empire and Diplomacy in the Sahara and the Hijaz (Stanford: Stanford University Press, 2016); Hatice Uğur, Osmanlı Afrikasi'nda Bir Sultanlık Zengibar (Istanbul: Kure Yayınları, 2005); Selim Deringil and Sinan Küneralp, eds., Studies on Ottoman Diplomatic History V: The Ottomans and Africa (Istanbul: The Isis Press, 1990); Ahmet Uçar, Güney Afrika'da Osmanlılar (Istanbul: Çamlıca, 2008).

steamship traffic passing through Suez.[17] Specifically, he described the four cities as "India's commercial centers" and "prominent commercial ports" on the Suez Canal route that passed by Ottoman provinces in the Red Sea.[18]

By the early twentieth century, interest in the growing eastern China and Pacific markets had led to a consular presence in Singapore. The decree appointing the first official consul-general in Singapore in 1900 trumpeted that city's role as "Indo-China's most important commercial port and the most frequented harbor on the route to the Far East."[19] These descriptions were probably crafted to convince cautious ministry officials that these distant cities deserved new investments in consular infrastructure. They reveal how important economic activity and links to busy maritime transportation networks were in justifying the investment of limited government resources. Whereas, relations with foreign Muslim populations were in the past managed by a variety of non-state actors—ranging from local intermediaries to temporary diplomatic envoys or itinerant religious figures and scholars—the imposition of colonial authority changed things and required an official presence. Intermediaries whose authority was based in formal bureaucratic institutions or whose actions were measured against international legal and diplomatic norms may have been less likely to be viewed as controversial or threatening to the authority of anxious colonial officials.[20]

Consular officials were ideally suited to regulating an environment in which the government's primary concerns revolved around issues of trade and immigration straddling the boundaries of territories within and outside their direct control. Although there was still a great deal of variety at this time in how various governments structured their diplomatic affairs, in general their consular institutions were founded on the granting of extraterritorial authority to an official who would mediate commercial disputes and act as a local diplomatic representative.[21] While the framework that Ottoman officials used to describe the candidate cities was primarily economic, the purpose of posting consulates there was not necessarily limited to the production of revenue or the promotion of trade. Their focus also encompassed the migration and transportation networks that

---

17. BOA, HR. SFR (3) 335/78 (17 Oct. 1887), doc. 2.
18. In this case, the documents used the terms *ticaretgâh* and *başlıca bandar-i ticaret*. BOA, İ. HR. 312/19941 (20 R 1306/24 Dec. 1888), doc. 3; BOA, HR. SFR (3) 335/78 (17 Aug. 1887), doc. 2.
19. BOA, İ. HR. 371/22 (8 M 1319/9 May 1901), doc. 1, "Hindi-Çini'nin en mühim bandar-i ticaret ve Aksa-i Şark tarikinin en işlek iskelesi."
20. Some measure of British wariness over the potential negative impact of allowing in unofficial envoys can be glimpsed in the 1877 warning of Sir Austen Henry Layard about the Ottoman delegation to Kabul: "If the Turks cannot send envoys and ministers openly then they will employ secret agents which are more to be feared." See Özcan, *Pan-Islamism*, 82.
21. Jan Melissen, "The Consular Dimension of Diplomacy," 1–4; Jan Helenus Ferguson, *Manual of International Law for the Use of Navies, Colonies, and Consulates*, vol. 2 (London: W.B. Whittingham, 1884), 123–25.

were a significant outgrowth of that economic activity and the main connective thread tying the empire's territories to the regions outside their direct control. In this context, Istanbul's consular interests were shaped by parallel concerns over the movement of Ottoman ships and subjects to outside ports and the movement of foreign ships and subjects back to the empire's provinces in places like Yemen, Hijaz, or Iraq.

The Hamidian Foreign Ministry's Efforts to Standardize Ottoman Consular Practices Worldwide

When the Porte expanded the reach of its consular representation into the Indian Ocean, it did so at the same time that Foreign Ministry officials were rolling out policies that sought to standardize and professionalize their consular offices around the world. While Ottoman sultans had appointed honorary consular agents in European cities since the late eighteenth century, the first salaried and "full-time" Ottoman consular positions were not created until 1838 in London and Marseilles.[22] Shortly thereafter, the consul in London made an early attempt to enumerate the duties of his new office through a document written in French consisting of twenty articles. It outlined the duties and responsibilities of European consuls as a model for his Ottoman colleagues. These developments inaugurated a series of alternating efforts to expand and regulate a growing network of consular offices. According to Sinan Kuneralp, in the aftermath of the Crimean War the Foreign Ministry endeavored to replace honorary consuls around the Mediterranean and the Adriatic with salaried officials. It also attempted to extend the reach of the office to new areas around the Black Sea and the Greek territories, and further regulate the duties expected of the growing number of consular officers.[23]

By the time the Foreign Ministry launched reforms in the Bombay office in 1870, their efforts to professionalize the consular service and standardize its practices were well underway in other regions. By 1871, the number of salaried Ottoman consular posts across the globe had risen to thirty-four and the honorary posts to seventy.[24] The consular system had grown so much by 1873 that the Foreign Ministry deemed it necessary to create a full-time Directorate of Consular Affairs to oversee and manage its increasing complexity.[25] In response to the

22. Kuneralp, "Le service consulaire Ottomane," 431–33, 438. Kuneralp highlights Marseilles' role in Levantine maritime trade and the 1838 Treaty of Balta Limanı with London as reasons for those consulates being the first to undergo reforms. The consulate that was opened in London in 1838 operated alongside the existing ambassadorial diplomatic mission established decades earlier. The two offices worked in tandem with different areas of responsibility through World War One.
23. Ibid., 431–33.
24. Ibid.
25. Ibid., 433–34; Findley, *Bureaucratic Reform*, 258–59.

strains caused by the continued growth and broad dispersal of consular agents by the end of that decade, Foreign Ministry officials began to consolidate efforts to regularize their consular policies and practices system-wide. In turn, the standards that they put in place would shape the evolution of the Indian Ocean consular offices as they expanded beyond Bombay in later decades.

In an attempt to bring greater coherence to the Foreign Ministry's consular practices worldwide, between 1882 and 1884, officials in Istanbul promulgated new, comprehensive consular regulations outlining the duties and procedures to be followed by consular officials. The first regulatory document was titled "Internal Regulation of Ottoman Imperial Consulates" (*Saltanat-ı Seniyye Şehbenderlerine Dair Nizamname-i Dahili*).[26] It included seventy-one articles divided into three sections detailing the administrative and financial organization of the consulates, a system for holding them accountable for misdeeds, and measures that created a formal distinction between salaried and honorary consuls.[27] The most important of these was the first section, which outlined ministry officials' idealized expectations for how the consular offices would be staffed and administered, what qualifications the consuls should possess, and what kinds of duties they would be expected to perform in their posts. Appended to the new regulations was an updated version of an 1860 document listing the prices to be charged for services rendered by the consular chancelleries.[28]

The final piece of the new regulatory framework was titled "Instructions to be sent to the consulates of the Ottoman Empire" (*Saltanat-ı Seniyye Şehbenderlerine Gönderilecek Talimat*).[29] The document was made up of three sections released over several months between 1883 and 1884.[30] These documents provided much more detailed instructions for how the consuls were expected to carry out the duties outlined for them in the earlier regulations. Together, these

---

26. "Saltanat-ı Seniyye Şehbenderlerine dair Nizamname-i Dahilidir," in *Salname-i Nezaret-i Umur-ı Hariciyye*, 4 vol. (Dersaadet: Matbaa-yı Osmaniye, 1318), 3:362–76; George Young, *Corps de droit Ottoman: Recueil des codes, lois, reglements, ordonnances et actes les plus importants du droit interieur, et d'etudes sur le droit coutumier de l'Empire Ottoman*, 7 vol. (Oxford: Clarendon Press, 1905), 3:1–10.

27. Ibid. The final section of the regulations included a list of ten articles detailing "Special Provisions Concerning Honorary Consular Posts." These provisions were included to specify the elements of training, duties, and jurisdictional authority that would distinguish the honorary representatives from the new class of salaried consular officials.

28. Ibid. See particularly Chapter 1, "Consulate Personnel," of Section 1, "Organization of the Consulates," 2–5. For the 1860 list of fees to be charged for consular services, see "Tarif des droits a percevoir dans les Chancelleries consulaires d l'Empire Ottoman," in ibid., 10–14.

29. "Saltanat-ı Seniyye Şehbenderlerine Gönderilecek Talimat," *Salname-i Nezaret-i Umur-ı Hariciyye*, 3:377-425; Young, *Corps de Droit Ottoman*, 3:14–40.

30. Dates cited here are based on Young, *Corps de Droit Ottoman*, 3:14. Section I was released January 1883, Section II December 1883, and Section III December 1884. According to Young, the three were promulgated together on the third date.

new measures attempted to make the once-motley collection of consular offices subject to an increasing amount of administrative direction and oversight implemented to varying degrees by the centralized bureaucratic structure in Istanbul.

An especially important component of the new regulations for the offices in the Indian Ocean was the strict separation created between official, salaried consular positions and their unpaid, honorary counterparts, as well as new standards to which each would be held in the training and qualifications required to take up the positions. The new measures included an implicit repudiation of the potential that honorary, unsalaried consuls could be compromised by conflicts of interest by requiring salaried consuls to be Ottoman subjects and forbidding them from engaging in commercial activities during their consular tenure under penalty of dismissal.[31] They also tried to establish new professional standards for applicants by making admission to the career subject to competitive exams and a licensing process carried out by the Foreign Ministry, with special consideration given to graduates of the Imperial Lycée at Galatasaray and the School of Civil Administration.[32] The desired result was to draw consular appointees from among the ranks of career professionals steeped in the diplomatic and legal traditions of the Ottoman bureaucracy in Istanbul, who were dependent on the government for their status and salary and motivated by promises of advancement within the bureaucracy to pursue their assignments with relative discipline and vigor.[33]

Standardizing and Expanding the Reach of Consular Offices in the Colonial Indian Ocean

As the government applied these new consular policies, the posts in Bombay and Batavia became integrated into an emerging network of bureaucrats working within the Foreign Ministry diplomatic cadre. These peripatetic career civil servants brought experience and skills developed in diverse regional posts to the offices in the Indian Ocean. Between 1882 and the First World War, a succession of eight consuls-general occupied the post in Bombay, while eleven served in Batavia. Each of these consuls was an Ottoman subject, primarily educated in Istanbul, with experience in either the Foreign Ministry bureaucracy in Istanbul or consular offices elsewhere in Europe or the United States.

31. See Article 3 of the consular regulations, ibid., 3:2. By forbidding the consuls to engage in commerce the ministry likely sought to ensure the officials' dependence on their government salary and eliminate the potential for financial conflicts of interest.
32. These were the Mekteb-i Sultani and Mekteb-i Mülkiye. For more on the important role that these schools played in training future government officials in the nineteenth century, see Benjamin Fortna, *Imperial Classroom: Islam, the State, and Education in the Ottoman Empire* (New York: Oxford University Press, 2002).
33. For a more skeptical assessment on whether this was likely, see Findley, *Bureaucratic Reform*, 283.

A handful of examples suffice to show the unusual career trajectories of some of the officials that passed through the consulates in Bombay and Batavia. Ali Galip Bey transferred from the Foreign Ministry Translation Bureau in Istanbul to become the first consul-general in Batavia in 1882.[34] After a three-year tenure in the Dutch East Indies, he was transferred to serve as the consul-general in Bombay. After a short stint, he was promoted to serve as the Foreign Ministry's director of mixed legal affairs in Istanbul.[35] Galip Bey has gained some notoriety in histories of the Dutch East Indies for his contentious interactions with the colonial government. When he was transferred from his position as consul-general in Batavia, it was rumored that the Porte made the move to alleviate pressure from Dutch colonial officials who were upset over Galip Bey's alleged involvement in "pan-Islamic activities."[36] His successor in Batavia, Ismail Zühdü Bey, transferred from a position as Ottoman commissioner in Serbia to the Dutch East Indies before being sent to Bombay upon Galip's departure for Istanbul.[37] Among the consuls who served in Batavia, three were later transferred to Bombay, a fourth was unsuccessfully nominated to become consul-general in Singapore, while others moved to and from consular posts as varied as Tabriz, Tbilisi, Liverpool, New York, and Barcelona. Their unique *curricula vitae* and career trajectories suggest that the officials chosen by the Ottoman government to represent their interests in politically sensitive Indian Ocean territories were not one-dimensional Pan-Islamic firebrands who might stir up trouble. Rather, they were part of an emerging group of career officials forming a nascent consular corps capable of meeting a diverse range of needs for the government in different contexts.

When the Porte began dispatching consular agents to the subcontinent and Southeast Asia in the 1870s and 1880s, it chose to expand an institution with which the Foreign Ministry enjoyed broad familiarity while adapting its use to new political contexts in the colonized territories of the Indian Ocean. The establishment of new, salaried consular offices in this region relied to some extent on a developing set of institutional and bureaucratic practices in the Foreign Ministry's more mature consular operations in Europe and North America. In addition, the ministry's growing cadre of legal advisors had at their disposal decades of precedent in the Porte's interactions with the British and Dutch imperial governments. The Porte drew on this experience to respond to the reticence and out-

---

34. BOA, İ. HR. 289/18146 (4 C 1300/12 April 1883).
35. BOA, İ. HR. 302/19182 (28 L 1303/30 July 1886). For a brief history of the office and its position within the Foreign Ministry, also see Findley, *Bureaucratic Reform*, 259–60.
36. For more on Galip Bey's alleged Pan-Islamic activities, see Karpat, *Politicization of Islam*, 236. If Pan-Islamic agitation was a primary reason for his dismissal from Batavia, it then seems an odd decision to transfer him to a position of higher status with a larger budget in Bombay, a city not unknown for its Pan-Islamic associations.
37. See BOA, İ. HR. 301/19085 (3 B 1303/7 April 1886).

right resistance of European powers who feared the potential disruptions of Pan-Islamic activity in the colonies. Extant treaties and consular norms established by other European governments proved to be a powerful tool in the hands of the Foreign Ministry's Office of Legal Counsel (Hukuk Müşavirliği İstişare Odası).

This resistance accompanied the appointment of the first salaried agent in Bombay in 1870, which broke with decades of Ottoman consular practice in India. In earlier decades, the Porte had relied on local notables to act as honorary consuls, beginning with appointments to Bombay and Calcutta in 1849,[38] and followed by representatives selected from among prominent Muslim merchants in Colombo (Sri Lanka) in 1863 and Singapore in 1864.[39] The figures that filled these posts were primarily merchants with extensive ties to local society. While they did not receive salaries directly from the Ottoman government, their appointments promised prestige associated with being named the local representative of the Ottoman sultan, and opportunities to recoup some of their expenses from the receipts of the consulate's chancellery.[40]

However, since the income that honorary consuls could derive from discharging their official duties was primarily limited to reimbursements for expenses associated with consular business, the majority of the honorary consuls' livelihood still came from a combination of personal wealth and local business ventures.[41] As a result, the honorary officials were forced to split their attention between official consular duties and personal business activities and were more likely to face conflicts of interest as a result. The appointment documents for Ali Mehmed Han, honorary Ottoman consul in Bombay from 1856 until his death in 1869, reported him to be "the owner of the Mazagon dockyard at present occupied by the P&O [steamship navigation] company."[42] A letter from J. Emerson Tennant, former colonial secretary of Ceylon (Sri Lanka) and member of Great

38. BOA, A. DVNS. ŞHB_D 1 (1217/1802), 41–42. The Calcutta office folded quite quickly and was not revisited until efforts to open another honorary consulate there in the 1880s.
39. For the Colombo consulate, see BOA, A. DVNS.ŞHB_D 1 (1217/1802), 84. For the Singapore consulate, see BOA, İ. HR. 208/11999 (16 S 1281/21 July 1864). The Singapore consul died just one year later, and his brother took his place in an unofficial capacity for more than a decade after.
40. See Article 59, Young *Corps de Droit Ottoman*, 3:9.
41. Ibid. Article 59 stated that the honorary consuls would not receive pay for their work, but could "retain the revenues of their chancery up to 500 *kuruş* per year." Thus the maximum amount available to honorary consuls was limited to a fraction of the annual salary guaranteed to their counterparts in remunerated consular positions. At the same time, while Article 3 of the regulations forbade salaried consuls from engaging in commercial activities, Article 60 stated explicitly that honorary consuls could engage in commerce. By thus limiting the amount that honorary consuls could earn from their consular duties, while at the same time allowing them to engage in commerce, the regulations ensured that holders of the honorary office would need to maintain their livelihoods by some means outside of their activities on behalf of the Porte.
42. BOA, İ. HR. 128/6504 (18 C 1272/25 Feb. 1856).

Britain's Board of Trade, was submitted to the Ottoman government in support of Ali Mehmed's nomination.[43] Similarly, the document recommending the honorary consul appointed in Singapore in 1864 described him as part of "the agency of Mr. Stanley, eldest son of Lord Stanley" and boasted that the proposed consul was "among the wealthiest merchants residing [in Singapore]."[44]

The wealth and connections of these honorary consuls would have provided advantages to the Ottoman government in local affairs. Well-connected locals could support themselves with minimal Ottoman investment and would likely have a modicum of access to wealthy and powerful individuals from various strata of the cities in which they resided. Likewise, they could also provide valuable intelligence and personal understanding of the power structures at play in the colonial state. Yet, those same factors could also become liabilities. The entanglement of their assets and livelihoods in local political and economic structures, for example, called into question how zealously or faithfully they would have acted in promoting the interests of distant Ottoman authorities over local colonial power or their own business or political ambitions.

By contrast, when the first salaried Ottoman consul—Hüseyin Hasib Efendi—arrived in Bombay in 1870, his salary and status were determined by his position in the Ottoman bureaucratic structure. Unlike his predecessors, Hüseyin Hasib had worked in the Foreign Ministry's Translation Bureau (Tercüme Odası) in Istanbul and was trained in and familiar with the administrative practices of the Ottoman civil bureaucracy. Perhaps most importantly, his status as a civil servant operating within the bureaucratic structure of the Ottoman state lent institutional support to his actions. Hüseyin Hasib's reports from the subcontinent reflect a level of attentiveness and professional skill that distinguished him from the honorary consuls that had preceded him and ensured that he was entrusted with greater responsibility and more sensitive assignments.[45]

The person most responsible for the shift in staffing the consular office in Bombay was Ahmed Midhat Pasha. During his tenure as the governor of Baghdad, the Tanzimat reformer and future grand vizier became increasingly interested in how Ottoman consular policies could support the government's interests in territories outside their control in Persia and the Indian subcontinent.[46] In an 1869 petition to the grand vizier, Midhat cited the importance of India in the commercial affairs of "the people of Iraq" and asked that a permanent represen-

---

43. Ibid.
44. BOA, İ. HR. 208/11999 (16 S 1281/21 July 1864).
45. BOA, HR. SFR(3) 48/8 (9 Jan. 1860); BOA, HR. SFR(3) 56/6 (12 Jan. 1861).
46. The petition was, in fact, one of three in which he advocated a shift to salaried consular agents in the region. The other two offices he proposed were in the neighboring Persian cities of Bushehr and Sine (Sanandaj). See BOA, İ. HR. 241/14279 (17 Ş 1286/22 Nov. 1869); BOA, İ. HR. 242/14954 (20 B 1288/5 Oct. 1871).

tative of the government be sent there to protect their interests.[47] He argued that the region's significance merited a full-time appointment of a qualified official who would be paid a salary of ten thousand *kuruş* from the imperial treasury.[48] Hüseyin Hasib's appointment the following year demonstrated Midhat's influence in the capital; the decree repeated verbatim the opening lines of his 1869 petition and even confirmed the very same salary that Midhat had proposed.[49]

During the ten years that Hüseyin Hasib served in the post, he established new benchmarks for the level of integration between the Bombay consulate and the Porte. His reports to Istanbul included information gleaned from diverse contacts in the British Indian government, itinerant Arab merchants, and people from various levels of local Muslim society.[50] He was tasked in at least two cases with providing logistical support to Ottoman diplomatic missions passing through Bombay on their way to Central Asia. Throughout the 1870s, he used his connections in the Emirate of Kashgar (1863–77) to keep Istanbul apprised of events there, and to provide updates on the status of several Ottoman soldiers serving as part of a military mission sent to assist the emir.[51] When the Ottomans sent a diplomatic delegation to Kabul in 1877, Hüseyin Hasib played an even more prominent role in facilitating the logistics and activities of the Porte's traveling representatives.[52]

Between taking up the post in 1870 and his departure a decade later, Hüseyin Hasib was the only salaried consul operating on behalf of the Ottoman govern-

47. BOA, İ. HR. 242/14354 (27 L 1286/30 Jan. 1870).

48. Ibid.

49. Midhat originally proposed an official from the Baghdad Telegraph Office to take the position, but the nominee declined to accept. See BOA, İ. HR. 246/14630 (3 B 1287/29 Sept. 1870).

50. See, for example, his report of a conversation with Arab merchants from several cities on the Persian coastline in BOA, I.HR 274/16634 (1 C 1294/15 June 1877).

51. See BOA, HR. SYS 4/36 (19 Oct. 1878). Incidentally, that mission travelled to Kashgar from Istanbul by way of Bombay and the Suez Canal just a few years earlier. Hüseyin Hasib maintained correspondence with Yakub Efendi, the emissary sent to Istanbul several times on behalf of the Islamic ruler of Kashgar and other Central Asian rulers, and produced several reports for Istanbul on his activity there and in India.

52. Hüseyin Hasib met the Porte's delegation at the docks in Bombay's Apollo Bunder (now Wellington Pier) alongside the British Municipal Commissioner in Bombay, hosted the delegation for several days at the consulate, and traveled north with them as far as Peshawar. For coverage of the delegation's time in India, see Özcan, *Pan-Islamism*, 78–88; S. Tanvir Wasti, "The 1877 Ottoman Mission to Afghanistan," *Middle Eastern Studies* 30, no. 4 (1994): 956–62. Hasib's role in the delegation is also mentioned in the accounts of several of the delegation's members. See BOA, İ. HR. 276/16873 (5 C 1295/6 June 1878); BOA, İ. HR. 296/18687 (25 S 1302/14 Dec. 1884). For the presence of the British officials, see BOA, İ. HR. 276/16873 (5 C 1295/6 June 1878), doc. 2; M. Cavid Baysun, "Şirvanizade Ahmed Hulusi Efendi'nin Efganistan Elçiliğine Aid Vesikalar," *Tarih Dergisi* (1952): 151. An individual identified in the last document only as "Mr. Grant" was presumably J.H. Grant who was described as "Acting Municipal Commissioner for the City of Bombay" in the *Bombay Civil List* of 1877.

ment in the region.[53] This began to change in the 1880s. The example set by the salaried official in Bombay loomed large as the Foreign Ministry tried to expand into other cities beginning in 1882. However, as Faiz Ahmed makes clear in his chapter in this volume, the Ottoman government was not free to determine the location of new consulates, and efforts to open offices in the interior of British India repeatedly failed.[54] The Porte's ability to dispatch consular representatives to particular areas was subject to negotiation with the governments of host countries and shaped by bilateral treaties granting each party access to their territory. In the case of Great Britain, an Ottoman consular presence in territories under British jurisdiction was secured as early as the Dardanelles Treaty, signed in 1809.[55] Article 8 of the treaty afforded the Porte the right to appoint "Consuls (*Shahbenders*)...at Malta, and in the Dominions of His Britannic Majesty where it shall be necessary."[56] The final clause of the article limited the posting of consuls to "Dominions...where it shall be necessary," but did not elaborate who would decide the criteria by which such a determination would be made. The Porte's experiences trying to open new consulates in Peshawar in 1877 and repeated attempts to open an office in Singapore, explored below, demonstrate how this ambiguity could complicate Ottoman consular expansion in the face of outright opposition from treaty partners like the British.

Despite treaty provisions that gave the Porte the right to dispatch consular agents to particular territories, the Ottomans were still restricted by the requirement to obtain an *exequatur* (certificate of recognition) from the host government approving an individual consul's nomination to any given city.[57] This restriction occasionally posed obstacles that were difficult if not impossible to overcome. For example, when the Ottomans attempted to install one of the members of the 1877 delegation to Kabul as consul-general in Peshawar, British Indian officials refused to approve the appointment of a second consular agent in western India by

---

53. During that period, there were honorary consuls working for various periods in the British Ceylonese port of Colombo (now in Sri Lanka) and in British Singapore.
54. Ahmed, "The British-Ottoman Cold War."
55. "The (Dardanelles) Treaty of Peace, Commerce, and Secret Alliance: Great Britain and the Ottoman Empire," in *Diplomacy in the Near and Middle East: A Documentary Record, 1535-1914*, ed. J.C. Hurewitz, 2 vol. (Princeton: D. Van Nostrand Company, Inc., 1956), 1:81–84.
56. Ibid., 1:83. The following clause linked Ottoman consuls' duties to the Porte's need to "manage and superintend the affairs and interests of merchants of the Sublime Porte." The article went on to promise to Ottoman consuls "similar privileges and immunities to those granted to English consuls resident in the Ottoman domains."
57. An *exequatur* is defined as an official recognition of a consul or commercial agent by the government of the country to which he is accredited, authorizing him to exercise his power. For the role of the *exequatur* as documentary approval of a consul's credentials, see Leira and Neumann, "The Many Past Lives of the Consul," 244.

claiming that, "Turkey had no commercial interest in the region."[58] That British officials cited commercial matters as a primary reason for rebuffing the Porte's interest in extending consular representation to the western Indian interior highlights how the ambiguous divide between a consul's commercial and diplomatic duties could create obstacles to the Porte's interest in expanding their consuls' reach in particular colonial territories.

Although the Ottoman Foreign Ministry never succeeded in opening an office in Peshawar, it had greater success negotiating with the Dutch government for the creation of a salaried consul-general post in Batavia. This highlights the increasing prominence of the Foreign Ministry's legal advisors and their reliance on legal precedents to carve out space for Ottoman diplomats. In February 1882, Foreign Ministry officials nominated a local merchant named Bağdatlı Seyyid Hızırzâde Seyyid Aziz Efendi as their honorary consul in Batavia. The edict detailing his nomination identified the candidate as an Ottoman subject engaged in commercial activity in the region.[59] According to a March report of that year from the director of consular affairs, the impetus for creating the honorary post was a request from the Ottoman Embassy to the Netherlands in The Hague. The directorate argued that as a result of "the arrogant treatment shown by the Dutch state to the Muslims of Java," the absence of an Ottoman agent in Batavia contributed to a situation in which "the rights of Ottoman subjects [were] being trampled upon."[60] However, due to budgetary concerns about the salary and expenses required to support a salaried consul, the Porte preferred to appoint an honorary representative already residing in the Dutch East Indies.[61]

58. Özcan, *Pan-Islamism*, 113–14. Also see, Ahmed, "The British-Ottoman Cold War"; Wasti, "The 1877 Ottoman Mission," 958–60. The consular registers do not indicate that there were any other attempts to appoint a consular agent to Peshawar. Özcan's argument that British pushback was what forced the Ottomans to "[resort] to the appointment of natives as honorary consuls" appears to not be the whole story based on the examples of Madras and Karachi outlined later in this section.

59. BOA İ. HR. 289/18146 (4 C 1300/12 April 1883), doc. 2 identified him as an Ottoman subject and mentioned his commercial activity. BOA İ.HR. 285/17778 (28 Ra 1299/17 Feb. 1882) includes the appointment document, which was the only instance in which the epithet "Bağdatlı" was applied to his name.

60. BOA İ. HR. 289/18146 (4 C 1300/12 April 1883), doc. 2. The document's phrasing is interesting since it makes no distinction between Javanese Muslims as a group and Ottoman subjects, which would have constituted a very small proportion of the former. While this would seemingly support the idea that the Ottomans viewed the Muslims of the East Indies as part of their purview, later reports written by the Ottoman consuls posted there were more circumspect in distinguishing the two groups.

61. Ibid. The report cited the necessary outlay of "at least nine thousand *kuruş* in salary and expenses like that given to the agent in Bombay" and argued that since such a sum could not be found in the coming year's budget, the new post should instead be administered by an honorary agent chosen from among the Ottoman subjects residing in the city who were engaged in local trade.

Whereas the Ottomans had initially proposed a modest consular office, the creation of a full-fledged Consulate-General in Batavia demonstrates how the Hamidian Foreign Ministry used diplomatic bureaucracy and substantive engagement with international law. Dutch authorities initially rejected the nomination of Seyyid Aziz, claiming that there were problems in the Ottoman *berat* (warrant) that proposed his post.[62] In response, the Porte sought counsel from one of the Foreign Ministry jurists. This was likely Carl Gescher, one of the two newly-hired legal advisors whose role in establishing the Office of Legal Counsel is described by Aimee Genell in this volume.[63] According to a report by the director of consular affairs, Gescher advised that there was no legal basis for Dutch opposition to the consular appointment. The *berat* in question contained the same provisions as those given to all Ottoman consular officials in Dutch and other territories. Since the Dutch had accepted the terms for Ottoman consuls elsewhere in Dutch territory, Gescher argued that they would have no valid reason to oppose the same document for the consul in Batavia. He advised that it would be beneficial to appoint another individual in place of Seyyid Aziz to determine if their opposition would be sustained. Following Gescher's advice, more than a year after the initial proposal to appoint an honorary consul to the island, the Foreign Ministry nominated an Ottoman bureaucrat from Istanbul, then employed in the Translation Bureau, as an official, salaried consular agent. That official, Ali Galip Bey, became the first of nearly a dozen Ottoman diplomats to occupy the post of consul-general in Batavia between 1883 and the conclusion of World War One.[64]

Despite their success in opening a new office in Batavia, the addition of a second salaried consular position in a major center in the Indian Ocean did not mark an irreversible trend toward the use of salaried officials in new posts. In fact, through the end of the 1890s most Ottoman proposals to open new consulates still privileged honorary positions that would pose less of a strain on the imperial budget. Even these more modest proposals were not always successful. The Ottoman government's struggle to post representatives to key ports like Singapore, Karachi, and Calcutta showed that even relatively more sympathetic treaty

---

62. Ibid. In fact, the director's phrasing hints at a deeper conflict between the two governments: "Because the Dutch state was unable to show that they had been unsuccessful in opposing the placement of an Ottoman government official on the aforementioned island, they objected to the contents of the *berat* given to Seyyid Aziz and refused to confirm the aforementioned appointment."

63. Ibid. The report identified him as *"hukuk müşaviri saadetlu Geşir efendi hazretleri."* Interestingly, the director's report was dated 27 March 1883 and described events at an unspecified earlier date. That would have placed it just before the official date of Gescher's appointment cited in Genell "The Well-Defended Domains," in this volume.

64. BOA, İ. HR. 289/18146 (4 C 1300/12 April 1883).

partners like the British could still create roadblocks for the Porte's attempts to expand their consular footprint.

Efforts to nominate an honorary consular official to represent Ottoman interests in Singapore illuminate the difficult path that such negotiations could take. In May 1882, just months after the first, unsuccessful attempts to install Seyyid Aziz Efendi in Batavia, the Foreign Ministry sought approval from the British government for Seyyid Juneid bin Omer al-Juneid to occupy an honorary consular position in Singapore that had been vacant for years.[65] The new nominee had been serving in the role unofficially since the death of his brother in 1865, who had died just a year after taking up the post.[66] By 1865, Seyyid Juneid had already made several unsuccessful attempts to get the Ottoman government to make his position official.[67] Remarkably, the appointment appears to have been ignored by the British until a verbal inquiry from the Ottoman ambassador in London caused Lord Granville to look into the matter in late 1884.[68] Even after the involvement of Lord Granville, Seyyid Juneid's appointment remained unconfirmed as late as August 1886, nearly four years after he was originally nominated for the position. A copy of an 1886 translated report to the Office of Legal Counsel states that the British expressed a desire to delay recognition of the appointment in Singapore on the condition that the Ottomans agree to extend British consular jurisdiction in Asia Minor.[69] Absent more documentation it remains unclear whether the British truly sought to leverage the Singapore appointment to extend their own consular jurisdiction in Ottoman lands or whether such a demand provided a ruse to delay approval of another Ottoman consul with access to a regional center of Pan-Islamic activity.

65. BOA, İ. HR. 286/17881 (5 B 1299/23 May 1882).

66. Quite a bit of literature has accumulated on the affairs of this Hadhrami Arab family in Singapore. For example, see Leif Manger, *The Hadrami Diaspora: Community-Building on the Indian Ocean Rim* (New York: Berghahn, 2010), 22–25; Ulrike Freitag, *Indian Ocean Migrants and State Formation in Hadhramaut* (Leiden: Brill, 2003), 204–13; Engseng Ho, *The Graves of Tarim: Genealogy and Mobility across the Indian Ocean* (Berkeley: University of California Press, 2006).

67. Juneid notified the Ottoman government that he had been acting in his brother's stead as early as 1867. See, BOA, HR. TO. 448/8 (12 Feb. 1867). In a letter included in BOA, HR. SFR (3) 200/1 (6 Nov. 1873), Juneid tried again to approach the Foreign Ministry via a memorandum to the Ottoman ambassador to London, Musurus Pasha, dated May 1873 in which he "respectfully request[ed] your Excellency's attention to my letter dated the last in which I brought to notice that my late brother died in Jidda in the month of May 1865 and that ever since his death I have been acting as Ottoman Vice Consul at this port under an appointment from him given on his departure." The 1882 nomination, thus, came nearly seventeen years after the surviving Juneid brother began performing his duties in an unofficial capacity!

68. BOA, HR. SFR (3) 305/15 (28 Oct. 1884).

69. BOA, HR. SFR (3) 316/100 (21 Aug. 1886).

Following these early setbacks, the Foreign Ministry did not succeed in opening a consulate in Singapore until March 1901, when the British government consented to the appointment of Ahmed Ataullah Efendi, an Ottoman subject born and raised in the British colonies in South Africa, as the first salaried consul-general posted to Singapore.[70] When he died in an automobile accident a few years later, the British refused to acknowledge the successor proposed by Istanbul and the post was once again left vacant.

New personnel guidelines contained in the regulations were adopted in the same year that the Ottoman government opened the new Consulate-General in Batavia and appointed an official to replace Hüseyin Hasib in Bombay. Established before many of the other outposts opened in the region, the new regulations had a clear impact on the structure of relations between the various offices in the region. By continuing to staff the offices in Bombay and Batavia with salaried officials instead of reverting to honorary figureheads, decision-makers in Istanbul ensured that future consular appointments were subjected to greater limitations. They also struggled to find qualified Ottoman subjects with sufficient rank and training who were willing to occupy the posts.

Safeguarding Ottoman Extraterritorial Rights and Regulating Movement between the "Well-Protected Domains" and the Colonial Indian Ocean

At the same time that Pan-Islamic discourses touted the unification of Muslim interests worldwide, European colonial powers claimed authority over growing numbers of Asian and African Muslims as their colonial subjects. Ottoman administrators were faced with the challenge of reconciling claims of global Islamic leadership under the caliphate with the emerging reality that foreign Muslims affiliated with colonial governments could pose a threat to Ottoman rule at home. Ottoman consuls in the colonial Indian Ocean were uniquely challenged to navigate the line between protecting the extraterritorial rights of Ottoman Muslims in foreign territories and managing the potential threat of foreign Muslims subject to colonial rule traveling between potentially hostile foreign jurisdictions and Ottoman domains.

The role that consular officials played in defending the rights of their subjects in foreign territories formed one of the most common rationales for Ottoman consular expansion in the Indian Ocean. Many of the consular appointment decrees based their arguments on the premise that a significant number of Ottoman subjects resided in places like India or Southeast Asia and consulates were a necessary means of protecting their rights. The petition for an office in Singapore claimed that "a portion of the population consists of Arabs of Ottoman nationality," while documents related to Batavia argued that "in the absence of an agent of

---

70. The position was given the same salary and expenses budget as the posts in Bombay and Batavia. BOA, İ. HR. 371/22 (8 M 1319/27 April 1901).

the Ottoman government there the rights of subjects of the Ottoman Empire are being trampled upon."[71] The form that these protections took differed according to the local context in which the consuls operated. In areas of the Dutch East Indies, where the classification of Arabs as "foreign Orientals" subjected them to onerous restrictions on movement and commercial activity, the consulates tended to play a more confrontational role in mediating disputes with local colonial authorities.[72] In other areas, consuls were primarily charged with helping Ottoman subjects navigate the local economy.[73] In this respect, consular expansion in the region was defined by an extension of the government's responsibilities to protect Ottoman subjects in territories that fell outside its formal jurisdiction.

The Ottoman government's efforts to craft and enforce regulations controlling the movement of Ottomans and foreigners across their borders were complicated by the dynamic transformations in the Indian Ocean realm that abutted the empire's southeastern frontiers. As increasing numbers of people moved between the Arabian Peninsula and various parts of Africa, the Indian subcontinent, and Southeast Asia, their movements raised new concerns in Ottoman government circles over security and stability in the Arabian provinces. These concerns required the government to increase its efforts to address potential problems prior to the arrival of foreign travelers in Ottoman ports. Realizing those goals proved especially challenging in the fraught political environment of the Indian Ocean, which was split between several colonial jurisdictions and a handful of more independent powers.[74]

71. BOA, İ. HR. 371/22 (8 M 1319/22 April 1901); BOA, İ. HR. 289/18146 (4 C 1300/12 April 1883). The Singapore document used the phrase "*tabiiyet-i osmaniye'de bulunan Araplar*" that could be translated as either "Arabs of Ottoman allegiance" or "Arabs of Ottoman nationality."

72. For examples of these restrictions, see Schmidt, "Pan-Islamism"; Eric Tagliacozzo, *Secret Trades, Porous Borders: Smuggling and States along a Southeast Asian Frontier, 1865–1915* (New Haven: Yale University Press, 2005), 146–51. The Southeast Asian consulates especially were the site of constant disagreements with the Dutch and English governments over how to define the limits of Ottoman nationality and how that impacted local individuals' status within colonial social structures.

73. For example, see BOA, HR. SFR(3) 335/78 (17 Aug. 1887) in which Bombay Consul-General Ismail argued that consuls were necessary to ensure that Ottoman merchants could remain competitive with their Indian counterparts. He claimed that for some time the Muslim merchants of India had been successful in opening the door to trade within Ottoman domains "to the extent that people from Madras [active] in Istanbul or people from Bombay [active] in Syria send a special representative to be of use in selling Indian goods and products there." He worried that without the intervention of Ottoman consular agents in a number of local ports, the benefits of such trade would continue to be restricted to the Indian merchants and that Ottoman merchants would remain excluded.

74. To be sure, officials in Anatolia or the Levant faced some of the same challenges across the Mediterranean, Aegean, and Black Seas in this and earlier periods that were partly mitigated by Ottoman consular offices in Greece, the Balkans, and Crimea. However, Ottoman administrators in Basra, Yemen, and Hijaz were further burdened by the headache of coordinating

The array of regulations governing consular affairs that were adopted between 1882 and 1884 intersected with other major regulatory reforms. Due to mobility between Ottoman and foreign domains, the regulations that most directly impacted consular operations in the Indian Ocean were the passport rules adopted or updated in 1844, 1869, 1884, and 1895.[75] In the absence of an Ottoman embassy east of Tehran, Ottoman consuls in Indian Ocean ports were the only official outlets from which foreign nationals could acquire the visa documents that the passport law required to cross Ottoman borders. Viewing the work of the Indian Ocean consulates within the context of these complementary and overlapping areas of regulatory reform helps explain why authorities in Istanbul continued to expend the effort and resources necessary to extend the office into distant parts of Asia and Africa.

In theory, diplomatic agents like the consuls had a straightforward role to play in helping to regulate travel to and from the Ottoman lands. Consuls were capable of issuing both passports and visas according to the administrative duties listed in the schedule of rates to be charged for various consular services.[76] However, the instructions that detailed the consuls' duties made clear that they were to issue passports only to Ottoman subjects whose status could be verified under strictly defined conditions.[77] The instructions issued to the consuls in 1883–84 contained an entire section of provisions on how to discharge their duties related to both passports and visas. These articles made an explicit distinction between passports for international travel, to which their regulations referred, and the "*mürûr tezkeresi* [internal passport] used for travel within the empire [which] shall in no case be used for travel abroad."[78] While the consuls

with adversarial British and Dutch colonial regimes in order to fulfill their obligations to facilitate the Hajj pilgrimage for scores of foreign Muslims.

75. The 1844 and 1869 versions are available in Aristarchi Bey, *Legislation Ottomane our recueil des lois, reglements, ordonnances, traits, capitulations et autres documents officiels de l'Empire Ottoman*, 7 vol. (Constantinople: Freres Nicolaides, 1874), 2:95–102. The 1884 version can be found in BOA, A. DVN. MKL 25/25 (15 R 1301/13 Feb. 1884). The 1895 version is in Young, Corps de Droit Ottoman, 2:263–68. For an overview of Ottoman passport legislation, see Nalan Turna, 19. *Yüzyıldan 20. Yüzyıla Osmanlı Topraklarında Seyahat, Göç ve Asayış Belgeleri: Mürûr Tezkereleri* (Istanbul: Kaknüs Yayınları, 2013).

76. See Young, *Corps de Droit Ottoman*, 3:10. Kuneralp "Le service consulaire Ottomane," 433, cites the presence of passports in the 1860 text but makes no mention of visas. Although visas were clearly part of the program by the revised 1884 version, without access to the original 1860 text I cannot tell if the visa provision was added later.

77. See Articles 49–54 in "Instructions to be Sent to the Consulates of the Ottoman Government" (*Saltanat-ı Seniyye Şehbenderlerine Gönderilecek Talimat*), *Salname-i Nezaret-i Umur-ı Hariciyye*, 3:377–425; Young, *Corps de Droit Ottoman*, 3:14–40. Also the special set of instructions to consuls annexed to the 1895 update of the passport law in Texte 35, ibid., 2:268–72.

78. Article 50, "Instructions to be Sent to the Consulates of the Ottoman Government," ibid., 2:268–72.

were told they could issue passports to Ottoman subjects intending to travel outside the consuls' jurisdictions, they were strictly forbidden from renewing the passports of Ottomans residing in their jurisdictions and were instructed to take possession of any *mürûr tezkeresi* that a traveler should present to them.[79] By contrast, visas would be issued to all travelers seeking to enter the empire. Thus, in practice, consuls would be required to issue visas far more often than they would be involved with the passport documents.

In the aforementioned 1869 update to the passport regulations, Ottoman consulates were identified as the only locations other than Ottoman embassies where foreigners could acquire visas that would allow them to enter Ottoman territory without a financial penalty.[80] This would pose a significant burden for travelers from South and Southeast Asia, since there were no Ottoman embassies and very few consular offices at the time. In practice, the provision was seldom enforced; in the unlucky event the provision was enforced, payment of the penalty was considered sufficient.[81] Uneven enforcement of the visa requirement and the existence of an alternative means of gaining legal entry provided little incentive for travelers to expend effort acquiring the necessary documents. However, an 1884 update to the passport regulations again placed the burden of seeking out Ottoman consuls on foreign travelers en route to Ottoman domains.[82] Although the regulations included an exemption for people from regions where there were no Ottoman embassies or consulates,[83] they concluded with a requirement that travelers who "in the course of their journey pass through an area in which an Ottoman consulate is found," must obtain a visa from the consular official in that region.[84]

Seen in that light, the repeated efforts of the Foreign Ministry to open offices in major Indian Ocean transportation hubs take on added significance. In addition to being located in cities where they would have access to large and diverse populations capable of providing useful information and services, the consuls would also be well-placed to fulfill their duties in providing visas even for those

79. Article 13 of 1895 instructions in Texte 35, ibid., 2:268–72.

80. Article 1, Aristarchi Bey, *Legislation Ottomane*, 2:95–96. The law demanded that "all foreigners entering the empire must have a passport bearing a visa provided by the Legation or one of the consulates of Turkey" or else they would be required to pay a penalty.

81. In some cases, pilgrims arriving in the Hijaz without the necessary visa documents appear to have been charged for a *mürûr tezkeresi* that was theoretically meant more for authorizing travel within the Ottoman territories. See Michael Christopher Low, "The Mechanics of Mecca: The Technopolitics of the Late Ottoman Hijaz and the Colonial Hajj" (Ph.D. diss., Columbia University, 2015), 283–91.

82. Selim Deringil has argued that this was one of the primary purposes of the consulates in South and Southeast Asia. See Deringil, "Legitimacy Structures," 351–52.

83. See Article 10 in BOA, A. DVNL. MKL 25/25 (15 R 1301/13 Feb. 1884).

84. Ibid., Article 11. The article also set the price of the visa at twenty *kuruş*.

travelers from outside their jurisdiction that were passing through the port. Since many of the steamships serving the Indian Ocean routes at that time made regular stops at ports of call between their origin and destination, it increased the likelihood that travelers would pass through at least one city with an Ottoman consulate.

It is clear from the documentary record that these provisions proved easier to plan than to implement in the Indian Ocean environment. The archives are littered with reports of provincial officials complaining of travelers arriving without passports or visas and consular officials seeking clarification of how they should apply the requirements in a variety of special circumstances.[85] These issues became particularly problematic when they involved Muslims traveling through India or Southeast Asia for the Hajj pilgrimage.[86] When the passport regulations were updated again in 1895, another article was inserted immediately after the revised visa provision that reiterated its application to "the passports of those who would go on pilgrimage either to Mecca or Medina, or to Jerusalem and the Holy Places."[87] While the provision originally set the price of the visa for pilgrims at the same twenty *kuruş* level applied to other visas, the government later reduced the amount charged to pilgrims to six *kuruş* under pressure from colonial governments and foreign Muslim groups.[88] Even with these regular updates and revisions, the Ottoman government's ability to apply the visa provisions to the populations traveling from India and Southeast Asia was never able to overcome the opposition that it faced from their foreign rivals. Yet, the desire to do so and the primary role that the consulates were supposed to play in regulating mobility continued to be a driving factor in Ottoman efforts to expand their consular footprint through the final years of the empire.

Conclusion

It is not a coincidence that the Porte's efforts to extend the reach of their consular services into the bustling colonial port cities of the Indian Ocean coincided with efforts within the Foreign Ministry to standardize bureaucratic practices and formalize engagement with the structures of international law. From the last decades of the nineteenth century through World War One, the Ottomans faced renewed threats of encroachment from an increasingly assertive European imperialism that took several forms: territorial, economic, and legal. While these de-

---

85. BOA, MV 151/10 (4 R 1329/4 April 1911); BOA, BEO 3820/286466 (5 Za 1328/8 Nov. 1910).
86. For more see Low "The Mechanics of Mecca," 283–91.
87. *Salname-i Nezaret-i Umur-ı Hariciyye*, 3:362–76, Article 12.
88. For a particularly pointed critique of the visa requirements from an Indian Muslim group, see BOA, HR. HMŞ. İŞO 65/22 (10 Ş 1331/15 July 1913). The letter, addressed to the consul in Bombay and signed by the "President de Comité du Hajj" in Bombay, lists several complaints about the visa fees and communicates the group's demand that the government "abolish this questionable tax" on the pilgrims' religious obligations.

velopments posed a potentially mortal threat to Ottoman authority within their domains, the increasingly global domination of European imperial powers also raised dire concerns over the Ottoman state's ability to continue protecting the lives and livelihoods of Muslim populations—Ottoman and foreign alike—that traversed the liminal zones on the empire's frontiers. Along the extended maritime zones of the empire's southeastern boundaries in the Arabian Peninsula, long-established networks of interregional commerce and migration via the waterways of the Indian Ocean meant that changes in the status quo even in seemingly distant territories could have major repercussions on the well-being of the Ottoman Arabian provinces bordering the Red Sea and the Persian Gulf.

While the Ottoman state had long found reasons to dispatch envoys to protect their interests in engaging with the large, commercially-active, Muslim populations that ringed the Indian Ocean, the posting of consular agents to semipermanent positions resident within those territories was a novel development of the later nineteenth century. Only in those later decades did the Porte deem it necessary to dispatch Ottoman subjects, versed in the empire's bureaucratic traditions and backed by the institutional authority of the government's ministries, to serve as official proxies acting on their behalf in interactions with foreign Muslims and European colonial authorities alike. As this chapter has shown, dispatching Ottoman consuls to strategic new trade and transit hubs was a key innovation in Istanbul's strategy of adjusting to the transformed status quo in the Indian Ocean. As colonial powers in the region expanded their claims to territorial control and restricted the ability of outside powers to access the markets and populations that they contained, governments with established interests in the region like the Ottomans were forced to seek new means of maintaining their own subjects' local status and access and to protect their frontiers from potential threats posed by encroaching rivals. In this case, the Ottomans could use the strategic advantages of pre-existing consular treaties, formalized bureaucratic practices, and, if necessary, the protections afforded by international legal precedent to carve out a niche for representatives of Ottoman governmental interests in the colonial jurisdictions of their European imperial rivals.

Concerns over the status of Muslim populations under colonial rule and the well-being of the global Islamic community were by no means absent from Istanbul's desires to increase their empire's presence in many parts of Asia and Africa. However, a myopic historiographical focus on the religious foundations of Ottoman interests in the broader world obscures the diverse set of motivations for engagement with South and Southeast Asia that were both novel for the sole remaining global Muslim empire of the era and similar to those that informed other global powers. That Istanbul would seek to maintain the integrity of centuries-old relationships with Muslim populations in South and Southeast Asia is hardly surprising; that they would elect to maintain those relationships by engaging in often intense, high-level legal negotiations just to send salaried government employees to live in territories under European imperial jurisdiction poses a number of more interesting questions about the Porte's motivations.

If the extension of Ottoman Islamic prestige had been the primary motivator in Istanbul's outreach to the colonial Indian Ocean in the late nineteenth century, any number of informal or covert intermediaries could have been employed to pursue the Porte's objectives. On the other hand, consuls were highly visible public figures whose activities would be constantly scrutinized by the colonial officials that governed the cities in which they resided. Consuls depended on the certification of the host government for the right to occupy their position and discharge their duties. A variety of internal Ottoman regulations and international legal norms governed what was considered acceptable behavior from consular agents in their foreign posts. These elements hardly seem conducive to the pursuit of an agenda that could undermine or contravene the objectives of the colonial governments within whose territories the consuls needed to operate. Yet throughout the period examined here, the Ottoman Foreign Ministry continuously pursued the expansion of their consular representation into new and more distant parts of the colonial Indian Ocean.

In the end, the Porte's attempts to extend its authority across the Indian Ocean were likely motivated by a combination of desires. To do so would be to burnish the sultan-caliph's Islamic credentials, and to achieve more prosaic objectives revolving around trade, security, and imperial prestige. However, analyses that privilege the Islamic components of those motivations over a simultaneous engagement with bureaucratic reforms, international legal structures, and nascent international diplomatic practices run the risk of casting the late Ottoman imperial government as a narrowly religious enterprise instead of the complex, adaptive, constantly transforming, Islamic empire reflected in the archival record.

10 Travel Documents, Mobility Control, and the Ottoman State in an Age of Global Migration, 1880–1915

David Gutman

In the past twenty years the passport has become the focus of intense scholarly inquiry. As these studies have revealed, the history and evolution of the passport provides critical insight into topics of profound interest to humanists and social scientists from a broad cross-section of disciplines such as modernity, identity, citizenship, and borders.[1] In his now classic work, *The Invention of the Passport*, sociologist John Torpey argues that the passport, a document which by the mid-twentieth century underpinned a vast, internationalized system of mobility control, emerged out of a process that began in the late eighteenth century with the French Revolution in which (European) states sought to exercise their control over movement both within and across their borders, a process he terms "monopolizing the legitimate means of movement."[2] Torpey contends that the emergence of the passport provides scholars with the opportunity to rethink the relationship between states and the societies over which they rule. For him, the passport, a document central to state efforts to identify populations to which they seek to provide protection and succor, and those they seek to exclude, is emblematic of the efforts of the modern nation-state to "embrace" the populations they govern.3 Furthermore, according to Torpey, the desire to control and document movement across borders through the use of passports, went hand-in-hand with the movement toward free and unhindered domestic mobility within European nation-states, a process that was fundamental in shaping modern notions of territoriality and borders.[4]

In portraying the international passport and its emergence as emblematic of the processes that gave rise to the modern liberal nation-state, Torpey contrasts

---

1. For example, see Jane Caplan and John Torpey, eds., *Documenting Individual Identity: The Development of State Practices in the Modern World* (Princeton: Princeton University Press, 2001); Adam McKeown, *Melancholy Order: Asian Migration and the Globalization of Borders* (New York: Columbia University Press, 2008); Craig Robertson, *The Passport in America: The History of a Document* (Oxford: Oxford University Press, 2010); John Torpey, *The Invention of the Passport: Surveillance, Citizenship and the State* (Cambridge, UK: Cambridge University Press, 2000).
2. Torpey, *Invention*, 6–10.
3. Ibid., 10–13.
4. Ibid., 20.

the passport used to govern international travel with documents employed by states to police domestic mobility. For him, such documents are hallmarks of illiberal regimes such as the Soviet Union or apartheid South Africa, whose use of such documents "constitute a reversion to practices generally abandoned by democratic nation-states by the twentieth century."[5] For Torpey, such documents are governed by dynamics other than those that gave rise to the modern international passport system. Torpey is by no means entirely incorrect to link the use of internal passports to repressive and undemocratic forms of rule.[6] Nonetheless, viewing such documents as divergent from a liberal-and Western-norm risks missing what they, like Torpey shows for the passport, can tell us about broader questions of modernization, borders, mobility (both domestic and international), and the relationship between state and citizen, in states that used them.

This chapter examines such themes through the prism of the Ottoman Empire's document-based system of internal mobility control—what I call the *mürûr tezkeresi* system.[7] More specifically, it examines the Ottoman state's use of the *mürûr tezkeresi* system in its efforts to prevent unsanctioned overseas migration among Maronite Christian subjects in Mount Lebanon and Armenians in the eastern Anatolian province of Mamuretülaziz between roughly 1880 and 1908. What emerges is a vivid picture of the many contradictions that shaped the post-Tanzimat Ottoman state during the rule of Sultan Abdülhamid II. Through a focus on the rise of international migration from these two regions, I show how the lines between domestic and international travel were blurred, and how the Ottoman government's attempts to create a standardized system of mobility control intended to be applied uniformly throughout the empire rendered the system largely ineffective as a tool to prevent overseas migration from these two imperial hinterlands which, despite their superficial similarities as primarily non-Muslim, mountainous regions, were viewed quite differently by the state. These efforts in turn reveal broader tensions and contradictions that underlay Ottoman rule in the post-Tanzimat era. These include the desire to limit and control certain forms of mobility while allowing for and even encouraging others; balancing efforts at legal standardization with the longer-standing imperial practice of flexible and locally-specific rule; and maintaining the Tanzimat-era promise to guarantee equal protection under the law for all imperial subjects in an era when the Ot-

---

5. Ibid., 160.
6. The literature that does exist on these documents, much of it from the Imperial Russian and Soviet cases, tends to reinforce this point. See Marc Garcelon, "Colonizing the Subject: The Genealogy and Legacy of the Soviet International Passport," in *Documenting Individual Identity*, 83–84.
7. For the purposes of this chapter, I prefer to refer to the Ottoman internal passport by its Ottoman name, *mürûr tezkeresi*, which roughly translates as "document of passage."

toman state viewed any hint of separatist politics among the empire's various ethno-religious communities as a serious threat.

The Ottoman case is especially compelling, because it allows for a comparison of two very different migration control regimes. As this study demonstrates, the Young Turk Revolution of 1908 ushered in a drastically different, liberalized approach to both domestic and international migration. The implementation of these policies was also beset by several tensions and contradictions, and as the First World War dawned, aspects of the Young Turk approach to mobility control began to resemble not only their Hamidian predecessors, but also the wartime policies of putatively liberal states such as Britain and France. As has recently been argued, the modern global system of mobility and border control, key to understanding the twentieth and twenty-first-century process of globalization, was founded on a series of tensions between nineteenth-century liberal discourses on individual freedom (including freedom of movement) and universal rights, and the desire to exclude those considered racially, culturally, or religiously inferior.[8] By understanding the *mürûr tezkeresi* system, and Ottoman mobility control efforts more broadly, as built upon similar tensions and contradictions, it is the aim of this chapter to consider the Ottoman case as part of rather than divergent from the broader global history of mobility and migration in the nineteenth and twentieth centuries.

The Emergence of the *Mürûr Tezkeresi* System in the Early Nineteenth Century

As Reşat Kasaba has argued, from its founding at the dawn of the fourteenth century through to its collapse in 1922, the Ottoman state's relationship with mobile populations both within and outside its frequently changing and often permeable borders was a key factor in shaping its rule. According to Kasaba, Ottoman centralization efforts in the eighteenth and nineteenth centuries were predicated in large part on the state's ability to exert greater control over mobile populations, whether through tribal sedentarization, refugee settlement, or by controlling migration between rural and urban spheres. By the dawn of the nineteenth century, documentary controls on mobility became a central component of the Ottoman modernization project.[9] According to Musa Çadırcı, the *mürûr tezkeresi*, the document that would underpin Ottoman efforts at controlling domestic mobility throughout much of the empire's final century, was first issued in the 1810s in an effort to control the number of impoverished peasants flooding the imperial capital in search of work. Such efforts grew in importance following

---

8. McKeown, *Melancholy Order*, 16–17, 289.
9. Reşat Kasaba, *A Moveable Empire: Ottoman Nomads, Migrants, and Refugees* (Seattle: University of Washington Press, 2009), 1–12.

the destruction of the janissary corps in 1826.[10] The janissaries, once a powerful infantry force key to the empire's rapid territorial expansion in the sixteenth century, had by the eighteenth century morphed into a major economic and political force in many of the empire's cities closely allied with urban artisans, and powerful enough to depose sultans and challenge state policies they saw as contrary to their interests.[11] Their destruction, carried out in a bloody massacre conducted by forces allied to the sultan, removed a major threat to the Ottoman state's efforts at strengthening and centralizing its power.[12] Those spared the sword were banished from the imperial capital and other major cities. By denying them access to the *mürûr tezkeresi*, the state sought to limit the ability of former janissaries to move through the empire.

With the advent of the Tanzimat Reforms following the 1839 Gülhane Rescript, the Ottoman state embarked on a much more ambitious effort at controlling mobility within its borders. In 1841, it promulgated the Men-i Mürûr Nizamnamesi (Regulations Pursuant to the Restriction of Movement), a comprehensive set of laws that would govern Ottoman mobility control efforts until the 1908 revolution. In its emphasis on standardization and universal applicability regardless of religious identity, the new law embodied the ethos of the Tanzimat reforms. Its provisions clearly placed control of domestic and international mobility squarely in the hands of the central state. The law required all who travelled in the Ottoman Empire beyond the district (*kaza*) level to be in possession of a *mürûr tezkeresi*; outlined how Ottoman subjects could obtain them; and detailed the information that was to be included in each *tezkere*.

The *mürûr tezkeresi* was the beating heart of the Men-i Mürûr Nizamnamesi, and it lay at the center of the law's effort to render domestic mobility visible to the state.[13] By requiring all subjects moving within the borders of the empire to possess a *mürûr tezkeresi*, the central state could now more clearly delineate between forms of mobility it saw as legitimate (i.e., trade, labor, and pilgrimage) and those it saw as illegitimate (i.e., banditry, smuggling, and vagrancy).[14] The

---

10. Musa Çadırcı, "Tanzimat Döneminde Çıkarılan Men'-i Mürûr ve Pasaport Nizâmnâmeleri," *Belgeler* 15, no. 19 (1993): 170–71.
11. For more on the political power of the janissary corps in the early nineteenth century, see M. Mert Sunar, "Cauldron of Dissent: A Study of the Janissary Corps, 1807–1828" (PhD diss., Binghamton University, 2006).
12. M. Şükrü Hanioğlu, *A Brief History of the Late Ottoman Empire* (Princeton: Princeton University Press, 2008) 58–60.
13. For a transliterated version of the Men'-i Mürûr Nizamnamesi, see Musa Çadırcı, "Tanzimat Döneminde Men'-i Mürûr," 173–78.
14. For a thorough discussion of the role of the mürûr tezkeresi system in controlling vagrancy, see Christoph Herzog, "Migration and the State: On Ottoman Regulations Concerning Migration since the Age of Mahmud II," in *The City in the Ottoman Empire: Migration and the Making of Urban Modernity*, ed. Nora Lafi et al. (London: Routledge, 2011), 120–21.

law also made a strict distinction between domestic and international mobility, requiring Ottoman subjects seeking to travel abroad to obtain special permission from the central government. The Ottoman state's suspicion of large-scale international mobility meant that only a small, connected and trustworthy minority of Ottomans could hope to obtain the state permission to travel abroad. In the decades following 1841, a series of amendments and alterations to the Men-i Mürûr Nizamnamesi would further distinguish between domestic and international travel, creating an entirely separate document, the *pasaport*, to govern the latter.[15] Although plagued from its inception by severe administrative and technological limitations, the Ottoman state's efforts to make visible and regulate all forms of mobility through the *mürûr tezkeresi* system, along with its efforts to firmly separate domestic and international migration, would face an especially acute challenge with the advent of cheap steamship travel in the mid-1880s and the possibilities it brought for average Ottomans to migrate abroad.

Mobility Documents and Efforts to Prevent Overseas Migration in the Late Hamidian Era

The Case of Mount Lebanon

In the late 1880s, officials in the Interior Ministry in Istanbul began receiving a spate of reports from officials stationed in port cities along the empire's eastern Mediterranean coast. Droves of villagers, primarily Maronite Christians from agricultural communities nestled in the interior highlands known as Mount Lebanon (Cebel-i Lübnan) were obtaining domestic travel documents that permitted them to travel to Egypt. Although under de facto British occupation, Egypt was still nominally a part of the empire and, thus, considered a "domestic" destination by the Ottoman state. According to the reports, many of these travelers ostensibly bound for Egypt never disembarked from the foreign steamships ferrying them to Alexandria or Port Said. Instead they remained on board, only disembarking when the ship reached a European transit port where these travelers would then board ships for destinations as varied as Mexico, Brazil, and the United States, places far removed from their mountain homes.[16] By

---

15. Herzog includes a detailed timeline of Ottoman laws concerning mobility. See ibid., 133. Passports were not required for international travel until the second and third decades of the twentieth century. The Ottoman pasaport document functioned like international passports issued by other states in this era, a diplomatic request for safe passage. Because of its high cost and difficulty to obtain, the Ottoman state was seeking to limit legal international travel to a small and privileged elite.

16. For example, see BOA.DH.MKT 1394 104, Interior Ministry to the Province of Syria and the Governorate of Mount Lebanon (29 Rebiülahir 1304/25 Jan. 1887); BOA.DH.MKT 1597 67, Interior Ministry to the Province of Syria and the Governorate of Mount Lebanon (20 Cemaziyelahir 1306/22 Feb. 1889).

the early 1890s, a veritable cottage industry of smugglers and agents had emerged in cities such as Beirut and Tripoli aiding those who wanted to travel abroad to obtain a *mürûr tezkeresi* under false pretenses.[17]

Between 1885 and 1915, well over 100,000 people departed Mount Lebanon and surrounding regions and migrated abroad.[18] A significant proportion of these migrants ended up in the United States. Large communities of Lebanese migrants also emerged in this period throughout Latin America, West Africa, and Europe. Akram Khater ties the onset of this migration to the decline of Mount Lebanon's once lucrative silk industry, and the promise of greater economic opportunity abroad. Through monetary remittances and the return of many thousands of these sojourners, this migration had a profound transformative effect on the society and culture of Mount Lebanon.[19] From the perspective of the Ottoman state, however, the widespread use of the *mürûr tezkeresi* to bypass Ottoman restrictions on international mobility undermined document-based efforts to monitor and police mobility and amounted to nothing less than a subversion of imperial law.

As Engin Akarlı has noted, the Ottoman response to the explosive growth of unsanctioned overseas migration from Mount Lebanon was both inconsistent and contradictory.[20] This confusion was in line with the state's broader ambivalence about the possible political and economic consequences of overseas migration, especially as it concerned the state's authority over the region. The Ottoman state had particular cause for concern regarding the political situation in the region. In 1860, the outbreak of violence between the Druze and Maronite communities on the Mount threatened to plunge the entire region from Beirut to Damascus into political chaos and religious conflict. Following the restoration of order, the Great Powers led by France used the massacre of Christians on the Mount and in Damascus during the events of 1860 as a pretext to intervene on behalf of their coreligionists in the Levant. In 1861, the Ottoman state was compelled to sever Mount Lebanon from the Province of Syria, declaring it a special administrative district, or mutasarrifate, governed directly from Istanbul with local administration split along sectarian lines.[21] Meanwhile, France

---

17. For further information on migration routes and the emergence of smuggling networks, see Engin Deniz Akarlı, "Ottoman Attitudes towards Lebanese Emigration, 1885–1910," in *The Lebanese in the World: A Century of Emigration*, ed. Albert Hourani et al. (London: I.B. Tauris, 1991), 109–38.

18. According to Akram Khater, in this period more than 200,000 Lebanese migrated to the Americas alone. See Akram Khater, *Inventing Home: Emigration, Gender, and the Middle Class in Lebanon, 1870–1920* (Berkeley: University of California Press, 2001), 1.

19. Ibid., 108–45.

20. Akarlı, "Ottoman Attitudes," 109–38.

21. Engin Akarlı, *The Long Peace: Ottoman Lebanon, 1861–1920* (Berkeley: University of California Press, 1993) 31–33, 148–49.

retained the right to intercede on behalf of the region's Christian populations. Unlike Egypt, where the Ottomans were but nominal sovereigns, the central state retained extensive control over the day-to-day affairs of Mount Lebanon. Nonetheless, its legitimacy in the region had been compromised both in the eyes of the local population and the Great Powers. Thus, while Ottoman officials were perturbed by the rapid growth of illegal commerce that emerged to help facilitate the outward flow of migrants,[22] they were especially anxious about the status of migrants who returned to the empire after having naturalized as citizens of a foreign power.[23] By the late nineteenth century, citizens of most western European states and the United States residing in the Ottoman Empire enjoyed wideranging extra-territorial legal protections as a result of capitulatory agreements between their governments and the Ottoman state. From the perspective of the Ottoman state, large-scale overseas migration, especially to places such as the United States where emigrants could rather easily naturalize as citizens, posed a major risk if migrants could then claim capitulatory protections as citizens of a foreign state upon returning to the empire.[24] Not wanting to generate more Great Power interest in the affairs of Mount Lebanon, this quickly became the overriding anxiety vexing the minds of Ottoman officials as increasing numbers of people left Mount Lebanon for destinations overseas.

Ottoman concerns about the possibly detrimental effects of overseas migration from Mount Lebanon went beyond anxieties concerning return. For example, reports from Ottoman consular officials based in various locations in Europe and the Americas complained of destitute Lebanese migrants wandering into their offices unable to continue their journeys due to lack of funds, and seeking help with the return trip home. In addition to fears that these broke migrants might sully the empire's reputation abroad, diplomats were concerned that financing the travels of migrants who had left Ottoman lands without securing official permission was not the best use of the state's limited funds.[25] In line with such fiscal considerations, various officials lamented that the use of the *mürûr*

22. Akarlı, "Ottoman Attitudes," 112–14.
23. Ibid., 130–33.
24. The 1869 Ottoman Citizenship Law banned subjects of the empire from adopting the citizenship of a foreign state without first securing the permission of the Ottoman state. This provision was motivated in part by a desire to prevent Ottoman subjects from claiming foreign citizenship in order to benefit from capitulatory privileges. Despite the law, the Ottomans could not prevent foreign states from recognizing the status of their citizens of Ottoman origin who naturalized without first seeking permission from the Ottoman state. See Feroz Ahmad, "Ottoman Perceptions of the Capitulations 1800–1914," *Journal of Islamic Studies* 11, no. 1 (2000): 7.
25. For example, see BOA.DH.MKT 1623 100, Interior Ministry to Office of the Grand Vizier (18 Ramazan 1307/18 May 1889); BOA.DH.MKT 1623 100 Interior Ministry to the Foreign Ministry (25 Cemaziyelevvel 1310/16 Dec. 1892). Also see Akarlı, "Ottoman Attitudes," 111.

tezkeresi for overseas migration was resulting in a significant loss in revenue as the official document permitting international travel, the *pasaport*, cost ten times more than the *mürûr tezkeresi*.[26] Such anxieties, however, were tempered by increasing evidence of migration's upside. In an 1889 report, the special governor of Mount Lebanon reported that while his office was taking steps to prevent the flow of local residents going abroad, the region was receiving the equivalent of 5,500 English pounds a week remitted from locals living and working abroad, an amount that was having an undeniably positive effect on the local economy.[27]

From the perspective of Ottoman state officials, however, such arguments about the seemingly salutary effects of migration on the economy of Mount Lebanon did not outweigh concerns about emigration from Mount Lebanon. Throughout the late 1880s and much of the 1890s, the Ottoman state focused on combating smuggling and tweaking the *mürûr tezkeresi* system in order to make misuse of the document more difficult. Barring residents of Mount Lebanon from obtaining a *mürûr tezkeresi* all together was entirely out of the question. The central state was careful to ensure that any amendments to the *mürûr tezkeresi* system adhered to the legal statutes that governed it. The system operated under the assumption that a *mürûr tezkeresi* was to be granted to any Ottoman subject of good character with ostensibly legitimate reasons for requesting one. Even as it was becoming clear that large numbers of Lebanese were taking out *mürûr tezkeresi* documents for the purpose of bypassing Ottoman restrictions on migrating abroad, extralegal proposals to restrict their access were denied. For example, the Interior Ministry rejected an 1887 proposal to deny all residents of Mount Lebanon the ability to procure a *mürûr tezkeresi* from officials based in coastal cities.[28] Similarly, in the face of numerous reports about the fraudulent use of *mürûr tezkeresi* documents obtained for travel to Alexandria, an 1889 Interior Ministry communiqué to officials in Syria and Mount Lebanon stated that residents of Mount Lebanon were not to be denied access to travel documents for

26. BOA.DH.MKT 1623 82, Interior Ministry to the Interior Ministry of the Egyptian Khedival Government (5 Mayis 1305/18 May 1889); BOA.DH.MKT 397 54, Office of the Grand Vizier to Interior Ministry (19 Zilhicce 1312/24 May 1895). The Ottoman state intentionally made the *pasaport* document expensive and difficult so as to severely limit the number of Ottoman subjects who could legally travel abroad. It is possible the official here was recommending that the state make it easier for Lebanese to obtain the pasaport while keeping the fee for the document the same, thus opening the door for the state to earn revenue off of migration from Mount Lebanon.

27. Report summarized in BOA.DH.MKT 1623 100 Interior Ministry to Office of the Grand Vizier (18 Ramazan 1307/18 May 1889).

28. BOA.DH.MKT 1394 104, Interior Ministry to the Province of Syria and the Governorate of Mount Lebanon (29 Rebiülahir 1304/1 Jan. 1887).

Egypt unless it was very strongly suspected (*kuvven maznun*) they may use the documents to migrate abroad.[29]

Some extraordinary measures were put in place to restrict access to *mürûr tezkeresi* documents.[30] For example, by the late 1880s, residents of Mount Lebanon seeking to obtain a *mürûr tezkeresi* were obligated to provide a third party guarantor, who was willing to cosign a surety that the applicant would not use the document to migrate abroad.[31] Guarantors initially did not face a serious penalty if the document was misused, and into the mid-1890s, residents of Mount Lebanon treated the requirement for a guarantor as little more than another nuisance added to the migration process.[32] Indeed, according to an 1894 report from the Interior Ministry, as long as a person in possession of a *mürûr tezkeresi* could demonstrate that the document had been obtained with a legal surety, that person could not be prevented from traveling, meaning port city officials could do little to stop ships from departing the eastern Mediterranean with significant numbers of Lebanese aboard en route to various overseas destinations.[33] In response, the office of the grand vizier approved a proposal that would require *mürûr tezkeresi* guarantors to pay a fifty gold lira cash bond. This sum would not be collected in every case of misuse, but rather only if the bearer fell into penury while abroad and sought financial assistance from an Ottoman consulate. According to the proposal, the fifty liras collected from the individual's guarantor would then be used to finance a return trip to Mount Lebanon.[34]

The proposal to require guarantors to pay a fifty lira cash bond amounted to a last ditch effort by Ottoman officials to deter misuse of the *mürûr tezkeresi* and to stem, at least in part, overseas migration from Mount Lebanon. The policy, however, had little effect, due in large part to the fact that in the wake of its implementation very few Lebanese migrants sought assistance from Ottoman consular officials.[35] Indeed, according to Akarlı, the failure of this policy marked an important turning point in the Ottoman state's response to Lebanese migra-

29. BOA. DH. MKT 1597 67, Interior Ministry to the Province of Syria and the Governorate of Mount Lebanon (20 Cemazeyilahir 1306/22 Feb. 1889).

30. Akarlı, "Ottoman Attitudes," 114.

31. For example, see BOA. DH. MKT 1394 104 Interior Ministry to the Province of Syria and the Governorate of Mount Lebanon (29 Rebiülahir 1304/25 Jan. 1887), BOA. DH. MKT 1597 67, Interior Ministry to the Province of Syria and the Governorate of Mount Lebanon (20 Cemaziyelahir 1306/22 Feb. 1889).

32. According to Akarlı, in 1892, a proposal from the governor of Mount Lebanon to levy a financial penalty on guarantors for the misuse of *mürûr tezkeresi* documents was rejected. Akarlı, "Ottoman Attitudes," 117.

33. BOA. DH. MKT 321 7, Interior Ministry to the Office of the Grand Vizier (21 Cemaziyelevvel 1312/20 Nov. 1894).

34. BOA. DH. MKT, Office of the Grand Vizier to the Interior Ministry (12 Recep 1312/14 Jan. 1895).

35. Akarlı, "Ottoman Attitudes," 121.

tion.[36] By the late 1890s, unable to stem the flow, the Ottoman state embarked on a very different strategy. In November 1898, the Ottoman state announced a new policy allowing residents of Mount Lebanon to obtain official permission to migrate abroad if they provided a signed guarantee that they would maintain their Ottoman citizenship, refrained from engaging in political activity the state deemed seditious, and agreed not to seek financial assistance from the state to return home.[37] According to documents from the highest echelons of the Ottoman bureaucracy, failure to prevent misuse of the *mürûr tezkeresi* along with the proliferation of people smuggling networks were primary factors driving the state's *volte face* on Lebanese migration.[38] In addition the state tacitly conceded that as long as migration remained an economically enticing option for the residents of Mount Lebanon, measures intended to keep them from leaving would continue to fail.[39] Thus, this dramatic change in policy amounted to an official acknowledgement of the realities on the ground. Nevertheless, by requiring a signed pledge, the state employed the same logic that undergirded its documentary system of policing mobility, namely rendering visible and affecting some degree of control over the movement of its subjects.

Indeed evidence suggests that with this more relaxed approach the state succeeded in curbing some of the problems it associated with clandestine migration. In 1901, officials in Mount Lebanon reported that as a result of the policy change fewer people from the region were seeking the services of smugglers, cutting into the bottom line of these black market operators. The report went on to suggest that the remaining clientele of these smugglers consisted largely of people who could not bother with the inconvenience of obtaining official permission to migrate.[40] Whether or not we accept the report's explanation for why some individuals continued to turn to enlist the aid of smugglers, it is likely that the new policy, by cutting out the need for the smuggler middleman and thus reducing the price of the migration process, provided an incentive for the Lebanese to obtain official permission. The Ottoman state's relatively liberal attitude toward overseas migration would remain confined to Mount Lebanon, however. Certainly, this abrogation of the laws that governed the empire-wide system of migration control flew in the face of the Tanzimat emphasis on legal standardization that undergirded the *mürûr tezkeresi* system, a fact not entirely lost on some

---

36. Ibid., 122.

37. Ibid., 124; also see BOA. İ. DH 1360 1316, Office of the Grand Vizier (1 Şaban 1316/15 Dec. 1898).

38. BOA. İ. DH 1360 1316, Decision of the Ottoman Council of State (12 Recep 1316/26 Nov. 1898); BOA. İ. DH 1360 1316, Office of the Grand Vizier (1 Şaban 1316/15 Dec. 1898).

39. BOA. İ. DH 1360 1316, Office of the Grand Vizier (1 Şaban 1316/15 Dec. 1898).

40. Report cited in BOA. DH. MKT 2562 38, Interior Ministry to Mount Lebanon (17 Şaban 1319/28 Nov. 1901).

Ottoman bureaucrats. For example, in May of 1902, the Porte's representative in Bulgaria requested clarification of the government's policy regarding the issuing of passports to Ottoman subjects seeking to travel to the United States. The official was apparently confused by conflicting information he had received about policies governing the granting of passports.[41] The Interior Ministry responded that only under very few circumstances were Ottoman subjects to be granted passports for travel to the United States, citing that country's ability to corrupt the morals of all who set foot there (*Amerika'ya gidenlerin ahlakı bozulmakta*). Surmising perhaps that the state's exceptional stance toward Lebanese migration was the source of the representative's confusion, the report went onto detail on the reasons for Mount Lebanon's exceptional treatment, pointing to the region's special administrative status and significant Christian population.[42]

The Case of the Harput Region

The decision to limit this policy to Mount Lebanon was driven by factors beyond the region's special administrative status and its majority Christian population. Essentially a concession on the part of the state that it could not bring a halt to the phenomenon, the relaxation of restrictions on Lebanese migration also reflected a broad sense that many of the state's anxieties regarding the issue had largely been assuaged. At the same time that such restrictions were being lifted in this highland district abutting the empire's eastern Mediterranean coastline, however, state officials were feverishly working to put an end to overseas migration from another of the empire's mountainous hinterlands. Beginning in the late 1880s, at nearly the same time reports were beginning to arrive in Istanbul detailing misuse of *mürûr tezkeresi* documents by residents of Mount Lebanon seeking to travel overseas, similar reports began to trickle in concerning Armenian residents of the province of Mamuretülaziz, located deep in the interior of east-central Anatolia. In July 1888, the governor of that province reported that local residents were using documents authorizing travel to Istanbul to help facilitate migration to the United States.[43] Another report claimed that over the first six months of 1888, at least seventy-two Armenians from the Anatolian city of Harput, located in Mamuretülaziz, had been arrested in Istanbul on suspicion of attempting to migrate to the United States. One-by-one these individuals were returned to their home communities in the Anatolian interior at consider-

41. BOA.DH.MKT 525 55, Office of the Commissioner for Bulgaria to Interior Ministry (23 Safer 1320/1 June 1902).

42. BOA.DH.MKT 525 55, Interior Ministry to Office of the Commissioner for Bulgaria (10 Rebiülevvel 320/18 June 1902).

43. BOA.Y.PRK.DH 2 86, Copy of Telegram from Mamuretülaziz Province to Interior Ministry (14 Temmuz 1304/26 July 1888).

able cost to the state treasury.[44] Between the late 1880s and the onset of the First World War, more than 75,000 Armenians departed the Ottoman Empire for the United States. The majority of these migrants, especially in the years before the 1908 Revolution, originated from in and around the twin cities of Harput/Mezre, the administrative center of Mamuretülaziz province. Not unlike their Lebanese counterparts, most Armenian migrants to North America in this period were young men seeking economic opportunity abroad, many of whom intended to eventually return to their home communities in the Ottoman east.[45]

From the perspective of the Ottoman state, Armenian migration abroad posed a uniquely grave threat to the political stability of the empire, as the onset of this phenomenon coincided with the emergence of several Armenian political groups such as the Armenakan Party (1885) and the Hunchakian Revolutionary Party (1887), organizations that quickly established branches in Western Europe and the United States.[46] In March 1888, the palace officially banned most Armenian travel to the United States, making a limited exception for those individuals seeking to travel there for trade purposes. The document echoed fears that Armenians migrating to the United States looking for work or seeking education might fall under the sway of "seditious" Armenian political organizations (*fesad komiteleri*) operating in an environment of "complete and total freedom" (*serbest ve hürriyet-i kamile*). Most concerning, according to the document, was the possibility that these migrants could then return to the empire where they threatened to "poison the minds" (*tesmim-i ezhane*) of their fellow countrymen.[47] The perception that migration and "seditious" politics were inextricably linked would shape Ottoman policy on Armenian migration for the remainder of Sultan Abdülhamid II's reign. Yet despite the urgency assigned to preventing Armenian migration abroad, as with the case of Mount Lebanon, the Ottoman state's response to this phenomenon was shaped by several seemingly insuperable tensions and contradictions.[48]

44. BOA.DH.MKT 1528 96, Interior Ministry to the Police Ministry (26 Zilkade 1306/04 Aug. 1888).
45. For more on Armenian migration from the Harput region, see David Gutman, "The Political Economy of Armenian Migration from the Harput Region to North America in the Hamidian Period, 1885–1908," in *The Ottoman East in the Nineteenth Century*, ed. Ali Sipahi et al. (London: I.B. Tauris, 2016), 45–66.
46. For a very dated but useful history and timeline of Armenian political organizations, see Louise Nalbandian, *The Armenian Revolutionary Movement: The Development of Armenian Political Parties through the Nineteenth Century* (Berkeley: University of California Press, 1963).
47. BOA İ. DH 1075 84332, Yıldız Palace Office of the Chief Scribe (18 Ramazan 1305/29 May 1888).
48. Although Maronite Christians from Mount Lebanon and Armenians from eastern Anatolia together comprised the vast majority of Ottoman migration to the Americas, Anatolian and Syrian Muslims, Assyrians, and various Balkan populations also migrated in relatively

In contrast to its relatively ambivalent view of Lebanese migration the state viewed the flow of Armenians overseas as a threat to the empire's stability. Nonetheless, in its effort to stop Armenian migration abroad, it employed a similar strategy centered on preventing misuse of the *mürûr tezkeresi*. In 1891, the office of the grand vizier reported that officials in areas of eastern Anatolia with high rates of unsanctioned overseas migration were requiring all Armenians who requested a *mürûr tezkeresi* to provide a cash bond (*kefalet-i nakdiye*) worth twenty gold liras.[49] This cash bond would be collected from the guarantor if it was found that the applicant used the *mürûr tezkeresi* for travel to a destination other than the one stipulated on the document. In this way, it differed from the 1894 proposal to require that Lebanese applicants obtain a fifty-lira cash bond, as that sum would only be collected to finance a return trip to the Ottoman Empire. An 1893 report from Mamuretülaziz claimed provincial officials were authorized to collect cash bonds if the bearer of a *mürûr tezkeresi* failed to register every three months with officials in the destination indicated on the document.[50] As officials in the interior were mandating cash bonds, their counterparts in various port cities requested that Armenians bearing documents for domestic destinations necessitating steamer travel be restricted to passage aboard ships flying the Ottoman standard.[51]

As in the case of Mount Lebanon, several factors limited the effectiveness of these efforts to modify the *mürûr tezkeresi* system in order to prevent Armenian migration. Key among these obstacles was the extra-legal nature of these modifications. In 1893, the governor of Mamuretülaziz complained that guaran-

high numbers. Especially in the aftermath of the 1898 decision to relax restrictions on Lebanese overseas migration, the Ottoman state's position in relation to the overseas migration of these groups lay somewhere in between its respective policies toward Lebanese and Armenian migration. In essence, the state endeavored to prevent unauthorized overseas migration from these groups, especially to the United States, out of concern for their moral and political well-being, while in limited cases authorizing travel for purposes of trade and education. For documents concerning overseas migration from the Balkans, see BOA.DH.MKT 2595 70, Interior Ministry to Police Ministry (20 Zilkade 1319/05 March 1902); BOA.DH.MKT 462 19, Interior Ministry to Office of the Grand Vizier (19 Zilhicce 1319/25 March 1902); BOA.DH.MKT 462 19, Interior Ministry to Office of the Grand Vizier (14 Cemaziyelevvel 1325/25 June 1907). For migration of eastern Anatolian Muslims, for example, see BOA.DH.MKT 107 35, Grand Vizier to Interior Ministry (18 Muharrem 1311/1 Aug. 1893).

49. BOA.Y.RES 55 53, Office of the Grand Vizier to Interior Ministry (7 Zilkade 1308/14 June 1891).

50. BOA.DH.MKT 41 5, Interior Ministry to Office of Grand Vizier (25 Zilkade 1310/11 June 1893); DH.TMIK.S 60 18, Interior Ministry Reform Commission to Office of the Grand Vizier (14 Eylül 1321/27 Sept. 1905).

51. BOA.DH.MKT 38 17, Office of the Grand Vizier to Interior Ministry (6 Zilhicce 1310/21 June 1893); BOA.DH.MKT 38 17, Province of Trabzon to Interior Ministry (11 Zilkade 1310/28 May 1893).

tors of travel documents that had been subsequently used to migrate abroad were successfully challenging efforts by provincial officials to collect cash bonds.[52] In order to collect the bonded money, officials were required first to seek the permission of local *Nizamiye* courts. Given that the cash bond requirement for the *mürûr tezkeresi* was adopted at the provincial rather than the imperial level and applied only to Armenian applicants, it clearly violated the legal regulations that governed the *mürûr tezkeresi* system. Thus, receiving permission from the courts to collect these cash bonds was a tall order given their extralegal nature of the requirement. In response, the Interior Ministry authorized officials in Mamuretülaziz to bypass the courts when seeking to collect on cash bonds.[53] Yet, questionable legality was not the only obstacles to the use of cash bonds. Eastern Anatolian Armenians provided a critical mobile labor source for many of the empire's most important economic centers such as Istanbul and the cotton boomtown of Adana. The money that these domestic migrants remitted to their home communities was immensely important to the economic health of local communities. As a result, officials in provinces such as Mamuretülaziz were hesitant to enforce measures that could restrict domestic mobility, a concern many in the Ottoman central state also shared.[54] Because of this reluctance, and despite the fact that the cash bond requirement had been mandated at the provincial level, by the first years of the twentieth century, officials in interior provinces ceased requiring sureties backed by cash bonds for Armenian residents wanting a *mürûr tezkeresi*.[55] Finally in 1902, the grand vizier outlawed the use of cash bonds altogether, citing the extralegal nature of the practice and concerns about possible corruption involved with its use.[56] Meanwhile, related efforts to restrict Armenian travel to Ottoman steamers were also rejected again out of concern that doing so would contravene Ottoman law and curtail the right to legitimate domestic mobility.[57]

Already by the mid-1890s, it was clear to many state officials that the *mürûr tezkeresi* was ineffectual as a tool for preventing unsanctioned migration abroad.[58] The Ottoman system of document-based mobility control was predicated on a clear division between domestic and international migration. Yet as

52. BOA.DH.MKT 41 5, Interior Ministry to Grand Vizier (18 Zilhicce 1310/3 June 1893).
53. BOA.DH.MKT 16 4, Interior Ministry to Grand Vizier (29 Şevval 1310/17 May 1893).
54. BOA.DH.TMIK.M 119 73, Province of Erzurum to Interior Ministry (29 Şevval 1319/8 Feb. 1902).
55. BOA.DH.TMIK.M 134 13, Interior Ministry copy of telegram from Mamuretülaziz (13 Teşrinievvel 1318/26 Oct. 1902).
56. BOA.MKT.MHM 654 11, Interior Ministry to Grand Vizier (26 Muharrem 1320/29 April 1902).
57. BOA.DH.TMIK.M 88 11, Interior Ministry to Police Ministry (16 Safer 1318/16 June 1900).
58. BOA.DH.TMIK.M 4 6, Interior Ministry Reform Commission to Provinces of Adana, Aleppo, and Beirut, and the Sub-province of Jerusalem (29 Nisan 1316/11 May 1896).

we have seen, the advent of the steamship age in the Ottoman Empire blurred the lines that separated these two forms of mobility. In the case of Armenian overseas migration, the Ottoman state was faced with a dilemma: While the Ottoman economy was heavily reliant on the ability of Armenians to move within the empire's borders for purposes of trade and labor, large-scale overseas migration of Armenians from the eastern provinces of Anatolia was viewed as a considerable threat that needed to be brought to a quick and decisive end. Any drastic alteration to the *mürûr tezkeresi* system to prevent misuse risked simultaneously limiting access to the document and by extension restricting "legitimate" domestic mobility, a problem that similarly plagued Ottoman efforts to put an end to outlawed overseas migration from Mount Lebanon. As a result, to confront the perceived threat posed by Armenian migration to the United States, the Ottoman state instead began adopting a different approach, tasking officials based in port cities along the Black Sea and Mediterranean coasts with the responsibility of preventing Armenian migrants from leaving the empire while bolstering coastal surveillance.[59]

Travel documents would nevertheless continue to play an important role in Ottoman efforts to bring Armenian overseas migration under some degree of state control. Meanwhile, beginning in 1896, in the aftermath of a series of uprisings and outbursts of anti-Armenian violence that swept much of the Ottoman East in the mid-1890s, the Ottoman state opened an avenue for Armenians to migrate legally to the United States. This new policy in no way resembled the relaxed stance toward Lebanese migration that the Ottoman state adopted in the same period. Rather, it reinforced the state's view that Armenian migration posed a unique threat to the empire. In return for a modified version of the *mürûr tezkeresi* that guaranteed safe passage to the Ottoman coast and unhindered access to a foreign steamer, prospective emigrants were obligated to forsake their Ottoman citizenship and vow never to return to the empire (*terk-i tâbiiyet ve avdet etmemek*). In addition, all rights to property were to be forfeited.[60] This became the preferred method of emigration of families, especially those with one member already in the United States. Indeed, as many such migrants had adopted United States citizenship while abroad, aiding families of naturalized citizens to apply for the modified *mürûr tezkeresi* became one of the principle jobs of American consular officials stationed in the region.[61] From the perspective of the Ottoman state, this policy had the effect of creating two streams of Armenian

59. For more on this issue, see David Gutman, "Armenian Migration to North America, State Power, and Local Politics in the Late Ottoman Empire," *Comparative Studies of South Asia, Africa, and the Middle East* 34, no. 1 (2014): 176–90.

60. BOA.DH.TMIK.M 20 59, Office of the Grand Vizier to Interior Ministry (18 Cemaziyelahir 1314/14 Oct. 1896).

61. See documents in Despatches from the US Consuls in Harput, 1904–1912. No. 84 350-10-7-3.

migration from eastern Anatolia, one sanctioned by the government and one not. This situation was reflected in the bureaucratic language used to refer to the two migration streams, with the verbs *hicret etmek* (emigration) used to refer to state-sanctioned emigration and *firar etmek* (escape or desertion) for migration undertaken illegally. The use of the *mürûr tezkeresi* in this capacity was more in line with the document's original function as a tool with which the state could sanction and render legible the mobility of its subjects. Thus, while these documents failed to prevent unsanctioned migration, they became critical tools in allowing the state to exercise some degree of control over the migration process.

In the case of both Mount Lebanon and eastern Anatolia, large-scale overseas migration allowed for by the availability of steamship transportation revealed the limitations of the Ottoman system of document-based mobility control. The series of statutes that governed the system reflected the Tanzimat emphasis on legal standardization and equal treatment before the law. This legal structure made it very difficult for Ottoman officials to modify the *mürûr tezkeresi* system to limit its misuse and enhance its ability to prevent overseas migration. As both cases also demonstrate, however, these efforts were also hamstrung by the Ottoman state's complex and often contradictory attitude toward the mobility of its citizens/subjects. The *mürûr tezkeresi* system was initially intended to serve as the state's primary tool for policing the line between legitimate and illegitimate mobility. The imperial economy's increasing reliance on a mobile labor force made it much more difficult for the state to prevent certain forms of mobility without restricting those it viewed as legitimate. This conundrum also deeply hampered state efforts to rely on the *mürûr tezkeresi* to prevent overseas migration.

Migration Control and Mobility Documents in the Aftermath of the Young Turk Revolution

The year 1908 would begin and end with the Ottoman Empire governed by two mobility control regimes that were, on the surface, radically different. In July of that year, a military coup led by a group of junior officers forced Sultan Abdülhamid II to relinquish much of his power and reinstate the long dormant Ottoman constitution, an event that would go down in history as the Young Turk Revolution. Among the first acts of the new regime was to grant to all Ottoman citizens freedom of mobility (*serbest-i seyrü seyahat*) both within and outside the empire's borders. The new policy brought an end to documentary requirements for both domestic and international travel. Deeply influenced by classical liberal thought that paired political freedom with economic freedom, the new regime viewed such requirements and especially the *mürûr tezkeresi* system as products of the despotic, illiberal *ancien régime*.[62] Not surprisingly, the Young Turks'

---

62. The *mürûr tezkeresi* system was officially abolished in July 1910. See Herzog, "Migration and the State," 121.

radically different response to migration, and especially to overseas migration, had an instant and profound impact on the dynamics of this phenomenon. This new approach, however, was not free of similar tensions and contradictions that plagued Ottoman policies toward mobility and migration in the Hamidian era.

The Young Turk Revolution spelled the end of distinctly Hamidian-era concerns about a link between overseas migration, especially to Western Europe and North America, moral degradation and revolutionary infiltration. The empire-wide policy of freedom of mobility officially nullified the differential treatment of overseas migration from Mount Lebanon and eastern Anatolia that characterized Ottoman policy under Abdülhamid II. Nonetheless, concerns about the possible negative impacts of unregulated overseas migration quickly emerged. For example, the scale and scope of Armenian migration to North America, no longer dependent upon smuggling networks to bypass Ottoman restrictions on their mobility, rapidly widened.[63] Port cities from Salonica to Jaffa saw the opening of travel agencies catering to the growing numbers of people from the Balkans and the eastern Mediterranean coast seeking to migrate abroad. Ottoman officials were concerned that the growing numbers of Ottoman citizens seeking to travel abroad were vulnerable to exploitation at the hands of unscrupulous migration and shipping agents.[64] Furthermore, the Young Turks' loosening of documentary requirements for international travel coincided with the efforts of several European and American states to restrict immigration especially from regions from Eastern Europe and the Middle East. For example, beginning in the final years of the first decade of the twentieth century, the United States government began requiring immigrants in European transit ports to pass medical examinations before being allowed to board transatlantic steamers. By 1909 and 1910, Young Turk officials and Ottoman consular staff in various European port cities were raising concerns that large numbers of Ottoman migrants risked being stranded en route to the United States with no means of support. Echoing their Hamidian counterparts, these officials also worried that the Ottoman state would be on the hook to finance the return to the empire of such stranded migrants.[65] The loss of military-aged men to overseas migration would become an issue of special concern especially following the 1911 Italian invasion of Libya, an event that would herald nearly fifteen years of constant warfare that would end in the empire's demise.[66]

---

63. BOA.DH 18-2 37, Interior Ministry to All Provinces (26 Nisan 1326/09 May 1910).
64. BOA.DH 18-2 37, Report of the Interior Ministry (16 Rebiülahir 1328/26 April 1910).
65. Ibid.; BOA.DH.MB.HPS.M 9 34, Copy of report from the Ottoman consulate at Fiume (Rijeka) (no date given).
66. This was less of a concern in the Hamidian period as the vast majority of non-Muslim subjects did not serve in the Ottoman military. Following the Young Turk Revolution, exemptions from military service based on religion were eliminated.

Concerns about the possible negative ramifications of unrestricted freedom of mobility led some to call for reinstating document-based controls especially for those seeking to leave the empire. In 1910, the Ottoman parliament passed a bill that required all Ottoman subjects travelling abroad to be in possession of a *pasaport*. The vote was eventually invalidated, and the passport was made optional.[67] The measure's failure to pass did not end all efforts to enforce some sort of documentary measures to prevent military-aged men from leaving the empire. Although the 1908 Revolution brought an end to the *mürûr tezkeresi* system, by 1912, the Young Turk government required all Ottoman citizens to present identification papers before boarding steamers at Ottoman ports. Men suspected of being military deserters faced arrest, and many apprehended at Ottoman ports were dispatched under armed guard to their assigned military battalions.[68] By 1914, provincial authorities were warning that the tightening restrictions on the ability of military-aged men to travel abroad was leading to the proliferation of people smuggling networks all along the Mediterranean and Black Sea coasts, conditions that were reminiscent of the response to Hamidian-era prohibitions on migration.[69]

Thus, with the First World War looming, the commitment to freedom of mobility in the aftermath of the Young Turk Revolution had begun to run aground on the Ottoman state's clear and present need for military manpower. In this way, however, the Ottomans were not alone. Throughout the years of the First World War, many western liberal democracies such as France, the United Kingdom, and the United States also introduced restrictions on the ability of their citizens to travel abroad, often resorting to the introduction of enhanced document-based controls, in order to preserve military manpower and preventing the movement of politically suspect individuals.[70] In the post-1908 Ottoman Empire, as in much of the western world, the pressures of war revealed the extent to which discourses of political and economic liberty in which freedom of movement was considered a key marker of civilization could not overcome the competing impulse of modern states to assert and maintain control over their constituent populations.[71]

Conclusion

It is tempting to read the 1908 Young Turk Revolution and its aftermath as a complete break with the Hamidian-era approach to mobility control. The

67. Herzog, "Migration and the State," 129.
68. BOA.DH.SN-THR 41 86, Ministry of War to Interior Ministry (18 Nisan 1328/1 May 1912).
69. BOA.DH.EUM.EMN 60 10, Governor of Jerusalem to Interior Ministry (17 Safer 1332/15 Jan. 1914); BOA.DH.EUM.EMN 60 10, Governor of Canık (Samsun) to Interior Ministry (1 Şubat 1329/14 Feb. 1914).
70. Torpey, *The Invention of the Passport*, 111–16.
71. See McKeown, *Melancholy Order*.

new regime dispensed with the *mürûr tezkeresi* system and relaxed restrictions on domestic and international mobility, aligning Ottoman policy with that of most Western European states. Indeed, the Young Turks understood their liberal policy on mobility and migration as a repudiation of the despotic and illiberal practices of the Ottoman *ancien régime*. This aligns broadly with Torpey's own understanding of internal mobility documents as byproducts of despotic and authoritarian regimes, fundamentally at odds with the policies and approaches to mobility control that gave rise to the modern passport system. This perspective, however, fails to capture the complexity of the *mürûr tezkeresi* system, and the ways in which it embodied the many tensions and contradictions that underlay the nineteenth-century Ottoman state's modernization and centralization efforts. The system was a central component of the Tanzimat-era reforms, and reflected the modernizing Ottoman state's push toward legal standardization. The Men-i Mürûr Nizamnamesi, the set of laws introduced in 1841 to govern use of the *mürûr tezkeresi*, outlined a system intended to apply equally to all Ottoman subjects, and that would allow the state to distinguish between legitimate and illegitimate mobility within its borders. This emphasis on legal standardization rendered it ineffective as a tool to prevent overseas migration from Mount Lebanon and Mamuretülaziz. Instead, the state was forced to turn to other measures that aligned with the different level of threat that the state perceived overseas migration from these two regions posed. When it came to the question of overseas migration, the *mürûr tezkeresi* system ran aground on the empire's much longer standing practice of tailoring its governing practices based on regional geographic, political, and demographic specificities.[72] The tensions and contradictions that rendered the *mürûr tezkeresi* system ineffective in preventing overseas migration from Mount Lebanon and Mamuretülaziz were born out of the many related threats, real and perceived, that the Ottoman Empire faced during the rule of Sultan Abdülhamid II. Overseas migration from Mount Lebanon, and the prospect of large numbers of Lebanese returning to the empire claiming foreign citizenship, stoked fears of increased foreign intervention in a region already the target of European imperial ambitions. Meanwhile, the Ottoman state viewed overseas migration from Mamuretülaziz as inextricably linked to the emergence of Armenian political organizations operating both within and outside the empire, and, thus, a clear and present danger to the political stability of the empire. These very different threats required different approaches to the problem of overseas migration from these two regions, circumstances the *mürûr tezkeresi* system was ill equipped to handle.

The Young Turk Revolution promised a constitutional fix to the many threats that the Ottoman Empire faced. In line with the new regime's liberal-

72. On the Ottoman legacy of flexible rule, see Karen Barkey, *Empire of Difference: The Ottomans in Comparative Perspective* (Cambridge, UK: Cambridge University Press, 2008).

ized approach to governance, the *mürûr tezkeresi* system was brought to an end, and Ottoman citizens were granted the freedom of domestic and international mobility. Yet, the persistent threat of war deepened tensions and contradictions within the Young Turk government's migration policies. Despite official policy allowing freedom of movement, by 1914, as the Young Turk government sought desperately to prevent the departure of military-aged men, its stance toward migration was in some ways more restrictive and illiberal than its Hamidian predecessors. While this shifting stance can be attributed in part to the increasingly authoritarian bend of the ruling Committee of Union and Progress, similar restrictive policies were adopted by several European nation-states in response to the growing threat of war. Indeed the tension between guaranteeing freedom of mobility and remediating perceived threats continues into the contemporary period. From terrorism watch lists to "smart" national IDs, in the second decade of the twenty-first century, governments across the world have proposed or instituted policies intended to bolster surveillance of and sometimes limit mobility within and outside their borders that have frequently been criticized as intrusive and discriminatory.[73] Given the parallels that can be drawn between the Ottoman case and the contemporary period, it is especially important not to dismiss the Ottoman experience as an unrepresentative outlier within the broader global history of migration and mobility control.

73. For example, the United States Transportation Security Administration No Fly List contains upwards of 50,000 individuals and has been criticized for its lack of transparency, and for barring individuals from commercial air travel on questionable grounds. For a summary of some of these criticisms, see Jared P. Cole, "Terrorist Databases and the No Fly List: Procedural Due Process and Hurdles to Litigation," (Washington, DC: Congressional Research Service, 2015). Recent scholarship has pointed toward the ways in which national identification cards embody the tension in democratic (and non-democratic) societies between individual liberty and state power in regards to mobility and other facets of daily life. See David Lyon and Colin Bennett, "Playing the ID Card: Understanding the Significance of Identity Card Systems," in Playing the Identity Card: Surveillance, Security and Identification in Global Perspective, ed. David Lyon and Colin Bennett (London: Routledge, 2008), 3–20. Meanwhile, civil libertarians have likened national ID cards to internal passports based on their surveillance. ("5 Problems with National ID Cards," American Civil Liberties Union, accessed 10 Aug. 2016, https://www.aclu.org/5-problems-national-id-cards).

11   "Claimed by Turkey as Subjects": Ottoman Migrants, Foreign Passports, and Syrian Nationality in the Americas, 1915–1925

Stacy D. Fahrenthold

IN APRIL 1917, the United States of America entered the First World War and called on its citizens to participate in an unprecedented military draft. The Selective Service Act of 1917 levied over two million troops to fight in Europe, and it commanded both native-born US citizens and foreign-born immigrants to register with American draft boards. As America's first experience with total mobilization, the draft raised new questions about the military eligibility and political loyalties of men living in the United States but holding foreign nationalities: German, Czech, and Slovak "enemy nationals," but also over 200,000 subjects of the Ottoman Empire then living in the United States.[1] Though America was never at war with the Ottoman Empire, Istanbul had recalled its ambassadors and severed diplomatic ties with Washington by 1917; Ottoman nationals, meanwhile, found themselves subject to new surveillance into their political activities, censorship of their ethnic press, and restrictions on their mobility culminating in a ban on cross-border travel by Ottoman subjects in 1918. Even as "neutral allies of the enemy," Ottoman migrants found that America's war effort complicated their lives considerably.

Nativists eager to draft "alien slackers" into the army opened the question of whether Ottoman migrants (as neutrals) were eligible for conscription and accused all who opposed the draft of cowardice.[2] Army Provost General Marshal

---

1. Of this number, around half were Arabs from Syria and Mount Lebanon, the rest being of Turkish, Armenian, and Kurdish extraction; see Akram Fouad Khater, *Inventing Home: Emigration, Gender, and the Middle Class in Lebanon, 1870–1920* (Berkeley: University of California Press, 2001), 8; Charles Issawi, "The Historical Backgrounds of Lebanese Emigration, 1800–1914," in *Lebanese in the World: a Century of Emigration*, ed. Albert Hourani and Nadim Shehadi (London: I.B. Tauris, 1992), 31l; Kemal H. Karpat, "The Ottoman Emigration to America, 1860–1914," *International Journal of Middle East Studies* 17, no. 2 (1985), 175–209.

2. "Alien Slackers May Not Escape Service," *New York Times*, 22 April 1917, 3; "Deportation of Alien Slackers," *Christian Science Monitor*, 1 Aug. 1917, 1; Nancy Gentile Ford, *Americans All! Foreign-Born Soldiers in World War I* (College Station: Texas A&M University Press, 2001), 60–61.

The Subjects of Ottoman International Law (2020): 216–237
DOI: 10.2979/subjectsottomaninternationallaw.0.0.12

Enoch Crowder initially opposed the impressment of "Turks" (a term unevenly applied to Ottoman nationals but also problematically connoted with Muslim) but left the matter of other Ottoman subjects open for debate.[3] In May 1917 congressional lawmakers examined whether the "national origins" status of Ottoman migrants could be used to determine which among them could be drafted, which could voluntarily enlist, and which should be policed and surveilled.[4] Building on a decade of legal precedent and working with migrant ethnic advocates in New York, Congress created a new legal distinction between "Syrians and Mount Lebanonites claimed by Turkey as subjects" and other Ottoman subjects, particularly Turkish- and Kurdish-speaking migrants from Anatolia.[5] A Syrian American legal exceptionalism was born.

Designed to delimit which among Ottoman migrants were eligible for conscription, the 1917 law drew a line between Ottoman subjects of Syrian origin and other migrants from the empire. Syrians gained enhanced rights to travel, to enlist, and to petition for US citizenship as a consequence. Ottoman Turks or Kurds, by contrast, were prohibited from departing the United States, ineligible for military service, and barred from naturalization. Syrian nationalists in the *mahjar* (diaspora) promoted the law as proof that the war effort "has prompted the American government to distinguish the Syrian and Lebanese from those who are clearly Turks," and they pushed for migrant men to enlist with the Entente in the name of Syria's national liberation.[6] Because the lawmakers who reclassified "Syrians and Mount Lebanonites" did so in order to conscript a subset of Ottoman immigrants, however, the new law did little to define who rightfully counted as Syrian. Similarly, it did not attempt to define geographic Syria, its territorial limits, or delimit the ethnic composition of its rightful claimants.

This chapter is a history of the Syrian American exception. It examines the origins of US legal ideas about Syria as a territory simultaneously *a part of* and *apart from* the Ottoman Empire. It traces the impact of the Syrian exemptions

3. *Second Report of the Provost Marshal General to the Secretary of War on the Operations of the Selective Service System to December 20, 1918* (Washington, DC: Government Printing Office, 1919), 86–88.
4. US legislation restricting immigrants on the basis of their geographic origins began with the Chinese Exclusion Act of 1882, but the language of "national origins" emerged in World War I as US authorities parsed immigrants eligible for the draft from ineligible aliens. As a mechanism of migration restriction, national origins provisions appeared in the Immigration Act of 1917 (in the creation of the Asiatic barred zone) and in the Immigration Act of 1924, which introduced annual quotas on the basis of national origins. The 1965 Immigration Act repealed the use of quotas. See Mai M. Ngai, *Impossible Subjects: Illegal Aliens and the Making of Modern America* (Princeton: Princeton University Press, 2004).
5. Na'um Mukarzil, "al-Lubnaniyyun wa-l-Suriyyun tujaha al-Khidma al-'Askariyya," *al-Huda* 1 June 1917, 3.
6. Ibid., 3.

from wartime laws that restricted the rights and movements of Ottoman immigrants and the legacy of these laws from the 1918 armistice through the Treaty of Lausanne. The reclassification of Syrians and Lebanese as national origins categories in US law opened kinopolitical opportunities for Arab migrants and activists, as well as for French diplomatic authorities looking to claim Syrian migrants for a post-Ottoman Middle East.[7] In the *mahjar*, Syrian migrant activists lobbied for progressively more thorough articulations of "Syrian" national origins to access US citizenship, to facilitate the repatriation of migrants to Syria after 1918, and to expand the borders of those territories in the months before the French Mandate. France granted passports to these Syrian migrants as one means of establishing a claim over Syria and Mount Lebanese territory between 1918 and 1920. And smugglers exploited these efforts to assist Ottoman Kurds and Turks in obviating a US ban on cross-border travel by Ottoman subjects in its territories.

From "Turkey in Asia:" the Origins of Syrian American Legal Exceptionalism

Ottoman migrants began arriving in the Americas as early as the 1860s but by the 1880s the number of annual arrivals reached mass proportions. By 1914, between 200,000 and 225,000 Ottoman subjects lived in the United States; between 100,000 and 130,000 of them were Arabs from Syria, Palestine, and Mount Lebanon.[8] Processed through New York City's Ellis Island, arriving Syrians usually settled first in lower Manhattan, joining the Syrian "mother colony" on Washington Street and finding ready employment in textile or leather factories, in small-time commerce, and in peddling.[9] Attempts at a more precise demographic estimate on the various groups arriving from the Ottoman Empire are difficult because immigration officials drew no distinction between Syrians and other groups also arriving from "Turkey in Asia:" Turks, Kurds, Armenians, and Sephardim, all travelling on Ottoman travel documents.[10] It was not until 1899 that US ports of entry classified "Syrians" as a distinct ethnic category, typically signifying Arabophone migrants from Syria, Mount Lebanon, and Palestine.[11]

---

7. See Thomas Nail, *The Figure of the Migrant* (Stanford: Stanford University Press, 2015).

8. Karpat, "The Ottoman Emigration," 183–84. Élie Safa, "L'émigration libanaise" (PhD diss., Université Saint Joseph, Beirut, 1960), 188–90.

9. Alixa Naff, *Becoming American: The Early Arab Immigrant Experience* (Carbondale: Southern Illinois University Press, 1993), 128–33.

10. Engin Akarlı, *The Long Peace: Ottoman Lebanon, 1861–1920* (Berkeley: University of California Press, 1993), 63; Karpat, "The Ottoman Emigration," 182; David Gutman, "Travel Documents, Mobility Control, and the Ottoman State in an Age of Global Migration, 1880–1915," in this volume.

11. Naff, *Becoming American*, 110. This was also the case in Argentina and Brazil; see Jeffrey Lesser, *Negotiating National Identity: Immigrants, Minorities, and the Struggle for Ethnicity in Brazil* (Durham: Duke University Press, 1999), 58; John Tofik Karam, *Another Arabesque:*

Critically, the "Syrian" category was an ethnic and racial one in 1899, and did not denote a connection to a national point of origin.[12] Because it lacked geographic specificity, the term was conflated with Arab Christianity and to American biblical ideations about the Holy Land, a messy, problematic ordering principle which was frequently contested in America's immigration courts. That said, the production of a Syrian racial category in US law opened new opportunities for Arab American migrants, who sought to distinguish themselves from other Ottoman migrants as a means of enhancing their access to American citizenship.

Before 1915, Syrian migrants petitioning for naturalization came up against three forces simultaneously: Ottoman laws requiring subjects abroad to seek permission to naturalize in their countries of domicile, the conflation of "Turkish" identity with Islam in US law, and the conflation of "Turkey in Asia" with the rest of the Asian continent facing a mounting restrictionist immigration regime.[13] These obstacles led Arab Christian migrant activists to seek classification of "Syrians" in the United States and racially white, a move which would enhance their naturalization rights while exempting them from legislation designed to limit Asian immigration to America and (in the eyes of America) from Ottoman laws designed to stop them from renouncing ties to the empire.[14] A series of racial prerequisite cases between 1909 and 1915 culminated with *George Dow v. United States* in 1915, which established that Syrians were racially white and thus could not be denied access to US citizenship.[15] The ruling based Syrian "whiteness" on the Christian identity of its claimants, a courtroom strategy designed by Dow's attorneys in collaboration with the Syrian American Association in New York City.[16]

The Dow ruling offered Syrian migrants a path to citizenship routinely denied to other Ottoman subjects, and it did so by conflating Syrian identity with Christianity and simultaneously confirming US legal understandings that

Syrian-Lebanese Ethnicity in Neoliberal Brazil (Philadelphia: Temple University Press, 2007), 26.

12. Akram Fouad Khater, "Becoming 'Syrian' in America: A Global Geography of Ethnicity and Nation," *Diaspora: A Journal of Transnational Studies* 14, no. 2 (2005): 301.

13. Ottoman laws requiring permission by subjects seeking to naturalize in their countries of domicile provided a flimsy obstacle for Syrians in the United States, a country which allowed immigrants to naturalize by unilaterally renouncing their previous nationality. On this Ottoman law, see Will Hanley, "What Ottoman Nationality Was and Was Not," in this volume; Gutman, "Travel Documents."

14. Sarah Gualtieri, *Between Arab and White: Race and Ethnicity in the Early Syrian American Diaspora* (Berkeley: University of California Press, 2009), 77–79.

15. Ibid., 58–61. Whiteness cases also appeared elsewhere in the Syrian diaspora, see Anne Monsour, *Not Quite White: Lebanese and the White Australia Policy, 1880–1947* (Teneriffe: Post Pressed, 2010).

16. Na'um Mukarzil and his brother, Sallum, were among the SAA's founding members and financiers. Gualtieri, *Between Arab and White*, 3–7.

"Turks" were defined primarily in connection to Islam. The US naturalization process rarely (if ever) observed Ottoman laws requiring its subjects abroad to obtain permission to renounce their nationality, but the 1915 ruling unambiguously cleared the way for Syrian migrants to unilaterally cut ties with the empire. Though it redefined "Syrian" as a racial-cum-religious category, it did not identify Syrians as sharing a national origin nor attempt to identify Syria as a place, Ottoman or otherwise. The ruling was unconcerned with defining Syria or its territorial limits, though at the same time Syrian migrants living in America still carried Ottoman passports and immigration documents identifying them as coming from "Turkey in Asia." What *Dow v. United States* did, however, was grant Syrian migrants the right to claim exemption from legal restrictions facing other migrants from the Ottoman Empire on the basis of their enhanced racial status. In 1915, America was still neutral in the First World War, but as the conflict progressed, by 1917 these restrictions multiplied and incentivized migrant activism to expand the logic of exemption into something approaching a Syrian American national origins category.

The United States remained in a state of armed neutrality until relatively late, declaring war on Germany in April 1917 and Austria-Hungary the following December. Despite not being at war with one another, diplomatic relations between America and the Ottoman Empire were frosty, particularly after Istanbul severed diplomatic relations with the country, recalled its diplomatic staff, and left the empire's affairs in the hands of the neutral Spanish Consulate of New York.[17] Though only Canada joined the war as a pro-Entente belligerent before 1917, Syrian, Armenian, Kurdish, and Turkish migrants of Ottoman nationality found themselves subject to intensifying official scrutiny across both North and South America.

Official surveillance of Ottoman nationals in the United States never reached the same levels it did in Canada, where thousands of ethnic Turks were interned in camps over concerns about their loyalties.[18] But the US Departments of State, War, and the Bureau of Investigation kept close surveillance on Syrian migrants travelling across American borders, particularly the US-Mexico border. Though largely left alone before 1914, US concerns about the possibility of pro-German sentiments among Ottoman migrants fed rumors that Mexico's Syrian communities might be smuggling propaganda to Texas or that they might even play a role

---

17. NARA RG 65.2.2, M1085, case 8000-306290, S. Bucha, "Fouat Mehmet: Formerly in the U.S. Army/ Intimidation by Supposed Turkish Consulate," Philadelphia, 14 Oct. 1918, 30.

18. Işıl Acehan, "Internment of Turks in Canada during WWI," *Proceedings of the International Institute of Social and Economic Sciences* 15 (2015): 18. Like Britain, Canada imposed a ban on new naturalization by Ottoman subjects and ethnic Turkish subjects living in its territories; Daniela L. Caglioti, "Dealing with Enemy Aliens in WWI," *Italian Journal of Public Law* 3, no. 2 (2011): 186.

in immigrant subversion against the US government. These fears stemmed from the fact that networks of Syrians managed a carrying trade between El Paso and Mexico, usually travelling on foreign passports.[19] The US Bureau of Investigation policed the border, subjecting migrants to extensive questioning and detaining those suspected of carrying illegal printed materials, illegitimate paperwork, or after 1917, of evading the Selective Service draft.[20]

Because it required able-bodied men to register for possible military impressment regardless of nationality, the 1917 Selective Service Act included provisions for classifying all foreign-born immigrants in the United States into one of three categories: declarants (migrants having declared their intent to naturalize but not yet US citizens), non-declarants (migrants maintaining a foreign nationality), and enemy aliens (foreign nationals from countries with which America was at war).[21] Implicit in this system was the expectation that immigrants would prove their loyalty to America by serving in the army unless they were legally ineligible. Enemy aliens were also required to file for exemptions when drafted. Because immigrant men often failed to obtain these exemptions, nearly 200,000 German, Austrian, and Czechoslovak immigrants were inducted and served in the army despite being legally ineligible.[22]

Migrants from the Ottoman Empire inhabited a particularly murky legal space because they fit imperfectly into the eligibility matrix arranged by the Selective Service Act. US Army Provost Marshal Enoch Crowder was reticent to open the draft to Ottoman nationals because, despite America's neutral stance toward Istanbul, the induction of Ottoman subjects risked their deployment against the empire's enemies. Ottoman subjects, Crowder reasoned, were particularly vulnerable to being labelled as traitors by their home government if they were inducted into American military service. Ottomans fighting for the US Army would also break Ottoman conscription and nationality laws if deployed

19. NARA RG 65.2.2, M1085, case 111694, Gus T. Jones, "Re: Syrian Activities: Order Refusing Permission to Depart for Mexico," El Paso, 9 March 1918, 5.
20. See NARA RG 65.2.2, M1085, case 43703, B.B. Stone, "Joseph Ayub: Departure of Syrians from Mexico," El Paso, 22 July 1917, 4–5; NARA RG 65.2.2, M1085, case 232-3145, Wm. Nennhoffer, "Re: George Coury/Dealing with Syrian Race in Mexico," El Paso, 14 June 1918. Ironically, Na'um Mukarzil was himself accused of pro-German sentiments while recruiting Syrian migrants in Mexico for military service with the French, NARA RG 65.2.2, M1085, Investigative Case Files of the Bureau of Investigation, case 83061, W.H. Yoakum, "N.A. Mokarzel: Loyalty of Syrian," New York City, 42, 45.
21. Craig Robertson, *The Passport in America: The History of a Document* (New York: Oxford University Press, 2010), 189–90.
22. Ford, *Americans All,* 56.

against Germany.[23] Such induction, he argued, could draw the United States into direct conflict with the Ottoman Empire.[24]

The Army's hesitance to induct Ottoman nationals ran up against a Congress seeking to broaden the pool of available military labor, as well as the persistent lobbying efforts of Syrian, Lebanese, and Armenian immigrant clubs to extend military service to Ottoman nationals on either a voluntary or compulsory basis. In New York City, Syrian recruiters navigated a stream of migrants through voluntary enlistment by having them take "first papers" (the Declaration of Intent) just before registering for the Army. Though still formally Ottoman nationals, declarant immigrants faced fewer restrictions in the process of voluntary enlistment than did non-declarants.[25] Émigré recruiters from the Syrianist, Lebanist, and Arab nationalist movements in the United States competed with one another for potential recruits for the US Army.[26]

As Congress debated the legality of drafting foreign nationals, émigré activists lobbied for a reclassification of Syria and Mount Lebanon and its migrants in the United States. They built on the logic of 1915's *Dow v. United States* to argue that migrants from Syria and Mount Lebanon were distinct from their Ottoman co-nationals, racially and politically. They invoked Mount Lebanon's prewar autonomy and Syria's Semitic and biblical pasts to advance the claim that Syrian migrants were an exceptional American immigrant population, aligned with America's war effort. Perhaps unsurprisingly, the Syrian American Association, the Syrian Union, the Lebanon League of Progress, and the Mukarzil brothers of New York City all advanced these ideas to policymakers; they had been the same men who financed George Dow's appeal and several others making the whiteness arguments two years earlier.[27]

Congress ultimately distinguished "Syrians and Mount Lebanese claimed by Turkey as subjects" from other Ottoman nationals in summer 1917, casting Syria and Mount Lebanon not as sovereign Ottoman territories but as contested spaces held by Istanbul also claimed by America's allies. It built on an American understanding of the pre-war mutasarrifate (*mutasarrıflık*) of Mount Lebanon as a legally autonomous province under French extraterritorial protection. This was also an implicit rejection of Istanbul's 1914 abolition of Mount Lebanon's autonomous status and an ambiguous understanding that while Syrian migrants typically carried Ottoman passports (*mürûr tezkeresi*), they were Ottoman-but-

---

23. *Second Report of the Provost Marshal General*, 86–88.
24. Na'um Mukarzil, "Fi Kull Yawm Khitab," *al-Huda*, 7 June 1917, 2.
25. Mukarzil, "al-Lubnaniyyun was-l-Suriyyun tujaha al-Khidma," 3.
26. On these respective nationalist movements and their diasporic connections, see Carol Hakim, *The Origins of the Lebanese National Idea* (Berkeley: University of California Press, 2013).
27. See Rev. Kalil A. Bishara, *The Origin of the Modern Syrian* (New York: al-Hoda Printing Press, 1914).

not-quite under US law.[28] The United States considered Syrians as immigrants first, potential Americans second, and as Ottoman subjects living outside the empire after that. By granting Syrians this national origin status, furthermore, Congress opened voluntary military service to them. Syrians and Lebanese were also drafted into the army, a move which produced friction with Ottoman consular authorities.

Ultimately, Congress's aim was not to define the borders of Syria or Mount Lebanon, but to classify migrants who originated from those vaguely-defined territories. There was no discussion about where "Syria" began and ended, and as a consequence the law conflated a racial understanding of Syrian identity with an emergent national origins category. It not only stopped short of defining what, precisely, made an Ottoman migrant in the United States a "Syrian" but was remarkably unconcerned with such questions. The following year, a second draft act built on this by extending instantaneous US citizenship to immigrant volunteers regardless of declarancy status. The 9 May 1918 Act,

> Entitle[d] all aliens in the service (including enemy aliens) to citizenship whether they have their first papers or not… when the application is granted, the soldier will immediately become a citizen, with all privileges and immunities of citizenship.[29]

By obviating the need for immigrants to be "declarant" prior to joining the service, the US Army expanded pathways for enemy aliens to enlist and, for Syrians of Ottoman nationality, a means towards coveted US citizenship. Syrian enlistees in 1918 came not only from migrant colonies in the United States but from Brazil, Argentina, Mexico, and Chile. Some travelled to the United States expressly to join and obtain American citizenship.

Turkish and Kurdish migrants also enlisted in the US Army during the First World War, though in much smaller numbers. Tasked with managing Ottoman affairs in America, the Spanish consul general in New York, Francisco Javier de Salas, continually protested the wrongful conscription of Ottoman nationals, including the conscription of Arab migrants then re-identifying themselves as Syrians to enhance their access to citizenship. Salas also contested the use of travel regulations, passports, and naturalization papers to impugn a rightful Ottoman sovereignty over its diaspora subjects, and his office pushed back against the heightened surveillance of Ottoman migrants and censorship of the ethnic press.[30] This also meant pushing back against the nationalist aspirations of New

28. Akarlı, *The Long Peace*, 61–63. On these passports, see Gutman, "Travel Documents."
29. War Department organizational records, 77th division records, Office of the Chief of Staff, memorandum 79, 21 May 1918, as cited in Ford, *Americans All*, 63. Parentheses in original.
30. Spanish Consul General Francisco Javier de Salas to N.A. Mokarzel, 20 March 1918. Letter reprinted in *al-Fatat*, 26 March 1918, 1.

York City's Arab committees. When the Lebanon League of Progress issued a circular to Syrians in the United States enjoining them to join the Army without fear because they were no longer Ottoman subjects, Salas responded with a public letter reminding his constituents that "my mission is to protect the interests of Turkish subjects in the district of New York whatever their race, creed, or political inclination is, and at the present moment, the Lebanonites are Turkish subjects, whether they like it or not."[31] The letter was widely circulated in the Arabic press and inspired a new Bureau of Investigation case over whether the Spanish Consul's act constituted an invitation to draft fraud.[32]

Though there were Syrian migrants who used enlistment as a means of erecting new documentary borders between themselves and the Ottoman state, there were also Syrians who expressed newfound belonging to the "Turkish" empire as a means of escaping American military impressment. The Syrian exemption could cut both ways: Syrians could describe themselves as distinct from the Ottomans or as an integral part of the empire as it suited them, frustrating the efforts of recruiters, diplomats, and federal investigators tasked with determining their military eligibility. A federal investigation into a suspected draft dodger named Naceep Mallouf is instructive. A printer living in Brooklyn, Mallouf was a declarant immigrant and thus considered eligible for the draft despite his Ottoman nationality. When called to service, Mallouf went to the Spanish Consulate and obtained a draft exemption, proclaiming his Ottoman nationality and military ineligibility. Mallouf's case raised eyebrows among federal investigators because, as a Syrian from Mount Lebanon who had formally declared his intention to become a US citizen, his self-presentation as a faithful Ottoman subject presented a contradiction.

Mallouf's 1918 testimony illustrates that although the Americans had begun to consider Syria as a territory distinct from Ottoman Turkey, the Spanish (acting as Ottoman agents) did not consider it so. Mallouf described how he obtained the exemption:

> A Turkish newspaper here published a notice from the Spanish Consulate that Syrians, being Turkish subjects, were not liable for United States military service... I went to the Spanish Consulate to see about this matter... I met a man who told me to make affidavit as to my Turkish citizenship and send it to the War Department, and I did so, and claimed exemption.

31. Salas to Mokarzel, 20 March 1918, 1.
32. NARA RG 65.2.2, M1085, case 36334, Perkins, testimonies of French Consul Goiran and Spanish Consul Gadol, "Naoum Mokarzel—French Consul—Spanish Consul, Alleged Interference of Spanish Consul with Selective Draft of Syrians in the United States," New York City, 28 Jan. 1918, 18–20.

Asked whether Mount Lebanon was an Ottoman possession, Naceep Mallouf replied, "Yes, Mount Lebanon has had some sort of autonomy, but only since 1866, [and] the Turkish Government abrogated that when the European War drew it into the conflict."[33] It was the 1914 abrogation that made him an ineligible Turkish subject.

Mallouf's argument about the Ottoman mutasarrifate of Mount Lebanon was a common one, used simultaneously by recruiters arguing for Syrian enlistments and by Syrians seeking to exempt themselves from the draft. American ideas about Mount Lebanon and, later, of Syria as legally disputed territory grew up from immigrant informants like Na'um Mukarzil, Shukri Bakhash, Ayyub Tabet, and the anonymous informant "Mr. Zaloom" who helped federal investigators interrogate Naceep Mallouf in 1918. These informants relied on arguments advanced in racial prerequisite cases that declared Syrian Arabs "white" and Mount Lebanon as legally autonomous territory under the mutasarrifate according to the 1864 Organic Law, a law backed by French diplomatic power.[34]

Interestingly, the US federal government remained divided unto itself on the question about whether Mount Lebanon was Turkish territory in 1918. Congress, the United States Army, the Department of Justice, and Bureau of Investigation converged on the notion that both Mount Lebanon and Syria were nominal—if disputed—Ottoman territories and that migrants from those places were not entirely Ottoman.[35] However, the Department of State's opinion contradicted this idea, and reflected the Spanish consulate's understanding that the Ottoman Empire continue to claim its migrants abroad as nationals. Policies based on these contradictory visions of Syria and Syrians brought US federal agencies into conflict. When the Bureau of Investigation sought the State Department's guidance on Syrian draft exemptions in April 1918, the only answer they received was a routine, "according to the Spanish Consulate's understanding, the citizens of Mount Lebanon are Turkish subjects and as such, they are under Spanish protections" and a subsequent unwillingness to assist with prosecution of draft dodgers.[36]

Jurisdictional disputes and inter-agency conflict involving immigration status was a defining feature of US domestic policy during the war; the case of Syria

33. Ibid., 16–17.
34. Ibid., 18.
35. Ottoman acknowledgements of provincial autonomy similarly opened up wartime opportunities for European powers to claim they were disputed spaces in the nineteenth century. See Michael Christopher Low, "Unfurling the Flag of Extraterritoriality: Autonomy, Foreign Muslims, and the Capitulations in the Ottoman Hijaz," in this volume; Aimee Genell, "Empire by Law: Ottoman Sovereignty and the British Occupation of Egypt, 1882–1923" (PhD diss., Columbia University, 2013), 7–12.
36. NARA, RG 65.2.2, M1085, case 36334, Perkins/DeWoody, Leland Harrison/Bielaski letter to DeWoody/Perkins, New York City, 14 April 1918.

(Ottoman or not) was not exceptional but typical in that regard.[37] Though Syrian migrants continued to be considered "Turkish" by the US State Department, they simultaneously were granted a distinct national origins category by immigration, legislative, military, and criminal justice officials. Syrians could selectively deploy either Ottoman or Syrian identities to enhance their opportunities to travel, to serve, or to exempt themselves from wartime restrictions. Although these laws represent a progressive recognition of "Syrian and Mount Lebanonite" as both a racial and a national origins category by 1918, exactly what constituted Syrian nationality remained remarkably ambiguous. To be "Syrian" identified a person through some combination of racial, ethnic, and religious markers that Ottoman nationals could claim—or repudiate—when it was practically expedient to do so. This usually meant seeking either inclusion or exclusion from the draft, but after the 1918 armistice Syrian activists broadened the kinds of claims they made. In 1919, for instance, émigré nationalists invoked the draft laws as proof of America's commitment to Middle Eastern nation-building. They pushed for President Wilson to take a League of Nations Mandate in Syria, to transfer laws defining Syrian identity in the United States into a proper Syrian nationality, and to work with migrants in America to reconstruct an independent post-Ottoman Syrian state. Syrian migrants, these groups argued in their petitions, would eagerly repatriate to the Middle East for the cause.[38]

The Ottoman Travel Ban, the Safe Conduct Passport, and Paper Syrians

Floating signifier or not, to be a Syrian in wartime America was to be granted exemption from some of the restrictions which governed everyday life for Ottoman nationals. Among these was a travel ban forbidding the departure of Ottoman subjects from US soil, including a ban on migrant repatriation to the homeland in 1918. The travel ban was imposed on all foreign nationals from countries hostile to America or allied with its enemies (the Ottoman Empire was the latter) in May 1918. Three features made this measure remarkable. First, the law contravened international travel norms and was ultimately imposed by executive order after complaints by the US Department of Justice. Second, although legislators allowed the ban to expire for German, Austrian, and other European nationals in 1918, they upheld the ban on Ottoman departures for months following the armistice to forestall migrant repatriation until after the conclusion of the Paris Peace Conference of 1919. Third and finally, Syrians were given provisions

---

37. Robertson, *The Passport in America*, 189–90.
38. See Abraham Mitrie Rihbany, *America Save the Near East* (Boston: Houghton, 1918), or petitions from the New Syrian National League of New York: NARA RG59 M367, roll 387, 763.72119/2740 Philip K. Hitti to Robert Lansing, Secretary of State, Washington, 22 Nov. 1918, 1; Abraham Rihbany, "Amirka fi-Suriya," *Mirat al-Gharb*, 19 Feb. 1919, 2; AANM ES1(5) Georges Khayrallah open letter, New York City, 7 April 1919.

to exempt themselves from the ban and leave American soil freely, regardless of actual nationality status, if they applied for a special French passport called the *sauf conduit*, or safe conduct passport.

The Travel Control Act of 22 May 1918 imposed specific restrictions on citizens and foreign nationals seeking to exit or enter the country and prohibited the departure of enemy aliens and their neutral allies (including Ottoman nationals) from US soil. Granting the president authority to limit all travel deemed "contrary to public safety," the act drew fire from the judiciary; the US attorney general, for instance, questioned the ban's legality on the basis of international prohibitions against measures inhibiting the departure of non-citizens.[39] In an August 1918 executive order (2932), President Wilson mandated that all "hostile aliens must obtain permits for all departures from, and entries to, the United States" from both their own consulates and the US Department of State.[40] The State Department, in turn, granted departure rights to "hostile aliens" only if they could prove medical incapacity or mental incompetence.[41]

In addition to the broad mandate of ensuring public safety, the Travel Control Act aimed to "control the transmission of information in and out of the country."[42] President Wilson extended the law after the 1918 armistice, citing its utility in preventing "entry of all improper and dangerous persons" during the war, expressing his concern that the ban would cease upon the declaration of peace.[43] Cross-border travel by Ottoman subjects was prohibited through the conclusion of the Paris Peace Conference of 1919, posing a serious imposition for Kurdish and Turkish migrants anxious to return home, reconnect with relatives, or see to household affairs after the conflict. The Department of Justice criticized President Wilson for extending a wartime measure through the 1918 armistice through executive powers; the Department of State, by contrast, supported the measure as a public safety necessity.[44]

In practice, though, the law contained within it the seeds for its own subversion. Just as with the overreaching US Selective Service Act of 1917, the travel ban drew immediate fire from neutral consulates as well as from America's allies.

39. Robertson, *The Passport in America*, 189–90. The act was also called the Wartime Measure Act, Passport Control Act, and the Entries and Departures Control Act of 1918.
40. *US Statutes at Large*, vol. 40, part 1: 559; Executive Order No. 2932, 8 Aug. 1918. Also see John Torpey, "The Great War and the Birth of the Modern Passport System," in *Documenting Individual Identity: The Development of State Practices in the Modern World*, ed. Jane Caplan and John Torpey (Princeton: Princeton University Press, 2001), 265; Robertson, *The Passport in America*, 191.
41. Robertson, *The Passport in America*, 194.
42. Ibid., 188.
43. "Continuance of the Passport Control System," *Congressional Edition* vol. 7610, doc. 79, 25 Aug. 1919.
44. Torpey, "The Great War and the Birth of the Modern Passport System," 265.

The State Department honored various means of exemption for allied nations; among them, the French safe conduct passport for Syrians seeking to repatriate to the Middle East by way of Paris. In wartime, this temporary French passport assisted with neutral commerce by French partners across maritime or land borders. Syrian migrant peddlers, for instance, carried these documents when conducting the carrying trade across the US-Mexico border or when shipping goods across the port cities of the Atlantic.[45] The passport bestowed its bearer with the promise of French diplomatic protection and acted as a letter of marque, and the French Consulate in New York offered them freely to Syrians as a potential subject population. Practically speaking, the safe conduct passport extended French sovereignty over Syrian travelers, negating Ottoman claims over these migrants and facilitating Syrian trade as well as the enlistment of Syrians into the French military. After the 1918 armistice, Syrian migrants eager to repatriate to the Middle East could obtain French safe conduct passports for that purpose; by the mid-1920s, these passports offered Syrian repatriates a fast track to claiming citizenship under the Mandate. In the months following the First World War, though, hundreds of ineligible Turks and Kurds also presented themselves as "Syrians" to obviate the travel ban.

Like many facets of the Syrian exemption, the safe conduct passport was a document of political expediency. The United States government allowed France to continue issuing these documents to Ottoman nationals in its territory on the basis that France then occupied Mount Lebanon, and that migrants from Syria and Mount Lebanon could opt into French diplomatic protection. Getting the passport required a vetting process delegated almost entirely to Syrian committees operating in New York City and Boston. Syrian petitioners appeared before these committees empowered by France to certify their connection to Syria, usually with the help of migration agents who advertised their services in the Arabic and Turkish language press. Importantly, these committees were not only French clients but nationalist political parties with a history of pro-French partnership: the Syria Mount Lebanon League for Liberation and the Lebanon League of Progress vetted candidates in addition to Maronite leaders (both lay and clerical).[46] Petitioners arrived with signatures from two witnesses stating that they knew the petitioner to be Syrian; the committee assessed the claim and signed the application, which the petitioner then brought to the French Consulate. Both the French

45. In El Paso, Texas, Bureau investigators watched Syrian cross-border traffic closely and placed French *sauf conduits* from Latin and South America under heavy scrutiny; see examples NARA, RG 65.2.2, M1085, case no. 111694, Gus T. Jones, "Syrian Activities: Order Refusing Permission to Depart for Mexico," El Paso, 15 March 1918, 5; NARA, RG 65.2.2, M1085, roll 6, case no. 241285, "Emile J. Couri," New York, 20 July 1918, 1–2; NARA, RG 59, M367, roll 223, 763.72112/7011, A. Michael, U.S Consul to Secretary of State, Rio de Janeiro, 22 Jan. 1919, 1–2.
46. NARA RG 65.2.2, M1085, roll 811, case 369154, Valkenburgh, "Fraudulent Passport Matter," French Consul Joseph Flamand testimony, Boston, 30 July 1919, 3.

Consulate and the US Department of State had to approve these documents, but the process was more or less summary and the work of vetting applicants happened within the confines of the Syrian committees.

From the perspective of the US government, Syrians traveling on French safe conduct passports were presumptive French colonial subjects; this was a continuation of wartime policies of honoring French diplomatic protection over Syrian migrants regardless of nationality.[47] They were routed through French ports, on French steamship lines, and destined for French-occupied Beirut. The French Consulates seem to have understood the passports as part of a wider project to claim Syrian and Lebanese repatriates for a possible French protectorate in the Middle East; on the rare occasion that they denied a Syrian a safe conduct passport in 1919, it was because the applicant was discovered to have ties to pro-independence or anti-French parties in the *mahjar*.[48] There were also Syrians who, noting this connection between French passports and French plans for a Middle Eastern mandate, petitioned the American commission at the Paris Peace Conference to halt the practice or else afford "Syrians and Arabians residing in [American] territories... all facilities of travel by land or sea by issuing to them their own permits or passports without reference to any other Government."[49]

The French safe conduct passport gave the Syrian committees tasked with vetting candidates an enormous amount of latitude to determine who was—or was not—Syrian. There was no discussion about what made a petitioner Syrian enough for the passport; claimants became Syrian if their documents had been stamped by the Syrian committees entrusted with this role, investing them with a remarkable amount of kinopolitical power. These activists not only wished to deepen the ties between Syrian migrants and the French; they also saw the passport as a means of defining who Syrians were, and where Syrian territory began and ended.[50] A surprise July 1919 discovery that dozens of Kurds from Diyarbakır had obtained French *sauf conduits* from New York's Lebanon League of Progress led the Spanish Consul General to file a complaint with the US Justice Department alleging that the Syrian committees vetting the special passports used them

47. This was also a remnant of US draft policies exempting Syrians who opted to serve in the French military instead; see Stacy Fahrenthold, "Former Ottomans in the Ranks: Pro-Entente Military Recruitment among Syrians in the Americas, 1916–1918," *Journal of Global History* 11, no. 1 (2016): 106; NARA, RG 65.2.2, M1085, roll 692, case 277009, Dunn, "Visa Investigation, Melham Maroum George," Portland, 30 Aug. 1918, 1.
48. NARA RG 59, M376, roll 409, 763.72110/4913, Marsh to Sec. of State Phillips, "Democratic Syrian Society Requests American Protectorate," Merida, 2 May 1919, 2–3.
49. NARA RG 59, M367, roll 398, 763.72119/4248, American Commission to Sec. of State Phillips, Paris, 22 March 1919, 1, capitalization in original.
50. NARA RG 59, M367, roll 137, 763.72/13046, "10th Rapport Conseil du l'Assemblee fédérale sur les mesures precises par lui en vertu de l'arrete federal du 3 aout 1914," 26 April 1919, 54–55.

to lay claim to lands within Turkish domain.[51] A six-month federal investigation turned up a smuggler who was filing applications for any Ottoman subjects who came from lands claimed as potentially French in the 1916 Sykes-Picot Agreement. The Justice Department saw this as a clear violation of US policy regarding who could rightly claim Syrian national origins, but the department's lawyers were unable to convict the smugglers because no legal precedent existed to differentiate Syrian territories from Turkish ones. This suggests that if passport laws were the means by which states claimed Syrian migrants for political projects, smugglers were also capable of exploiting the necessary ambiguities in these laws to conduct their own business. Smuggling was not a resistance act, but a feature of a kinopolitical system dependent on a Syria without borders.

Federal investigators also suspected the Syrian committees that vetted French safe conduct passports of asserting a kinopolitical agenda. Bureau of Investigation agent Robert Valkenburgh argued to his superiors in October 1919 that the Lebanon League of Progress had offered known Kurds the safe conduct passport in order to expand French-claimed territories as "Syria" as far as Adana and Diyarbakır. Valkenburgh reasons these passports would bolster French claims to those territories as its war indemnity, an argument France was making at the Paris Peace Conference.[52] Valkenburgh pushed the Department of State to allow his office to investigate New York's Lebanon League of Progress on this line, without success.

Syrians were not the only group of Ottoman subjects who circumvented the travel ban by seeking foreign diplomatic protection; similar provisions were made for Armenian migrants, who could obtain American passports as protected persons in the wake of the genocide.[53] But the French foreign consulates in the United States were especially invested in putting French travel documents into Syrian and Lebanese hands. Very often, the same committees vetting Syrians for the passport simultaneously circulated petitions for a pro-French Mandate in the Levant, illustrating a desire to create a French Syria through a diasporic proliferation of papers.[54] The same Syrian committees produced pro-French propaganda and had served as pro-French military recruiters during the war. The

51. NARA, RG 65.2.2, M1085, Valkenburgh, "Fraudulent Passport Matter," Boston, 30 July 1919, 3.

52. NARA, RG 65.2.2, M1085, roll 811, case no. 369154, Valkenburgh briefing, Boston, 29 Oct. 1919, 2–3.

53. The Department of State and Bureau of Investigation vetted their requests, primarily to verify the Armenian identity of applicants and reject Turkish applicants. See NARA RG 65.2.2, M1085, roll 808, case 367163, "Application for Passport to Leave U.S.," Providence, 10 July 1919, 1–3; NARA RG 65.2.2, M1085, roll 792, case 358938, "Passport Matter: Sarkis Deroian," Cincinnati, 16 April 1919, 1–3.

54. Simon Jackson, "Diaspora Politics and Developmental Empire: the Syro-Lebanese at the League of Nations," *Arab Studies Journal* 21, no. 1 (2013): 169–71; Andrew Arsan, "This Age is

French invested an enormous amount of kinopolitical power which was vested into their client Syrian committees, effectively granting them with the authority to define who the Syrians were and where Syria began and ended by virtue of passport control. At the same time, though, France issued the *sauf conduits* only to Syrians who came from territories France claimed as her future Mandate, and saw the passport project as a means of legitimating its claim over the migrants' homeland. Because America allowed the provision of safe conduct passports to "non-Turkish" Ottoman minorities defined in religious or racial terms, furthermore, the order essentially transformed into a prohibition on Muslim travel into and out of the United States, targeting specifically the movements of Ottoman migrants.[55]

Lausanne and French Attempts to Domesticate the Diaspora

The League of Nations ultimately awarded France control over both Syria and Mount Lebanon at the San Remo Conference in April 1920. France set about establishing itself in the Levant, defeating Emir Faysal's Arab nationalist forces at the Battle of Maysalun in July 1920, creating Greater Lebanon that September, and soon after establishing the federated states of Syria. Though France relinquished its earlier claims to Diyarbakır, Syria's northern border remained porous and fuzzy until 1921, when Mandate authorities negotiated with Turkey to draw a boundary running between Diyarbakır and Aleppo.[56]

Persistent historiographic images of Syrian and especially Lebanese migrants as supportive of the French Mandate are themselves a construction of French diplomats and the émigré groups who collaborated with them.[57] The contrasting reality was that the emigrants overwhelmingly opposed foreign Mandates in general and French rule in particular. As they articulated new states in the Levant, France faced the task of asserting its authority over diasporic Syrians and Lebanese, a hostile subject population beyond the reach of conventional containment methods and whose mistreatment could (and did) draw diplomatic fire upon Paris from its allies. French administrators during the Mandate's first five years understood the *mahjar* as a place which needed to be policed, contained, and if possible, cut away from the emergent Syrian and Lebanese states. Towards

the Age of Associations: Committees, Petitions, and the Roots of Interwar Middle Eastern Internationalism," *Journal of Global History* 7, no. 2 (2011): 186–87.

55. In an interesting counterpoint, Ottoman Jews and Armenians seeking passports to travel from Greek Salonika to the United States encountered difficulties because of their nationality in 1917; see Devin Naar, "From the 'Jerusalem of the Balkans' to the *Goldene Medina*: Jewish Immigration from Salonika to the United States," *American Jewish History* 93, no. 4 (2007): 460–61.

56. John McHugo, *Syria: A History of the Last Hundred Years* (London: Saqi Books, 2014), 70.

57. Andrew Arsan interrogates this assumption in *Interlopers of Empire: The Lebanese Diaspora in French Colonial West Africa* (New York: Oxford University Press, 2014).

these ends, the French employed travel documents as a means of embracing the Mandate's supporters in the diaspora while shunning potential troublemakers. The provision or refusal of passports to Syrian and Lebanese migrants abroad was vested into French foreign consulates in countries with significant Arab populations. Each was given its own dragoman whose job it was to parse friend from foe.[58]

Émigrés seeking to repatriate from abroad applied not for nationalization, but for safe conduct passports of a type similar to those tendered during the First World War. Critically, the documents legally marked repatriates as French colonials traveling under French protection, not as nationals of the new Mandate states (Lebanon would not get its first nationality laws until 1925).[59] The French passports caused simmering and recurrent waves of protest in the Syrian colonies abroad, and migrant leaders demanded more formal national recognition under the terms promised them by Article 3 of the League of Nations Mandate charter.[60] In Greater Lebanon, French High Commissioner Henri Gouraud had been eager to claim Lebanese abroad for demographic reasons, registering emigrants in the largely-Christian communities of the Americas for Lebanon's first census in 1921.[61] Lebanese who registered with the census could later apply for repatriation to Lebanon, but it did not confer automatic nationality to Lebanese emigrants, nor guarantee them suffrage or other citizenship rights.[62] Taken in this light, the 1921 census was largely a French project to create a confessional balance that France saw as favorable to the continuation of its rule in Greater Lebanon.

The Mandate's policies were even less forthcoming to Syrian emigrants, and the French consulates abroad mostly saw their work in the *mahjar* as surveillance

---

58. The British imposed a similar style of documentary politics in Mandate Palestine; see Lauren Banko, *The Invention of Palestinian Citizenship, 1917–1948* (Edinburgh: Edinburgh University Press, 2016).

59. On Lebanon's Arrêté 2825 (1924) and Nationality Law of 1925, see Rania Maktabi, "The Lebanese Census of 1932 Revisited: Who Are the Lebanese?" *British Journal of Middle Eastern Studies* 26, no. 2 (1999): 25–26.

60. Ministère des Affaires Etrangères, *Rapport sur la Situation de la Syrie et du Liban, Année 1924*, 54.

61. 9 Feb. 1921 Telegram Circulaire du Président du Conseil aux Agents Diplomatiques et Consulaires de la République Fraçaise en Amérique. M.A.E., E-Levant 1918–1929, Syrie-Liban, Vol. 130, ff. 81bis–83bis. Reproduced in Eliane Fersan, "L'Émigration Libanaise aux États-Unis: d'Aprés les Archives du Ministère de Affaires Étrangères de France" (PhD diss., Université Saint-Esprit de Kaslik, 2006), 163–64; "Population du Grand Liban," *Correpondance d'Orient*, 15–30 May 1922, 270. Also see Maktabi, "The Lebanese Census of 1932 Revisited," 224–52.

62. "Les élections municipales au Grand Liban," *Correspondence d'Orient* 237–38, 15–30 June 1922, 337; Kais Firro, *Inventing Lebanon: Nationalism and the State Under the Mandate* (London: I.B. Tauris, 2003), 77–78; Arrêté 1307, article 26, "De l' électorat et de l'inéligibilité," reproduced in *Correpondance d'Orient* 287–88, 15–30 June 1922, 366.

and policing of political opponents, especially the Arab nationalists organizing in Latin America. The consulates did what they could to contain Arab activism within Latin America, halting Syrian repatriation by rejecting travel permits and threatening denationalization for emigrants who spoke publically against the Mandate. The objective was to sever the ties of protest and politics which bound Syria to its diaspora because, while there were pro-French collaborators in the *mahjar*, the majority of Syrians and Lebanese abroad contested France's right to rule.

The first time that a post-Ottoman nationality was offered to Syrian and Lebanese migrants abroad came with the Treaty of Lausanne in 1923. Under Articles 34 and 36, former Ottoman nationals were given the right to exercise a nationality option within three years of the document's signing, regardless of their country of domicile.[63] In theory, this provided a mechanism for former Ottoman subjects to become formally Syrian or Lebanese abroad and to gain the unobstructed right to repatriation. In practice, however, France's consulates screened would-be repatriates, placing obstacles in the path of known nationalists. Similarly, it was more difficult for Syrian migrants to exercise the option than it was for Lebanese, emigrants who tendered their registration receipt from Lebanon's 1921 census as proof of their national origins. The Lebanese case was further complicated by the fact that the 1921 census was widely boycotted by Lebanese Druze and Muslims.[64] Access to legal repatriation was most freely available to Lebanese Christians by consequence, with gradations of difficulty filtering through every other population of would-be returnees. Because France employed no such legitimation strategy in Syria (which it ruled through overwhelming military force), Syrian emigrants usually carried Ottoman documents or none at all; they were also subject to more careful screening when exercising their nationality option.

Former Ottomans who did not claim a new nationality as Syrian or Lebanese could naturalize in their countries of domicile, and this is what most Arab migrants did in the Americas in the 1920s (although a third or perhaps half of Lebanese migrants did ultimately return to Lebanon).[65] Nativism was on the rise in the United States, Brazil, and Argentina, and restrictions mounted on the entry of new migrants into those countries.[66] The 1924 Johnson-Reed Act effectively ceased new legal immigration of Syrians into the United States, but laws govern-

63. Rania Maktabi, "State Formation and Citizenship in Lebanon: The Politics of Membership and Exclusion in a Sectarian State," in *Citizenship and the State in the Middle East: Approaches and Applications*, ed. Nils August Butenschon, Uri Davis, and Manuel Sarkis Hassassian (Syracuse: Syracuse University Press, 2000), 148.
64. Maktabi, "State Formation and Citizenship in Lebanon," 161; Meir Zamir, *Formation of Modern Lebanon* (London: Croom Helm, 1985), 98.
65. Khater, *Inventing Home*, 111–12.
66. On Syrians targeted for immigration restriction, see Steven Hyland, *More Argentine than You: Arabic-Speaking Immigrant in Argentina* (Albuquerque: University of New Mexico Press, 2017); Karam, *Another Arabesque*; Gualtieri, *Between Arab and White*.

ing the naturalization of Syrians already domiciled there remained comparative-
ly permissive.[67] After waiting out the war, the peace settlement, and negotiations
with the French Mandate, Syrian migrants in the United States naturalized in
unprecedented numbers after 1923. Many of them simply refused to register as
citizens of French Syria and Lebanon. They saw this status as accepting French
colonialism, an outcome only slightly preferable to the default for Ottomans who
failed to opt into a nationality before the Treaty's 1926 expiration: to theoretically
revert to a Turkish nationality neither they nor the Turkish Republic wanted for
them.[68]

Access to optional nationality became an even more fraught issue with the
eruption of the Great Syrian Revolt in 1925, a repudiation of French rule broadly
supported by Syrian migrants in the Americas.[69] Argentina's former Ottoman
consul general, Emir Amin Arslan (cousin to Shakib Arslan and Fu'ad Arslan),
led Syrian protests against the French in Buenos Aires and was rumored to be
providing material support to Druze revolutionaries in the Hawran.[70] The French
saw Arslan as a dangerous foe, and the Buenos Aires consulate monitored him
closely; officer Shukri Abi Sa'ab routinely denied Arslan's applications to travel outside of Argentina or to return to Syria.[71] When Arslan led two thousand
Syrians through the streets of Buenos Aires to arrive at the consulate following
France's October 1925 bombardment of Damascus, the Mandate responded by
threatening Argentina's entire Syrian community—over 110,000 people—with
denationalization, severing any claims that emigrants had to their homeland.[72]

France's threatened mass denationalization essentially looked like a refusal
to honor émigré nationality claims from Argentina; it would have transformed

67. Not for want of trying, however. Naturalization challenges continued in 1924. See "Declares Syrians Can Become Citizens: Judge Wilkerson Also Says Armenians are Eligible," *New
York Times* 28 June 1924, 15.

68. Like the Lebanese Nationality Regulation of 1925, the Turkish Nationality Act 1312/1928
combined *jus sanguinis* with a territorial concept of nationality, but the 1928 law was the first
time that post-Ottoman Turkey integrated the logic of descent into its nationality laws. The
French Consulate's 1926 threat that Argentina's Syrians would turn Turk seems to have been
an empty threat. Zeynep Kadirbeyoğlu, "Changing Conceptions of Citizenship in Turkey," in
Citizenship Policies in the New Europe, ed. Rainer Bauböck, Bernhard Perchinig, and Wiebke
Sievers (Amsterdam: Amsterdam University Press, 2007), 433.

69. Reem Bailony, "Transnational Rebellion: the Syrian Revolt of 1925–1917" (PhD diss., University of California, Los Angeles, 2015).

70. Maria Narbona, "The Development of Nationalist Identities in French Syria and Lebanon:
A Transnational Dialogue with Arab Immigrants to Argentina and Brazil, 1915–1929" (PhD
diss., University of California, Santa Barbara, 2007), 44–45.

71. Arslan's 1926 manifesto against the French prompted an intensification of the consular
surveillance of his activities in Latin America; see Emin Arslan, *La Revolución Siria Contra el
Mandato Francés* (Buenos Aires: Imp. Radio Correintes, 1926).

72. Ibid., 120.

the Syrian colony into Turkish nationals, theoretically making the Turkish Republic responsible for governing them.[73] Both the Argentinian and the Turkish government protested the proposed measure and loudly questioned France's breach of international legal norms. Though the French walked back the idea in early 1926, France did not suddenly strive to honor the nationality claims of Syrian emigrants following the incident. Emigrant leaders in that community consistently protested mistreatment by the French Mandate's consular offices in Buenos Aires through the 1920s.[74]

Conclusion

In the decade following the 1915 case, *Dow v. United States*, the logic of Syrian exemption facilitated the construction of a practical Syrian nationality in the *mahjar*. Wartime laws building on *Dow* opened opportunities for Syrian migrants to renounce their ties to the Ottoman state and also gave France a means of claiming Syrian migrants abroad as potential French colonials for the purposes of state-building in the Levant. The 1923 Treaty of Lausanne attempted to replace this system by standardizing the process of asserting new nationalities in the post-Ottoman international order. In practice, however, Lausanne delegated the task of determining which Arabs abroad would become citizens to the French Mandate, a decision which abetted France's paper-based expulsion of Syrian migrants for political purposes.

This chapter has ventured into the logic of Syrian exemption from the *Dow* ruling, through the construction of the French Mandate in the early 1920s. US laws marking "Syrians and Mount Lebanonites claimed by Turkey as subjects" as a distinct class exempt from prohibitions imposed on Ottoman subjects set up an opportunity for French authorities seeking control over Syria and for their emigrant partners. Syrian activists saw the exemption as a means of renouncing ties to the Ottoman Empire and of entering into new relationships of rights and sovereignty with the United States through military recruitment. They also invoked the exemption to travel freely at a moment of heightened travel restriction. The United States of America and its army saw the opportunity to enlist, induct, and deploy Syrian migrants as military labor. The French Foreign Ministry saw the language of exemption as a convenience allowing them to claim certain Ottoman

---

73. Narbona, *The Development of Nationalist Ideologies*, 137.

74. The Mandate's Buenos Aires dragoman, Shukri Abi Sa'ab, wrote a memo to his superiors describing the high commissioner's reticence to honor emigrant nationality claims as a pervasive threat to French legitimacy in Syria; Abi Sa'ab as cited in Narbona, *The Development of Nationalist Ideologies*, 137. Though granted greater access to the nationality option, Lebanese emigrants were also denied nationality for political reasons; see Butrus Kairuz and *Jama'iyyat al-Ittihad al-Maruni* to Patriarch Ilyas Butrus Huwayyik, 26 Nov. 1928 letter, Archives of the Maronite Patriarchate, Bkerke, Lebanon, Huwayyik Collection, Folder 89, Latin America, number 368.

migrants under the regime of protection. They issued safe conduct passports as part of a system to claim Syrian migrants for the purposes of establishing sovereignty over their lands of origin. In sum, the new legal category offered kinopolitical opportunities to all who invoked it, including the smugglers who exploited the law's ambiguities to repatriate ineligible Turks and Kurds to Diyarbakır.

The end of the Ottoman Empire, the emergent hegemony of optional nationality post-Lausanne, and the expectation that former Ottomans would assert a single nationality ended the period of the Syrian American exceptionalism. And in 1924, the Johnson-Reed Act's passage in the United States illustrates a broader endorsement of regionally specific immigration on the principle not of racial categories but of national origins. The Johnson-Reed Act set annual quotas for sending states based on a percentage of migrants registered on the 1890 US census; Syria's quota was 100, the minimum allowable under the act.[75] New migrants continued to leave French-ruled Syria and Lebanon through the 1920s, and the threat of emigration was at the top of the French Mandate's list of concerns before the 1925 Syrian Revolt; the continuing political influence of émigrés abroad was another.[76]

In those anxieties about Syrian mobility, the French Mandate closely resembled its Ottoman predecessor. In attempting to manage subject populations living abroad, both polities confronted the fundamental weaknesses of extraterritoriality in a uniform world of nation-states. The Ottoman Empire had made several attempts to refract its diplomatic power and legal sovereignty over migrant populations abroad. The legal exceptionalism that Syrian Arabs in the United States exercised—and indeed, expanded through successful lobbying—demonstrates the limitations inherent in an imperial project to "cast shadows of sovereignty" beyond their realms.[77] US laws governing the naturalization of foreign nationals empowered Syrians with the means to unilaterally renounce their ties to the empire; the exigencies of the First World War motivated larger numbers of these migrants to do so. In an ironic twist, the same US laws which disempowered the Ottoman Empire's sovereignty over its migrants abroad allowed the French Foreign Ministry to claim them. France claimed Syrian migrants as they sought to repatriate home, seeing in them a means of bolstering its claims on the Arab Middle East. Had they examined the Ottomans' recent history of attempts to domesticate the diaspora, however, the French might have foreseen what was to

75. Ngai, *Impossible Subjects*, 29; Naff, *Becoming American*, 123.

76. Ministère des Affaires Étrangères, *Rapport sur la Situation de la Syrie et du Liban, Juillet 1922– Juillet 1923* (Paris: Imprimerie Nationale, 1924), 9.

77. Lauren Benton, "Shadows of Sovereignty: Legal Encounters and the Politics of Protection in the Atlantic World," in *Encounters Old and New: Essays in Honor of Jerry Bentley*, ed. Alan Karras and Laura Mitchel (Honolulu: University of Hawaii Press, 2017) as cited by Lâle Can and Michael Christopher Low, "The 'Subjects' of Ottoman International Law," in this volume.

come: migrants once eager to oppose Ottoman authority from abroad turned out to be equally suspicious of French rule.

Afterword
Ottoman International Law?

Umut Özsu

WHAT EXACTLY DOES it mean to speak of "Ottoman international law"? Are we to assume that Ottoman jurists, diplomats, and bureaucrats consciously dedicated themselves to the cultivation of a distinct approach to the study and practice of international law? Or that something like an Ottoman "school" of international law came to emerge in response to the empire's complex and frequently ambiguous arrangements with other powers, regardless of whether particular Ottoman authorities understood themselves to be contributing to such a project? Perhaps the point is not so much that Ottoman officials sought to develop a unique form of international law, one that would enable them to articulate and rationalize their state's interests, but that the Ottoman Empire served as a particularly robust site of experimentation for European and American actors, offering a laboratory for a range of different legal innovations? If nothing else, it is hard to deny that it was to a great degree in relation to the Ottoman Empire that minority protection, humanitarian intervention, and coordinated population transfer came to be conceptualized in international legal terms during the course of the nineteenth and early twentieth centuries. In this sense, state institutions, social networks, and commercial relations throughout the empire may well have played a significant role in the development of international legal thinking, even if it is difficult to characterize authorities in Istanbul and elsewhere as driven by a desire to formulate a "specifically Ottoman" approach to international law.

Students of Ottoman history have typically not posed questions of this sort. In fact, to the extent that they have been broached at all, these and other questions have been considered only recently, with a new group of scholars paying increasing attention to the international (and not simply domestic) facets of Ottoman legal practice.[1] Interestingly, this turn toward international law—a turn that

1. From a varied and rapidly growing literature, see Tetsuya Toyoda, "L'aspect universaliste du droit international européen du 19ème siècle et le statut juridique de la Turquie avant 1856," *Journal of the History of International Law* 8 (2006): 19–37; Mark Toufayan, "Empathy, Humanity and the 'Armenian Question' in the Internationalist Legal Imagination," *Revue québécoise de droit international* 24 (2011): 171–91; Eliana Augusti, *Questioni d'Oriente: Europa e Impero ottomano nel Diritto internazionale dell'Ottocento* (Naples: Edizioni Scientifiche Italiane, 2013); Aimee M. Genell, "Empire by Law: Ottoman Sovereignty and the British Occupation of Egypt, 1882–1923" (PhD diss., Columbia University, 2013); Mustafa Serdar Palabıyık, "The Emergence of the Idea of 'International Law' in the Ottoman Empire before the Treaty

The Subjects of Ottoman International Law (2020): 238–245
DOI: 10.2979/subjectsottomaninternationallaw.0.0.13

contributors to this volume are doing much to bolster and deepen—has occurred at a time when the historiography of international law is itself in the process of undergoing systematic revision and expansion.

For some time now, scholars of international law have observed a marked "turn to history" in their discipline. The causes and consequences of this "turn"—distinguished by a growing number of articles, monographs, edited volumes, and even whole journals[2]—have elicited different responses, and there is no workable consensus as to its theoretical and methodological implications. To take but one example, the field of international law has recently begun to play host to a lively and occasionally acrimonious debate about the merits and drawbacks of Cambridge School intellectual history. Some have sought to defend such contextualism, claiming that the historiography of international law is characterized by inordinately high levels of abstraction and that the discipline's core concepts—statehood, sovereignty, territory, jurisdiction, self-determination, and so on—cannot be understood independent of the specific circumstances in which they emerged and were first deployed. Others have voiced skepticism with respect to this position, arguing that strict adherence to the kind of contextualism popularized by Quentin Skinner fails to capture the distinctiveness of legal reasoning,

of Paris (1856)," *Middle Eastern Studies* 50 (2014): 233–51; Faiz Ahmed, "Istanbul and Kabul in Courtly Contact: The Question of Exchange between the Ottoman Empire and Afghanistan in the Late Nineteenth Century," *Osmanlı Araştırmaları: The Journal of Ottoman Studies* 45 (2015): 265–96; Nobuyoshi Fujinami, "Georgios Streit on Crete: International Law, Greece, and the Ottoman Empire," *Journal of Modern Greek Studies* 34 (2016): 321–42. Two contributors to the present volume also contributed to a recent special issue of the *Journal of the History of International Law*; see "International Legal Histories of the Ottoman Empire," ed. Umut Özsu and Thomas Skouteris, *Journal of the History of International Law* 18 (2016): 1–145. For broader discussions, also see Cemil Aydın, *The Politics of Anti-Westernism in Asia: Visions of World Order in Pan-Islamic and Pan-Asian Thought* (New York: Columbia University Press, 2007); Turan Kayaoğlu, *Legal Imperialism: Sovereignty and Extraterritoriality in Japan, the Ottoman Empire, and China* (Cambridge, UK: Cambridge University Press, 2010); Samera Esmeir, *Juridical Humanity: A Colonial History* (Stanford: Stanford University Press, 2012); Mostafa Minawi, *The Ottoman Scramble for Africa: Empire and Diplomacy in the Sahara and the Hijaz* (Stanford: Stanford University Press, 2016); Sarah Abrevaya Stein, *Extraterritorial Dreams: European Citizenship, Sephardi Jews, and the Ottoman Twentieth Century* (Chicago: University of Chicago Press, 2016); Joshua M. White, *Piracy and Law in the Ottoman Mediterranean* (Stanford: Stanford University Press, 2017).
2. For a sense of this diverse and voluminous body of scholarship, especially see Martti Koskenniemi, *The Gentle Civilizer of Nations: The Rise and Fall of International Law 1870–1960* (Cambridge, UK: Cambridge University Press, 2001); Gerry Simpson, *Great Powers and Outlaw States: Unequal Sovereigns in the International Legal Order* (Cambridge, UK: Cambridge University Press, 2004); Antony Anghie, *Imperialism, Sovereignty, and the Making of International Law* (Cambridge, UK: Cambridge University Press, 2005); Stephen C. Neff, *Justice among Nations: A History of International Law* (Cambridge, MA: Harvard University Press, 2014). Brill began publishing the *Journal of the History of International Law* in 1999.

particularly the degree to which precedential argument relies upon the creative interpretation and "anachronistic" application of past cases.[3] Debates of this sort show no signs of disappearing, let alone being resolved.

One of the signature characteristics of this revived interest in the history of international law has been an explicit concern for the way in which jurists from different states and regions have interpreted and sought to develop international law. Frequently dubbed "comparative international law," the study of different national and regional approaches to international legal doctrine and practice has attracted considerable attention.[4] Among other things, this new wave of scholarship has generated a complex literature that often prioritizes the role of "peripheral" and "semi-peripheral" actors in the production of legal ideas and institutions.[5] Some scholars who work in this vein accord pride of place to the critique of Eurocentrism, disputing claims to the effect that international legal norms have historically been generated in a European core and subsequently disseminated to various extra-European peripheries, where they have been resisted or internalized through one or another means. Others concede that international law is an elite enterprise dominated by jurists affiliated with class-riven, geopolitically dominant states, but nevertheless underscore the importance of unearthing the mechanisms whereby such law is appropriated and resignified by jurists representing less powerful states.

This volume represents one of the few sustained and collaborative efforts to analyze the Ottoman Empire's shifting engagement with international law from what may broadly be described as a "comparative international law" perspective. The contributions attend not only to the way in which Ottoman actors sought to absorb and adapt Euro-American international law (ultimately as part of the

---

3. For a taste of the debate, see Anne Orford, "On International Legal Method," *London Review of International Law* 1 (2013): 166–97; Martti Koskenniemi, "Histories of International Law: Significance and Problems for a Critical View," *Temple International and Comparative Law Journal* 27 (2013): 215–40. Also see Alexandra Kemmerer, "'We do not need to always look to Westphalia...': A Conversation with Martti Koskenniemi and Anne Orford," *Journal of the History of International Law* 17 (2015): 1–14.

4. See Anthea Roberts, *Is International Law International?* (Oxford: Oxford University Press, 2017); Anthea Roberts, Paul B. Stephan, Pierre-Hugues Verdier, and Mila Versteeg, eds., *Comparative International Law* (Oxford: Oxford University Press, 2017). Also see Martti Koskenniemi, "The Case for Comparative International Law," *Finnish Yearbook of International Law* 20 (2009): 1–8; Boris N. Mamlyuk and Ugo Mattei, "Comparative International Law," *Brooklyn Journal of International Law* 36 (2011): 385–452.

5. On increased attention to the role of legal and other actors from the "semi-periphery," especially see Arnulf Becker Lorca, *Mestizo International Law: A Global Intellectual History 1842–1933* (Cambridge, UK: Cambridge University Press, 2015). For a politico-economic discussion, see Umut Özsu, "From the 'Semi-Civilized State' to the 'Emerging Market': Remarks on the International Legal History of the Semi-Periphery," in *Research Handbook on Political Economy and Law*, ed. Ugo Mattei and John D. Haskell (Cheltenham: Edward Elgar, 2015), 246–59.

empire's integration into the world capitalist order), but also to the way in which they attempted to develop novel legal rules and techniques, in some cases on the basis of existing Ottoman practices and traditions. While their specific topics differ in a number of respects, each contributor expresses a strong interest in questions of nationality, citizenship, and, more generally, Ottoman "subjecthood." The legal dimensions of such questions are notoriously wide-ranging, not least because they involve matters of private international law—an exceptionally intricate body of rules for inter-jurisdictional disputes and transactions—in addition to public international law. The way in which these and related questions were handled in Ottoman and post-Ottoman contexts has not been explored, at least not to a satisfactory degree.

At first glance, this dearth in the relevant scholarship might strike some students of the history (and theory) of international law as little more than a "blindspot"—a "regional" deficiency in the available literature that is bound to be rectified, later if not sooner. On closer inspection, though, it reveals itself to be more than that. The Ottoman Empire was an immensely rich site for working through the knotty problems of status and affiliation that large chunks of public and private international law have been developed to resolve. From the Capitulations and mixed courts to the status of *millets* before and after the Tanzimat reforms, it was partly through the tangled and overlapping rules of international law that the late Ottoman Empire's transformation and subsequent disintegration were analyzed and articulated. There are a variety of reasons why the Ottoman context has not received the attention it requires. Undoubtedly, though, it is partially a function of the fact that the history of international law, both public and private, remains a preponderantly Eurocentric endeavor. This is the case in spite of the appearance of a number of studies in recent years on specifically non-European traditions and episodes.[6] The chapters in this volume are a most welcome addition in that regard, expanding and augmenting a growing literature on extra-European experiences with international law through a series of incisive, empirically rich analyses of the Ottomans' participation in the game of international law.

Despite differences in their topics and modes of analysis, the chapters are undergirded by several tendencies. Two are especially significant for the purpose of developing a finer appreciation of the Ottoman Empire's engagement with international law. The first is a common appreciation of the fact that Ottoman

---

6. For example, see Liliana Obregón, "Completing Civilization: Creole Consciousness and International Law in Nineteenth-Century Latin America," in *International Law and Its Others*, ed. Anne Orford (Cambridge, UK: Cambridge University Press, 2006), 247–64; Kayaoğlu, *Legal Imperialism*; Becker Lorca, *Mestizo International Law*; Lauri Mälksoo, *Russian Approaches to International Law* (Oxford: Oxford University Press, 2015); Umut Özsu, *Formalizing Displacement: International Law and Population Transfers* (Oxford: Oxford University Press, 2015).

authorities invested in international law as a means of defending the interests of their empire. The second is a shared desire to accord law a more prominent place in our understanding of the processes through which new, often "national" modes of identification came to arise in the Ottoman context.

The Ottomans were keenly aware of the fact that many leading Western jurists of the late nineteenth and early twentieth centuries distinguished between "civilized," "semi-civilized," and "uncivilized" states, with the Ottoman Empire and other weak but nominally sovereign non-Western states typically being placed in the intermediate category. This, however, did not diminish their interest in international law. After all, if international law constituted and lent legitimacy to the claims of imperial expansion, it also, they believed, formalized and provided symbolic machinery for the claims of imperial resistance. The promise of de jure sovereignty, the central concept of public international law (and arguably all modes of international law), appeared to many Ottoman lawyers and policymakers as a key defensive tool—the cornerstone of a multi-pronged effort to reinforce the independence and territorial integrity of a state that had become vulnerable to great-power rivalry and the dynamics of centrifugal nationalism. Such faith in international law was—and is—anything but uncommon. Not unlike the way in which Japanese and subsequently Chinese and other actors struggled to slough off "unequal treaties" and win recognition for various territorial claims, Ottoman officials were determined to rid themselves of their capitulatory regime, stave off the empire's retreat from the Balkans and Caucasus, and contain political and financial intervention in their domestic affairs from European powers. Nor was this stance entirely misplaced. While international law has never been anywhere as "even-handed" as many have thought, its core normative commitment to sovereign equality and non-intervention provided Ottoman officials with important arguments, even when their European counterparts operated under the (widely shared) assumption that the Ottoman Empire fell short of the kind of "civilization" requisite for the enjoyment of "full" sovereignty. At the very least, international law seemed to promise the logic of performative contradiction: it was not always easy for European powers to talk the talk of equality and sovereignty while running roughshod over the Ottomans' international rights to equality and sovereignty.

This commitment to international law marked much of Ottoman diplomatic strategy until the empire's final decade. Indeed, it was only with the 1912–13 Balkan Wars and the outbreak of the First World War—and the hardening of the Committee of Union and Progress' programs of Turkish nationalism and state-centralization—that this commitment underwent significant erosion.[7] It was also marked by a certain belief in legal positivism—the theory that law is

---

7. For a convincing account of this transformation, see Mustafa Aksakal, *The Ottoman Road to War in 1914: The Ottoman Empire and the First World War* (Cambridge, UK: Cambridge

best understood as an outgrowth of state authority, not a reflection of some set of deep-seated moral principles that endow it with normative weight. In the context of international law, this tendency manifested itself in a preference for international treaty law over customary international law, the body of legal rules that arise from general and consistent practices of states that are viewed to be legally obligatory. Regarding the latter as vague and prone to the kind of interpretational fluidity that often favors more powerful parties, this penchant for treaty law was in turn expressed in the publication of large, multi-volume compendia like Gabriel Noradounghian's magisterial *Recueil d'actes internationaux de l'Empire ottoman*,[8] the closest the Ottomans ever came to producing something on par with Baltic-Russian jurist Friedrich (Fedor) Martens' gargantuan *Recueil des traités et conventions conclus par la Russie avec les puissances étrangères*.[9] Aimee Genell is thus correct to observe in her study of the Ottoman Foreign Ministry that for much of the late nineteenth and early twentieth centuries, Ottoman international lawyers drew upon positive international law, particularly treaty law, in an effort to shield the empire from aggression and encroachment. Similarly, Jeffery Dyer is fully justified in arguing that the Ottomans' insistence upon dispatching consular representatives to Bombay, Batavia, and other major cities in South Asia were partly intended to leverage international legal mechanisms of inter-state diplomacy for the purpose of expanding Ottoman political power and religious prestige.

Consider now the second of the two tendencies identified above, namely the desire to grasp the role of law in the Ottoman Empire's reconfiguration during the late nineteenth and early twentieth centuries in accordance with "modern" frameworks of legal identity and association. It is now well-recognized that nationalism was a relative latecomer to the Ottoman context. While the Ottoman state had for centuries demanded allegiance from its subjects through a number of means, it was only in the final decades of the nineteenth century that explicitly ethno-linguistic (as opposed to confessional) modes of collective identification came to secure enough mass appeal to present Ottoman authorities with what they typically regarded as a serious structural threat (and also, at least occasionally, a serious political opportunity). What is considerably less understood, though, is that this transformation—which has been studied from a variety of social, political, and economic perspectives over the years—was to a significant

University Press, 2010). On this see Aimee Genell, "The Well-Defended Domains: Eurocentric International Law and the Making of the Ottoman Office of Legal Counsel," in this volume.

8. Gabriel Noradounghian, ed., *Recueil d'actes internationaux de l'Empire ottoman*, 4 vols. (Paris: Librairie Cotillon F. Pichon, 1897–1903).

9. F. Martens, *Recueil des traités et conventions conclus par la Russie avec les puissances étrangères*, 15 vols. (St. Pétersbourg: Imprimerie du Ministère des voies de communication, 1874–1909).

degree mediated and formalized by competing conceptions of international law. What is more, as Will Hanley notes, in regard to matters of nationality legislation, the Ottomans were anything but latecomers. Illuminating the way in which debates about "subjecthood" were intertwined with modernization and state-building efforts, the contributors demonstrate that the Ottoman struggle against intervention and extraterritoriality cannot be understood fully without appreciating the central role played by international law in reconstituting what it meant to be "Ottoman" (not to mention "Muslim," "Turkish," and so on).

The chapters in this volume realize this objective in different ways. Faiz Ahmed and David Gutman focus upon debates about the legal dimensions of diplomatic intercourse and public administration—the construction and maintenance of consulates, the granting of passports and domestic travel documents, the exercise of the right of diplomatic protection in respect to nationals in foreign territories, and a host of related issues. Ahmed trains his lens on British and Ottoman claims to jurisdictional authority over Central and South Asian Muslims, while Gutman writes about the *mürûr tezkeresi*, a domestic travel document the late Ottomans used to standardize mobility controls in line with their post-Tanzimat drive to further bureaucratize state functions. Similarly, Michael Christopher Low analyzes competing Ottoman and British arguments about the application of the Capitulations and the general law of consular protection to the question of the status and rights of non-Ottoman Muslims visiting or residing in the Hijaz. Home to Islam's holiest two cities but typically constituted as an "exceptional" frontier territory in domestic and international law, the Hijaz was thought to be a potential site not only for the expansion of Pan-Islamist and anti-European sentiment but also of intrigue against Istanbul. As a result, Ottoman authorities regularly resisted British jurisdictional claims in respect of Muslim colonial subjects in the province. Will Smiley suggests that eighteenth- and early nineteenth-century treaties with the Russians led to significant reconfigurations of state-subject relations within the Ottoman Empire long before the Tanzimat. In his view, inter-imperial treaty provisions involving the release of Ottoman captives served as a medium through which ruler and ruled came to think their relations anew. Will Hanley analyzes the 1869 Nationality Law and its proposed revision in the first decade of the twentieth century. The 1869 legislation was a bold attempt to reconfigure the conditions under which nationality could be acquired and lost, and Hanley argues that both it and the proposed revision of 1909—which was never implemented—constituted an attempt to reinforce sovereignty in the face of pervasive anxieties about extraterritoriality. Julia Stephens charts the way in which migrants and other "mobile subjects" navigated the empire's complex legal terrain during the nineteenth century, facilitating the modification of prevailing conceptions of sovereignty, territoriality, and nationality in the process. In the place of a top-down study of inter-imperial rivalry in which questions of citizenship and nationality are settled definitively in established centers of legal authority, hers is an on-the-ground history of shifting allegiances, evolving identities, overlapping jurisdictional arrangements, and complex networks of institutions. Lâle Can focuses upon the thorny debates surrounding the legal status of Afghans, Bukharans, and other Central Asian Muslims who lived within the Ottoman Empire in the late nineteenth century. Against Russian and British efforts to exercise "protective" authority over such persons, and also in response to the "affiliation switching" and "forum shopping" to which this phenomenon gave rise, Istanbul sought to limit the ambit of extraterritoriality and consular power. Stacy Fahrenthold considers many of the same questions from the perspective of US law during the First World War, demonstrating that the reclassification of persons of Syrian heritage in the United States fostered new opportunities for social and political mobilization within diaspora communities. In addition to cleaving those who were thereby categorized as "Syrian" from other "Ottomans," a development that had wide-ranging implications for their individual and collective identities, this legal change had direct consequences for state-building efforts in the Levant, with French authorities claiming Syrian migrants as potential colonial subjects. The cumulative result is a set of eye-opening discussions of identity formation and reformation through law. International law has never been merely an instrument for the coordinated regulation of inter-state relations; it has also been a means of reconfiguring the link between the state and the individual, with far-reaching implications for the latter's self-understanding.

Notwithstanding the all-too-familiar nineteenth-century rhetoric of the "sick man of Europe," the Ottoman Empire was a powerful and ambitious imperial actor, one with deep-seated and multi-faceted investments in international law. For a structurally fragile state, international law offered a vital medium and instrument of statecraft, with abstract principles of formal equality and reciprocity promising to provide something of a buffer against encroachment and internal partition. Given the vehemence with which Ottoman authorities of various ideological stripes sought to ensure fidelity to Istanbul during the empire's final decades, it should come as no surprise that international law should also have been marshalled on behalf of the project of ensuring the entrenchment of a new and supposedly tighter connection between the Ottoman state and the Ottoman subject. This volume gives us much to ponder.

Select Bibliography

Abou-el-Haj, Rifa'at A. "The Formal Closure of the Ottoman Frontier in Europe: 1699–1703." *Journal of the American Oriental Society* 89, no. 3 (1969): 467–75.

Abu-Manneh, Butrus. "Sultan Abdülhamid and the Sharifs of Mecca, 1880–1890." *Asian and African Studies* 9, no. 1 (1973): 99–123.

Afyoncu, Erhan. "Necati Efendi: Târih-i Kırım (Rusya Sefâretnâmesi)." Master's thesis, Marmara University, 1990.

Ahmad, Feroz. "Ottoman Perceptions of the Capitulations, 1800–1914." *Journal of Islamic Studies* 11 (2000): 1–20.

———. *The Young Turks and the Ottoman Nationalities: Armenians, Greeks, Albanians, Jews, and Arabs, 1908–1918*. Salt Lake City: University of Utah Press, 2014.

Ahmed, Faiz. *Afghanistan Rising: Islamic Law and Statecraft between the Ottoman and British Empires*. Cambridge, MA: Harvard University Press, 2017.

———. "Istanbul and Kabul in Courtly Contact: The Question of Exchange between the Ottoman Empire and Afghanistan in the Late Nineteenth Century." *Journal of Ottoman Studies* 45 (2015): 265–96.

Ahmed Reşid. *Hukuk-ı Umumiye-i Düvel*. Istanbul: Arkadaş Matbaası, 1928.

———. "Kapitülasyonlar." *Dârülfünûn Hukuk Fakültesi Mecmuası* 6/37 (1928): 1–38.

———. "Kuvve-i Müessese Nazariyyesi." *Dârülfünûn Hukuk Fakültesi Mecmuası* 6/38 (1928): 1299–328.

———. "La condition des étrangers dans la République de Turquie." *Recueil des cours* 4 (1933).

———. "Les droits minoritaires en Turquie dans le passé et le present." *Revue générale de droit international public* (1935): 293–341.

Aitchison, Charles Umpherston, ed. *A Collection of Treaties, Engagements, and Sanads Relating to India and Neighbouring Countries*. 12 Vol. Calcutta: Office of the Superintendent of Government Printing, India, 1892.

Akarlı, Engin. *The Long Peace: Ottoman Lebanon, 1861–1920*. Berkeley: University of California Press, 1993.

———. "The Problems of External Pressures, Power Struggles, and Budgetary Deficits in Ottoman Politics under Abdülhamid II, 1876–1909." PhD diss., Princeton University, 1976.

Akkor, Mahmut. "I. Dünya Savaşında Çeşitli Ülkelerdeki Türk Esir Kampları." Master's thesis, Sakarya University, 2006.

Aksakal, Mustafa. "Not 'by those old books of international law, but only by war': Ottoman Intellectuals on the Eve of the Great War." *Diplomacy and Statecraft* 15, no. 3(2004): 507–44.

———. *The Ottoman Road to War in 1914: The Ottoman Empire and the First World War*. New York: Cambridge University Press, 2010.

Aksan, Virginia H. *Ottoman Wars 1700–1870*. London: Longman, 2007.

Aktepe, M. Münir, ed. *Mehmed Emnî Beyefendi (Paşa)'nin Rusya Sefâreti ve Sefâret-Nâmesi*. Ankara: Türk Tarih Kurumu, 1974.

Alavi, Seema. *Muslim Cosmopolitanism in the Age of Empire*. Cambridge, MA: Harvard University Press, 2015.

al-Daulah, Iqbal. *Iqbal-i Farang: Dar Shamma-yi Siyar-i Ahl-i Farang ba Farhang*. Calcutta: Matba-yi Tabi, 1249 AH.

Allworth, Edward et al., eds. *The Personal History of a Bukharan Intellectual: The Diary of Muhammad-Sharif-i Sadr- Ziya*. Leiden: Brill, 2004.

Anghie, Anthony. *Imperialism, Sovereignty, and the Making of International Law*. Cambridge, UK: Cambridge University Press, 2002.

Anscombe, Frederick F. *The Ottoman Gulf: The Creation of Kuwait, Saudi Arabia, and Qatar*. New York: Columbia University Press, 1997.

Aral, Berdal. "The Ottoman 'School' of International Law as Featured in its Textbooks." *Journal of the History of International Law / Revue d'histoire du droit international* 18 (2016): 70–97.

Aristarchi Bey. *Legislation Ottomane our recueil des lois, reglements, ordonnances, traits, capitulations et autres documents officiels de l'Empire Ottoman*. 7 Vol. Constantinople: Freres Nicolaides, 1874.

Arminjon, Pierre. *Étrangers et protégés dans l'Empire ottoman*. Paris: A. Chevalier-Maresq & cie, 1903.

Arsan, Andrew. *Interlopers of Empire: The Lebanese Diaspora in Colonial French West Africa*. New York: Oxford University Press, 2014.

Arslan, Emin. *La Revolución Siria Contra el Mandato Francés*. Buenos Aires: Imp. Radio Correintes, 1926.

Augusti, Eliana. *Questioni d'Oriente: Europa e Impero ottomano nel Diritto internazionale dell'Ottocento*. Naples: Edizioni Scientifiche Italiane, 2013.

Aydın, Cemil. *The Idea of the Muslim World: A Global Intellectual History*. Cambridge, MA: Harvard University Press, 2017.

———. *The Politics of Anti-Westernism in Asia: Visions of World Order in Pan-Islamic and Pan-Asian Thought*. New York: Columbia University Press, 2007.

Aydıngün, İsmail and Esra Dardağan. "Rethinking the Jewish Communal Apartment in the Ottoman Communal Building." *Middle Eastern Studies* 42, no. 2 (2006): 319–34.

Bailony, Reem. "Transnational Rebellion: the Syrian Revolt of 1925–1917." PhD diss., University of California, Los Angeles, 2015.

Balcı, Sezai. *Babıali Tercüme Odası*. Istanbul: Libra Kitapçılık, 2013.

———. "Bir Osmanlı Ermeni Aydın ve Bürokrati: Sahak Abro (1825–1900)." In *Osmanlı Siyasal ve Sosyal Hayatında Ermeniler*. Edited by İbrahim Erdal and Amhet Karaçavuş. Istanbul: IQ Kültür Sanat Yayıncılık, 2009.

Banko, Lauren. *The Invention of Palestinian Citizenship, 1917–1948*. Edinburgh: Edinburgh University Press, 2016.

Barak, On. *On Time: Technology and Temporality in Modern Egypt*. Berkeley: University of California Press, 2013.

Barfield, Thomas. *Afghanistan: A Cultural and Political History*. Princeton: Princeton University Press, 2010.

Barkey, Karen. "Aspects of Legal Pluralism in the Ottoman Empire." In *Legal Pluralism and Empires, 1500–1850*. Edited by Lauren Benton and Richard Ross. New York: NYU Press, 2013.

———. *Empire of Difference: The Ottomans in Comparative Perspective*. Cambridge, UK: Cambridge University Press, 2008.

Başaran, Betül. *Selim III, Social Control and Policing in Istanbul at the End of the Eighteenth Century*. Leiden: Brill, 2014.

Baysun, M. Cavid. "Şirvanizade Ahmed Hulusi Efendi'nin Efganistan Elçiliğine Aid Vesikalar." *Tarih Dergisi* (1952): 147–58.

Becker, Seymour. *Russia's Protectorates in Central Asia: Bukhara and Khiva, 1865–1914*. Cambridge, MA: Harvard University Press, 1968.

Bedir, Murteza. "Fikh to Law: Secularization through Curriculum." *Islamic Law and Society* 11, no. 3 (2004): 378–401.

Benton, Lauren. *Law and Colonial Cultures: Legal Regimes in World History, 1400–1900.* Cambridge, UK: Cambridge University Press, 2002.

———. "Shadows of Sovereignty: Legal Encounters and the Politics of Protection in the Atlantic World." In *Encounters Old and New in World History: Essays Inspired by Jerry H. Bentley.* Edited by A. L. Karras, L. J. Mitchell, and J. H. Bentley. Honolulu: University of Hawaii Press, 2017.

Benton, Lauren, Adam Clulow, and Bain Attwood, eds. *Protection and Empire: A Global History.* Cambridge, UK: Cambridge University Press, 2017.

Berki, Osman Fazû. "Türk Vatandaşlığı Kanununun Aslî Tabiiyete Müteallik Hükümleri." *Ankara Üniversitesi Hukuk Fakültesi Dergisi* 7, no. 1–2 (1950): 146–59.

Beşikci, Mehmet. *The Ottoman Mobilization of Manpower in the First World War: Between Voluntarism and Resistance.* Leiden: Brill, 2012.

Bishara, Kalil A. *The Origin of the Modern Syrian.* New York: al-Hoda Printing Press, 1914.

Bitis, Alexander. *Russia and the Eastern Question: Army, Government, and Society, 1815–1833.* Oxford: Oxford University Press, 2006.

Boeck, Brian J. "Identity as Commodity: Tournaments of Value in the Tatar Ransom Business." *Russian History* 35, no. 3/4 (2008): 259–66.

———. *Imperial Boundaries: Cossack Communities and Empire-Building in the Age of Peter the Great.* Cambridge, UK: Cambridge University Press, 2009.

Brimnes, Niels. "Beyond Colonial Law: Indigenous Litigation and the Contestation of Property in the Mayor's Court in Late Eighteenth-Century Madras." *Modern Asian Studies* 37, no. 3 (2003): 513–50.

Broadley, A. M. and Frederick Villiers. *How We Defended Arabi and His Friends: A Story of Egypt and Egyptians.* London: Chapman and Hall, 1884.

Brotton, Jerry. *The Sultan and the Queen: The Untold Story of Elizabeth and Islam.* New York: Penguin Books, 2017.

Burbank, Jane. "An Imperial Rights Regime: Law and Citizenship in the Russian Empire." *Kritika* 7, no. 3 (2006): 397–431.

Buzpınar, Ş. Tufan. "Abdulhamid II and Amir Hussein's Secret Dealings with the British, 1877–1880." *Middle Eastern Studies* 31 no. 1 (1995): 99–123.

———. "Opposition to the Ottoman Caliphate in the Early Years of Abdülhamid II: 1877–1882." *Die Welt des Islams* 36, no. 1 (1996): 59–89.

Câbi Ömer Efendi. *Câbî Târihi (Târîh-i Sultân Selîm-i Sâlis ve Mahmûd-ı Sânî) Tahlîl ve Tenkidli Metin.* Edited by Mehmet Ali Beyhan. Ankara: Türk Tarih Kurumu, 2003.

Çadırcı, Musa. "Tanzimat Döneminde Çıkarılan Men'-i Mürûr ve Pasaport Nizâmnâmeleri." *Belgeler* 15, no. 19 (1993): 153–72.

Campos, Michelle. *Ottoman Brothers: Muslims, Christians, and Jews in Early 20th Century Palestine.* Stanford: Stanford University Press, 2010.

Can, Lâle. *Spiritual Subjects: Central Asian Pilgrims and the Ottoman Hajj at the End of Empire.* Stanford: Stanford University Press, 2020.

Çankaya, Ali. *Mülkiye Tarihi ve Mülkiyeliler.* Ankara: Örnek Matbaası, 1954.

Caplan, Jane and John Torpey, eds. *Documenting Individual Identity: The Development of State Practices in the Modern World.* Princeton: Princeton University Press, 2001.

Çetin, A. Atilla, ed. *Devlet ve Memleket Görüşlerim.* Istanbul: Çamlıca, 2011.

Çetinsaya, Gökhan. "The Ottoman View of British Presence in Iraq and the Gulf: The Era of Abdülhamid II." *Middle Eastern Studies* 39, no. 2 (2003): 194–203.

Ceylan, Ayhan. *Osmanlı Taşra İdarî Tarzı Olarak Eyâlet-i Mümtâze ve Mısır Uygulaması.* Istanbul: Kitabevi, 2014.

Chatterjee, Indrani. *Gender, Slavery, and Law in Colonial India.* Oxford: Oxford University Press, 1999.

Chatterjee, Nandini. "Muslim or Christian? Family Quarrels and Religious Diagnosis in a Colonial Court." *American Historical Review* 117, no. 4 (2012): 1101–22.

Chatterjee, Partha. *The Black Hole of Empire: History of a Global Practice of Power.* Princeton: Princeton University Press, 2012.

Çiçek, M. Talha. "Negotiating Power and Authority in the Desert: the Arab Bedouin and the Limits of the Ottoman State in Hijaz, 1840–1908." *Middle Eastern Studies* 52, no. 2 (2016): 250–79.

Clancy-Smith, Julia. *Mediterraneans: North Africa and Europe in an Age of Migration, c. 1800–1900.* Berkeley: University of California Press, 2012.

Cogordan, George. *Droit des gens: la nationalité au point de vue des rapports internationaux.* 2nd ed. Paris: L. Larose et Forcel, 1890.

Cohen Julia Phillips. *Becoming Ottoman: Sephardi Jews and Imperial Citizenship in the Modern Era.* New York: Oxford University Press, 2014.

Cole, Juan R.I. "'Indian Money' and the Shi'i Shrine Cities of Iraq, 1786–1850." *Middle Eastern Studies* 22, no. 4 (1986): 461–80.

Colley, Linda. *Captives: Britain, Empire and the World, 1600–1850.* London: Jonathan Cape, 2002.

Davis, Robert C. *Christian Slaves, Muslim Masters: White Slavery in the Mediterranean, the Barbary Coast, and Italy, 1500–1800.* Basingstoke: Palgrave Macmillan, 2003.

Davison, Roderic H. *Essays in Ottoman History, 1774–1923: The Impact of the West.* Austin: University of Texas Press, 1990.

———. "'Russian Skill and Turkish Imbecility': The Treaty of Kuchuk Kainardji Reconsidered." *Slavic Review* 35 (1976): 463–83.

Deringil, Selim. *Conversion and Apostasy in the Late Ottoman Empire.* Cambridge, UK: Cambridge University Press, 2012.

———. "Legitimacy Structures in the Ottoman State: The Reign of Abdülhamid II (1876–1909)." *IJMES* 23, no. 3 (1991): 345–59.

———. "The Ottoman Empire and Russian Muslims: Brothers or Rivals?" *Central Asian Survey* 13 (1994): 409–16.

———. "'They Live in a State of Nomadism and Savagery': The Late Ottoman Empire and the Post-Colonial Debate." *Comparative Studies in Society and History* 45, no. 2 (2003): 311–42.

———. *The Well-Protected Domains: Ideology and the Legitimation of Power in the Ottoman Empire, 1876–1909.* London: I.B. Tauris, 1999.

Deringil, Selim and Sinan Küneralp, eds. *Studies on Ottoman Diplomatic History V: The Ottomans and Africa.* Istanbul: Isis Press, 1990.

Dubois, Colette. "The Red Sea Ports During the Revolution in Transportation, 1800–1914." In *Modernity and Culture: From the Mediterranean to the Indian Ocean.* Edited by Leila Tarazi Fawaz and C.A. Bayly. New York: Columbia University Press, 2002.

Ekmekçioğlu, Lerna. *Recovering Armenia: The Limits of Belonging in Post-Genocide Armenia.* Stanford: Stanford University Press, 2016.

———. "Republic of Paradox: The League of Nations Minority Protection Regime." *IJMES* 46, no. 4 (2014): 657–79.

Eraslan, Cezmi. *II. Abdülhamid ve İslam Birliği: Osmanlı Devleti'nin İslam Siyaseti, 1856–1908.* Istanbul: Ötüken, 1991.

Erbakan, Cevat. *1736–1739 Osmanlı-Rus ve Avusturya Savaşları*. Istanbul: Askeri Matbaa, 1938.

Erdem, Y. Hakan. "'Do Not Think of Them As Agricultural Labourers': Ottoman Responses to the Greek War of Independence." In *Citizenship and the Nation-State in Greece and Turkey*. Edited by Thalia G. Dragonas and Faruk Birtek. London: Routledge, 2005.

Esmeir, Samera. *Juridical Humanity: A Colonial History*. Stanford: Stanford University Press, 2012.

Fadel, Mohammad. "International Law, Regional Developments: Islam." In *Max Planck Encyclopedia of Public International Law*. Oxford: Oxford University Press, 2010.

Fahmy, Ziad. "Jurisdictional Borderlands: Extraterritoriality and 'Legal Chameleons' in Precolonial Alexandria, 1840–1870." *Comparative Studies in Society and History* 55, no. 2 (2013): 305–29.

Fahrenthold, Stacy. "Former Ottomans in the Ranks: Pro-Entente Military Recruitment among Syrians in the Americas, 1916–1918." *Journal of Global History* 11, no. 1 (2016): 88–112.

Farnie, D.A. *East and West of Suez: The Suez Canal in History 1854–1956*. Oxford: Oxford University Press, 1969.

Farooqi, Naimur Rahman. *Mughal-Ottoman Relations*. Delhi: Idarih-i Adabiyat, 2009.

Faroqhi, Suraiya. *Pilgrims and Sultans: The Hajj under the Ottomans*. London: I.B. Tauris, 2014.

Ferguson, Jan Helenus. *Manual of International Law for the Use of Navies, Colonies, and Consulates*. Vol. 2. London: W.B. Whittingham, 1884.

Fersan, Eliane. "L'Émigration Libanaise aux États-Unis: d'Aprés les Archives du Ministère de Affaires Étrangères de France." PhD diss., Université Saint-Esprit de Kaslik, 2006.

Findley, Carter V. *Bureaucratic Reform in the Ottoman Empire: The Sublime Porte 1789–1922*. Princeton: Princeton University Press, 1980.

———. *Ottoman Civil Officialdom: A Social History*. Princeton: Princeton University Press, 1989.

Firro, Kais. *Inventing Lebanon: Nationalism and the State under the Mandate*. London: I.B. Tauris, 2003.

Fisher, Alan W. "Muscovy and the Black Sea Slave Trade." In *A Precarious Balance: Conflict, Trade, and Diplomacy on the Russian-Ottoman Frontier*. Edited by Alan W. Fisher. Istanbul: Isis Press, 1999.

Fisher, Michael Herbert. *A Clash of Cultures: Awadh, the British, and the Mughals*. New Delhi: Manohar, 1987.

———. *Counterflows to Colonialism: Indian Travellers and Settlers in Britain, 1600–1857*. Delhi: Permanent Black, 2004.

Flournoy, Richard and Manley Hudson, eds. *A Collection of Nationality Law of Various Countries as Contained in Constitutions, Statutes and Treaties*. New York: Oxford University Press, 1929.

Fodor, Pál. "Piracy, Ransom Slavery and Trade: French Participation in the Liberation of Ottoman Slaves from Malta during the 1620s." *Turcica* 33 (2001): 119–34.

Ford, Nancy Gentile. *Americans All! Foreign-Born Soldiers in World War I*. College Station: Texas A&M University Press, 2001.

Fortna, Benjamin C. *Imperial Classroom: Islam, the State, and Education in the Late Ottoman Empire*. New York: Oxford University Press, 2002.

Freitag, Ulrike. "Helpless Representatives of the Great Powers? Western Consuls in Jeddah, 1830s to 1914." *Journal of Imperial and Commonwealth History* 40 (2012): 357–81.

———. *Indian Ocean Migrants and State Formation in Hadhramaut.* Leiden: Brill, 2003.

Fujinami, Nobuyoshi. "The First Ottoman History of International Law." *Turcica* 48 (2017): 245–70.

———. "Georgios Streit on Crete: International Law, Greece, and the Ottoman Empire." *Journal of Modern Greek Studies* 34 (2016): 321–42.

Gelvin, James and Nile Green, eds. *Global Muslims in the Age of Steam and Print.* Berkeley: University of California Press, 2014.

Genell, Aimee M. "Empire by Law: Ottoman Sovereignty and the British Occupation of Egypt, 1882–1923." PhD diss., Columbia University, 2013.

———. "Ottoman Autonomous Provinces and the Problem of 'Semi-Sovereignty' in European International Law." *Journal of Balkan and Near Eastern Studies* 18, no. 6 (2016): 533–49.

Gescher, Carl. "Egypten." *Jahrbuch der Internationalen Vereinigung für vergleichende Rechtswissenschaft und Volkswirtschaftslehre zu Berlin Jahrbuch der Internationalen* 8 (1904): 1489–1505.

Ginio, Eyal. "Piracy and Redemption in the Aegean Sea during the First Half of the Eighteenth Century." *Turcica* 33 (2001): 135–47.

Göçek, Fatma Müge. *Denial of Violence: Ottoman Past, Turkish Present, and the Collective Violence against Armenians, 1789–2009.* Oxford: Oxford University Press, 2015.

Gong, Gerrit. *The Standard of Civilization in the International Society.* Oxford: Clarendon Press, 1984.

Green, Nile. "The Hajj as Its Own Undoing: Infrastructure and Integration on the Muslim Journey to Mecca." *Past and Present* 226 (2015): 193–226.

———. "Spacetime and the Industrial Journey West: Industrial Communications and the Making of the 'Muslim World.'" *American Historical Review* 118, no. 2 (2013): 401–29.

Gualtieri, Sarah. *Between Arab and White: Race and Ethnicity in the Early Syrian American Diaspora.* Berkeley: University of California Press, 2009.

Gürpinar, Doğan. *Ottoman Imperial Diplomacy: A Political, Social and Cultural History.* London: I.B. Tauris, 2013.

Gutman, David. "Armenian Migration to North America, State Power, and Local Politics in the Late Ottoman Empire." *Comparative Studies of South Asia, Africa, and the Middle East* 34, no. 1 (2014): 176–90.

———. "The Political Economy of Armenian Migration from the Harput Region to North America in the Hamidian Period, 1885–1908." In *The Ottoman East in the Nineteenth Century.* Edited by Ali Sipahi et al. London: I.B. Tauris, 2016.

Hakim, Carol. *The Origins of the Lebanese National Idea.* Berkeley: University of California Press, 2013.

Hall, T.E., ed. *The European Concert in the Eastern Question: a Collection of Treaties and Other Public Acts.* Oxford: Clarendon Press, 1885.

Hanley, Will. "Foreignness and Localness in Alexandria, 1880–1914." PhD diss., Princeton University, 2007.

———. *Identifying with Nationality: Europeans, Ottomans, and Egyptians in Alexandria.* New York: Columbia University Press, 2017.

———. "International Lawyers without Public International Law: The Case of Late Ottoman Egypt." *Journal of the History of International Law* 18 (2016): 98–119.

———. "Papers for Going, Papers for Staying: Identification and Subject Formation in the Eastern Mediterranean." In *A Global Middle East: Mobility, Materiality and Culture in the Modern Age, 1880–1940.* Edited by Liat Kozma, Avner Wishnitzer, and Cyrus Schayegh. London: I.B. Tauris, 2014.

———. "When Did Egyptians Stop Being Ottomans? An Imperial Citizenship Case Study." In *Multilevel Citizenship*. Edited by Willem Maas. Philadelphia: University of Pennsylvania Press, 2013.

Hanna, Nelly. *Making Big Money in 1600: The Life and Times of Ismail Abu Taqiyya, Egyptian Merchant*. Syracuse: Syracuse University Press, 1998.

Hanioğlu, M. Şükrü. *A Brief History of the Late Ottoman Empire*. Princeton: Princeton University Press, 2008.

Harris, George S. *Atatürk's Diplomats & Their Biographies*. Istanbul: Isis Press, 2010.

———. "Cementing Turkish-American Relations: The Ambassadorship of (Mehmet) Münir Ertegün." In *Studies in Atatürk's Turkey*. Edited by George S. Harris and Nur Bilge Criss (Leiden: Brill, 2009).

Hayne, M.B. *The French Foreign Office and the Origins of the First World War 1898–1914*. Oxford: Oxford University Press, 1993.

Hennings, Jan. *Russia and Courtly Europe: Ritual and the Culture of Diplomacy, 1648–1725*. Edinburgh: Edinburgh University Press, 2016.

Herzog, Christoph. "Migration and the State: On Ottoman Regulations Concerning Migration since the Age of Mahmud II." In *The City in the Ottoman Empire: Migration and the Making of Urban Modernity*. Edited by Nora Lafi et al. London: Routledge, 2011.

Hickok, Michael Robert. *Ottoman Military Administration in Eighteenth-Century Bosnia*. Leiden: Brill, 1997.

Hitzel, Frédéric. "Osmân Ağa, captif ottoman dans l'Empire des Habsbourg à la fin du XVIIe siècle." *Turcica* 33 (2001): 191–213.

Ho, Engseng. *The Graves of Tarim: Genealogy and Mobility across the Indian Ocean*. Berkeley: University of California Press, 2006.

Horowitz, Richard S. "International Law and State Transformation in China, Siam, and the Ottoman Empire during the Nineteenth Century." *Journal of World History* 15, no. 4 (2004): 445–86.

Huber, Valeska. *Channelling Mobilities: Migration and Globalisation in the Suez Canal Region and Beyond, 1869–1914*. Cambridge, UK: Cambridge University Press, 2013.

Hülagü, M. Metin. "Topal Osman Nuri Paşa Hayatı ve Faaliyetleri, 1840–1898." *Ankara Üniversitesi Osmanlı Tarihi Araştırma ve Uygulama Merkezi Dergisi* 5 (1994): 145–53.

Hurewitz, J.C., ed. *Diplomacy in the Near and Middle East: A Documentary Record, 1535–1914*. 2 Vol. Princeton: D. Van Nostrand Company, Inc., 1956.

Hussain, Nasser. *The Jurisprudence of Emergency: Colonialism and the Rule of Law*. Ann Arbor: University of Michigan Press, 2003.

Hyland, Steven. *More Argentine than You: Arabic-Speaking Immigrant in Argentina*. Albuquerque: University of New Mexico Press, 2017.

İhsanoğlu, Ekmeleddin. *Darülfünun: Osmanlı'da Kültürel Modernleşmenin Odağı*. Istanbul: IRCICA, 2010.

İnal, M.K. *Osmanlı Devrinde Son Sadriazamlar*. Istanbul: Milli Eğitim Basımevi, 1965.

İnalcık, Halil. "Yaş Muahedesinden Sonra Osmanlı-Rus Münasebetleri: Rasih Efendi ve Ceneral Kutuzof Elçilikleri." *Ankara Üniversitesi Dil ve Tarih-Coğrafya Fakültesi Dergisi* 4, no. 2 (1946): 195–203.

Iordachi, Constantin. "The Ottoman Empire: Syncretic Nationalism and Citizenship in the Balkans." In *What Is a Nation?: Europe 1789–1914*. Edited by Timothy Baycroft and Mark Hewitson. Oxford: Oxford University Press, 2006.

Isin, Engin Fahri. "Citizenship after Orientalism: Ottoman Citizenship." In *Citizenship in a Global World: European Questions and Turkish Experiences*. Edited by Fuat Keyman and Ahmet İçduygu. London: Routledge, 2005.

Ismail, Fehmi. "The Making of the Treaty of Bucharest, 1811–1812." *Middle Eastern Studies* 15, no. 2 (1979): 163–92.

Issawi, Charles. "The Historical Backgrounds of Lebanese Emigration, 1800–1914." In *Lebanese in the World: a Century of Emigration*. Edited by Albert Hourani and Nadim Shehadi. London: I.B. Tauris, 1992.

Itzkowitz, Norman and Max Ethan Mote, eds. *Mubadele: An Ottoman-Russian Exchange of Ambassadors*. Chicago: University of Chicago Press, 1970.

Jackson, Simon. "Diaspora Politics and Developmental Empire: the Syro-Lebanese at the League of Nations." *Arab Studies Journal* 21, no. 1 (2013): 166–90.

Jahn, Karl. "Zum Loskauf Christlicher Und Türkischer Gefangener Und Sklaven Im 18. Jahrhundert." *Zeitschrift Der Deutschen Morgenländäsche Gesellschaft* 111 (1961): 63–85.

Jalal, Ayesha. *Self and Sovereignty: Individual and Community in South Asian Islam since 1850*. New York: Routledge, 2000.

Kadirbeyoğlu, Zeynep. "Changing Conceptions of Citizenship in Turkey." In *Citizenship Policies in the New Europe*. Edited by Rainer Bauböck, Bernhard Perchinig, and Wiebke Sievers. Amsterdam: Amsterdam University Press, 2007.

Kane, Eileen. *Russian Hajj: Empire and the Pilgrimage to Mecca*. Ithaca: Cornell University Press, 2015.

Karam, John Tofik. *Another Arabesque: Syrian-Lebanese Ethnicity in Neoliberal Brazil*. Philadelphia: Temple University Press, 2007.

Karpat, Kemal H. "Millets and Nationality: The Roots of the Incongruity of Nation and State in the Post-Ottoman Era." In *Christians and Jews in the Ottoman Empire*. Edited by Benjamin Braude and Bernard Lewis. New York: Holmes & Meier Publishers, 1982.

———. "The Ottoman Emigration to America, 1860–1914." *IJMES* 17, no. 2 (1985), 175–209.

———. *The Politicization of Islam: Restructuring Identity, State, Faith, and Community in the Late Ottoman State*. Oxford: Oxford University Press, 2001.

———. "Yakub Bey's Relations with the Ottoman Sultans: A Reinterpretation." *Cahiers du Monde russe et soviétique* 32 (1991): 17–32.

Kasaba, Reşat. *A Moveable Empire: Ottoman Nomads, Migrants, and Refugees*. Seattle: University of Washington Press, 2009.

Kayaoğlu, Turan. *Legal Imperialism: Sovereignty and Extraterritoriality in Japan, the Ottoman Empire, and China*. Cambridge, UK: Cambridge University Press, 2010.

Kern, Karen M. *Imperial Citizen: Marriage and Citizenship in the Ottoman Frontier Provinces of Iraq*. Syracuse: Syracuse University Press, 2011.

Kévorkian, Raymond H. "Gabriel Noradounghian (1852–1936): extraits des memoires recueillies par Aram Andonian." *Revue d'histoire arménienne contemporaine* 1(1995).

Khater, Akram Fouad. "Becoming 'Syrian' in America: A Global Geography of Ethnicity and Nation." *Diaspora: A Journal of Transnational Studies* 14, no. 2 (2005): 299–331.

———. *Inventing Home: Emigration, Gender, and the Middle Class in Lebanon, 1870–1920*. Berkeley: University of California Press, 2001.

Khodarkovsky, Michael. *Russia's Steppe Frontier: The Making of a Colonial Empire, 1500–1800*. Bloomington: Indiana University Press, 2002.

Kim, Hodong. *Holy War in China: The Muslim Rebellion and State in Chinese Central Asia, 1864–1877*. Stanford: Stanford University Press, 2004.

Konan, Belkıs. "Osmanlı Devletinde Yabancıların Kapitülasyonlar Kapsamında Hukuki Durumu." PhD diss., Ankara University, 2006.

Köremezli, İbrahim. "Kırım Harbi Sırasında Rusya'daki Esir Osmanlı ve Müttefik Askerleri (1853-1856)." *Belleten* 77, no. 280 (2013): 983-1030.

Köse, Osman. *1774 Küçük Kaynarca Andlaşması*. Ankara: Türk Tarih Kurumu, 2006.

Koskenniemi, Martti. "The Case for Comparative International Law." *Finnish Yearbook of International Law* 20 (2009): 1-8.

———. *The Gentle Civilizer of Nations: The Rise and Fall of International Law 1870-1960*. Cambridge, UK: Cambridge University Press, 2002.

———. "Histories of International Law: Significance and Problems for a Critical View." *Temple International and Comparative Law Journal* 27 (2013): 215-40.

Kostopoulou, Elektra. "Armed Negotiations: The Institutionalization of the Late Ottoman Locality." *Comparative Studies of South Asia, Africa and the Middle East* 33, no. 3 (2013): 295-309.

Kuehn, Thomas. *Empire, Islam, and Politics of Difference: Ottoman Rule in Yemen, 1849-1919*. Leiden: Brill, 2011.

Kuneralp, Sinan. *Son Dönem Osmanlı Erkân ve Ricali, 1839-1922: Prosopografik Rehber*. Istanbul: Isis Press, 1999.

Kuneralp, Sinan and Emre Öktem, eds. *Chambre des conseillers légistes de la Sublime Porte: Rapports, avis et consultations sur la condition juridique des ressortissants étrangers, le statut des communaités non musulmanes et les relations internationals de l'empire ottoman*. Istanbul: Isis Press, 2012.

Kurtynova-D'Herlugnan, Liubov. *The Tsar's Abolitionists: the Slave Trade in the Caucasus and Its Suppression*. Leiden: Brill, 2010.

Landau, Jacob. *The Politics of Pan-Islam: Ideology and Organization*. Oxford: Clarendon Press, 1990.

Leira, Halvard and Iver B. Neumann. "The Many Past Lives of the Consul." In *Consular Affairs and Diplomacy*. Edited by Jan Melissen et.al. Leiden: Martinus Neijhoff Publishers, 2011.

Lewis, Mary Dewhurst. *Divided Rule: Sovereignty and Empire in French Tunisia, 1881-1938*. Berkeley: University of California Press, 2013.

———. "The Geographies of Power: The Tunisian Civic Order, Jurisdictional Politics, and Imperial Rivalry in the Mediterranean, 1881-1935." *Journal of Modern History* 80 (2008): 791-830.

Litvak, Meir. "Money, Religion, and Politics: The Oudh Bequest in Najaf and Karbala, 1850-1903." *IJMES* 33, no. 1 (2001): 1-21.

Lohr, Eric. *Russian Citizenship: From Empire to Soviet Union*. Cambridge, MA: Harvard University Press, 2012.

Lorca, Arnulf Becker. *Mestizo International Law: A Global Intellectual History 1842-1933*. Cambridge, UK: Cambridge University Press, 2015.

Low, Michael Christopher. "Empire and the Hajj: Pilgrims, Plagues, and Pan-Islam under British Surveillance, 1865-1908." *IJMES* 40, no. 2 (2008): 269-90.

———. "The Mechanics of Mecca: The Technopolitics of the Late Ottoman Hejaz and the Colonial Hajj." PhD diss., Columbia University, 2015.

———. "Ottoman Infrastructures of the Saudi Hydro-State: The Technopolitics of Pilgrimage and Potable Water in the Hijaz." *Comparative Studies in Society and History* 57 (2015): 942-74.

Maas, Willem, ed. *Multilevel Citizenship*. Philadelphia: University of Pennsylvania Press, 2013.

Macalister-Smith, Peter. "Bio-Bibliographical Key to the Membership of the Institut de Droit International, 1873–2001." *Journal of the History of International Law* 5 (2003): 77–159.

Maier, Charles S. "Consigning the Twentieth Century to History: Alternative Narratives for the Modern Era." *American Historical Review* 105, no. 3 (2000): 807–31.

Makdisi, Ussama. "Ottoman Orientalism." *American Historical Review* 107, no. 3 (2002): 768–96.

Maktabi, Rania. "The Lebanese Census of 1932 Revisited: Who Are the Lebanese?" *British Journal of Middle Eastern Studies* 26, no. 2 (1999): 219–41.

———. "State Formation and Citizenship in Lebanon: The Politics of Membership and Exclusion in a Sectarian State." In *Citizenship and the State in the Middle East: Approaches and Applications.* Edited by Nils August Butenschon, Uri Davis, and Manuel Sarkis Hassassian. Syracuse: Syracuse University Press, 2000.

Mamlyuk, Boris N. and Ugo Mattei. "Comparative International Law." *Brooklyn Journal of International Law* 36 (2011): 385–452.

Manger, Leif. *The Hadrami Diaspora: Community-Building on the Indian Ocean Rim.* New York: Berghahn, 2010.

Martens, F. *Recueil des traités et conventions conclus par la Russie avec les puissances étrangères.* 15 Vol. St. Pétersbourg: Imprimerie du Ministère des voies de communication, 1874–1909.

Masters, Bruce. *Christians and Jews in the Ottoman Arab World: The Roots of Sectarianism.* Cambridge, UK: Cambridge University Press, 2001.

———. "The Sultan's Entrepreneurs: The Avrupa Tuccaris and the Hayriye Tuccaris in Syria." *IJMES* 24, no. 4 (1992): 579–97.

Matar, Nabil. *Turks, Moors, and Englishmen in the Age of Discovery.* New York: Columbia University Press, 1999.

Mazower, Mark. *Governing the World: The History of an Idea.* New York: Penguin, 2012.

McHugo, John. *Syria: A History of the Last Hundred Years.* London: Saqi Books, 2014.

McKeown, Adam. *Melancholy Order: Asian Migration and the Globalization of Borders.* New York: Columbia University Press, 2008.

Melissen, Jan. "The Consular Dimension of Diplomacy." In *Consular Affairs and Diplomacy.* Edited by Jan Melissen et.al. Leiden: Martinus Neijhoff Publishers, 2011.

Merry, Sally Engle. "Colonial Law and Its Uncertainties." *Law and History Review* 28 (2010): 1067–71.

Metcalf, Thomas R. *Imperial Connections: India in the Indian Ocean Arena, 1860–1920.* Berkeley: University of California Press, 2007.

Meyer, James H. "Immigration, Return and the Politics of Citizenship: Russian Muslims in the Ottoman Empire, 1860–1914." *IJMES* 39, no. 1 (2007): 15–32.

———. "Speaking Sharia to the State: Muslim Protesters, Tsarist Officials, and the Islamic Discourses of Late Imperial Russia." *Kritika* 14 (2013): 485–505.

———. *Turks across Empires: Marketing Muslim Identity in the Russian-Ottoman Borderlands, 1856–1914.* Oxford: Oxford University Press, 2014.

Milovidov, B.P. "Turetskie Voennoplennye v Rossii v 1812 Goda." *Voprosy Istorii* 10 (2008): 91–96.

Minawi, Mostafa. *The Ottoman Scramble for Africa: Empire and Diplomacy in the Sahara and the Hijaz.* Stanford: Stanford University Press, 2016.

———. "Telegraphs and Territoriality in Ottoman Africa and Arabia during the Age of High Imperialism." *Journal of Balkan and Near Eastern Studies* 18, no. 6 (2016): 567–87.

Monsour, Anne. *Not Quite White: Lebanese and the White Australia Policy, 1880–1947.* Teneriffe: Post Pressed, 2010.

Moore, Erin. *Gender, Law, and Resistance in India.* Tucson: University of Arizona Press, 1998.

Moreland, W.H. "The Shahbandar in the Eastern Seas." *Journal of the Royal Asiatic Society of Great Britain and Ireland* 4 (1920): 517–33.

Morieux, Renaud. "French Prisoners of War, Conflicts of Honour, and Social Inversions in England, 1744–1783." *The Historical Journal* 56, no. 1 (2013): 55–88.

Morkva, Valeriy. "Russia's Policy of Rapprochement with the Ottoman Empire in the Era of the French Revolutionary and Napoleonic Wars, 1792–1806." PhD diss., Bilkent University, 2010.

Morrison, Alexander. "Metropole, Colony, and Imperial Citizenship in the Russian Empire." *Kritika* 13 (2012): 327–64.

———. *Russian Rule in Samarkand, 1868–1910: A Comparison with British India.* Oxford: Oxford University Press, 2008.

Mukherjee, Mithi. *India in the Shadows of Empire: a Legal and Political History, 1774–1950.* New Delhi: Oxford University Press, 2010.

Naar, Devin. "From the 'Jerusalem of the Balkans' to the *Goldene Medina*: Jewish Immigration from Salonika to the United States." *American Jewish History* 93, no. 4 (2007): 435–74.

Naff, Alixa. *Becoming American: The Early Arab Immigrant Experience.* Carbondale: Southern Illinois University Press, 1993.

Naff, Thomas. "Reform and the Conduct of Ottoman Diplomacy in the Reign of Selim III, 1789–1807." *Journal of the American Oriental Society* 83, no. 3 (1963): 295–315.

Nail, Thomas. *The Figure of the Migrant.* Stanford: Stanford University Press, 2015.

Nalbandian, Louise. *The Armenian Revolutionary Movement: The Development of Armenian Political Parties through the Nineteenth Century.* Berkeley: University of California Press, 1963.

Narbona, Maria. "The Development of Nationalist Identities in French Syria and Lebanon: A Transnational Dialogue with Arab Immigrants to Argentina and Brazil, 1915–1929." PhD diss., University of California, Santa Barbara, 2007.

Neff, Stephen C. *Justice among Nations: A History of International Law.* Cambridge, MA: Harvard University Press, 2014.

Ngai, Mai M. *Impossible Subjects: Illegal Aliens and the Making of Modern America.* Princeton: Princeton University Press, 2004.

Noradounghian, Gabriel. *Recueil d'actes internationaux de l'empire ottoman.* 4 Vol. Paris: F. Pichon, 1897–1903.

Norton, Claire. "Lust, Greed, Torture, and Identity: Narrations of Conversion and the Creation of the Early Modern Renegade." *Comparative Studies of South Asia, Africa and the Middle East* 29, no. 2 (2009): 259–68.

Numan, Nurtaç. "The Emirs of Mecca and the Ottoman Government of Hijaz, 1840–1908." Master's thesis, Boğaziçi University, 2005.

Ochsenwald, William. *Religion, Society, and the State in Arabia: The Hijaz under Ottoman Control, 1840–1908.* Columbus: Ohio State University Press, 1984.

Orford, Anne. "On International Legal Method." *London Review of International Law* 1 (2013): 166–97.

Osmanağaoğlu, Cihan. *Tanzimat Dönemi İtibarıyla Osmanlı Tâbiiyyetinin (Vatandaşlığının) Gelişimi.* Istanbul: Legal, 2004.

Özcan, Azmi. *Pan-Islamism: Indian Muslims, the Ottomans and Britain, 1877-1924*. Leiden: Brill, 1997.

Özkaya, Sevda. *Süveyş Kanalı: XIX. Yüzyılda Doğu Akdeniz'de Bir Rekabet Unsuru (Osmanlı Arşivi Göre)*. Istanbul: Bilge Kultur Sanat, 2015.

Özsu, Umut. *Formalizing Displacement: International Law and Population Transfers*. Oxford: Oxford University Press, 2015.

———. "From the 'Semi-Civilized State' to the 'Emerging Market': Remarks on the International Legal History of the Semi-Periphery." In *Research Handbook on Political Economy and Law*. Edited by Ugo Mattei and John D. Haskell. Cheltenham: Edward Elgar, 2015.

———. "Ottoman Empire." In *The Oxford Handbook of the History of International Law*. Edited by Bardo Fassbender and Anne Peters. Oxford: Oxford University Press, 2012.

———. "The Ottoman Empire, the Origins of Extraterritoriality, and International Legal Theory." In *The Oxford Handbook of the Theory of International Law*. Edited by Florian Hoffman and Anne Orford. Oxford: Oxford University Press, 2016.

Özsu, Umut and Thomas Skouteris, ed. "International Legal Histories of the Ottoman Empire." *Journal of the History of International Law/Revue d'histoire du droit international* 18 (2016).

Özyüksel, Murat. *The Hejaz Railway and the Ottoman Empire: Modernity, Industrialisation, and Ottoman Decline*. London: I.B. Tauris, 2014.

Palabıyık, Mustafa Serdar. "The Emergence of the Idea of 'International Law' in the Ottoman Empire before the Treaty of Paris (1856)." *Middle Eastern Studies* 50, no. 2 (2014): 233–51.

———. "International Law for Survival: Teaching International Law in the Late Ottoman Empire (1859–1922)." *Bulletin of the School of Oriental and African Studies* 78, no. 2 (2015): 271–92.

Pálffy, Géza. "Ransom Slavery along the Ottoman-Hungarian Frontier in the Sixteenth and Seventeenth Centuries." In *Ransom Slavery Along the Ottoman Borders: (Early Fifteenth-Early Eighteenth Centuries)*. Edited by Géza Dávid and Pál Fodor. Leiden: Brill, 2007.

Parolin, Gianluca Paolo. *Citizenship in the Arab World: Kin, Religion and Nation-State*. Amsterdam: Amsterdam University Press, 2009.

Payk, Marcus. "Institutionalisierung und Verrechtlichung: Die Geschichte des Völkerrechts im späten 19. und frühen 20. Jahrhundert." *Archiv für Sozialgeschichte* 52 (2012): 861–83.

Peirce, Leslie. "Abduction with (Dis)honor: Sovereigns, Brigands, and Heroes in the Ottoman World." *Journal of Early Modern History* 15 (2011): 311–29.

Pennell, Richard. "The Origins of the Foreign Jurisdiction Act and the Extension of British Sovereignty." *Historical Research* 83 (2010): 465–85.

Philliou, Christine. *Biography of an Empire: Governing Ottomans in an Age of Revolution*. Berkeley: University of California Press, 2010.

Pitts, Jennifer. "Empire and Legal Universalisms in the Eighteenth Century." *American Historical Review* 117, no. 1 (2012): 92–121.

Qafisheh, Mutaz M. *The International Law Foundations of Palestinian Nationality: a Legal Examination of Nationality in Palestine under Britain's Rule*. Leiden: Martinus Nijhoff, 2009.

Rafeq, Abdul-Karim. "Ownership of Real Property by Foreigners in Syria, 1869 to 1873." In *New Perspectives on Property and Land in the Middle East*. Edited by Roger Owen. Cambridge, MA: Harvard University Press, 2001.

Rai, Mridu. *Hindu Rulers, Muslim Subjects: Islam, Rights, and the History of Kashmir.* Princeton: Princeton University Press, 2004.

Reid, Anthony. "Nineteenth Century Pan-Islam in Indonesia and Malaysia." *The Journal of Asian Studies* 26, no. 2 (1967): 267–83.

Reynolds, Michael A. "Buffers, Not Brethren: Young Turk Military Policy in the First World War and the Myth of Panturanism." *Past and Present* 203 (2009): 137–79.

———. *Shattering Empires: The Clash and Collapse of the Ottoman and Russian Empires 1908–1918.* Cambridge, UK: Cambridge University Press, 2011.

Rihbany, Abraham Mitrie. *America Save the Near East.* Boston: Houghton, 1918.

Roberts, Anthea. *Is International Law International?* Oxford: Oxford University Press, 2017.

Roberts, Anthea, Paul B. Stephan, Pierre-Hugues Verdier, and Mila Versteeg, eds. *Comparative International Law.* Oxford: Oxford University Press, 2017.

Robertson, Craig. *The Passport in America: The History of a Document.* New York: Oxford University Press, 2010.

Rodogno, Davide. *Against Massacre: Humanitarian Interventions in the Ottoman Empire, 1815–1914.* Princeton: Princeton University Press, 2012.

Rogan, Eugene. *Frontiers of the State in the Late Ottoman Empire: Transjordan, 1850–1921.* Cambridge, UK: Cambridge University Press, 1999.

Rothman, E. Natalie. *Brokering Empire: Trans-Imperial Subjects between Venice and Istanbul.* Ithaca: Cornell University Press, 2012.

Rothschild, Emma. *The Inner Life of Empires: An Eighteenth-Century History.* Princeton: Princeton University Press, 2011.

Safa, Élie. "L'émigration libanaise." PhD diss., Université Saint Joseph, Beirut, 1960.

Sahadeo, Jeff. *Russian Colonial Society in Tashkent: 1865–1923.* Bloomington: Indiana University Press, 2007.

Şahin, Canay. "The Rise and Fall of an *Ayân* Family in Eighteenth Century Anatolia: The Caniklizâdes (1737–1808)." PhD diss., Bilkent University, 2003.

Saldanha, Jerome A. ed. *The Persian Gulf Précis.* 8 Vol. Gerrards Cross: Archive Editions, 1986.

Salname-i Nezaret-i Umur-ı Hariciyye. 4 Vol. Dersaadet: Matbaa-yı Osmaniye, 1318.

Salzmann, Ariel. "Citizens in Search of a State: The Limits of Political Participation in the Late Ottoman Empire." In *Extending Citizenship, Reconfiguring States.* Edited by Michael P. Hanagan and Charles Tilly. Lanham, MD: Rowman & Littlefield Publishers, 1999.

Santha, K. S. *Begums of Awadh.* Varanasi: Bharati Prakashan, 1980.

Saray, Mehmet. *The Russian, British, Chinese and Ottoman Rivalry in Turkestan: Four Studies on the History of Central Asia.* Ankara: Turkish Historical Society Printing House, 2003.

Sartori, Paolo and Ido Shahar. "Legal Pluralism in Muslim-Majority Colonies: Mapping the Terrain." *Journal of the Economic and Social History of the Orient* 55, no. 4/5 (2012): 637–63.

Savigny, Friedrich Carl von. *Private International Law, and the Retrospective Operation of Statutes: A Treatise on the Conflict of Laws, and the Limits of Their Operation in Respect of Place and Time.* Translated by William Guthrie. 2nd Ed. Edinburgh: T. & T. Clark, 1880.

Schmidt, Jan. "Pan-Islamism between the Porte, the Hague, and Buitenzorg." In *Through the Legation Window 1876–1926: Four Essays on Dutch, Dutch-Indian and Ottoman History.* Istanbul: Nederlands Historisch-Archaeologisch Instituut, 1992.

Second Report of the Provost Marshal General to the Secretary of War on the Operations of the Selective Service System to December 20, 1918. Washington, DC: Government Printing Office, 1919.

Sharafi, Mitra. "The Marital Patchwork of Colonial South Asia: Forum Shopping from Britain to Baroda." *Law and History Review* 28, no. 4 (2010): 979–1009.

Shaw, Stanford J. *Between Old and New: The Ottoman Empire under Sultan Selim III, 1789–1807.* Cambridge, MA: Harvard University Press, 1971.

Simpson, Gerry. *Great Powers and Outlaw States: Unequal Sovereigns in the International Legal Order.* Cambridge, UK: Cambridge University Press, 2004.

Şimşir, Bilal N. *Lozan Telgrafları.* Ankara: TTK Yayınları, 1990.

Slight, John. *The British Empire and the Hajj, 1865–1956.* Cambridge, MA: Harvard University Press, 2015.

Smiley, Will. "'After Being so Long Prisoners, They Will Not Return to Slavery in Russia': An Aegean Network of Violence between Empires and Identities." *Journal of Ottoman Studies* 44 (2014): 221–34.

———. "The Burdens of Subjecthood: The Ottoman State, Russian Fugitives, and Interimperial Law, 1774–1869." *IJMES* 46, no. 1 (2014): 73–93.

———. *From Slaves to Prisoners of War: The Ottoman Empire, Russia, and International Law.* Oxford: Oxford University Press, 2018.

———. "Let *Whose* People Go? Subjecthood, Sovereignty, Liberation, and Legalism in Eighteenth-Century Russo-Ottoman Relations." *Turkish Historical Review* 3, no. 2 (2012): 196–228.

———. "War without War: The Battle of Navarino, the Ottoman Empire and the Pacific Blockade." *Journal of the History of International Law / Revue d'histoire du droit international* 18 (2016): 42–69.

———. "When Peace Comes, You Will Again Be Free: Islamic and Treaty Law, Black Sea Conflict, and the Emergence of 'Prisoners of War' in the Ottoman Empire, 1739–1830." PhD diss., Cambridge University, 2012.

Solanki, Gopika. *Adjudication in Religious Family Laws: Cultural Accommodation, Legal Pluralism, and Gender Equality in India.* Cambridge, UK: Cambridge University Press, 2011.

Somel, Selçuk Akşin. "Osman Nuri Paşa'nın 17 Temmuz 1885 Tarihli Hicaz Raporu." *Tarih Araştırmaları Dergisi* 18/29 (1996): 1–38.

Sonyel, Salahi R. "The Protégé´ System in the Ottoman Empire." *Journal of Islamic Studies* 2 (1991): 56–66.

Sousa, Nasim. *The Capitulatory Régime of Turkey: Its History, Origin, and Nature.* Baltimore: Johns Hopkins University Press, 1933.

Spagnolo, John T. "Portents of Empire in Britain's Ottoman Extraterritorial Jurisdiction." *Middle Eastern Studies,* 27 (1991): 256–82.

Stein, Sarah Abrevaya. "Citizens of a Fictional Nation: Ottoman-Born Jews in France during the First World War." *Past & Present* 226, no. 1 (2015): 227–54.

———. *Extraterritorial Dreams: European Citizenship, Sephardi Jews, and the Ottoman Twentieth Century.* Chicago: University of Chicago Press, 2016.

———. "Protected Persons? The Baghdadi Jewish Diaspora, the British State, and the Persistence of Empire." *American Historical Review* 116 (2011): 80–108.

Stephens, Julia. *Governing Islam: Law, Empire, and Secularism in South Asia.* Cambridge, UK: Cambridge University Press, 2018.

Sturman, Rachel. *The Government of Social Life in Colonial India: Liberalism, Religious Law, and Women's Rights.* Cambridge, UK: Cambridge University Press, 2012.

Sugar, Peter F. "The Ottoman 'Professional Prisoner' on the Western Borders of the Empire in the Sixteenth and Seventeenth Centuries." *Études Balkaniques* 7, no. 2 (1971): 82–91.

Sunar, M. Mert. "Cauldron of Dissent: A Study of the Janissary Corps, 1807–1828." PhD diss., Binghamton University, 2006.

Tagliacozzo, Eric. *The Longest Journey: Southeast Asians and the Pilgrimage to Mecca.* Oxford: Oxford University Press, 2013.

―――. *Secret Trades, Porous Borders: Smuggling and States along a Southeast Asian Frontier, 1865–1915.* New Haven: Yale University Press, 2005.

Tahsin Paşa. *Sultan Abdülhamid: Tahsin Paşa'nın Yıldız Hatıraları.* Istanbul: Boğaziçi Yayınları, 1999.

Tezcan, Baki. *The Second Ottoman Empire: Political and Social Transformation in the Early Modern World.* Cambridge, UK: Cambridge University Press, 2010.

Thornton, Thomas. *The Present State of Turkey.* London: Joseph Mawman, 1809.

Thum, Rian. *The Sacred Routes of Uyghur History.* Cambridge, MA: Harvard University Press, 2014.

Tolasa, Harun. *Temeşvarlı Osman Ağa: Bir Osmanlı Türk Sipahisi ve Esirlik Hayatı.* Istanbul: Akçağ Yayınları, 2004.

Toledano, Ehud. *The Ottoman Slave Trade and Its Suppression: 1840–1890.* Princeton: Princeton University Press, 1983.

Torpey, John. "The Great War and the Birth of the Modern Passport System." In *Documenting Individual Identity: The Development of State Practices in the Modern World.* Edited by Jane Caplan and John Torpey. Princeton: Princeton University Press, 2001.

―――. *The Invention of the Passport: Surveillance, Citizenship and the State.* Cambridge, UK: Cambridge University Press, 2000.

Toufayan, Mark. "Empathy, Humanity and the 'Armenian Question' in the Internationalist Legal Imagination." *Revue québécoise de droit international* 24 (2011): 171–91.

Toyoda, Tetsuya. "L'aspect universaliste du droit international européen du 19ème siècle et le statut juridique de la Turquie avant 1856." *Journal of the History of International Law* 8 (2006): 19–37.

Travers, Robert. *Ideology and Empire in Eighteenth-Century India: The British in Bengal.* Cambridge, UK: Cambridge University Press, 2007.

Turna, Nalan. *19. Yüzyıldan 20. Yüzyıla Osmanlı Topraklarında Seyahat, Göç ve Asayış Belgeleri: Mürur Tezkereleri.* Istanbul: Kaknüs Yayınları, 2013.

Uçar, Ahmet. *Güney Afrika'da Osmanlılar.* Istanbul: Çamlıca, 2008.

Uçarol, Rifat. *Gazi Ahmet Muhtar Paşa (1839–1919): Askeri ve Siyasi Hayatı.* Istanbul: Derin Yayınları, 2015.

Uğur, Hatice. *Osmanlı Afrikası'nda Bir Sultanlık Zengibar.* Istanbul: Kure Yayinları, 2005.

Unat, Faik Reşit, ed., "Şehdi Osman Paşa Sefaretnamesi." *Tarih Vesikaları* 1 (1941–42): 66–80.

Van den Boogert, Maurits. *The Capitulations and the Ottoman Legal System: Qadis, Consuls, and Beratlıs in the 18th Century.* Leiden: Brill, 2005.

Wasti, Tanvir. "The 1877 Ottoman Mission to Afghanistan." *Middle Eastern Studies* 30, no. 4 (1994): 956–62.

Weiss, Gillian. "Barbary Captivity and the French Idea of Freedom." *French Historical Studies* 28, no. 2 (2005): 232–64.

―――. *Captives and Corsairs: France and Slavery in the Early Modern Mediterranean.* Stanford: Stanford University Press, 2011.

White, Joshua M. *Piracy and Law in the Ottoman Mediterranean*. Stanford: Stanford University Press, 2017.

Whitman, James Q. *The Verdict of Battle: The Law of Victory and the Making of Modern War*. Cambridge, MA: Harvard University Press, 2012.

Yanıkdağ, Yücel. *Healing the Nation: Prisoners of War, Medicine and Nationalism in Turkey, 1914–1939*. Edinburgh: Edinburgh University Press, 2013.

———. "Ottoman Prisoners of War in Russia, 1914-22." *Journal of Contemporary History* 34, no. 1 (1999): 69–85.

Yasamee, F.A.K. *Ottoman Diplomacy: Abdülhamid II and the Great Powers, 1878–1888*. Istanbul: Isis Press, 1996.

Yeniçeşmeli Hâfız Fâik Efendi. *İstanbul'dan Bombay'a bir Osmanlı Fırkateyni'nin Keşif Seyahati*. Edited by Ali Ergun Çınar. İstanbul: Kitabevi, 2014.

Yılmazer, Ziya, ed. *Sânî-Zâde Târîhî: 1223–1237/1808–1821*. Istanbul: Çamlıca, 2008.

Young, George. *Corps de droit Ottoman: Recueil des codes, lois, reglements, ordonnances et actes les plus importants du droit interieur, et d'etudes sur le droit coutumier de l'Empire Ottoman*. 7 Vol. Oxford: Clarendon Press, 1905.

Yurdusev, A. Nuri, ed. *Ottoman Diplomacy: Conventional or Unconventional?* Basingstoke: Palgrave Macmillan, 2004.

Zamir, Meir. *Formation of Modern Lebanon*. London: Croom Helm, 1985.

Zandi-Sayek, Sibel. *Ottoman Izmir: The Rise of a Cosmopolitan Port, 1840–1880*. Minneapolis: University of Minnesota Press, 2012.

Contributors

FAIZ AHMED is an Associate Professor in the Department of History at Brown University, Providence, RI. He is the author of *Afghanistan Rising: Islamic Law and Statecraft between the Ottoman and British Empires* (Harvard University Press, 2017). His current book project examines the history of relations between the Ottoman Empire and the United States, as seen from Ottoman perspectives.

LÂLE CAN is an Associate Professor in the Department of History at the City College of New York, CUNY and the CUNY Graduate Center. She is the author of *Spiritual Subjects: Central Asian Pilgrims and the Ottoman Hajj at the End of Empire* (Stanford University Press, 2020).

JEFFERY DYER is a PhD candidate in the Department of History at Boston College, Chestnut Hill, MA. His dissertation is titled "The Ottomans in the Age of Empire."

STACY D. FAHRENTHOLD is an Assistant Professor in the Department of History at the University of California, Davis. She is the author of *Between the Ottomans and the Entente: the First World War in the Syrian and Lebanese Diaspora, 1908–1925* (Oxford University Press, 2019).

AIMEE M. GENELL is an Assistant Professor in the Department of History at the University of West Georgia, Carrollton, GA. She presently is completing a manuscript titled *Empire by Law: The Ottoman Origins of the Mandates System in the Middle East.*

DAVID GUTMAN is an Associate Professor in the Department of History at Manhattanville College, Purchase, NY. He is the author of *The Politics of Armenian Migration to North America, 1885-1915: Sojourners, Smugglers, and Dubious Citizens* (Edinburgh University Press, 2019).

WILL HANLEY is an Associate Professor in the Department of History at Florida State University, Tallahassee, FL. He is the author of *Identifying with Nationality: Europeans, Ottomans, and Egyptians in Alexandria* (Columbia University Press, 2017).

MICHAEL CHRISTOPHER LOW is an Assistant Professor in the Department of History at Iowa State University, Ames, IA. He is the author of *Imperial Mecca: Ottoman Arabia and the Indian Ocean Hajj* (Columbia University Press, 2020).

UMUT ÖZSU is an Associate Professor in the Department of Law and Legal Studies at Carleton University, Ottawa, ON, Canada. He is currently completing a manuscript titled *Completing Humanity: The International Law of Decolonization*. He is also the author of *Formalizing Displacement: International Law and Population Transfers* (Oxford University Press, 2015).

KENT F. SCHULL is an Associate Professor in the Department of History at Binghamton University SUNY, Binghamton, NY. He is the author of *Prisons in the Late Ottoman Empire: Microcosms of Modernity* (Edinburgh University Press, 2014) and co-editor of *Living in the Ottoman Realm: Empire and Identity, 13th to 20th Centuries* (Indiana University Press, 2016) and *Law and Legality in the Ottoman Empire and Turkish Republic* (Indiana University Press, 2016).

WILL SMILEY is an Assistant Professor of Humanities at the University of New Hampshire. He is the author of *From Slaves to Prisoners of War: The Ottoman Empire, Russia, and International Law* (Oxford University Press, 2018), and the coeditor (with John Fabian Witt) of *To Save the Country: A Lost Treatise on Martial Law* (Yale University Press, 2019).

JULIA STEPHENS is an Associate Professor in the Department of History at Rutgers University, New Brunswick, NJ. She is the author of *Governing Islam: Law, Empire, and Secularism in South Asia* (Cambridge University Press, 2018). Her second book project is tentatively titled *Worldly Afterlives: Death and Diaspora in the Indian Ocean*.

ROBERT ZENS is a Professor in the Department of History at Le Moyne College, Syracuse, NY. He has co-edited three books, including *Law and Legality in the Ottoman Empire and Turkish Republic* (Indiana University Press, 2016). Presently he is completing a manuscript entitled *Rogues, Rebellions, and Reforms in the Ottoman Empire, 1699–1815*.

Index

Printed and bound by CPI Group (UK) Ltd, Croydon, CR0 4YY

13/04/2025